LITERARY PATERNITY,

LITERARY FRIENDSHIP

UNIVERSITY OF NORTH CAROLINA
STUDIES IN THE GERMANIC LANGUAGES
AND LITERATURES

Initiated by RICHARD JENTE (1949–1952),
established by F. E. COENEN (1952–1968),
continued by SIEGFRIED MEWS (1968–1980),
RICHARD H. LAWSON (1980–1985), and
PAUL T. ROBERGE (1985–2000)

JONATHAN M. HESS, Editor

Publication Committee: Department of Germanic Languages

Send orders to:
The University of North Carolina Press
P.O. Box 2288, Chapel Hill, NC 27515-2288

For other volumes in the "Studies" see pages 413–15.

Number One Hundred and Twenty-Five

UNIVERSITY OF NORTH CAROLINA STUDIES IN

THE GERMANIC LANGUAGES AND LITERATURES

Literary Paternity, Literary Friendship

Essays in Honor of Stanley Corngold

EDITED BY GERHARD RICHTER

The University of North Carolina Press

Chapel Hill & London 2002

The University of North Carolina
Studies in the Germanic Languages
and Literatures wishes to express its
appreciation of the generous assistance
provided by Princeton University and
Professor Harold Shapiro, its former
president, in the publication of this
volume.

Manufactured in the United States of
America

The paper in this book meets the guidelines for permanence and durability of
the Committee on Production Guidelines
for Book Longevity of the Council on
Library Resources.

Frontispiece: Photograph by Regine
Corngold.

"Of National Poets and Their Female
Companions" by Herman Rapaport was
initially published in *Future Crossings:
Literature between Philosophy and Cultural
Studies,* ed. Krzysztof Ziarek and Seamus
Deane (Evanston: Northwestern Univer-
sity Press, 2000), and is reprinted here by
permission.

"Old Father Jupiter: On Kleist's Drama
Amphitryon" by Gerhard Kurz appeared
in an earlier German version in *Gewagte
Experimente und kühne Konstellationen.
Kleists Werk zwischen Klassizismus und
Romantik,* ed. Christine Lübkoll and
Günter Oesterle (Würzburg: König-
hausen und Neumann, 2001), and is
reprinted here by permission.

Library of Congress
Cataloging-in-Publication Data
Literary paternity, literary friendship :
essays in honor of Stanley Corngold /
edited by Gerhard Richter.
    p. cm. — (University of North Carolina
studies in the Germanic languages and
literatures; no. 125)
Includes bibliographical references.
ISBN 0-8078-8125-2 (alk. paper)
1. German literature — History and
criticism.   2. Paternity in literature.
3. Friendship in literature.
PT285 .L57   2002   2001057825

06 05 04 03 02   5 4 3 2 1

CONTENTS

Literary Paternity,
Literary Friendship

The text can be read without its father's guarantee.

— Roland Barthes

1 Introduction

Literary Paternity, Literary Friendship

GERHARD RICHTER

Ich glaube, Du hast es nicht genug begriffen, daß Schreiben meine einzige innere Daseinsmöglichkeit ist.
—Franz Kafka, in a letter to Felice Bauer, 20 April 1913

From any perspective, Stanley Corngold, whose life and achievements as a scholar, teacher, and friend the following essays celebrate, is an exception. He is an exception in these times of methodological dogma and professed certainty not only because he approaches both his work and his empirical life with an uncommon curiosity and infectious openness but also because, more than most scholars, he works to keep his ideas and perspectives perpetually in strategic flux. This fluidity of thinking and writing, which grows out of a sense of responsibility to the difficulty of his objects of study, is only matched by the rigor and intellectual integrity that also have come to be his trademark. Ian Balfour puts it well apropos of Corngold's most recent book, *Complex Pleasures: Forms of Feeling in German Literature* (1998), when he writes that "elegance and intelligence meet on virtually every page," while the "prose is pellucid, flexible, and sinuous at the same time."[1] From the perspective of the productive tensions that traverse all his writings, the idea of a *Festschrift* is almost an oxymoron—at least when one hears in this word not only the denotation of a worthy feast but also the echoes of *festschreiben,* to arrest something in writing for good. After all, one of the lessons of Corngold's work is that there is very little that is *festgeschrieben* once and for all, that does not deserve to be carefully reread and passionately rethought, again and again. This rereading and rethinking is propelled by an ethical impulse—the *cura,* which Heidegger tells us lies at the heart of all worry—that contents itself neither with the received wisdom of conventional disciplinary perspectives nor with the false promise of closure offered by this or that system.

The essays gathered in this volume honor Stanley Corngold by focusing on the twin problems of literary friendship and literary paternity. It is appropriate that these twin themes should stand at the core of a volume in his honor, both because he has addressed them in his variegated critical writings and because these tropes conspire to yield a perspective from which many of his more general intellectual concerns come metonymically into view. Corngold's celebrated work on Franz Kafka, for instance, includes meditations, directly or indirectly, on questions of friendship and paternity, relation and offspring, proximity and distance. Moreover, honoring Corngold, who has always been both highly aware of, and vigilantly guarded vis-à-vis, the most recent developments in critical theory, with a volume on these twin themes is particularly timely in the current critical situation. Here, the problems of friendship and paternity occupy a central position in discussions of ethics, politics, art, and literature, as well as the relationship between the public and the private sphere. One could even say that with the numerous publications of books and essays on these topics, paternity and friendship have become privileged tropes in contemporary critical and historical debates.[2]

While friendship has been a central issue in the history of Western ethical and political discourses in philosophy and literature—from Plato and Cicero via Montaigne, Bacon, and Kant all the way to Nietzsche, Freud, Simmel, Blanchot, and beyond—it has only recently begun to become visible as a sphere in which to consider the possibility of a subject that strives to act ethically and responsibly, even without recourse to an essential groundedness or a stable metanarrative. The subject of friendship emerges in contemporary theory, for example, in Jacques Derrida's recent *The Politics of Friendship,* as constantly confronted with an otherness, an alterity that traverses even the self. As such, it provides a prime territory in which to rearticulate such contested notions as community, democracy, and responsibility.

Paternity, like friendship, has a long literary and philosophical history, from Plato's *Phaedrus*—where it is discussed in its relation to writing—through Nietzsche and Kafka to the postmodernists. Concrete and metaphoric paternity allows us to raise essential questions about the status of the "origin," the ethics and politics of responsible production, the status of the "author," the empirical versus the simulated or written personality, the discourse of disowning, constructions of the self through an other, the concept of reproduction, the relation of failed (literary) paternity to the sublimations of destruction, and the ideological attempts to differentiate between proper offspring and bastard forms. Corngold himself has energetically contributed to these debates, both in the form of regular seminars at Princeton University, where students eagerly flock to his course on "Literary Paternity: Nietzsche, Kafka, Benjamin," and in the form of essays addressed to a wider scholarly community, most recently in his work on "Nietzsche, Kafka, and Literary Paternity."[3] In this regard, the essays that follow not only address but *perform* the topic of this volume: the texts written by Corngold's friends and colleagues implicitly enact what is at stake in friendship, while the contributions by his former students, whether their explicit topic is friendship or paternity, are implicated in the structure of a certain literary paternity.

To pay tribute to Stanley Corngold with a volume addressing issues that he has helped to define also means to celebrate more generally his distinguished career as an influential scholar and teacher. His career began when he earned a doctorate in Comparative Literature from Cornell University in 1969 with a dissertation on *The Intelligible Mood: A Study of Aesthetic Consciousness in Rousseau and Kant*. His studies at Cornell were preceded by his college years at Columbia University, from which he graduated with an honors degree in English in 1957. He also studied at the University of London, England, again Columbia University, and the University of Basel, Switzerland. Since 1966, he has taught at Princeton University, where today he is a professor of German and Comparative Literature. The remarkable accomplishments of his career have been recognized by a large number of awards and distinctions, from National Endowment for the Humanities fellowships to Guggenheim Foundation awards, and from election to P.E.N. to membership in the Academy of Literary Studies. While Corngold always has regarded himself first and foremost as an *American* scholar — even during those times when German departments in this country still saw themselves, in an inversion or internalization of the fatherly gaze, as filial extensions of their putatively more powerful paternal departments in Germany — he frequently has taught and lectured to appreciative audiences around the world: among other sites, Germany, England, France, Belgium, Hong Kong, Hungary, Mexico, Switzerland, Spain, the Netherlands, and Israel. But all these achievements and external validations seem hardly adequate to gauge Corngold's influence on several generations of students and colleagues, who cannot imagine the German Department at Princeton or, indeed, the field of German studies more generally, without his energy and presence.

For Princeton undergraduate students from a variety of fields, it has long been considered a special treat, for instance, to enroll in Corngold's German and Comparative Literature 320: "The Romantic Quest," a course that has become something of a cult phenomenon. Anchored in an innovative consideration of central works of the modern European literary tradition, this course includes, among others, detailed readings of works by Goethe, Byron, Flaubert, Stendhal, Nietzsche, and Th. Mann, and the ways in which each alludes to the others in their constructions of the self and their quest for greatness. I had the good fortune of being invited more than once to be a preceptor (what in the academic world outside of Princeton is called a teaching assistant) for this course, and I recall vividly the unusual enthusiasm and depth of reflection that Corngold's lectures inspired in his students. It seemed that he would spend an equal amount of time and mental energy worrying about the remarks and questions from a first-year undergraduate student of literature as he would fielding questions from audiences at his many national and international distinguished lectures. Yet in "The Romantic Quest," more was at stake than a rereading of a series of canonical works in masterful lectures. Students intuitively felt that, for Corngold, reading these texts was not a sterile and detached academic exercise, but a matter of great and immediate ethico-political relevance deserving of sustained personal involvement and rational passion. Here was a teacher who fussed and worried about each sentence, each word it seemed, and who would not allow facile wisdoms of any sort to occlude the responsibility and the calling he felt in relation to every text he caringly explicated with students. After all, it became clear to all participants in this course that this was not just the "Romantic Quest" but also, for several decades now, Stanley Corngold's quest. It was as though he enacted for his students what Nietzsche once identified as his "epistemological starting point," that is, the "[p]rofound aversion to reposing once and for all in any total view of the world. Fascination of the opposing point of view: refusal to be deprived of the stimulus of the enigmatic."[4]

From the wide range of Corngold's graduate seminars at Princeton, perhaps the most influential ones are those concerned with the work and intellectual orbit of Kafka. Both in his teaching and his prolific writings on the

Prague author, Corngold emphasizes the tension between Kafka's relentless compulsion to write, what Kafka called his *Schriftstellersein* or "being-as-a-writer," and his growing awareness that this writing can never fully achieve what it sets out to accomplish, falling short of its own goal with a rigor, however, that delivers a self-reflexive commentary on its own internal contradictions. Indeed, Corngold's scholarship on Kafka continues to be the most influential aspect of his work and, although there has sprung up a veritable "Kafka industry" since the 1950s, Corngold belongs to a handful of scholars worldwide who can be counted among the elite of Kafka's critics. In this country, his teaching and writing on Kafka have had a decisive impact on generations of students and scholars, and on both lay and scholarly audiences. His landmark 1972 translation of Kafka's *The Metamorphosis* made available to readers of English a faithful yet lucid rendering of Kafka's peculiar German that is second to none among modern literary translations. The recently sold 1-millionth copy of Corngold's translation speaks volumes, literally, about its usefulness to generations of readers.[5]

Yet simultaneously, on the more strictly critical side, the importance of his far-ranging scholarly work from the 1973 *The Commentators' Despair: The Interpretation of Kafka's "Metamorphosis"* to the 1988 *Franz Kafka: The Necessity of Form* cannot be overstated. Such classic essays as "*The Metamorphosis:* Metamorphosis of the Metaphor," one of Corngold's best texts, remain touchstones for all readers concerned with the properly rhetorical dimension of Kafka's writing. What draws readers to his work is the rare combination of broad theoretical awareness and critical intensity that allows his work not only to place theory and practice into a new and unexpected constellation, but also simultaneously to transform both of these terms. In Corngold's work, there is no easy "application" of a preformulated theory or system to a given text. His work enacts the ways in which every text constitutes not simply an instantiation of a theoretical point, but rather a subversive provocation to any attempt at systematic classification or generic closure. As Corngold once wrote, "Kafka's most marked contribution to modern art and culture is to the way in which the subject of writing has become Writing, the way in which reflection on the act of writing has become ontological, not psychological, ranging from metaphysical reference to technical aspects of its production."[6] Elsewhere, he teaches us that the "attitude of identifying with what originates in the act of writing even or especially in spite of local intention suggests — mutatis mutandis — Kafka's aesthetic of suffering."[7] For those who are acquainted with Stanley Corngold's personality and biography, such sentences make it ever more difficult to distinguish between him and Kafka. There is something within many of us that wishes to claim that, in ways that far transcend the incidental or even the scholarly, he *is* Kafka.

In a critical climate when ideological hostilities, critical *Gleichschaltung*, and the dogmas of conformity reign supreme, Corngold's approach to his work defies classification. It is certainly a far cry from the philological pieties of the traditional Germanist stance but, for all its theoretical rigor, is not really at home in any of the critical fads or well-rehearsed newer idioms either. His 1986 *The Fate of the Self: German Writers and French Theory*, with its provocative readings of Hölderlin, Dilthey, Nietzsche, Kafka, Th. Mann, Freud, and Heidegger, is a good example of his innovation and subversion of critical orthodoxies. But Corngold's unusually individualistic perspective has never been an easy position to occupy. Precisely because he pledges allegiance to no recognizable dogma, he has always precariously and rather uncomfortably sat not only, as they say in English, between a rock and a hard place, but also, as they say in German, *zwischen allen Stühlen*. Never content with discipleship, Corngold has been criticized by proponents of every conceivable critical school.

While he was decisively influenced by the rhetorical ways of reading laid out by his doctoral adviser, Paul de Man, he also has significantly departed from de Man's manner of reading and has even written a series of texts addressing what he perceived as ethical and theoretical blind spots in his mentor's œuvre and the ways of thinking it opened up.[8] But at the same time, de Man's influence on his critical sensibilities remains visible, and his friends, colleagues, and students often cannot escape the impression that it would be hard to imagine anyone taking de Man's work more seriously or studying it with greater care and urgency even today, when the fortunes of rigorous rhetorical criticism have shifted and a more culturally-oriented hegemony has installed itself. On a biographical level, then, Corngold experienced the pleasures and tensions in relation to the paternal superego of his *Doktorvater*, or thesis adviser, that he subsequently would theorize in his scholarly work on paternity in Nietzsche, Kafka, and others. It is as though he remained close to de Man precisely by not following him. For Corngold, to do justice to de Man's deconstructive project, it too must be deconstructed.

In the process, Corngold has done much to introduce contemporary rhetorical scholarship into a discipline that all too often exhibited an aversion to the demands of close reading and a resistance to theory.

While all of Corngold's works wrestle self-consciously with the relations of rhetoric or figurative language and the larger philosophical claims that the text in which they are embedded attempts to make, he explicitly thematizes this vexed relationship in his 1991 novel *Borrowed Lives*. Coauthored with Irene Giersing, this "critical fiction" presents itself as an enactment of various issues in literary criticism and philosophical aesthetics. It tells the story of an uneasy history professor, Paul van Pein (in whose name the empirical location of the Princeton German Department, East Pyne Hall, resonates) and his quixotic quest in the South of France for creative originality, stable identity, carnal pleasure, and a readable life unmarred by the threats of inauthenticity. Brilliantly allegorizing issues of contemporary literary theory and philosophy, the novel traces the vicissitudes of the written self, satirizes the academic marketplace, and constantly points to the ways in which "the honey of experience" cannot be thought in separation from the postmodern chiastic reversal that links identity and its absence in the space of language. The novel situates itself in the interstices between the writing self and its narrative presentation in a self-conscious gesture that inscribes it in the critical metafictions produced by literary theoreticians such as Steiner, Eagleton, Sontag, Eco, and Burgess. At times, it even rivals David Lodge's acclaimed academic romance *Small World*.

The spirit of *Borrowed Lives,* which ineluctably intertwines the demands of the theoretical with the passion of the personal, animates Stanley Corngold's entire perspective on intellectual life. This critical stance is not simply a matter of subjective predilection, it was also shaped by the political circumstances and the social milieu in which he came of age.[9] When Corngold began studying Yeats with Lionel Trilling at Columbia in the 1950s, the Cold War was already in full swing in the United States. Having grown up in Brooklyn with a mother who was born to Ukrainian parents during their ship journey to New York harbor and a father hailing from Harlem, Manhattan, he decided to enroll in the Regular Naval Reserve Officers Training Corps. This program, which would help to finance his college education, turned out to be in the Cold War business of producing not critical thinkers but nationalistic scholar-warriors, or "scholwars," as Corngold calls them for short. As a nonconformist Jewish intellectual in the militaristic, brutal, and often arbitrary environment of Columbia's scholwars, he was early on sensitized to the absurdity of what amounted to what he calls the American "military-educational complex." Here, he got an early taste of the Eisenhower era, since the later American president was already president of the university where Corngold's intellectual persona initially was shaped. Because graduate school at that time seemed like an extension of military service and U.S. Cold War indoctrination, he decided finally to realize his long-held dream of living in Europe, albeit under the patronage of the Army. Stationed at an Army base near Heidelberg as a drill sergeant and English instructor, Corngold experienced firsthand the absurd logic by which it seemed to have "become necessary in an age of increasingly complex warfare to raise the technical consciousness of the officer class; but another consideration was in play: legislators believed that a generally heightened literacy among officers and soldiers would be pleasing and impressive to the semi-occupied countries in postwar Europe, supposing that it is better to be ordered about by a scholwar than by some thug who cannot tell 'Lapis Lazuli' from a Bofors gun." Here, Corngold was repulsed by the "merger of values of the university and 'military': American expatriates teaching at such camps could not fail to confuse the authentic content of their work (rhetoric and composition) with its inauthentic circumstances — the fact that their workplace, the classroom, was enclosed by barbed wire and guarded by bayonets."[10] In the early 1960s, the U.S. National Defense Education Act, created in part in response to the perceived threat of the Soviet Union, which, since the 1957 Sputnik success, had made giant leaps forward in technology and education, made it possible for Corngold, as for many others of his generation, to attend graduate school. But even in graduate school the subterranean structures of power and domination, both in the Army and in the educational milieu of the time, continued to provide the impetus for a restless critical mind and an ever-vigilant reader of the textual and political networks that work upon us as human agents. This critical stance, and the oppositional spirit lodged within it, has never left Corngold.

In some of his more recent work, such as "The Melancholy Object of Consumption," Corngold explicitly applies this oppositional spirit to an analysis of the properly cultural phenomena of consumption and the capitalist exploitation even of such seemingly private emotions as depression.

By way of penetrating and exposing the political logic of such productions of the cultural text as Omaha Steaks and Pfizer Pharmaceuticals, he comes to the following conclusion: "All complex industrial societies rule by non-coercive coercion, whereby political questions become disguised as cultural ones and as such become insoluble. I have been talking about a prevalent and ubiquitous melancholy (in its radical form, satanism) under capitalism in an age of technical reproduction. This is a political question. Its ostensible cure proceeds today by means of further commodification—indeed, even the commodification of melancholy (or satanism) itself. But this solution, occurring through commodities—pseudospecifics which are actually generics—in this way becomes a cultural one and hence, in its own terms, insoluble. At this point what is called for, in the West as well as in the East, is an exercise of radical political thinking."[11] In this more recent work, the traditions of rhetorical and cultural-political criticism meet in unexpected and fruitful ways. Indeed, Corngold here sets the conceptual standards for what a future critical analysis of culture and textuality, conceived politically and theoretically in postmimetic terms, might look like.

It is this kind of irreverent critical urgency, combined with the far-reaching insights abundantly offered by his scholarship and his unusual dedication to and encouragement of his students' and colleagues' intellectual development, that have made Stanley Corngold one of the most influential and admired American literary scholars of his generation. In this spirit, the purpose of the current volume is to celebrate and pay tribute to this remarkable life and œuvre by rigorously revisiting the twin themes of literary friendship and literary paternity. The first section of the book is a conceptual meditation on the very idea of friendship. In John H. Smith's experimental dialogue, some of the main philosophical positions concerning friendship are creatively laid out in the form of a fictional dialogue among friends embracing conflicting theoretical viewpoints. In this way the philosophical dialogue on friendship both casts into sharp relief and enacts the central issues it raises. Smith's conceptual dialogue clears the way for the following parts of the volume.

The second section, "Literary Archaeologies (I): Codes of Friendship and Paternity in German Classicism," devotes itself to modern forms of friendship and paternity as they emerge in what arguably remains the key period of German literature. Here, Walter Hinderer explores the concepts of friendship and love in Schiller and Hölderlin, analyzing the ways in which these themes were not only created as discursive "codes," as Niklas Luhmann's systems-theoretical studies have argued, but also the ways in which these themes carried within themselves the tools to challenge these dominant codes. The dynamic tensions that Hinderer sets into sharp relief are exemplified and further explored in Peter Uwe Hohendahl's reflections on the formative role of the father in German Classical literature, specifically in plays by Goethe and Schiller. Hohendahl demonstrates that their literary production is interlaced with the contemporary discursive formations surrounding the notion of the father and that their imbrication with contemporary codes can be traced on the linguistic and structural levels of *Iphigenie auf Tauris* and *Die Braut von Messina*. While Hohendahl focuses on the figure of the father in concrete literary terms, Mark Roche explores a more mediated form of paternity. He investigates the paternal role that Plato plays for one of German Classsicism's central and enigmatic texts, Hölderlin's *Hyperion*. Analyzing the ways in which Hölderlin mobilizes a number of previously unrecognized allusion's to Plato, Roche shows how Hölderlin both appropriates and inverts a number of positions found in his literary "father" in order to construct his own variety of Idealism. The creative tensions that traverse the relationship between Hölderlin and Plato are recast in more concrete terms in Karin Schutjer's analysis of a specific relation of literary paternity, that of Goethe, the "father" of German literature, and his "literary" daughter Bettina Brentano von Arnim. Cunningly intertwining the story of Goethe and his "daughter" with a contemporary account of a father-daughter conflict, Schutjer explores issues of differentation, agency, and the internalization of the other from a psychoanalytically inflected perspective.

The third section, "Literary Archaeologies (II): Codes of Friendship and Paternity in German Romanticism," extends the historical and conceptual range of the previous section by revisiting a number of key texts of German Romantic authors writing in the uneasy wake of Classicist paradigms. As a piece of Romantic writing, Brentano's *Godwi* is characterized, as John Lyon demonstrates, by a movement toward a form of aesthetic mediation that is inseparable from the possession of the father, even when it seems maternally focused on the surface. Gerhard Kurz's analysis of Jupiter as a father figure in Kleist's *Amphitryon* confirms this predominance of paternity in post-classicist writing, and Jochen Hörisch's witty analysis of the discourses on the undecidability of love and friendship in Romantic writers such as Achim von Arnim adds these two concepts to the orbit of predominant concerns.

While the gender- and sexuality-specific dimensions in discourses of friendship and paternity resonate through several of the essays in the previous parts of the book, the fourth section, "Languages of Friendship and Sexual Identity," confronts these issues head-on. Robert Tobin's historical account of the development of friendship in relation to the rise of sexual identity usefully sets the stage for the three essays that follow: Herman Rapaport's Heideggerean meditation on the concept of national poets in relation to their female companions; John Neubauer's analysis, centered on Hans Blüher, of images of friendship in the often conflictual relations among the problematic categories of Germans, Jews, and Gays; and Gail Finney's examination of women's comedy between Marxian and Freudian analyses. Together, these essays suggest that there can be no thinking of friendship and paternity that does not strive to come to terms with the elusive dimensions of sexuality and gender that traverses these concepts.

The fifth section, "Simulations of Friendship and Paternity, Claims of Responsibility: The Case of Hannah Arendt," presents two studies that focus on Arendt as a key thinker of the responsibilities that these concepts entail. David Halliburton strategically traces themes in Arendt's work that speak directly to the issue of responsibility and friendship, such as the neighbor, the brother, the comrade, the enemy, and even ethics itself. Liliane Weissberg then performs a kind of case study for Arendt's ideas of friendship when she illuminates the complex relations between Arendt and Walter Benjamin.

The sixth and final section of the volume, "Textual Paternity and Friendship: Figures of Reading," convenes a number of projects that allow us to rethink issues of friendship and paternity after Arendt. Here, Rafaël Newman and Caroline Wiedmer confront questions of paternity versus autocreation in terms of quests for authenticity, alternate memory, and witnessing in the controversial Holocaust writings of Binjamin Wilkomirski and Daniel Ganzfried. Donald Brown's reflections on friends and mentors brings into a suggestive constellation significant moments in Dante, Proust, and Nietzsche that speak to the "infinite distance" without which no friendship can be thought. And while Howard Stern's rhetorical reading of Sholem Aleichem's *Tevye the Dairyman* focuses on the tropes that inscribe this novel deeply into the heart of the joys and sorrows of fatherhood, Laurence Rickels explores issues of paternal transference, the gift, and the horror of the middlebrow, with an emphasis on Paul de Man and the reception of Goethe's *Faust*. Taking up such psychoanalytic categories, Kiarina Kordela meditates on the possibility of the democratic father within figurative speech as she places Freud and Sophocles into a fruitful constellation. Finally, Mark Anderson focuses on what he calls a "sadomasochistic model of aesthetic pleasure" that becomes visible as the enduring yet rarely acknowledged signature of the paternities of Enlightenment. This semiotic paternity of the Gothic, in which knowledge and its undermining are inexorably intertwined, becomes especially urgent in the juxtaposition of Stoker's *Dracula* and Kafka's *Der Verschollene*. Together, the essays collected in this volume, then, offer both comprehensive conceptual discussions and specific analyses of certain key texts that have played a decisive role in shaping our modern culture's engagement with friendship and paternity.

What Stanley Corngold's life and work, along with his good humor, wit, and critical engagement, will have meant for those who have come into contact with them remains to be fully understood. The selected bibliography of his publications as well as the list of Ph.D. dissertations that he has directed in German and in Comparative Literature, both appended to this volume, are impressive registers that speak to this meaning. But, at the same time, these lists are hardly adequate to convey the deep friendship and admiration that students and colleagues feel for Stanley Corngold or to acknowledge the many debts to him that cannot be repaid. Yet it is precisely through the vexed logic of the gift — the many gifts he has given us, but also the gifts that can never be repaid without canceling themselves — that we here record our gratitude and affection for him.

NOTES

1. Ian Balfour on the back cover of Stanley Corngold, *Complex Pleasures: Forms of Feeling in German Literature* (Stanford, Calif.: Stanford University Press, 1998).

2. To name only a few representative recent publications: Jacques Derrida, *Politics of Friendship*, transl. George Collins (London: Verso, 1997); Peter Murphy, ed., *Friendship. A Special Issue of The South Atlantic Quarterly* 97:1 (Winter 1998); Peter Fenves, ed., *Politics of Friendship. A Special Issue of Eighteenth-Century Studies* 32:2 (Winter 1998–99); Gerhard Richter, "Siegfried Kracauer and the Folds of Friendship"

The German Quarterly 70:3 (Summer 1997): 233–46; Wolfram Mauser and Becker-Cantario, eds., *Frauenfreundschaft, Männerfreundschaft: Literarische Diskurse im 18. Jahrhundert* (Tübingen: Max Niemeyer, 1991); and Dieter Lenzen, *Vaterschaft: Vom Patriachat zur Alimentation* (Reinbeck bei Hamburg: Rowohlt, 1991).

3. See Stanley Corngold, "Nietzsche, Kafka, and Literary Paternity," in *Nietzsche and Jewish Culture,* ed. Jacob Golomb (London and New York: Routledge, 1996), 137–57.

4. Friedrich Nietzsche, *The Will to Power,* transl. Walter Kaufmann and R. J. Hollingdale (New York: Random House, 1967), 262.

5. Compare further the reflections in Stanley Corngold, "A Bug's Life: Thoughts on Having Sold a Million Copies of *The Metamorphosis*," *Princeton Alumni Weekly* (27 January 1999): 24–25.

6. Stanley Corngold, *Franz Kafka: The Necessity of Form.* (Ithaca, N.Y.: Cornell University Press, 1988), 2n5.

7. Corngold, *The Fate of the Self: German Writers and French Theory* (New York: Columbia University Press, 1986), 178.

8. See, among others, his "Error in Paul de Man," in *The Yale Critics: Deconstruction in America,* ed. Jonathan Arac, Wlad Godzich, and Wallace Martin (Minneapolis: University of Minnesota Press, 1983), 90–108, as well as his "On Paul de Man's Collaborationist Writing," in *Responses: On Paul de Man's Wartime Journalism,* ed. Werner Hamacher, Neil Hertz, and Thomas Keenan (Lincoln: University of Nebraska Press, 1989), 80–84, and "Paul de Man on the Contingency of Intention," in *(Dis)Continuities: Essays on Paul de Man,* ed. Luc Herman, Kris Humbeeck, and Geert Lernout (Amsterdam: Rodopi, 1989), 27–42.

9. Here, I draw on the autobiographical reflections found in Stanley Corngold, "Remembering Paul de Man: An Episode in the History of Comparative Literature," in *Building a Profession: Autobiographical Perspectives on the Beginnings of Comparative Literature in the United States,* ed. Lionel Gossman and Mihai Spariosu (Albany: State University of New York Press, 1994), 177–92.

10. Ibid., 182.

11. Stanley Corngold, "The Melancholy Object of Consumption," in *Violence and Mediation in Contemporary Culture,* ed. Ronald Bogue and Marcel Cornis-Pope (Albany: State University of New York Press, 1996), 33.

PART I.

Voices of Friendship:
A Conceptual Dialogue

2 Good Willing and the Practice of Friendship — A Dialogue[1]

JOHN H. SMITH

Four friends from graduate school — Ida (the Idealist), Cynthia (the Synthesizer), Dee (the Deconstructionist), Skip (the Skeptic) — meet in the basement restaurant where years before they used to gather at least once a week.

SKIP: It's been quite a while since we've sat together around a pitcher of beer. Just being here brings back memories of the arguments we had after St.'s[2] seminars. Nothing like a good argument.

IDA: I recall some of the last meetings were particularly heated. St. even came along sometimes to continue the debates. What I appreciated was the way there was something at stake in those discussions, like the fate of the self or the status of misreading.

DEE: *You* might have liked them, but after a while they got so tedious. I remember the old St., that is, the young one, before your time, when he was more playful, when signifiers slipped and tropes reigned everywhere.

CYNTHIA: I can't say I fully share your appreciation of *those* good old days, but I agree they got a lot of us thinking in new and interesting directions. The important thing for now, though, is that we're here, after all these years, having gone our different directions yet nonetheless sharing some common experiences that make it possible for the conversation to continue. It's almost as if we're picking up where we left off. A toast to friendship! And to St.!

DEE: Speaking of friendship, have you seen Derrida's *Politics of Friendship?*

IDA: Sure. But talk about tedious. Hundreds of pages of ramblings. I confess that I read more than I wanted, always hoping that the next page might develop a sustained argument.

DEE: If there are hundreds of pages it's because Derrida was pursuing hundreds of the possible "infinite interpretations" that, as he says, Nietzsche

opens up for us, interpretations in keeping with the "great unending ma-
ieutic tradition of *Lysis*."[3] For Derrida it's a question of filiation, genealogy, and problematic paternity that can't be traced without questions
arising.[4] After all, it's the very heritage of a long discourse, a wandering course, a "zigzag . . . history-without-history"[5] of friendship from
Heraclitus to Schmitt, Plato to Blanchot, that Derrida is exploring.

IDA: Wandering, rambling, discourse. . . . The point is, can you actually *say*,
on the basis of your reading of the text, what friendship, not to mention
the "politics of friendship," *is* according to Derrida. If there is no clearer
concept at the end, if we are left in the undecidable realm of the "perhaps," then we can neither accept nor argue the case. Seems like a dark
night with lots of gray cows to me.

DEE: It's ironic that you, with your Platonic leanings, would criticize Derrida for this, but, I assume, not reject the *Lysis* for coming up with the
same basic point — friendship is perhaps best approached without any
expectation of developing a clear concept of what it is. This openness
makes for a good dialogue — and I remind you that even Derrida dabbles
at one point in a minidialogue[6] — and a challenging hermeneutics. The
impossibility of providing a definition doesn't mean there's no friendship. After all, Socrates ends with an ironic gesture, pointing out that the
dialogue partners are in the situation of considering themselves friends
even though they have a difficult time explaining what that actually
means.[7]

IDA: You fail to mention that Plato refers to this situation as "ridiculous," a
characterization I take more seriously than you. This particular dialogue
of Plato's might be commonly celebrated for its open-ended character;
but I would read that as Plato's indication that the real work must now
begin — namely development of a positive understanding of the issue or
concept at hand since it's "ridiculous" to go about our business without
a clear idea of what it is. You seem to be comfortable with talking about
something that *is;* you just can't say *what* it is?

DEE: Maybe that's the paradox that Derrida is getting at every time he opens
a seminar with the apostrophe: "O friends, there are no friends."[8]

SKIP: But Dee, it seems to me that you are yourself not being consistent.
After all, if you want to criticize the notion that there *is* some concept
"out there," some "ideal friendship" that could be optimally defined,
then you really need to abandon that idea fully. You seem to leave it

hanging, as if Derrida wants to say that it's out there but he just despairs at grasping it. If you want to avoid the *Ding an sich* completely, then you have to drop the philosophical fiction that some "it" is the topic of conversation—whether it can be depicted clearly or not.

IDA: In which case Derrida is left with nothing to talk about? That *would* explain why it's so tedious.

SKIP: No. He has himself to talk about. Sure he is always mentioning the great maiuetic tradition, Aristotle's heritage, etc., as if *that* were the object of his discussion. But the filaments and threads that make up his text—and it *is* a very richly woven one, I must admit—are his own. We're following *his* mind, *his* thinking, *his* associations, *his* questions.

IDA: And why would we want to do *that?* Shouldn't we rather focus on the matter at hand, the *res,* or *Sache,* and not the person?

SKIP: Well, there's one reason I could give that's associated with the very topic of his text: you do it because you're tolerant of a "friend's" discourse. Almost every great thinker has pointed out that friendship is about complete openness and communication. The possibility of "mutual self-disclosure" could even be said to be at the heart of all friendship, so what better way for Derrida to deal with the topic and to try to engage the reader than to offer his text as an example of such self-revelation?[9] Of course, there's also the cynical reason (indicated in the title of his text): the "politics" of the academy give him the status of the "to-be-read" whether we want to or not. Even you, Ida, seemed to imply that you continued reading almost against your own will. To be honest, I'm not sure we can rule this out—or that Derrida wants us to rule out the implications of power. Given the context of power, some authors just have more authority.

DEE: But aren't you just bringing back some kind of metaphysics of subjectivity by implying that we are to treat the book "like a friend," whereby he/it speaks to us and we get to know the contours of his/its mind? You seem to be relying on an unacceptable notion of the text as the *vouloir-dire* of the author. I would say, rather, that the discourse tying the text and reader, or, to continue your analogy, the friends together, is itself not a product of the speakers' individual minds. We see less *Derrida's* intentions or *vouloir-dire* than the traditions of statements about friendship (or enmity) as they intersect with or cite each other through the centuries, forming a network of "it is said's" that come together in a Montaigne or Nietzsche. We make the choice to read a text within a certain context (called tradition in the old days) that actually limits the choice we made. The individual author and individual reader play a much less significant role than you imply. Rather, it's a massive discursive knot, not a subjective trajectory, which we follow in the text. Precisely this hermeneutic model — if it still counts as hermeneutics — would provide a different analogy for friendship, which is itself a way to "tie the knot."

CYNTHIA: Let me get a word in. I like the ideas that both Dee and Skip are suggesting, but we need to be more careful about the terms we use. Otherwise Dee's critique would overshoot its mark, striking more than it should. She's right to question an overly individualistic interpretation of either reading or friendship. But depending on just how we see the "tolerance of a 'friend's' discourse" or the *vouloir dire*, we may or may not fall into the metaphysics of subjectivity.

IDA: Good, someone has finally called for conceptual clarification here. Can we begin with the simple question since the possibility has been raised of a "friendly" reading of Derrida: Just what's involved with friendship? That's the issue he's supposed to be addressing, but in fact skirts.

DEE: Or explodes?

SKIP: Or debunks?

CYNTHIA: Or explores, but without the proper tool?

IDA: Whoa! I can't stand these pithy phrases that might get the like-minded to nod but which don't offer any real content for the rest of us. Let's slow down just a bit and work this through. I get to start. Derrida himself refers to Aristotle, but, interestingly, never manages to mention the definition offered in the *Nicomachean Ethics;* namely, friendship is mutually recognized good will. I offer this as a powerful conceptualization that we need to address. Doesn't this idea function as a kind of sine qua non of the friendship relation?

DEE: Obviously Derrida doesn't want to address this definition since that would bring us back to the metaphysics of subjectivity.

SKIP: He would also have his reservations about the "goodness" of that will.

CYNTHIA: I wish he had developed it since it would raise. . . .

IDA: Sorry for cutting you off, Cynthia, but I'm not going to let Dee and Skip dismiss the definition so fast. What's wrong with this definition? Beginning with Aristotle, who insists that friendship must rely on *proairesis* and *bouleusis,* on the faculty of decision, of deliberation or reflective choice.[10] There's a lot of meaningful reflection on this. It takes into account some of the obvious aspects of friendship. For example, it is a "willed" relationship in the sense that people enter into it of their own free wills (as opposed to parent-child or legally defined ones). No one would want to call a relationship a friendship if the individuals were being compelled to interact. Indeed, loss of freedom to be in a friendship, because of the other's claims, or needs, or expectations, would be a typical reason for its demise.

DEE: That sounds fine, but I don't see how you could possibly want to reintroduce the notion of free will into a discussion these days. Even the great philosophers of the will, from Augustine through Schopenhauer and Nietzsche, end up disputing the notion of its "freedom." You seem to be implying that the individual agent stands "outside" all relationships, or at least stands outside those that are not imposed on him or her, and then "chooses" to enter into friendships. But the deconstruction of the subject, the rejection of a notion of the "doer behind the deed" (to cite Nietzsche), makes this untenable. For example, is the individual outside the relationship, waiting to choose to enter into a friendship, "friendly" already or not? If so, then the relationship of friendship in fact preexists the friendship in a way that's problematic for you. If not, then the gap between being outside and inside a friendship seems, if not infinitely wide, infinitely deep and unbridgeable. That is, I just don't understand how a nonfriend could then will to be a friend. Derrida makes the point that we may not even be able to speak about a "self," or in your terms, a will, before there is a friend — or enemy.[11] No friends (or enemies) without the notion of the self, but no notion of the self without the others with whom we stand in a friendly or hostile relation. When the self is always already implicated in a discursive relationship with the other, how can there be a free will? So friendship is indeed a self-deconstructing paradox.

SKIP: But you shouldn't stop there, Dee. I think it *is* possible to account for the existence of friendship, but not in the way Ida implied. The problem with her starting point is not necessarily with the notion of "will," but with such attributes as "free" or "good." Nietzsche, after all, does proclaim that there is no such thing as the "free will," but nonetheless remains the philosopher of the will to power. Let me remind you of the exchange between Derrida and Gadamer in Paris in 1981.[12] Gadamer claimed that the "good will" was necessary for understanding to take place, whereas Derrida implied that one could never rule out the will to power in any interaction. Applied to our context, the individual, as I suggested, is not "free" to choose a friendship or not. On this we agree. But then what does make the supposed friendship happen? I'd say there is always a will to power operating that draws people into relationships that then get defined in any number of ways. If the will to power gets satisfied in a certain way, it gets the designation "friendship." And as odd as this might sound, my view does account for the intuitive experience so many of us have that our friendships are/were "inevitable." As in falling in love, becoming friends often happens *to* us — less a matter of *our* good will than being *willed* by the interaction.

IDA: But neither of your positions get us anywhere. Dee leaves us still with the fact of this relationship and, like Derrida, with a whole lot of questions but no clarification for how it happens. She can merely shift words around, but in the end, the statement that we can't choose friendships because we're always already friends (or however you want to formulate the paradox) doesn't explain anything. And you, Skip, who would otherwise sniff out metaphysical assumptions in others, have a strong ontological odor yourself since you imply some kind of substratum of "will to power" underlying the subject and object (the two friends) and the relation between them (their friendship).

CYNTHIA: This *is* like old times — the same old positions are getting played out here that we rehearsed, for example, when we argued about the possibility of *Bildung* after St.'s seminar on *Wilhelm Meister.* Ida has done us a service by raising Aristotle's definition, but let's make sure you all mean the same thing when you refer to the terms used there so that we can understand the nature of the value judgments you're making about those terms. Dee, why the charge of the "metaphysics of subjectivity"? This seems to be a critique that can quickly silence an opponent, but might thereby close off avenues for exploration.

DEE: I suppose I should let Ida speak. I'm assuming that she sees this "good will" as something like an intentional state of mind, that is, a subjective condition of the friend, an attitude one "possesses." Am I right?

IDA: That's basically right. I'd see the will as a fact of individual beings endowed with consciousness. It is what is, so to speak, dearest to us. This is why Epictetus argued for our own good will as the only thing we can be sure of in a friendship.[13] Epictetus rejects all outward signs of friendship, leaving him only the inner goodness of the individual as the guarantee. As Kant says, the will allows human beings to pursue and make real objects that they represent to themselves as desirable.[14] Like the *cogito,* the *volo* is indubitable since even if you *wanted* to doubt it. . . .

DEE: Yeah, we get the point. That's an old argument that also seems to silence all opposition. But there are equally old arguments that quickly show the groundlessness of your supposedly solid ground; to wit, doesn't the individual have to will his or her own will, since if I don't want to want, then I'll never want some thing, and then that will needs in turn to be willed, and so. . . .

CYNTHIA: Fine, we get your infinite-regress argument already. But where does that lead you (except to silence *your* opposition, as if Ida could be silenced!). The groundlessness of willing (or what Schelling called the *Abgrund* and *Ursein* of the free will)[15] doesn't make it go away. All you show is that we can't define it *merely* subjectively. That's why the metaphysics of subjectivity has been undermined for a good two hundred years. But don't we get a clue from Ida herself that willing is, by definition, never just the state of the individual's mind since, in Kant's definition, it is always implicated with some object and some representation of the object and some representation of the (future) self as having that object and maybe some reason why the self wants that object (because of prior experience or experience of others), etc. This seems much more complex than a "state of mind." German has the nice distinction between *Wille* and *Willkür,* the latter being the kind of arbitrary, willful free will to choose that has been shown to be an insufficient starting point for thinking about the self. *That* metaphysics of subjectivity is rightly criticized by means of variations of Dee's argument; but. . . .

SKIP: And this is where I come in. I waited for you to deconstruct the subject, the way Nietzsche followed upon fifty years of arguments against Cartesian dualism. And now the ground is clear for some nonsubjective principle (if we want to call it that) to emerge, hence the "will to power." The individual's "good will" can always be reduced to forces and power relations that exceed the mind of the individual. Hobbes already argued this. The consequences might not be pleasant since "friendships" and other forms of social interactions are created out of fear or greed, that is, out of the play of forces into which the individual is placed and where he or she must survive, and *not* out of some "good will."[16]

CYNTHIA: I think you're jumping the gun on the will's demise since I'm not sure the ground is cleared in that way. Just because willing and good will are not *only* subjective (that is, can't be grounded in a subjective principle and shouldn't be reduced to *Willkür*) doesn't mean that they are *not at all* subjective. Good will can be co-constitutive of the self insofar as it is a state that we are *in* in the double sense of that phrase. It is a condition that exceeds our intentionality but then disposes us to be a certain way. Good will is neither independent of the "play of forces" nor reducible to them. Dee's circular reasoning above — can't have a friendly disposition without a friend but can't have a friend without a friendly disposition — should be embraced dialectically, not used as grist for a deconstructive mill. Derrida himself implies this when he refers to the "heteronomic trust" that makes up friendship, a trust that exceeds the *cogito*.[17] But it is "trust," or "good will," nonetheless and the origin of a subjectivity mixed with otherness. After all, anyone with an appreciation for the trials of adolescence can see how the individual wills of youth emerge only out of a complex and intimate exchange of wills with their friends.[18] The subject is not there from the start "radiating" good will, so to speak; but once good will is there, the subject takes on a certain formation that allows a self to interact differently, differentially (not just in conformity) with the environment.

SKIP: What kind of adolescence did *you* have? Once you rather define the "intimate exchange of wills" as *peer pressure*, a different view of the tenuous origins of selfhood emerges.

IDA: Fine, both of you show me that I have to modify my position. But you should know me better than to assume I would adopt a position that we know from St.'s seminars was abandoned in the early nineteenth century. That is, my statement might have looked like that of a subjective idealist, but that can't have been my real intention since I would insist that the will (or ego) is actually *transcendental,* that is, a condition of our being. That's where my argument above was going before you cut me off. People critique the Cartesian ego as if it were the actual one Descartes found sitting alone in his dark room. Rather, he found the principle that, as Kant says, the "'I think' must be able to accompany" all my acts of consciousness — so, too, the "I will." And it's *this* that is the "ideal" behind the great discussion of friendship. These a priori conditions of our

subjective condition are not themselves subjects. Nor are they objects in
the world.

DEE: But that removes it from the world of temporality in which our consciousness actually unfolds. If there's one thing we've learned from phenomenology through poststructuralism, it is the need to account for the
differing/deferring effect of time. And friendship, of all things, is radically temporal. In fact, the temporal structure of friendship is incred-
ibly complex, so much so that far from being "timeless," this "good will"
is overburdened with all sorts of time. Friendship seems to be in the
present, but in fact is always being projected or put off into the future; for
example, the notion of fair-weather friends implies that *real* friendship
can only exist at some point in the future when it can be tested. Derrida
even shows, based on Cicero's reference to a projected friend's eulogy,
that there is a bizarre (and impossible) future perfect tense involved: You
are my friend because you will have demonstrated your friendship in
what you say about me after I die. Not to mention the nostalgia attached
to discussions about *past* friendships, the ones that most often do get
discussed.

SKIP: Ergo, the subject's will, good or not, dissipates into a nonentity. What
Dee's argument shows is that we're barking up the wrong tree by thinking of friendship and the will in subjective *or* transcendental terms. The
temporality that unfolds in a friendship is neither determined by the
individual subject nor accounted for by some transcendental will; rather
it arises out of the power conditions and relations that shift differentially. We only register them *après coup,* by which I mean that when we
find ourselves in a particular arrangement, we say "We are friends." This
might appear to be a statement of our being (who we are), but in fact
describes the condition we are in.

CYNTHIA: Temporality is in fact a key feature, and it's good we bring it in.
But even if it does have serious consequences for Ida's argument, I don't
think it's as serious as you two claim. I know that the word "will" might
tempt us to think of the, rightly discredited, view of a faculty psychology, and it's *this* view that temporality wreaks havoc on. There is no part
of the mind called the "will" that just exists outside of time. This is why
it's probably best to think more in terms of "willing" as a process or activity or practice. Such a notion of practice might also allow us to avoid

Skip's tendency to reduce everything to states and conditions. Let's play this out with an example: Two kids on the shore, each daring the other to enter the cold water first, until they decide that they'll enter together. A familiar scenario, right? I'd like to see it as a model for how friendship and good willing get enacted.

IDA: A scenario that shows the way the transcendental is not some spooky metaphysical thing, but a precondition that inheres in the most concrete. After all, if there were not a good will to cooperate between the two — and I stress "between" since it enjoins both without being "in" either — then the agreement or understanding (in the sense of *Einverständnis*) would not work. We see this whenever one of the kids in fact acts out of malevolence, letting his or her "friend" run off alone into the water while he or she stands on the shore laughing at the gullible (and cold and wet) other. Such an act is a betrayal, which implies that a priori a bond or pact has been broken.

SKIP: And how would you purport to explain this all-to-often and very painful experience of the failure of the compact to work? Is it not the very disparity in the power between the two that allows the one to hold back at the expense of the other? If I can refer to one of your favorites, Ida, even Hegel bears me out indirectly. Echoing Aristotle, he says to his young students in the Nuremberg *Gymnasium* that friendship rests on equality and the common interest in some task.[19] This implies the priority of the real conditions, interests, goals — in short, power. That is, where there is a balance of power between the two, or a common interest (overcoming the fear of the cold water), there will be a state in which they will jump together and that state will be interpreted as good will, friendship, etc.

DEE: I hate these kinds of examples. Concocted to give an air of concreteness to the discussion, they remove the complex linguistic interplay of social relations from the example only to say: "So you see, we can do without language. . . ." They remind me of analytic philosophy, a game I'm not interested in playing.

CYNTHIA: For all your talk about temporality, your ad hominem gesture doesn't do a very good job allowing us to see how possibilities for friendship unfold. Let's work with the example some more (and *not* as analytic philosophers, necessarily). Sure, one kid could trick the other by holding back and laughing. Happens all the time. But how often could he get away with it? The bond I spoke of is not just *there,* but must develop over time and can indeed be disrupted, as when the one "friend" betrays the other all of a sudden because of the presence of a third person he wants to impress at the "friend's" expense. If that happens too often, the friendship comes to an end. The fact that these scenarios unfold over time, and that they are repeated — iterated, with variations — doesn't undermine the significance of friendship, but, on the contrary, shows why friendship has so often been considered paradigmatic for understanding human nature and relationships. Precisely the complex temporality being played out on the beach — each kid thinking about the past experiences, the amount of faith to be placed in the present, and the projections for the future — is the key to understanding the status of good willing and friendship. It's wrong to reduce the friendship to any one aspect or to assume that this complexity undermines friendship itself.

DEE: I again offer my feeble protest to the entire construct of the example. You want to say something here about the "will" of the kids involved here and think you can do so without appealing to the innumerable gestures and interpretive acts that take place in this little dance between "friends" on the shore. They can only surmise the other's will by "reading" the other's language, even if only body language. If you rule that out, you're getting as abstract as Ida.

CYNTHIA: Yes, the example is simplified, but your points don't destroy its value. We just need to be clear that the kind of good willing I'm talking about is not latent, simply needing to be expressed as if it were some pure potentiality. That strikes me as the movie fantasy version. Rather, it is developed (*gebildet?*) over time and only exists in its being "spread out" over time and between the subject and others. Unfortunately, we're lulled into believing that it's conceivable that someone really "has" good will, inside, but just can't show it for some reason, and so it needs to be "brought out." Not by chance, one of the more popular movies recently, which was structured with this all too typical narrative, was called, punningly, *Good Will Hunting.* I couldn't agree more that it's riskier than this, however, because it involves the kind of intricate interpreting that Dee's talking about, and there's nothing there. . . .

SKIP: Exactly. . . .

CYNTHIA: No, wait. There's nothing there except the activity of exploring the mutual recognition of the other. I suspect Aristotle would have accepted this interpretation. Seen in this way, friendship becomes not an entity or a relationship, but a *practice*. Hence, we also needn't argue about whether it's an entity or a nonentity. Friendship would thus best be understood in the broad anthropological terms of Bourdieu. Practices, which he sees as accounting for the way people create social cohesion and meaning, serve to move between the false subjectivist and objectivist dichotomy we've also been exploring. I like his understanding of the way people begin relationships out of proximity, consistency, and effectiveness and then develop practices that are flexible, yet, which over time "dispose" the agents to behave in certain ways. The relationships aren't fixed in stone, but need to be "maintained" and always reassessed.[20] That's what the kids on the beach are doing, and what adolescents are consumed by. This "maintenance work" in the case of friendship involves a certain give and take, an openness and intimate self-disclosure, that we can call "good willing." So my notion of good willing is not nearly as abstract as Ida's after all. But it also doesn't dissipate into uselessness. On the contrary, willing as practice is precisely what engages us with others and the world. At one point Derrida talks about the way friendship is often linked to *habitat,* the place where we are; but I prefer to see it as a question of *habitus,* the way we live.[21]

IDA: And yet, all this talk about practice doesn't relieve us from the responsibility of formulating guidelines. Kant says we need the good will to be based on *principles* to guide our friendships, otherwise we'll be like the "uneducated," those who move in and out of friendships, who break up just in order to have the pleasure of reuniting.[22] Sure it unfolds for them over time, but randomly, contradictorily. Only a deeper kind of understanding can avoid this kind of emotional imbalance.

SKIP: That's all too harmonious for me, and in fact the apparent harmony masks something. Note how Kant introduces class divisions into friendship. Your appeal to "principles" is actually full of its own biases, and the supposed rational will that would form the basis of "real" friendship is thus nothing but the *habitus* of the middle class. Moreover, we can use the example Cynthia raised, and the way it shows that friendships can go wrong, to focus on another point. The rivalry that often emerges in friendships is typically gender or sexually based. "Good will" is underwritten by desires that it can barely repress. We've left this out entirely, or I should say, we're tending to hide it. Did you all notice how Cynthia made the kids on the shore, at least the "betrayer," male? I don't think that's by chance. Even though he doesn't seem to do much with it, or about it, Derrida himself raises this issue a couple of times, for example, reminding us that the couples that make up "ideal" friendships are usually male-male or that the tradition on friendship is like a "desert" filled with only men.[23] It's remarkable how blind the tradition has been to this basic structuration of friendship. I confess I could hardly get through Kracauer's *Über die Freundschaft* because it was all coded male without the slightest awareness of its own gender bias. For example, friendship is constantly being contrasted with romantic love with a woman, the implication being that the real friends are straight men. This blindness to gender in the conception of friendship goes hand in hand with the blindness to the power that informs the friendships. No wonder the will, with all its macho implications, plays such a major role in the tradition. Moreover, even if I wanted to adopt the terms that are being used for the moment, I'd have to insist that where there's will there's desire, and that introduces much more than "good" will.

IDA: But why should gender play a role? I agree that any implication that real friendship is a male thing is problematic, as would any sense that there's some special status to female friendship. The transcendental conditions for friendship are gender-neutral precisely because they are not empirical. And to reduce everything to desire defeats all possible argumentation — your own included — not to mention the fact that it becomes a despicable approach to human beings. The model, by no means worthy of emulation in my estimation, of such a reductive view of friendship would be Freud, who in both theory and practice seems to have had your notions in mind, Skip. For all of Freud's insights into desire and the unconscious, it didn't do wonders for his friendships. He could only look at friendship as displaced desire, something that serves a temporary purpose but which then must be overcome if the self is to develop its powers.[24] And perhaps to his questionable credit, he acted accordingly.

DEE: Both of you make me feel uncomfortable. Ida because she would deny the categories of gender, Skip because he'd impose them. In both cases there's a kind of essentializing, either of a neutered will or of "male" and "female" desires. Your kind of exchange gets played out at our institutions as the paradoxes of identity unfold in identity politics and its

neutralizing other. The reason to raise these categories of sexual difference, and they do need to be raised, Ida, is to demonstrate their disruptive power, not their absoluteness. As Derrida says, if friendship is
a fraternity, what happens when the "sister" is introduced? Does that
make her another "brother"? Does it undermine the fraternal order?[25]
Such questions leave the debate over the essential nature or insignifi-
cance of gender categories behind. At that point, it's not obvious just
what "brotherhood" or "sisterhood" even refer to, except for some dif-
ferential operation that can't be stabilized. And I don't see how a notion
of the will—male, female, neuter—would help you here since precisely
such "master concepts" (already a telling phrase!) can't account for their
own internal complexity.

CYNTHIA: All right, then let's make the concepts more dialectically complex. The interactive model I proposed would account for the change
that can occur in friendships and for the role gender plays. And by implication, could even help us with the institutional debates you hint at.
So many of the great works on friendship point out that there are two aspects: there is the "enduring character" of "undying friendships" and the
"changeableness" of even the most intimate and strongest relations. Unfortunately, most writers tend to think of these aspects as mutually exclusive. Moreover, these two aspects are coded as male and female, so no
wonder that men and women have different kinds of friendship. It's also
no wonder that the canonical tradition is blind to women's interactions
that don't fit into the codification of woman as fickle. But in their essence,
friendships display, or are sustained by, what Amélie Rorty called "dynamic permeability." The "historicity" of friendships is granted, I would
say, by the necessarily temporal unfolding of good willing, which clearly
can't be a one-time thing. After all, would it really be a sign of bad will to
imply to someone: "I need show you good will only once." And because
it is expressed over time, this good willing is implicated in scenarios
and scripts and representations of possible interactions. These become
what Teresa de Lauretis has called the "practice of love." Her interest in
such practices (a word she could make more use of than in the title of
her book!) leads her to pragmatic and semiotic theories that, in a way
that parallels Bourdieu, allow her to mediate between the subjectivism
of psychoanalysis and the objectivism of more structuralist approaches
to gender and sexuality.[26] The nongendered phenomenon of willing (by

which I don't mean something "autonomous," but that point where the self interacts with the world) gets unfolded in gendered and sexualized ways thanks to the interaction of the individuals with the scripts they perform. Unfortunately, there is a tendency to see the performative nature of these interactions as abolishing the idea of the will, rather than to understand good willing precisely as performance, or to avoid inappropriate and distracting emphasis on the theatrical, on practice.

IDA: But this unfolding over time nonetheless still needs a principle of regulation. There are all sorts of "practices" or ways for people to interact. But we want to understand, and maybe even foster, a particular *kind*, namely, *good* will, and that presumes an ethical stance, which, I would think, applies to men and women alike.

SKIP: You just want some way of controlling the power investments that would otherwise lead at times to a dangerous interpenetration. But those dangers are part of it.

DEE: It's not just power and danger. There must be a random element in this temporal unfolding, some unpredicatiblity or, if you will, undecidability, the Derridean "perhaps," which is both a condition of friendship and its undermining. This undecidability must permeate the decision itself, ironically, if it is indeed to be a "free" decision at all. Otherwise, the will that you would have as the basis of friendship becomes a vain attempt to impose a rationality (will, in the sense of commanding) that you clearly can't intend.

CYNTHIA: I can only partially agree with you two. First of all, let me point out that you, Dee, also do seem to accept some notion of a free will that you would have deconstructed earlier.[27] Second, I think the dynamism involves the unfolding of dangers vis-à-vis both the self and other, and this is what makes the freedom relative, not absolute. I'd like to see good will as an active state of "being-there-for" the other. It's telling that Heidegger, for all his exploration of the ways human existence links both activity and passivity (for example, his notion of *Gelassenheit*) doesn't have a notion of *Dasein-für;* it's telling, that is, about his own moral character that such an engagement with the Other is lacking. What Hume refers to as the "benevolent or softer affections"[28] has no place in his thought.

DEE: The will as active *and* passive. So you also embrace the paradox.

CYNTHIA: Yes, dialectically. But my point is that the notion of will, always in the sense of "willing" and never as a substantive entity or faculty, captures best this duality, so there's no reason to "deconstruct" it. When I said earlier that I wished Derrida had introduced it in his analysis of friendship, I meant that he seems occasionally, in those passages that I like because they do provide cognitive content and not just the meanderings of his richly contoured mind, to be getting at such a notion. He coins a term, you'll recall, "lovence" (*aimance*) to get at the "middle voice" between activity and passivity that would be the basis of friendship (7).[29] He relates this to the act of making a decision (68–69), which exhibits the precise structuration we are looking at. This point of intersection and interaction between self and world, where we exhibit an "active passivity" that might be linked to "attentiveness" or, to use a term Derrida has explored a great deal, "responsibility," to the Other, is what I mean by will. And a case could be made that most of the Western tradition also, as a whole, develops such an interactional model.

DEE: But responsibility can't be isolated in the subject.

CYNTHIA: I couldn't agree more. That's why willing here is a more complex concept than subjectivity. Derrida and others always critique Kant on the "good will," accusing him of his fixation on autonomy, and rightly so, to the extent that Kant himself overly stresses that. But if we look at how Kant sees the will as having to be realized, carried out in reality, we see he might not be so far off from Derrida after all. The good will that is the basis of friendship, for Kant, makes us not just "in principle" but also "practically" involved with the well-being of the other person.[30] I would emphasize the "practical" here. And Kant admits that this is not a guarantee of happiness; things can (and will) go wrong; but this practical and emotional openness can make one "worthy" of happiness.

SKIP: Doesn't the "practical" imply interests? This is the kind of calculating rationality that turns friendship into an imposition of wills.

DEE: Right. You'll recall that Derrida criticized Gadamer on precisely those grounds. There's a slippage between the "good will" and the "will to power." Kant, for all his insistence on the purity of the good will, slips in here a pragmatic perspective that Adorno and Horkheimer saw all too well in the *Dialectic of the Enlightenment*.

IDA: I'll defend Kant here against your misinterpretations. You're wrong to interpret "practical" in this reductive way; in fact, he means *ethical*. The interest we should have in the well-being of the other, Kant is arguing, is dictated to us by our "practical" — not by "instrumental" — reason.

Ultimately, this could be seen as a maxim ("Have and be good to your friends!") that is justified by the categorical imperative, since if we *didn't* follow that maxim, that is, if no one did, we would find ourselves in a state of pure self-interest that would in fact *not* be in our best interest.

CYNTHIA: That may very well be Kant's meaning here. But why not also tease out a different reading, one that might not be so abstractly rational as yours, Ida, but which avoids the pitfalls of Skip's and Dee's doubts. I would see "practical" here in terms of practices. Good will does also need to be objectified. Like practices, good willing inhabits a space between the subjective (since practices are directed by our intentions) and the objective (since they can't be just in our minds). My willingness to work for my friend's well-being must be enacted or embodied *in practices*. The reason is that we are human beings and our wills are endowed with both a material and a rational side. Thus, Ida's call (in keeping, certainly, with a legitimate reading of Kant) for "principles" is not enough. It's more a question of unsystematizable tact, or tactics. As Amélie Rorty stresses, only the messy reality of our interactions, and not some abstract principle of reason, can decide the fate of our friendship.[31]

IDA: True. This is Hegel's critique of Kantian morality in general. The good will needs to be "played out" in the real world.

CYNTHIA: Kant's problem was that all too often he could only see nothing but an impossible choice between chaos (pathology) or principles (rules). Not unlike the two of you, Dee and Ida. Instead, one could consider a mediating notion or function. De Certeau's distinction between *strategies* as calculated acts predicated on the attempt to gain a mastery of will and power and *tactics* as *inter*actions is useful. The former recall a notion of the will that he finds very limited. And we all seem to concur on that point. The latter, however, introduce a complex idea of agency. We might strategize in the abstract, but tactics unfold only in interaction with others in specific contexts. To use a word from Kant, they are always "heteronomous," although this does not mean that we, as agents, don't have a role in their playing out.[32] Here, in a way that brings me back to Derrida, we have an interesting fusion of discussions of war (that's where "tactics" play a role, as de Certeau points out) and friendship. And it's interesting that Derrida and de Certeau refer to some of the same issues in Clausewitz.[33] But I like the way de Certeau does it: not in order to deconstruct the relationship between friendship and hostility, but to bring out this "playing on the other," or as he says, "making do" with the other. That would be the very essence of good willing.

SKIP: I like it. Friendship is just something one does. Maybe that's why we speak of "making friends." It's an activity that can't be grasped by any *vita contemplativa*. We sit together, we drink, we talk. And if we do all these things in a certain way, with a certain balance of power and interests, then we call the interaction "friendly."

CYNTHIA: Your characterization of what "we're doing" does indeed hit close to home. The bottom line for me would be whether or not we can even account for the very conversation and activities we are engaged in right now. Otherwise, we fall prey to Habermas's critique of Foucault and much postmodern thought, namely its failure to apply its own terms to its own activity.[34] That's what the notion of good will is trying to do — account for what we're up to. After all, if we didn't show a certain amount of good will toward each other, would we even bother to explore these positions together?

IDA: Excellent. I appreciate your call for transcendental grounding. I'd given up on you, since you seem to be a mere pragmatist. The a priori conditions of our "friendly" interaction could be carefully delineated. We all share a set of experiences and ideas and common language that make our communication possible. When I sense that Derrida no longer wants to participate in a real dialogue, I close the book. His claim to want to be misunderstood does strike me as a case of *bad will*.[35]

DEE: Needless to say (and even *that* phrase demonstrates my point, as you'll see), your drive toward discursive self-reflexivity remains highly questionable for two reasons (at the least; I'll control myself). First, can we really enunciate the conditions of our enunciations without falling into the same old infinite regress that bored everyone earlier? Don't we need to have an agreement on some a priori in order to pursue the a priori together, etc. And second, Cynthia's rhetoric of the "bottom line" betrays her in a significant way, since it shows how, despite the talk of "transcendental" arguments etc., she's working with a restricted economy that would impose a stopping point, and precisely that effort undermines itself. Derrida, on the contrary, is interested in tapping into an "economy without reserve" in the history of friendship.[36]

SKIP: Right, so stop trying to ground your positions Cynthia and Ida. All you're doing is trying to silence the rest of us with *your* good will. But

I would add to you, Dee, stop trying to lead us into infinite regresses. Let's just go about our business.

CYNTHIA: I'm closer to you than you think, Skip, and I should be careful about assuming my critique of the inability to account for our very activity as a call for transcendentalism. My point is that we can still make the effort to describe our business even as we're engaged in it, can't we? Why can't one of the practices we are engaged in be precisely the reflection on practices? There's no reason for that "theorizing" to have a qualitatively different epistemological or ontological status, or to attain an absolute stability beyond all practice. Instead, it can grow out of practices and itself be an "art" of theorizing.[37] Those engaged in this "second-order" practice would be related to Gramsci's "organic intellectual" — one engaged "in active participation in practical life, as constructor, organiser, 'permanent persuader.'"[38] And with that reference, we seem to come back to where we started, namely to the very basis of our own conversation: to mutually recognized good will, or better, to mutual good willing. There's no reason to presume any real or ideal consensus awaiting us at the end of our conversation or underlying it in any special way. But we also don't get anywhere if we presume some kind of "dissensus,"[39] a kind of underlying *bad* will. Rather, what I see operating here is an openness to each other, an attentiveness and a drive for self-disclosure that recognizes the potential for change and failure. Sometimes it works, sometimes it doesn't. Sometimes it works for a while, and then falls apart. Kind of like St.'s seminars. Practicing good willing takes time and repeated efforts.

SKIP: And the fact that we're willing to explore these positions together time and again tells us something about our friendship — at least up to now. I guess in the end we can be grateful that St. brought us together in this spirit.

DEE: Or in this spirit of "willingness," even though we seem to be playing out these ideas with a kind of repetition compulsion, willy-nilly, as it were.

IDA: Maybe we are carrying on his legacy. Our intellectual friendship is his living will and testament.

NOTES

1. I would like to express my gratitude to my colleague, Ermanno Bencivenga (Philosophy, UCI), for sharing his enthusiasm for philosophical dialogues.

2. A fictional professor at a fictional Ivy League university.

3. Jacques Derrida, *The Politics of Friendship* (London: Verso, 1997), 77.

4. Derrida, 176–77.

5. Derrida, 221.

6. Derrida, 149.

7. Plato, *Lysis:* ". . . we have made ourselves rather ridiculous today. . . . Though we conceive ourselves to be friends with each other . . . we have not as yet been able to discover what we mean by a friend" (223b). *The Collected Dialogues of Plato,* ed. Edith Hamilton and Huntington Cairns (Princeton: Princeton University Press, 1961).

8. Derrida on the conclusion of *Lysis,* 155.

9. Lawrence Thomas, "Friendship and Other Loves" in Neera Kapur Badhwar, *Friendship: A Philosophical Reader* (Ithaca: Cornell, 1993), 48–64.

10. See Derrida, 198.

11. Derrida's question: "without an enemy, and therefore without friends, where does one then find oneself, *qua* a self?" (77).

12. First documented in *Text und Interpretation: Deutsch-französische Debatte,* ed. Philippe Forget (Munich: Fink, 1984). In English, with different responses, *Dialogue and Deconstruction: The Gadamer-Derrida Encounter,* ed. Diane P. Michelfelder and Richard Palmer (Albany: State University of New York Press, 1989).

13. Epictetus in *Of Friendship: Philosophic Selections on a Perennial Concern,* ed. Marshell Carl Bradley and Philip Blosser (Wolfeboro, N.H.: Longwood Academic, 1989).

14. Kant's definition of will, for example, in the introduction to the *Kritik der praktischen Vernunft, Kants Werke, Akademie Textausgabe,* volume 5 (Berlin: Walter de Gruyter & Co, 1968): "welcher ein Vermögen ist, den Vorstellungen entsprechende Gegenstände entweder hervorzubringen, oder doch sich selbst zu Bewirkung derselben (das physische Vermögen mag nun hinreichend sein, oder nicht), d.i. seine Causalität, zu bestimmen" ("which is an ability either to produce objects that correspond to ideas or at least to determine itself to effect them, i.e. to be its own causality [regardless of whether the physical capability is sufficient to produce the objects]," 29).

15. Schelling, *Abhandlung über das Wesen der menschlichen Freiheit und die damit zusammenhängenden Gegenstände* (Frankfurt: Suhrkamp, 1988).

16. Hobbes: "We must therefore resolve, that the original of all great and lasting societies consisted not in the mutual good will men had towards each other, but in mutual fear they had of each other" (from *Leviathan,* in *Of Friendship,* 216).

17. "Heteronomic trust exceeds the reflexive forms of knowledge and consciousness of a subject, all the certitudes of an *ego cogito.*" Derrida, 195.

18. Adrian Durnham, "Friendship and Personal Development" in *The Dialectics of Friendship,* ed. Roy Porter and Sylvana Tomaselli (London and New York: Routledge, 1989), 92–110.

19. "*Freundschaft* beruht auf Gleichheit der Charaktere, besondern des Interesses, ein gemeinsames *Werk* miteinander zu tun." Hegel, *Rechts-, Pflichten-, und Religionslehre für die Unterklasse,* part 1, §67 (Theorie-Werkausgabe, vol. 4, 271).

20. "To escape from relativism without falling into realism, we may posit that the constants of the field of potentially useful relationships (i.e. those that are actually usable, because spatially close, and useful, because socially influential) cause each group of agents to tend to keep up by continuous maintenance-work a privileged network of practical relationships . . ." (39). Pierre Bourdieu, *Outline of a Theory of Practice* (Cambridge: Cambridge University Press, 1977).

21. Derrida, 17.

22. "the rabble brawl and make up . . . for they need to squabble in order to relish the sweetness of unity in reconciliation" (151). Kant, §46, *Metaphysik der Sitten,* Part II, *Kants Werke, Akademie Textausgabe,* Vol. 6 (Berlin: Walter de Gruyter & Co., 1968).

23. Derrida: "Even if there are more than two of them, the model (*exemplar*) will most often be furnished by a twosome, by some great couples of friends. Always men. Well, more often than not, and that is what counts . . ." (78). Or again, referring to Schmitt, but more generally applicable: "Not a woman in sight. An inhabited desert, to be sure, an absolutely full absolute desert, some might even say a desert teeming with people. Yes, but men, men and more men, over centuries of war and costumes. . . . In vain would you look for a figure of a woman, a feminine silhouette, and the slightest allusion to sexual difference" (155–56).

24. Graham Little, "Freud, Friendship, and Politics," in *The Dialectics of Friendship,* ed. Roy Porter and Sylvana Tomaselli (London: Routledge, 1989), esp. 148.

25. "And the sister? Would she be in the same situation? Would she be a case of fraternity?" Derrida, 149.

26. The use of Peirce, for example, "may serve to articulate Freud's privatized view of the internal world of the psyche with Foucault's eminently social view of sexuality." Teresa de Lauretis, *The Practice of Love: Lesbian Sexuality and Perverse Desire* (Bloomington: Indiana University Press, 1994), xixf.

27. "[Science and conscience] are unable to determine the leap of decision without transforming it into the irresponsible application of a programme, hence without depriving it of what makes it a sovereign and free decision. . . ." Derrida, 219.

28. In *Of Friendship,* 245–46.

29. He points out that a contemporary poet had also used this neologism, without mutual influence.

30. Kant writes: "It is easy to see that this [the association of friendship as equal and mutual love and respect] is an ideal whereby friends are united through a morally good will in such a way that each is concerned, both *practically* and emotionally, with the well-being of the other." *Metaphysik der Sitten,* §46.

31. "It is only the details of [a particular friendship] that can determine what would be rational, what would be appropriate, what would constitute (whose?) thriving. No general philosophical conclusions about the presumptive connections between ratio-

nality, appropriateness, and thriving can possible help [friends] determine just what corrections rationality recommends or requires as appropriate to their condition." In Badhwar, 88.

32. De Certeau writes: "No delimitation of an exteriority, then, provides [tactics] with the condition necessary for autonomy. The space of a tactic is the space of the other. Thus it must play on and with a terrain imposed on it and organized by the law of a foreign power." Michel de Certeau, *The Practice of Everyday Life*, trans. Steven Randall (Los Angeles: University of California Press, 1984), 37.

33. Derrida, 147.

34. In Jürgen Habermas, *Der philosophische Diskurs der Moderne* (Frankfurt am Main: Suhrkamp, 1985), Lecture 10.

35. Derrida, 218–19.

36. ". . . an *economy without reserve* is *unleashed,* announcing . . . the arithmetical challenge of arithmetic, the indivisibility that induces a desire for an *infinite* multiplication of the subject. . . . For it is due to the internal logic of the indivisibility of the soul in the couple of friends: 'This is what we cherish in friendship [according to Augustine], and we cherish it so dearly that in conscience we feel guilty if we do not return love for love . . . , asking no more of our friends than these expressions of goodwill (*praeter indicia benevolentiae*)." Derrida, 187.

37. De Certeau, Part II, Chapter V.

38. Antonio Gramsci, *Selections from the Prison Notebooks,* edited and translated by Quintin Hoare and Geoffrey Nowell Smith, (New York: International Publishers, 1971), 10.

39. Lyotard, *The Differend: Phrases in Dispute,* trans. Georges van den Abeele (Minneapolis: University of Minnesota Press, 1988). Also Bill Readings, *The University in Ruins* (Cambridge, Mass.: Harvard University Press, 1996), Chapter 12.

PART II.
Literary Archaeologies (I):
Codes of Friendship and
Paternity in German Classicism

3   Connotations of Friendship and Love in Schiller's *Philosophical Letters* and Hölderlin's *Hyperion*

WALTER HINDERER

Translated by Edward T. Potter

For Stanley Corngold, in friendship

Within the context of the German Enlightenment, love is often associated with the middle-class value of virtue. In the *Introduction to Ethics* (*Einleitung zur Sittenlehre*), Christian Thomasius speaks of "sensible or rational love [vernünftiger Liebe]" or "true love [wahrer Liebe]," which alone guarantees the intended goal: the "bliss of composure."[1] In contrast to French semantics, love in the German and the English contexts is spiritualized, idealized, and moralized, and sexuality is sublimated. Gellert's novel *Life of the Swedish Countess of G.* (*Leben der schwedischen Gräfin von G.*) is paradigmatic for the codification of love before 1750, for the main characters in this novel put the instructions of Thomasius into practice. Strong emotions endanger not only reason (the central value in the middle-class conception of morality), but also the ideal of courtly *constantia,* which was transposed into the middle-class realm and which extends far into the eighteenth century as the concept of Christian Stoicism (Justus Lipsius). In order to steer "restless and passionate longing" in the right directions and to alter the function of the energies of desires, love is bound tightly to reason. Even Schiller's *Love and Intrigue* (*Kabale und Liebe*) illustrates the extent to which erotic and sexual love was primarily considered a courtly phenomenon in the eighteenth century. The idealization of the semantics of love clearly has a political facet as well. Within this context, it is remarkable that Christian Fürchtegott Gellert, who functioned as a *Praeceptor Germa-*

niae in addition to Gottsched, subjected the concept of "sensible or rational love" to surprisingly fundamental criticism in an essay, although this
concept, not insignificantly, served to moderate desire.[2] On the one hand,
he criticizes in this essay a "sensual love which concerns merely the body
[sinnliche Liebe, die bloß auf den Körper geht]" as the "preoccupation of
small and infertile souls"; on the other hand, he denounces a "spiritual love
which is coupled only with the characteristics of the soul [geistige Liebe,
die sich nur mit den Eigenschaften der Seele gattet]" as "a fantasy of arro-
gant students who are ashamed that heaven has given them a body, which
they would not, if their words had to be backed up by actions, abandon
for ten souls."[3] Christoph Martin Wieland would later openly and furtively
smuggle "sexual love [Geschlechtsliebe]" as a topic into religious-pietistic
semantics. The codifications of love in the German context are, however,
not quite as clear and free of inconsistencies as Niklas Luhmann considers
them to be in his stimulating comparative study *Love as Passion* (*Liebe als
Passion*).[4] It is especially in literature that functions that are critical of codes
and whose goal it is to change the socially sanctioned semantics, appear
side by side with code-forming functions.

What Luhmann observes in a corresponding development in England
can be claimed, however, for a particular phase within the German context
as well: "Love as duty is reformulated into love as fondness and brought
into line with the ideal of friendship,"[5] whereby the difference between the
genders seems almost to become blurred in the sphere of friendship relations. Even the chief ideologue of the Storm and Stress movement, Johann
Gottfried Herder, influenced by Rousseau, would eventually programmati-
cally recommend in his essay "Love and Selfhood" [*"Liebe und Selbstheit"*]
(1781): "Love is meant to invite us to friendship, love itself is meant to become the most heartfelt friendship."[6] Not insignificantly, this is also valid
for marriage. Goethe's *Werther* and Jacobi's *Woldemar* (1779) demonstrate
that a dichotomy between marriage and spiritual friendship still exists in
the eighteenth century. Just as Lotte views Werther as her soul mate, so too
does Woldemar think of Henriette as his soul mate. Admittedly, in both
cases, the protagonists experience characteristic crises, which only serve to
demonstrate that, not insignificantly, it is sentimental tendencies that put
the connotation of friendship and love to a crucial test. Apparently, friendship cannot permanently satisfy "the burning desire for *a human heart*"[7]

either. Werther, with his demand that the emotions be absolutely supreme, becomes, in the end, the victim of his boundless passion. That does not, admittedly, mean that the narrative strategy therefore favors "sensible or rational love," the view of Albert. Rather, rational love and sentimental love are clearly being brought into a fictional course of conflict for which there seems to be no solution other than suicide or murder, as is demonstrated by the story of the love-stricken farmhand that was inserted into the novel. "Love and faithfulness, the most beautiful human sentiments," says the commentary, had in fact "transformed [themselves] into violence and murder."[8]

How, on the other hand, love and friendship as sentimental social phenomena move closer together within the emotional value of joy, the "sister of humanity," is illustrated by Klopstock's Asclepiadic ode "Lake Zurich" ("*Der Zürchersee*"), which appeared in 1750 and which had a paradigmatic effect on the younger generation. From the aesthetic experience of nature to the experience of "Haller's Doris," the poem leads up to the climax of the last five stanzas, in which a reorganization of the codification of "rational love" occurs. Friendship is placed above love and virtue as the supreme value: "O, in this way, we build huts of friendship here!" it says in the last stanza. "Eternally we lived here, eternally! The shady forest / Changed itself into Tempe for us / That valley into Elysium!" Whereas Schiller later draws a parallel and identifies love in its "utmost relevance"[9] with Elysium, it is friendship here, as Albert Salomon explains in detail, that expands itself to become the substratum of a way of life in the eighteenth century.[10] There can, however, be no question that, in the end, it is love and not friendship that characterizes the code for intimacy. Luhmann is correct in assuming "that friendship, in spite of all the privatization of, and all the distinction between, everyday and peculiar friendship (Thomasius), proves itself [impossible] to delimit or to be distinguished from other things."[11] This constellation was only to be plausible for a limited time and was, in the literary and philosophical discourse on love, exposed again and again to attempts that ultimately led to a "differentiation of differences" and, because of this, to the expansion of the semantic code. In the following sections, I wish to examine such attempts at differentiation more closely, using two examples: Schiller's *Philosophical Letters* (*Philosophische Briefen*) (I and II) and Hölderlin's novel *Hyperion* (III).[12]

I

Within the context of the German Enlightenment, friendship develops as a code of interaction that can perform a social, intellectual-historical, philosophical, pedagogical, or metaphysical function. In combination with the discourse on love, the code places itself in the service of a strategy of avoidance, which distinctly ignores sexuality and sensuality. As the example of Klopstock's ode demonstrates, the code implies a potential for emotion in sentimentality that does not only make the old concept of "rational love" possible, but also transcends it and elevates it to the metaphysical. Not only does the friendship of souls [Seelenfreundschaft] have a socializing function, it also has a religious one: it changes Tempe into Elysium.

Schiller's *Philosophical Letters,* the beginnings of which extend back as far as his days at the Karl's School, represent a characteristic variant of this change. In the "Prefatory Statement" ("Vorerinnerung,") the young writer remarks that "reason [has . . .] its epochs, its fates," just as the heart does, but "its history [is . . .] handled considerably less often." In other words: "One seems to be satisfied with developing the passions in their extremes, aberrations, and consequences, without taking into consideration how exactly they are connected with the system of thoughts of the individual" (NA 20:107). The cause of moral deficiencies is located, for Schiller, in a one-sided and false philosophy. It is not via the heart or the feelings that false convictions are corrected, but rather through an "enlightened intellect." In short, this means that "the head must educate the heart [der Kopf muß das Herz bilden]." The correspondence between Julius and Raphael is meant to provide a paradigm for this. He begins with the portrayal of a sentimental friendship in which separation triggers an intellectual and psychological crisis in Julius. While the "discourse of absence" is traditionally "held by the woman" in the codification of love, as Roland Barthes emphasizes,[13] the "always present *I,*" the Julius who remains behind, is constituted in view of the "continually absent *you.*" The absent Raphael takes on the position of the love object, and the lamentation of Julius, who remains behind, signals the situation: "I am loved less than I myself love."[14] He roams lonely through "the melancholy area," which mirrors his inner state. One could, in fact, suggest along with Barthes that the "man who is waiting there and suffering because of it [. . . is] in a wondrous manner feminized."[15] Absence leads not only to a yearning for the "physical presence" of the absent object, but also "to the formulation of a fiction with diverse roles (doubts, reproaches, impulses of desire and melancholy)."[16] The memory is called upon metaphorically to translate the absence of the object, which is experienced as painful, into presence even up to the "uneasy scene [of their] separation" (NA 20:109). Like a lover, Julius calls out the name of the absent one and is enraged when he does not answer. The memory of past happiness, of "the bold ideal [of their] friendship," of their commonality, only makes the loss more apparent. Even the act of writing as an attempt at mourning does not seem to be sufficient. The letter from Julius is a failed love-text,[17] inasmuch as the elegiac tone at the beginning, the Greek *pothos,* turns into a litany of reproaches, the lament into accusation. "You have stolen from me the faith that gave me peace. You have taught me to despise, when I used to worship" (NA 20:110).

Raphael has obviously recast Julius ideologically and turned him from a self into an Other, which only functioned as long as the signifier of the Other was present. In retrospect, Julius extols his earlier naive existence and temperament, which now seem to him a "blissful, paradisiacal time," since he "still staggered through life blindfolded, like a drunkard" (NA 20:109). In other words, he "*felt* and was happy," but Raphael had "taught [him] to think," and now he finds himself "on the way to mourning [the day of his] creation." Although his friend has, in this way, raised him from a lower level of existence to a higher one, he struggles against his newly found independence, which throws him back onto himself. The paradigm shift from childlike faith to rationalism has already been accepted and formulated in a positive, confessional manner at the end of the first letter: "My reason is everything to me now, my sole guarantee for divinity, virtue, immortality" (NA 20:111). With the example of this friendship, which, as far as semantics are concerned, is both emotionally and philosophically charged, Schiller represents a person's attainment of maturity as the most important process within his or her individual history, as a leave-taking from the naive way of thinking that characterizes the level of the child and the youth anthropologically, via the transition to the sentimental level, to maturity. Raphael led Julius, in the words of Kant, "out of the guardianship of nature into the state of freedom."[18] If he was previously merely "a good son [of his] house, a friend to [his] friends, a useful member of society," then Raphael has "transformed [him] into a citizen of the universe." He now carries, as he writes, his "imperial throne in [his] mind" and honors reason as the supreme value, as "the sole monarchy in the spirit world" (NA 20:111).

This position in the discourse of the letter soon undergoes a new revision, however, by means of the sudden insight into the anthropologically qualified "dialectics of the Enlightenment." Human beings, proceeds Julius's argumentation, are "bound [to] the rigid, unchangeable, clocklike mechanism of a mortal body" in spite of their "free intellects which soar upwards," and he ascertains, "this God is expelled into a world of worms" (NA 20:112). In the replies of Karl von Moor in *The Robbers* (*Die Räuber*), the young Schiller had already formulated this fundamental criticism of the principle of Enlightenment optimism as supported by Leibniz and Alexander Pope. I have "seen people," the robber explains to a follower, "their beelike cares and their gigantic projects—their godlike plans and their mouselike business dealings, the wondrously strange race for bliss . . . ; this confused lottery of life . . . —Zeroes are what is drawn out—in the end, there was no winner in it."[19] The discrepancy between "expectations and their fulfillment" and the restricted nature of human existence (NA 20:112) expose Julius to the "terrible abyss of doubts," as well. It is precisely the philosophy of reason that illuminates the dark dungeon like "a torch" and which first made him conscious of the misery in which he finds himself. Julius compares himself to the "disastrously curious Oedipus" and quotes the oracle: "May you never find out who you are" (NA 20:112). Nothing lasts forever, he now argues; the "present moment is the gravestone of all the past ones," and "a lover's rendezvous is a skipped heartbeat in a friendship." The compulsion to recall impresses the loss even more distinctly upon his consciousness as he reproaches Raphael: "You have torn down a hut which was inhabited and set up a splendid dead palace in its place" (NA 20:113).

Yet Raphael, in his reply, diagnoses Julius's spiritual "crisis" as absolutely necessary. A friendship without interruption would have been "too much for the lot of a human being" anyway. "Deprivation," he says, represents an important element within the school of life, and the sickness from which he suffers can be healed "only through himself alone," "in order to be safe from any relapse." It is not a coincidence that he chose the most favorable moment for his "enlightenment," when "body and mind" found themselves "in the most marvellous bloom" (NA 20:114). He was "*instinctively good, good from inviolate moral grace,*" but the level of the graceful and naive way of thinking was "not worthy" of him, and Raphael demands notes from him in order to be able better to judge the causes of his complaints. What Raphael then receives from Julius is an idealistic essay, which he had drafted in the "happy hours [of his] proud enthusiasm" (NA 20:115) and whose content had been called into question by his materialist afflictions. Julius comments pessimistically on his "Theosophy" in the following manner: "It is the wooden scaffolding of the stage when the lighting is gone. My heart sought a philosophy for itself, and the imagination slipped its dreams in" (NA 20:115). Julius confesses, in other words, that the materialist doubt regarding the imperial throne of "reason" triggered a reduction of the self to such an extent that he himself lost faith in his own capabilities. On the one hand, friendship led him to the high point of his life, to Kant's "departure of men and women from their self-induced mental immaturity," to an idealistic philosophy. On the other hand, this high point unexpectedly changes into the low point, into a materialistic way of thinking, when his friend leaves him. Julius finds himself in a similar situation to the one that Max in Schiller's *Wallenstein* ascribes to the main character, even while the themes are different:

> The bonds of old love shall break,
> [They will] not gently come undone, and you desire to make the tear,
> The painful tear, even more painful for me!
> You know I have not yet learned
> To live without you — . . .
> (*Wallenstein's Death* [*Wallensteins Tod*], III.23)

Julius experiences his separation from Raphael not only as a withdrawal of love but also as a psychological and intellectual shock to his system of meaning. Teaching and friendship are connected to Raphael's person to such an extent that Julius only believes himself to be an Other as long as the Other is present. The very moment when Raphael leaves him is when he discovers the other position to be an illusion, and he longs to return to his original position.[20] His "Theosophy" is not only an idealistic confession of faith, but also a document of his friendship without which the "Theosophy" would not have come into being. This clearly demonstrates that friendship already connotes other values here such as love, education, and ideals, just as will be the case later in Romanticism. In the "Letters on Don Carlos" ("Briefe über Don Carlos"), Schiller was to represent the phenome-

non from Carlos's perspective in this manner: "Fate gave him a friend—
a friend in the decisive years, when the flower of the mind unfolds, when
ideals are received, and when the moral sense purifies itself. . . . This serene
humane philosophy, which the prince on the throne wants to bring into
practice, is thus a product of friendship" (HS 2:252).

As Schiller himself explains, friendship, like love, is subordinated to a
higher purpose in this piece, that is, to the "dissemination of a purer, gentler
humanity," and it is subordinated to such an extent that both love and
friendship must sacrifice something or sacrifice themselves. When Schiller
suggests that Posa "loves the human race more than [he loves] Karl," this
could also be said of Raphael in relation to Julius. While Posa is primarily
interested in the idea of the human being, Raphael pleads in favor of the
idea of reason. For both, the friend is, to a certain extent, "the focal point at
which all his ideas of that composite whole are gathered." In the "love of *one*
being," Julius, too, experiences a "general, all-encompassing philanthropy
concentrated in one single jet of flame" (HS 2:240f.). If friendship, according to the perspective in the "Letters on Don Carlos," affords the "complete enjoyment [of the] ideal,"[21] then this applies to Raphael and Julius as
well. The "Theosophy" can, for this reason, also be read as an "enthusiastic
blueprint"[22] for friendship, for there is room neither for skepticism nor for
materialism as a way of thinking. The "huts of friendship" are meant to be
"eternal dwelling places," not "gravestones" of a moment (NA 20:112). If the
texts of the letters reflect the crisis of friendship and of ideology, then the
philosophical text represents the birth of idealism from the spirit of friendship. It is not coincidental that its actual addressee remains Raphael, the
Other, throughout.

II

The "Theosophy" reformulates theodicy as "an aesthetic conception of
the world," "in which the imagination has become a person's actual organ
of knowledge."[23] It is the beginning of a development in which theodicy's
legal battle for the rational institutions of the world is transferred onto the
philosophy of history, philosophical anthropology, and philosophical aesthetics.[24] Odo Marquard summarized the facts in the following formula:

"*The justification of the world depends henceforth on the justification of the self and this, in turn, on its capacity for the resolution of antinomies.*"[25] In the "Theosophy of Julius," God is in fact still a point of reference, so that one cannot yet speak of a "theodicy without God" as in the context of transcendental philosophy.[26] It is not merely being claimed here, as in mysticism, that God is dependent upon the human self, it is virtually being propagated that God is born by means of human powers. Already in Schiller's youthful philosophy, the person, the self, is the place where "an infinitely divided God" (NA 20:124) finds the way back to unity. When Schiller, even as early as in his dissertation *Philosophy of Physiology* (*Philosophie der Physiologie*), defines the destiny of the human being as "similarity to God" (NA 20:10), he raises the human being to the task of uniting once again "the divine self," which has "broken [itself] into countless feeling substances" (NA 20:123f.) in nature, the reproduction of the divine substance. The magical elemental force that fulfills the task of "reversing the separation" (NA 20:124) is precisely love. Love represents "the ladder," as Julius comments, "upon which we clamber upwards towards similarity to God" (NA 20:124).

The "Theosophy" treats various subchapters ("The World and the Thinking Being [Die Welt und das denkende Wesen]," "Idea [Idee]," "Sacrifice [Aufopferung]," and "God [Gott]") on its way to the central theme of the work, "Love" [Liebe]. Schiller took from the few philosophical writings that he read around this time[27] "always only the things," as he writes in a letter to Körner (15 April 1788), "that allow themselves to be felt and treated in a poetic manner" (J 2:41). Admittedly, love and friendship belonged to the concepts that particularly occupied Schiller from the *Anthology for the Year 1782* (*Anthologie auf das Jahr 1782*) up until *Don Carlos*. Love is defined by Schiller in the "Theosophy" as the "desire for someone else's happiness," as an "exchange of personality . . . a confusion of beings" (NA 20:119). Love is the precondition for the possibility of similarity to God. This "omnipotent magnet in the spirit world" unites the "entirety of creation" in the personality (NA 20:119), and it is stated in subjunctive *potentialis*: "If every human being loved all human beings, then each individual would possess the world" (NA 20:121). By taking up Shaftesbury's and Locke's thoughts, Julius consolidates this approach to a universal formula for a philosophy of life based on the expansion and contraction of the self.[28] "Egotism and love," we learn, "divide humanity into two extremely different races, the boundaries of which never run into one another. Egotism establishes its focal point within itself; love plants it outside itself in the axis of the eternal whole. Love aims at unity; egotism is loneliness" (NA 20:122f.).

For Julius, "unselfish love [uneigennützige Liebe]" represents without a doubt the supreme value, and he imagines himself to be lost without it. If he had to give up his faith in love, then ideas such as divinity, immortality, and virtue would be meaningless, for a "spirit that only loves itself is an atom swimming in immeasurable *empty* space" (NA 20:122). In the poem "Friendship" ("Die Freundschaft"), which specifically refers to a projected novel made up of letters from Julius to Raphael, the following lines, which are also quoted in the "Theosophy," are most relevant:

> —Dead groups are we—when we hate;
> Gods—when we lovingly embrace each other![29]

Here, friendship is declared to be a "jubilant alliance of love," in which the self gazes in admiration at itself in the "you," as the world and the universe are mirrored "more beautifully" and "more charmingly" in the Other.[30] In his interchanges with Raphael, Julius acquires the former's "great sentiments," and he thus becomes enriched by the qualities of the love object (NA 20:120). "With satisfaction, I recognize my sentiments in the mirror of your own," Julius comments on the process, "but with fiery longing, I devour the higher ones, which I am lacking in" (NA 20:121). In other words, friendship and love seek to compensate for deficiencies and to promote development toward perfection, toward the restitution of the lost totality. For this reason, Julius also wants to raise "brotherly love [Bruderliebe]," friendship, to a program for humanity, for it is only through love, as expressed in the chorus of "The Triumph of Love," that "people [become] like gods" and that "the earth [becomes] the kingdom of heaven."[31] In addition to this, love can achieve effects that seem to contradict human nature. Julius would definitely be capable, he maintains, for example, in the section called "Self-Sacrifice," of increasing his "own happiness by means of a sacrifice" for "someone else's happiness," that is, to sacrifice his life for his friend. At this early level of his philosophical reflections, Schiller wants to demonstrate the independence in principle both of the magnetic power of love as well as of the human self. Toward the end of the "Theosophy," Julius also calls his program a "confession of faith [of his faculty of] reason," which was prompted by Raphael (NA 20:126). This may seem all the more astonishing since it is precisely "love" and "friendship," rather than "reason" that are declared in the various sections to be the most important powers in human existence. Strictly regarded, however, they are functions of the self, too — as much of one's own self, in fact, as of the other's self.

Toward the end of his essay, the writer emphasizes its speculative outline character and its subjective perspective to his correspondent: "The world, as I have painted it here, is perhaps not real anywhere except in the mind of your Julius" (NA 20:126). In view of the fact that all knowledge amounts "to a conventional deception" anyway, he insists, however, upon the general validity "of every exercise of the power to think," for "every product of the mind, each thing woven by the wit [has] an irrefutable right in this greater meaning of creation" (NA 20:126, 128). Julius is making a plea here for pluralism, the variety of interpretations that, after all, can be traced back to the diversity of the Creator, and Julius claims sententiously: "Each of reason's skills, even in error, increases its skill in receiving the truth" (NA 20:129).

Yet strictly speaking, a secret goal lies behind the outline of the "Theosophy": the birth of the powers of imagination, which basically fulfills all the conditions attributed to love and friendship. It is not coincidental that Schiller declares in a letter to Reinwald on 14 April 1783: "Every work of literature is nothing other than an enthusiastic friendship or a Platonic love for a creation of our own head" (J 1:112). In this sense, friendship and love are nothing other "than a sensual confusion of beings." Just as God loves Himself "in the outline, the *signified* in the *sign*,"[32] and perceives "His great, infinite *self* strewn throughout infinite nature" (J 1:113), so too do poets love and perceive themselves in their outlines, in their creations. Friendship and love are, when understood in this way, only "a different effect of the power of literature." In other words: "That which we feel for a *friend* and what we feel for a hero in our literary works is precisely that. In both cases, we lead ourselves through new situations and paths, . . . we see *ourselves* in other colors, we suffer for *ourselves* in other bodies" (J 1:114). In anticipation of early Romannticism, love and friendship in the "Theosophy" become a sign, a linguistic "outline" of nature. Just as the "thought of God" writes itself out in its diversity in nature, so too is it the task "of all thinking beings" "to recognize the original sign [in this diversity] . . . , the unity in the arrangement" (NA 20:115). The first section of the "Theosophy" is thus about the readability of the world[33] or the "hieroglyph of a power" that makes people godlike (NA 20:116). With the help of nature, world history, and art, the ciphers of the "thinking being," allow themselves to be deciphered (NA 20:116).

Körner's commentary on the "Theosophy" continues the *Philosophical Letters* and, at the same time, ends them. As Raphael, he uncovers the weaknesses of the outline yet nonetheless rates it an important step on the path "towards a higher *freedom of the spirit*" (NA 21:156). He now also considers Julius-Schiller capable of accepting the Kantian critique of pure reason.[34] He does, however, vent noticeably harsh criticism on the sentence "that it is the supreme destiny of humanity to gain a premonition of the spirit of the Creator of the world in his work of art." Raphael, alias Körner, insists upon the fundamental difference between the universe and a work of art: "The universe is not a *pure* copy of an ideal like the completed work of a human artist. The latter rules despotically over the lifeless material which he needs in order to make his ideas perceptible to the senses," while "in the divine work of art[,] . . . the characteristic value of each of its components [is] protected" (NA 21:159). The divine creation characterizes "*life* and *freedom*" ["*Leben* und *Freiheit*"] to the greatest possible extent, and it is "never more sublime than when its ideal seems to be most unsuccessful." Yet, in a letter in which he discusses Körner's statement on the "Theosophy" in detail, Schiller responds that their views are by no means as different as Körner assumes (J 2:42). In the fourth letter *On the Aesthetic Education* (*Über ästhetische Erziehung*), Schiller would later modify this aspect of his early statement of belief by making almost word-for-word use of reflections of his friend Körner, alias Raphael. The discourse on friendship in the *Philosophical Letters* will thus be continued both in aesthetic discourse as well as in poetic practice.

III

Hölderlin's epistolary novel *Hyperion,* which appeared in two volumes in 1797 and 1799, stands without a doubt in the tradition of Goethe's *Werther* and Rousseau's *New Heloise,* but it radicalizes and clearly carries on the beginnings of Schiller's projected novel "made up of the letters of Julius to Raphael."[35] Like Schiller in the *Philosophical Letters,* Hölderlin tells the story in *Hyperion* of the development of his protagonist. The role of teacher

—in Schiller, it is the correspondent Raphael—is taken on by Adamas for Hyperion. Whereas Raphael educates his pupil Julius to maturity, Adamas introduces Hyperion "to Plutarch's world of heroes [one moment], and to the magical land of the Greek gods the next." (B 1:302). In both cases, the story of the development of the protagonists is presented in an elegiac tone arising from the difference of historical distance. A fundamental philosophico-anthropological concept of Schiller's can, moreover, be discerned in the structural principle of Hölderlin's novel, which the younger compatriot in the fragment of *Hyperion* defines as "an eccentric path" in the following manner: "There are two ideals of our existence: a state of supreme simplicity, in which our needs harmonize reciprocally with themselves and with our powers and with everything with which we are connected *by means of the very organization of nature* without our assistance, and a state of supreme education, in which the same thing would take place with infinitely duplicated and intensified needs and powers *by means of the organization which we are capable of giving ourselves*" (B 1:439f.).

If Raphael refers to "reason" as the highest level, then Adamas introduces not only the example of the "beautiful ancient world," but he also familiarizes his pupil with the "God within us" (B 1:305), a central anthropologico-metaphysical term that appears both in Wieland and especially in Schiller's work *On Grace and Dignity* (*Über Anmuth und Würde*).[36] Already in Schiller, friendship and love fulfill an educative function, which Hölderlin, along with the Romanticists Novalis, Friedrich Schlegel, and Schleiermacher, takes up. The loss of friendship and love throws the protagonists Julius and Hyperion back into their own interiority and exposes them to despair. Hyperion, too, laments the loss of original unity: "I have become so properly rational here with you, have learned to distinguish myself thoroughly from that which surrounds me, am now isolated in the beautiful world, am thus thrown out of the garden of nature, where I grew and throve, and am drying out in the midday sun" (B 1:298). The state of supreme simplicity is played off against the state of supreme education. As in Julius's case, doubt turns into despair, hope into hopelessness: "That people in their youth believe the goal to be so close! It is the most beautiful of all the deceptions with which nature helps to strengthen the frailty of our being" (B 1:299). Just like Julius, Hyperion sees everything through the lens of his sentiments (B 1:334), in the color of the state in which he finds himself at the moment. The negative aspect of the world can be traced back to the inner deficiencies of the person as well. The destiny of humanity, characterized precisely by the highest objective, suddenly leads to nothingness in a moment of despair. "O you poor ones," laments Hyperion, for example, in a letter, "who feel it, who do not like to talk about human destiny, who are utterly and so deeply moved by the nothingness that prevails over us, so thoroughly recognize that we are born for nothingness, that we love a void, believe in a void, slave away for nothingness, in order to gradually pass over into nothingness. . . . But I [can] not overcome it, the screaming truth. Have I not convinced myself twice? When I look into life, what is the end of everything? Nothing. When I soar in spirit, what is the highest of all things? Nothing" (B 1:332f.).

The discrepancy of the human existence between worm and God,[37] which Albrecht von Haller and Klopstock thematize, just as Goethe and Schiller do later, also belongs in *Hyperion* to the dissonances that await resolution. The enthusiasm of friendship, combined with the decision in favor of political activity, seems to be able to overcome the disastrous dichotomy. "What? God is supposed to be dependent on a worm?" exclaims Alabanda, thirsty for action, the "God in us, for whom infinity opens up to make a path, is supposed to stay and wait until the worm gets out of his way?" (B 1:316). Friendship carries the connotation of the *vita activa* and the concept of "joy" here, the latter differing from the depiction in Klopstock's ode in that it is understood here in *Hyperion,* as in Schiller's *Don Carlos,* as a correlate of political intent (B 1:317). Adamas refers his pupil Hyperion to his heart as the location where the beautiful lost world can find a new place for itself, and he holds up Apollo, the god of the sun, as his model,[38] whereas Alabanda leads his friend, who is the same age and to whom he is bound in an effusive youthful friendship, out from his internal world into the external world of contemporary history. Adamas's sentimental request ("What is loss, if human beings find themselves in their own world in this way? In us is everything" [B 1:4]) that one produce the lost world in oneself, as Schiller demands in *On Naive and Sentimental Poetry* (*Ueber naive und sentimentalische Dichtung*), is juxtaposed with Alabanda's enthusiastic action, which is similarly propagated by Fichte in his *Science of Knowledge* (*Wissenschaftslehre*). "The sons of the sun nourish themselves on their [own] deeds," it is said within the context of the friendly alliance; "they live on victory; with their own spirit, they rouse themselves, and their strength is their joy" (B 1:317).

Hyperion and his companion in combat, Alabanda, go into raptures like the youthful heroes of Schiller about "colossal designs" and about a positive change in the social and political plight of their time. In the political discourse of the two friends, it is, however, remarkable that they clearly differ in their conceptions of the projected new state. Alabanda even seems to smile critically at the equally romantic and utopian plan of his friend, which would grant the state less power, binding it to "love and the mind" and making it, to a certain extent, into a "new church" (B 1:319f.). It is no coincidence that soon afterwards the two friends engage in a major altercation: They "destroyed the garden of [their] love by force" (B 1:325). But Hyperion experiences the loss of his friend and the disappointment as a psychological crisis. The result is mourning and melancholia. It comes to a "withdrawal of interest for the external world" and to a "reduction of self-esteem."[39] In short, the loss of the object leads him to the loss of self. In a letter to Bellarmin, Hyperion visualizes his situation thus: "There is a falling silent, a forgetting of all existence, where it seems to us as if we had lost everything, a night of our soul where no glimmer of a star, where not even a rotten piece of wood shines for us" (B 1:329). Hyperion is commenting here on the transition from the expansion of the self to the reduction of the self, which, in contrast to the "Theosophy of Julius" ("Theosophie des Julius"), stands in the pursuance of the eccentric path in the dialectics of internalization and externalization, of extreme interior orientation to extreme exterior orientation. Hyperion is attempting to formulate this as an anthropological law. "If the life of the world indeed consists in the alternation between unfolding and closing," he supposes, "in flight from and return to oneself, why not the human heart as well?" (B 1:325).

If his friendship with Alabanda had aroused the hope for a better future, for positive political change, then, with their separation, he lost "[his] faith in everything great" (B 1:328f.). On the other hand, the work of mourning releases the heteronomous self once again, and in the second book of *Hyperion,* triggered by the context of Greece, the interior world of the protagonist receives a new impetus (B 1:334f.). This positive phase reaches its climax in the encounter with Diotima. Whereas in the relations between friends, Adamas represents first and foremost internal moral concepts and Alabanda represents external moral concepts, Hyperion's love for Diotima opens up a new means of access to the world: to nature and beauty. She represents for him a sort of Lethe, from which he "drank the oblivion of existence" and through which his "disposition full of contradictions" found peace (B 1:345f.). This love becomes the most important thing in the world, and he believes that he can do without gods or people. He pronounces ego-centrically: "What does the shipwreck of the world concern me; I know of nothing save my blessed island" (B 1:373).

The classic code of the "language of the eyes"[40] is a part of Hölderlin's grammar of love, but the linguistic expressions fail in the face of the in-tense experience. "One is ashamed of one's language." "One would like to become a musical sound and merge in One Heavenly Hymn;" and further: "And what should we speak of? We saw only each other. We shied away from talking about ourselves" (B 1:340). While Diotima's original form of communication is song (B 1:342), Hyperion speaks in retrospect of "conver-sations of the soul" as the principal discourse of love. In the course of their togetherness, Diotima admittedly gains in linguistic skill. An "exchange of personality, a confusion of beings" (NA 20:119) takes place between them. Diotima's oneness with nature and Hyperion's linguistic skill and sentimen-tal inner conflict, "the holy, free, youthful life of nature" and the "gloomy wandering" (B 1:412f.) are interchanged, the Other made into the Own. However, Hyperion's mind, signaled metaphorically in the novel by fire, will in the end destroy Diotima's nature. As quiet as she was in life, so is she "eloquent" in her death, as she herself comments in her final letter.

If the loss of the world and meaning has driven Hyperion into a crisis, then love balances out the losses. Love generates a new world and a new meaning, collects "the scattered powers . . . all into One golden Mean" and makes one "all-knowing," "all-seeing," "all-transfiguring" (B 1:360, 363). Al-though Hyperion makes these observations himself, he remains, however, "blind" in his love as well, in contrast to Diotima. Diotima understands him better than he does himself, and she interprets his friendship with Adamas and Alabanda completely correctly as compensatory actions. He was look-ing for a "more beautiful world" and "embraced" this world in his friends. "You did not want any people, believe me," explains Diotima, "you wanted a world," and she prophesies to him: "Your last place of refuge will be a grave" (B 1:353). She alludes to the temporal nature of friendship and love, which he, in idealistic delusion, not only deems a concentrate made up of "golden centuries," but he also raises the prevailing representative in ideal-istic blindness to the status of a god. The "slightest doubt about Alabanda" drove him of necessity to desperation and changed his "great joy into dreadful sorrow" (B 1:353). Indirectly, she gives him to understand that he is with-drawing the living foundation from their love out of idealistic exuberance. In the end, she does in fact draw a connection between her death and this course of events. She is of the opinion that Hyperion would have "had the power to bind [her] to the earth. . . . One [of his] heartfelt glances would have held [her] fast, One [of his] expressions of love would have made [her] a happy, healthy child once again." Without Hyperion, she can no longer exist; she mistakenly believes him, forever separated from her, to be on the way "to former freedom" (B 1:426f.). It also becomes clear here that more of Hyperion passed over into Diotima's being than vice versa. At the end of the novel, both Hyperion's beloved and his friend sacrifice themselves for him.

Diotima designates Hyperion as the educator of the people (B 1:375), just as Schiller's Raphael referred his friend Julius to art. Hyperion preaches his "mysteries" of beauty, love, art, and religion (B 1:365) and expands the discourse on love, art, and religion in this way to a political discourse: "without such a love of beauty, without such religion, every state is a dried-out skeleton without life or spirit, and all thought and action are a tree without a top, a column whose capital has been struck off" (B 1:365). This statement refers back to both Schiller's "aesthetic state" as well as to elements in the "Theosophy of Julius," where love also carries a political connotation. In the important reports in the first volume of the second book, an additional aspect of love presents itself. Love leads Hyperion to more profound insights, which Diotima "premonitorily" apprehends. When he, taking up an ancient example of friendship, sums up the function of love and friendship in the formula, "Love gave birth to millennia full of living people; friendship will give birth to them once again," Diotima indicates her equally spontaneous and instinctive understanding by condensing the formula slightly and repeating it, as it were, like an echo. While she succeeds in identifying herself with Hyperion to such an extent that she endangers her own identity, sufficient elements of his own self remain in effect in his exchange with her. When Hyperion claims that he has become like her, Diotima answers with superior insight: "But you must become a bit quieter for me" (B 1:359).

For Hyperion, Diotima is the embodiment of beauty, of the "One differentiating within itself" (Heraclitus), and she is therefore, for him, the guarantor of art and religion (B 1:365ff., 383). She helps him to attain the self-knowledge that he is lacking. Rather than judging his deficiencies objectively or evaluating his skills correctly, he misjudges himself continually. For this reason, Diotima warns him at the end of the novel: "Don't misjudge yourself! The lack of material held you back. It didn't happen fast enough. That cast you down" (B 1:373).[41] She therefore advises him to go to Athens, Italy, Germany, and France in order to acquire what he is missing, that is, knowledge of human nature and the stuff of life. She regards this type of educational journey as a necessary prerequisite for his calling as an artist and educator of the people (B 1:374–75). Although he at first concedes that Diotima is correct ("But I still must go away in order to learn. I am an artist, but I am not skillful. I mold [things] in my mind, but I do not yet know how to guide my hand") (B 1:375) and seems to recognize that he is still in need of a realistic basis for an idealistic aesthetic mission, he nonetheless follows Alabanda's call to take part in the political uprising almost without any hesitation (B 1:377) so that "the new world" can spring up from "the root of humanity" (B 1:374). Though he had just been praising his love for Diotima as the supreme value for which he had forgotten everything else, he now criticizes it: "I have become too idle, . . . too peace-loving, too heavenly, too lethargic!" (B 1:378). Not only does love come into conflict with friendship, but the *vita contemplativa* comes into conflict with the *vita activa,* the aesthetic sphere ("the holy theocracy of the beautiful") with the political sphere. Diotima criticizes this sudden turnaround as "vain high spirits" and prophesies shrewdly: "The wild combat will tear you to shreds, beautiful soul; you will age, blessed spirit! And at the end, weary of life, [you will] ask: where are you all, you ideals of youth?" (B 1:379).

In *Hyperion,* Hölderlin is playing on variants of the sentimental classical and Romantic love codifications.[42] Love is associated with nature, art, religion, and knowledge. In his friendship with Alabanda, Hyperion falls victim to the deception of being strong "like a demigod." He feels himself to be "like a conqueror" between Diotima and his friend and intends to surround them like his prey (B 1:390f.). Yet, the two friends celebrate Diotima's "festival" and the love between her and Hyperion. With Diotima and Alabanda, two discourses on love are being presented that are in competition with each other in different phases of the eighteenth century. On the one hand, friendship guarantees the ennoblement of love (Herder); on the other hand, it constitutes a three-way relationship (Jacobi, Goethe), which becomes anathema to the Romantic semantics of love with its binary distribution of roles. Schleiermacher summarized the difference between love and friendship in the following formula: "Love is intent on making one out of two; friendship is intent on making two out of each one."[43] This discrepancy could also be claimed in Hölderlin's *Hyperion*. Just as the protagonist offsets the loss of an ideal world in his friendship with Adamas and Alabanda and projected a "better time" (B 1:353) into each of these friendships, so too does Alabanda admit to Hyperion in his confessions about his life (B 1:416ff.) that "only their friendship [was his] world, [his] worth, [his] glory." Strictly speaking, only Diotima attains the "oneness" of "I" and "you," of the self and the Other in love, whereas, Hyperion misunderstands her again and again as a projection of his "beautiful dreams." What Diotima says about his friends also holds true for his love for her: "The loss of all the golden centuries, just as you felt them, pressed together into One happy moment, the spirit of all the spirits of a better time, the strength of all the powers of the heroes, all this is supposed to be replaced for you by one single person, one human being!" (B 1:353).

Not insignificantly, love and friendship illustrate *a tergo* the faults and deficiencies of Hyperion. The text signalizes how a hidden competition comes into being among the people involved, not only, in fact, from Diotima's perspective (B 1:397f.), but also from the perspectives of Hyperion (B 1:388f., 397) and of Alabanda (B 1:420). When Diotima exhorts her lover not to forget how to love, Hyperion writes to her that Alabanda is flourishing "like a bridegroom." After the military action is fully defeated, Alabanda rejects a life together as a threesome because he fears that he will fall in love with Diotima in his radical way. He describes the danger as follows: "I betrayed my obligations for the sake of my friend; I would betray my friendship for the sake of love. For the sake of Diotima, I would betray you and, in the end, murder Diotima and myself because we were indeed not One" (B 1:420). Although Alabanda considers himself, based on his energetic nature, to be incapable of the oneness of love, the question posed by Hyperion, who should actually know better, is nonetheless surprising: "O why can I not give her [Diotima] to you?" (B 1:417). Would he really have sacrificed his relationship with Diotima for the sake of friendship?

With regard to love and friendship, the end of the epistolary novel presents us with a chiastically arranged solution. Just as Diotima sacrifices herself for Hyperion and his friendship, so too does Alabanda sacrifice himself for his friend and his friend's love. Love and friendship, as differently as they are codified in the novel, bring forth effects that, in the words of Schiller's

"Theosophy," "seem to contradict their nature" (NA 20:122). Divested of all temporality, life and death merge in the "eternal love" ["ewigen Liebe"] that, according to Diotima, holds all natures together and links all beings. This metaphysical codification of love gains acceptance above all within the context of Romanticism. "Since the origin of life is, however, at the same time the point of its return as well," as Günther Dux describes the situation, "that unity comes into being which, more than any other unity, characterizes Romanticism: the unity of love and death."[44] Although the work of mourning drives Hyperion to alienation from himself and to estrangement from the world (B 1:430), the end of the novel presents us once again with a dialectic turnaround as well as with a sign of hope on a higher level: "We represent a finished thing in flux; we separate the great chords of joy into changing melodies" (B 1:428). This is the legacy of Diotima and, via a more profound oneness with her, Hyperion finally does reach that "state of supreme education" ["Zustand der höchsten Bildung"] (B 1:439f.), the level at which his love-text becomes a philosophy of life:

> The discord in the world is like strife between lovers. Reconciliation exists in the midst of the dispute, and all that has been separated finds itself together once again.
>
> The blood vessels divide and return to the heart, and Everything is united, eternal, ardent life (B 1:439).

NOTES

1. See Werner Schneiders, *Naturrecht und Liebesethik. Zur Geschichte der praktischen Philosophie im Hinblick auf Christian Thomasius* (Hildesheim and New York: G. Olms, 1971), 117–82.

2. Ibid., 171.

3. Quoted in Paul Kluckhohn, *Die Auffassung der Liebe in der Literatur des 18. Jahrhunderts und der deutschen Romantik* (Halle a. S.: Max Niemeyer, 1922), 159.

4. Niklas Luhmann, *Liebe als Passion. Zur Codierung von Intimität* (Frankfurt am Main: Suhrkamp, 1988), 163–82.

5. Ibid., *Liebe als Passion*, 102–3.

6. Johann Gottfried Herder, *Schriften zu Philosophie, Literatur, Kunst und Altertum 1774–1787,* vol. 4 of *Werke,* ed. Jürgen Brummack and Martin Bollacher (Frankfurt am Main.: Deutscher Klassiker Verlag, 1994), 414.

7. Friedrich Heinrich Jacobi, *Woldemar. Faksimiledruck nach der Ausgabe von 1779* (Stuttgart: J. B. Metzler, 1969), 238–39.

8. Johann Wolfgang von Goethe, *Die Leiden des jungen Werther,* vol. 6 of *Goethes Werke: Hamburger Ausgabe in 14 Bänden,* 7th ed. (Hamburg: C. Wegner, 1968), 95.

9. On the term "utmost relevance," see Hartmann Tyrell, "Romantische Liebe—Überlegungen zu ihrer 'quantitativen Bestimmtheit,'" in *Theorie als Passion. Niklas Luhmann zum 60. Geburtstag* (Frankfurt am Main: Suhrkamp, 1987), 571ff.

10. Albert Salomon, "Der Freundschaftskult des 18. Jahrhunderts in Deutschland: Versuch zur Soziologie einer Lebensform," *Zeitschrift für Soziologie* 8 (1979): 279–308.

11. Luhmann, *Liebe als Passion,* 105.

12. The references to Schiller's and Hölderlin's works are given with both the respective volume number and the respective page number or numbers within the text in parentheses. The following abbreviations have been used: NA = *Schillers Werke: Nationalausgabe,* 43 vols., ed. Julius Petersen, Lieselotte Blumenthal, and Benno von Wiese (Weimar: Hermann Böhlaus Nachfolger, 1943). H = Friedrich Schiller, *Sämtliche Werke,* 8th ed. 5 vols. ed. Gerhard Fricke and Herbert G. Göpfert with Herbert Stubenrauch (Munich: Hanser, 1987). J = Fritz Jonas, ed., *Schillers Briefe,* 7 vols. (Stuttgart: Deutsche Verlags-Anstalt, 1892–96). B = [Friedrich] Hölderlin, *Werke und Briefe,* ed. Friedrich Beißner and Jochen Schmidt, 3 vols. (Frankfurt am Main: Insel, 1969).

13. Roland Barthes, *Fragment einer Sprache der Liebe* (Frankfurt am Main: Suhrkamp, 1988), 27ff.

14. Ibid., 27.

15. Ibid., 28.

16. Ibid., 30.

17. See Barthes, 265.

18. Immanuel Kant, *Werke in zehn Bänden,* ed. Wilhelm Weischedel (Darmstadt: Wissenschaftliche Buchgesellschaft, 1968) 9:92.

19. *Robbers* III. 2.

20. On this general point, see Barthes, 240ff.

21. HS 2:243; see also NA 20:113, 16–17.

22. See HS 2:253.

23. Benno von Wiese, *Schiller* (Stuttgart: J. B. Metzler, 1959), 105.

24. Odo Marquard, *Abschied vom Prinzipiellen* (Stuttgart: Reclam, 1981), 47.

25. Odo Marquard, *Transzendaler Idealismus, Romantische Naturphilosophie, Psychoanalyse* (Cologne: Verlag für Philosophie J. Dinter, 1987), 83.

26. Marquard, 81.

27. For this, see NA 21:160ff.

28. For this, see John Locke, *An Essay Concerning Human Understanding,* collated and annotated by Alexander Campbell Fraser (New York: Dover Publications, 1959), 1:304–5., 340–41. "But hatred or love, to beings capable of happiness or misery, is often the uneasiness or delight which we find in ourselves, arising from their very being or happiness" (Ibid., 1:304).

29. Friedrich Schiller, ed., *Anthologie auf das Jahr 1782,* 1st ed., facsim. ed., ed. Katharina Mommsen (Stuttgart: J. B. Metzler, 1973), 150. On this topic, see also the poem "The Triumph of Love, a Hymn (Der Triumf der Liebe, eine Hymne)," ibid., 58–68.

30. Ibid., 149.

31. Ibid., 58.

32. See NA 20:126–27.

33. For this, see Hans Blumenberg's interpretation, which emphasizes different features. Hans Blumenberg, *Die Lesbarkeit der Welt* (Frankfurt am Main: Suhrkamp, 1981), 220–21.

34. See Schiller's letter to Körner dated 15 April 1788 (J 2:42).

35. Schiller, *Anthologie*, 148.

36. This, the first longer aesthetic work of Schiller's, was read by Hölderlin while he was working on his epistolary novel.

37. See NA 20:112.

38. B 1:304; see also NA 20:116.

39. On the analysis of the symptom, see Sigmund Freud, *Psychologie des Unbewußten*, vol. 3 of the *Studienausgabe*, ed. Alexander Mitscherlich, et al. (Frankfurt am Main: S. Fischer, 1975), 198, 201.

40. For this, see Luhmann, *Liebe als Passion*, 29.

41. For this, see also Raphael-Körner, NA 21:158–59.

42. On this topic, see Walter Hinderer, ed., *Codierungen von Liebe in der Kunstperiode* (Würzburg: Königshausen & Neumann, 1997), 8–19, 312–31.

43. Quoted in Kluckhohn, *Auffassung der Liebe*, 429.

44. Günter Dux, *Geschlecht und Gesellschaft. Warum wir lieben* (Frankfurt am Main: Suhrkamp, 1994), 432ff.

4 German Classicism and the Law of the Father

PETER UWE HOHENDAHL

I

Poststructuralist critics have regularly targeted German classicism for its presumed celebration of humanism, a position that, as the argument goes, deliberately covers up the deeper concerns and problems of the historical period around 1800. Schiller's idealism has been especially singled out for polemical treatment directed against his mature plays as well as his theoretical writings.[1] But also Goethe's understanding of *Menschlichkeit* and *Bildung* has come under severe criticism by scholars who feel that the concept of development toward mature adulthood included unacknowledged but fundamental losses in the formation of the subject.[2] Indeed, the stakes of this debate seem to be very high since it deals with the construction of the modern subject, as the more insightful readers have pointed out.

Both historical and literary scholarship have shown that fundamental social and cultural transformations occurred around 1800 in Central and Western Europe.[3] Its most violent manifestation was the French Revolution in its successful attempt to destroy the ancien régime and replace it with a new social and political system whose ramifications went far beyond the rise of the French bourgeoisie as the victorious new class. Clearly those countries that were not immediately touched by the political upheavals of the Revolution, among them most of the German states, felt the impact and had to come to terms with the political and social changes that occurred in France.[4] They extended to the areas of education and law, gender construction and ethics, but also to literary production and aesthetic perception, areas in which the response of German intellectuals became especially important and far-reaching. Although the ancien régime was allowed to survive in Germany after 1789 in varying degrees, the German principalities were confronted with the disintegration of established structures and had to deal to some extent with ideas that were fundamentally hostile to the traditional social and cultural order. In many instances the events of 1789 simply accelerated the impact of these discourses, forcing monarchs and governments to articulate their responses in terms of new discursive formations.

The field of education would be one example,[5] but it would also pertain to the attempts at legal reforms and ideas to rethink the structure of the family.[6] The question of paternal authority had become controversial under the regime of the Revolution.[7] The analogy between the power of the monarch and the authority of the father, firmly established in older political theory, especially had lost its unquestionable validity in the revolutionary republic. It was not accidental that the new concept of freedom and equality was enunciated in the name of brotherhood. In this respect the execution of the king was a decisive symbolic turning point of the French Revolution,[8] a turning point that was duly and critically noted by the majority of the German intellectuals who had initially sympathized with the struggle of the revolutionaries to create a better and more humane society.[9] The fall of the king suggested a lack of law and the threat of anarchy.

I want to argue that German classicism, far from being the highly elevated and socially free-floating literary style that historians have frequently sought to construct, was very much intertwined with these larger contemporary issues. My argument does not propose, however, that this connection can be understood in terms of an immediate reflection or response, not to mention a political intervention. These attempts do exist,[10] but they are less relevant for the understanding of the position of German classicism than those works that follow their own poetic and aesthetic concerns without regard for an immediate impact on the political discourse of the time. I propose therefore to read two plays, more than once described as the epitome of the classical style, by focusing on the role of the father. This emphasis will foreground aspects of these plays that shed light on the fundamental structural changes that occurred between 1780 and 1815. The first play, that is, Goethe's *Iphigenie auf Tauris,* was conceived during the 1770s and completed in its final form by 1787, in other words, before the French Revolution. Schiller's play, on the other hand, followed almost two decades later. *Die Braut von Messina,* while mentioned by Schiller as a plan already in 1801 in a letter to his friend Körner, was finally written and published in 1803.[11] What these plays have in common, however, is an interest in the revival of the Greek tragedy, an obvious element in the case of *Iphigenie,* which relies for its material on ancient sources, among them Euripides, and thereby also competes with the Greek author.[12] In the case of Schiller, on the other hand, the interest in Greek culture seems to be primarily a formal one, namely the experiment of a modern author to write a tragedy that deliberately makes use of the chorus since it was an intrinsic part of Greek tragedy.[13] With respect to the content, Schiller preferred to keep a distance between his work and the myth that formed the basis of the ancient tragedy. Yet this conscious decision did not remove him from the very concerns that determined the core of Greek tragedy, just as Goethe's decision to remove the plot from the contemporary scene, did not detach him from modern definitions of subjectivity.[14] When we understand these plays as decidedly modern explorations of premodern cultures (Greek and medieval) we are in both instances confronted with the crucial role of the father, not simply as a matter of plot structure and character analysis, but with his central function as the embodiment of the law.

The fact that in both plays the real father (as a person) is dead when the action begins does not diminish his importance for the drama. In fact, the opposite seems to be true. On the symbolic level, his death increases his relevance for the structure of the drama. Since the father figures, that is, Agamemnon and the prince of Messina, are not foregrounded in the development of the plot, interpreters have by and large focused their attention on the interaction between the members of the younger generation, in particular on the feud between the brothers in Schiller's play and the relationship between Iphigenie and Orest in Goethe's drama. Indeed, at the thematic level, the father figures seem to belong primarily to the past: an older order that was characterized by violence and abuse. The action of the drama, on the other hand, appears to offer a different outlook. While this observation is pertinent in the case of *Iphigenie,* it is less clear to what extent the generational difference implies a difference in attitude in *Die Braut von Messina.* One could argue that the sons, Manuel and Cesar, while trying to overcome the posture of their father, ultimately repeat the paternal pattern of violence in their own actions. In fact, they are less successful in upholding the law than their father. Still, as I will argue, the brothers make a serious attempt to subdue the state of civil war through establishing a brotherly bond suggested by their mother. It is the ultimate failure of this new maternal bond that marks the end of the play, where the sons are symbolically swallowed by the still open grave of their father.

The transformation from an older, in this case, mythic law to a new law of human communication through emotional transparency is openly the theme of Goethe's play, as a comparison with Euripides' drama will make clear.[15] While Euripides places the emphasis on the difference between Greek culture and the cruel customs of the barbarians, which have to be defeated through cunning, Goethe shifts the emphasis toward the internal conflict of Greek culture. Greek civilization is as much involved in the blind repetition of crime and guilt that characterizes the barbarian order. The extreme horrors of the family of Tantalus that Iphigenie discloses in her dialogue with Thoas and the emotional pathology of Orest, who feels persecuted by the Erinyes for the murder of his mother, indicate the enduring power of the old law. Ultimately there seems to be no fundamental difference between the culture of the Taurians and that of the Greeks. Therefore, the defeat of the old law, the theme of Goethe's play, cannot be structured along the lines of a Greek identity that can be set off against a foreign, less valuable culture. Thus we will have to address how Goethe's play performs the metamorphosis that Euripides' play simply structures according to preconceived notions of cultural difference.

There is no obvious parallel to this constellation in Schiller's play since the cultural and ethnic differences between the ruling princes, who are of Norman extraction, and the mass of the indigenous population are used in a very different way. The text points to an idyllic past determined by peace and harmony with nature before the intrusion of the Normans. But this state is no longer available in the contemporary world of feudal hierarchies and power struggles. Hence the Schillerian question is whether there can be a future peaceful order without simple regression to the idyllic state. Whether there is an answer to this question is controversial among Schiller scholars. I will argue that the transformation actually does not take place. The tragic ending defines the impossibility of establishing a new law. The law of the dead father is questioned but not broken.

II

Goethe's drama shares with that of Euripides an untragic ending. Iphigenie and Orest are allowed to return to Greece. But there the similarity ends. While in Euripides' play the Greeks owe their rescue exclusively to the intervention of Athena after the failure of the ruse, Goethe reconceives the motivation for the decision of Thoas to let the Greek party leave. Pylades' plan to flee with Orest and Iphigenie while Thoas and his army are waiting for the ritual purification of the sacrificial victims fails because Iphigenie decides to give the plan away (IV:4). Her refusal to betray Thoas, to treat him, as it were, not as a barbarian who deserves to be outwitted, but as a subject of equal value, changes the development of the plot in the fifth act. Thoas, after regaining control over the prisoners and his priestess, not only must decide the fate of the prisoners, but he must make up his mind about the significance and meaning of traditional law. To sacrifice Orest and Pylades, as he had menaced in anger, implies the return to the old order of guilt and retribution that had characterized his culture before the arrival of Iphigenie. The custom of human sacrifice that had already been abolished under the influence of the Greek priestess threatens to return, seemingly justified by the betrayal of Iphigenie and her relatives. Greek civilization, as Thoas points out not without some justification, only gives the impression of a higher degree of cultivation while its ground is as bloody and inhumane as the world of the barbarians. But is is precisely not the old law of Greek myth that Iphigenie mentions in her discussion with Thoas. When Thoas invokes an old law that demands human sacrifce (V:3), Iphigenie responds by suggesting the existence of a prior law:[16]

> Wir fassen ein Gesetz begierig an,
> Das unsrer Leidenschaft zur Waffe dient.
> Ein andres spricht zu mir, ein älteres,
> Mich dir zu widersetzen; das Gebot
> Dem jeder Fremde heilig ist.
>
> (1832–35)

> We are most willing to appeal to laws
> When we can make them weapons of our wishes.
> I know another law, one still more ancient,

Which tells me to resist you: by that law
All strangers are considered sacred.

(1832–36)

In fact, the older law is older only in the sense of being more fundamental and therefore more demanding than the rule of ritual human sacrifice,
whether it is applied among the Taurians or among the Greeks, for instance,
when Agamemnon was prepared to sacrifice his own daughter for the benefit of the Greek war expedition. Iphigenie's plea to Thoas to spare the lives
of the prisoners therefore calls on her own experience as the victim of a
ritual killing in order to persuade the king of the futility of ritual violence.
("Beschönige nicht die Gewalt," [1856] / "Enough! Why lend false colour to
an act / Of force . . .") The dialogue of the fifth act, dominated by the exchanges between Thoas and Iphigenie, brings about the change of mind in
Thoas that finally enables Iphigenie to leave the Taurians with her brother
and Pylades without fear of retribution. Yet it is only the consensus of the
king, his willingness to embrace and support Iphigenie's departure with his
"lebt wohl [fare well]" (2175), the final words of the drama that confirm the
acceptance of the new law.

This resolution of the dramatic conflict has been celebrated as the victory
of humanism because the heroine overcomes the forces of barbarism.[17] But
can this solution indeed function as a model for a politics of humanism?
Its application in the social world might be deemed as naive at best when
real lives are at stake, for what is the likelihood that the king does not carry
out his threat to have the prisoners executed. Brecht's play *Der gute Mensch
von Sezuan* reflects exactly on this dilemma of idealism when the heroine
can maintain her position of purity and goodness only by splitting herself
into two personae, where the "bad" cousin has to do all the unfriendly and
mean things to guarantee the survival of the good woman and her child.
In the "real" world, the claims of idealism do not carry much weight. But
it is precisely this pragmatism that points to the weakness of an interpretation of Goethe's play that posits it as a model for political ethics. Iphigenie's
near-fatal decision to abandon the agreed-upon plan of cunning by telling
Thoas the ruse responds to a different cultural and moral configuration,
clearly a modern one that Euripides could not have shared or even understood. What is at stake here is the possibility of complete transparency in
the interaction between human beings and especially between members of

a family. To be sure, Euripides' play invokes family relations, in particular the relationship between Orest and his sister. Yet they are not in the same sense at the center of the tradegy as they are in Goethe's *Iphigenie,* which cannot conceal its proximity to the modern domestic tragedy.

It is not accidental therefore that Goethe introduces two elements that are completely missing in Euripides: first, the love interest of Thoas in Iphigenie and second, Iphigenie's attitude toward Thoas. These elements are skillfully combined to move the action along. It is Thoas's wish to marry Iphigenie and her refusal to accept his proposal that bring about the decision of the angry king to return to the custom of human sacrifice. At the same time, Iphigenie's insistence to see in Thoas a second father motivates her resolution to tell him the secret plan. In other words, for Iphigenie there are two families, namely her family of origin, that is, the family of Tantalus, and her filial relationship to Thoas, whose trust she has won and in whom she has faith. While the first family depends on bonds of blood, the second relies on a spiritual bond. In both instances Iphigenie is aware of her filial duty, but there is a substantial difference in its nature: While the bonds of the family of origin are imposed on her and leave her only the role of the victim or unsuccessful rescuer, Iphigenie's sense of duty in her attitude toward Thoas empowers her to take action and to resist the return of the old law through the very figure of Thoas, whom she had previously persuaded to give up human sacrifice. The plot elements that Goethe added suggest the need for a rereading of the play, in which the role of the father receives greater emphasis.

In the context of Greek myth, the story of the family of Tantalus and in particular the fate of Orest, who is called upon to revenge the death of his father by killing his own mother, points to a shift from a matrilinear to a patrilinear definition of the family.[18] The power of the Erinyes, whose persecution Orest cannot escape even after the ritual purification by the court in Athens, represents an older matriarchal law, which then was superseded by the patriarchal law of the Olympian gods (in Euripides' tragedy embodied by Pallas Athene). Now the killing of the father emerges as the most severe crime, a crime for which neither Orest nor Iphigenie is responsible. Still, the Greek myth, as it is represented by Euripides, does not fundamentally challenge the law of guilt and retribution. It only shifts the emphasis from the mother to the father.

I want to argue that Goethe's drama, through its reconfiguration of the role of the father, does indeed challenge the concept of law as it is defined in myth.[19] For this reason, his play revises the concept of the imaginary as well as the symbolic father, to use Lacanian terminology,[20] by introducing a second father figure. While Agamemnon and Thoas are initially similar — namely, both grounded in the old law of sacrifice — they ultimately become rather different figures. Iphigenie's bond with the dead, murderous father, which incidentally she never denies or rejects, is replaced by the attachment to Thoas, the spiritual father, who finally grants her independence and freedom. Therefore, this transition, which begins to emerge in the first act and comes to fruition only in the last scene of Act V, has to be considered in more detail.

Iphigenie's struggle with Thoas, first about his feelings toward her and later about the fate of the Greek prisoners, involves more than the character of the man who has held her as a prisoner in his country. In the crucial scene (IV:4), it becomes quite clear that Thoas figures as an imaginary father as well, who has replaced the dark image of Agamemnon. By calling him "mein zweiter Vater" (1641) ["my second father" (1642)], Iphigenie invokes a different kind of relationship in which she becomes the subject. For Iphigenie this new father image is closely linked to a new cultural and legal order without human sacrifice and instrumental rationality. This is precisely the instance where she differs from Pylades, who presents his plan as justified by fate:

> Du weigerst dich umsonst; die ehrne Hand
> Der Not gebietet und ihr ernster Wink
> Ist oberstes Gesetz dem Götter selbst
> Sich unterwerfen müssen. Schweigend herrscht
> Des ewgen Schicksals unberatne Schwester.
>
> (1680–84)

> It is vain to resist; the brazen hand
> Of stern Necessity, its supreme law
> Must overrule us, for the gods themselves
> Obey it. Silently it reigns, the sister
> Of everlasting Fate, and heeds no counsel.
> Bear what it has imposed upon you, do
> What it commands.
>
> (1680–86)

It is the image of the second father that encourages her to define her own independent position in the conflict between the Greeks and the Taurians. Against Pylades' invocation of fate as the ultimate measure of human existence, she sets her claim for a subjective but irreducible ethical norm based on her "Bild [image]" of the father and, by extension, that of the gods. Contemplating her situation after Pylades has left her, she exclaims to the gods:

Rettet mich
Und rettet euer Bild in meiner Seele.
(1716–17)

Save me, and save your image in my soul!
(1717)

It is noteworthy that the parental relationship is exclusively emphasized by Iphigenie (Thoas prefers to see her as a woman and future wife). To put it differently, the relationship is not a given one but rather a process. Iphigenie has created the image of the second father in order to define her own ethical identity, a ground that can no longer be destroyed by the law of fate. Hence, in a reversal of the traditional pattern, the figure of the new father has to be educated. Iphigenie has persuaded Thoas to relinquish the old custom of sacrificing all foreigners. But in the play, Thoas resists the completion of this education when his understanding of the relationship to Iphigenie is not accepted by her. When Thoas questions her right to claim superiority for Greek culture, Iphigenie replies:

Es hört sie [die Stimme der Wahrheit und Menschlichkeit, PUH] jeder
Geboren unter jedem Himmel, dem
Des Lebens Quelle durch den Busen rein
Und ungehindert fließt —
(1939–42)

All men can hear it [the voice of truth and human kindness, PUH],
    born in any land,
If they have hearts through which the stream of life
Flows pure and unimpeded —
(1940–42)

By shifting the argument from Thoas's doubt about the supremacy of Greek law to the claim of a universal concept of truth and humanity, which will by definition include the barbarians as well as the cultivated Greeks, she reinforces her definition of the father as a spiritual force. Thoas the man is not at the center of her concerns, but the concept of Thoas as a generous and feeling father.

> O reiche mir die Hand zum Friedenszeichen.
>
> . . . .
>
> Um Guts zu tun braucht's keiner Überlegung.
>
> . . . .
>
> Der Zweifel ist's der Gutes böse macht.
> Bedenke nicht, gewähre wie du's fühlst.
> (1987–92)

> Oh now make peace with me, give me your hand!
>
> . . . .
>
> Why need we ponder whether to do good?
>
> . . . .
>
> It is by doubt that good is turned to evil.
> Do not reflect; give as your heart dictates!
> (1987–92)

By stressing the need for an emotional decision, Iphigenie blocks the recourse to a form of rationality that is built on the old law as, for instance, Pylades had invoked it. Now the trust of the daugther is expressed in terms of a discourse of feeling. Yet we have to note that the content of this discourse is the universal claim for a humane order that replaces the mythic law of guilt and retribution.

The symbolic father in whose name the law is imposed and who regulates desire intervenes in Goethe's play by virtue of someone incarnating this function, but in a veiled fashion. In this instance, however, it is not the discourse of the mother who mediates between child and law, but the discourse of the daughter, who finds herself in the position of an orphan in search of her own imaginary father. Iphigenie's wish to return to Greece with her brother, who is the last surviving male descendant of the family, reinforces the patrilinear symbolic order. At no point is she tempted to speak in the name of the mother or to take up the cause of the violated mother against her brother. Still, there is a strong element of rejection in Iphigenie's actions, namely her stern refusal to yield to the demands of fate as an inescapable power.

III

Schiller's play, by contrast, moves toward a tragic ending with the suicide of Don Cesar after he killed Don Manuel in a fit of jealousy. While philosophically-oriented Schiller criticism has tended to view this ending as an affirmation of a moral resolution of the play,[21] a number of more recent interpretations have taken issue with this reading and suggested that Cesar's state of mind before he takes his own life does not permit such a conclusion.[22] Yet this critical disagreement remains irresolvable as long as the explications of the play focus exclusively on the interaction of the characters. While references to other tragedies of Schiller such as *Maria Stuart* and Schiller's theoretical essays are helpful to support interpretative claims, they are by no means compelling. One can with equal justification advance another line of argument in which the concept of fate is given a more prominent role: The tragic ending proves the intended proximity of the drama to Greek tragedy (especially to *Oedipus the King* by Sophocles as the quintessential analytic play). In this reading the characters are, of course, perceived as objects of fateful connections rather than as subjects who are called upon to make moral decisions.[23] It may turn out, however, that these interpretations are ultimately more compatible than commonly assumed. The mediating element could be the very configuration that defines Sophocles' Oedipus play, that is, the Oedipal triangle.[24] However, the basic conflict between the father and the son who desires his mother, as Freud has described the dramatic constellation in more abstract terms,[25] remains more hidden in Schiller's play by the fact that the initial rivalry for the love of the mother is shifted toward the brothers and then replaced by the quarrel of Don Manuel and Don Cesar for the love of the mysterious young woman, who turns out to be no other than their lost sister. The threat of mother-son incest would be replaced by the menace of brother-sister incest as the underlying violation of the law. Yet this potential infraction, which the dead father tried to avoid by his order to have the younger daughter killed immediately after her birth, only repeats the act of the father, who took away and married the bride of his own father. For this reason, the ancestor had cursed the family. This curse then is acknowledged in the play by the dreams of the father and the mother about the future of the family. While these dreams seem to stand in opposition (extinction of the family in the dream of the father, and strengthening of the family in the mother's dream), they actually predict the same event: the fatal conflict among the brothers over the love of their sister. The power of desire, at the center of which is the mother, respectively the sister, drives the action to the expected tragic ending.

Some Schiller critics have resisted this interpretation by arguing that its affinity to a Greek concept of fate could not reflect Schiller's understanding of subjectivity as it is documented in his other dramas.[26] I want to suggest, however, that Schiller's play derives its dramatic conflict precisely from the underlying but unrecognized Oedipal triangle in which the protagonists strive to overcome the curse of guilt by establishing a new and different order for family and state. They ultimately fail in this attempt since they remain entangled in the mire of desire. In other words, the point of departure for the reading of the play should be the dead father in his relationship to his wife and his children.

All references in the drama to his attitude and his actions show him as a strong but also reckless and self-centered ruler who does not hesitate to exert his power in violent forms when he deems it necessary. The most egregious deed is of course the decision to have his own daughter killed because she might be a threat to the dynasty. At the same time, he is capable of suppressing the destructive rivalry and hostility among his sons. It is not accidental, therefore, that civil war breaks out immediately after his unexpected death. This is the situation at the opening of the play when Isabella, his widow, has to consult with the elders about the present calamity. Her summary of the former husband's life places the emphasis on his function as ruler:[27]

Nicht dreimal hat der Mond die Lichtgestalt
Erneut, seit ich den fürstlichen Gemahl
Zu seiner letzten Ruhestätte trug,
Der mächtigwaltend dieser Stadt gebot,

Mit starkem Arme gegen eine Welt
Euch schützend, die euch feindlich rings umlagert.

(13–18)

The moon its luminous form has not yet twice
Renewed since I my princely spouse conducted
Down to his final resting place, the same
Who ruled this city with his strong arm against
A world that hemmed you hostilely about.

(13–18)

As it turns out, protection was needed as much against the actions of his own sons, whose rivalry did not respect the bounds of the law:

Zwar weil der Vater noch gefürchtet herrschte,
Hielt er durch gleicher Strenge furchtbare
Gerechtigkeit die Heftigbrausenden im Zügel,
Und unter *eines* Joches Eisenschwere
Bog er vereinend ihren starren Sinn.

(34–38)

While yet their father, fear-inspiring, ruled,
He held their wayward turbulence in check
By the dread justness of his own impartial sternness.
Beneath a single yoke of iron weight
He bent their stubborn spirits to a union.

(34–38)

The forceful but violent law of the ruler could only repress, but not heal, the hatred among his sons. Therefore, his death results in civil war leaving the unprepared mother with the task of restoring peace and order. Her approach differs markedly from that of her husband. Where the latter used force, she implores her sons to stop the fighting.

Ich warf mit dem zerrißnen Mutterherzen
Mich zwischen die Ergrimmten, Friede rufend —
Unabgeschreckt, geschäftigt, unermüdlich
Beschickt ich sie, den einen um den andern,
Bis ich erhielt durch mütterliches Flehn,
Daß sies zufrieden sind, in dieser Stadt

Messina, in dem väterlichen Schloß,
Unfeindlich sich von Angesicht zu sehen,
Was nie geschah, seitdem der Fürst verschieden.

(81–89)

And with my shattered mother's heart I threw
Myself between the madmen, crying Peace!
Undaunted, eagerly, and tirelessly
I sent word to them, first one then the other,
Till I prevailed with my maternal pleas
That they consent to meet each other in
Messina and in their paternal castle
Without hostility, a thing which had
Not happened since the Prince their father died.

(81–89)

Although she has chosen the "väterliche Schloß" as the appropriate place for the restoration of peace, her diplomatic procedure relies on suggestions and supplication, thereby preparing the stage for a peaceful resolution of the conflict, but also, as it turns out, unknowingly preparing the ground for the return of the hatred.

Isabella appears to succeed in bringing her sons together and thereby ending the civil war because she follows a more personal strategy. Where the father used force, she appeals to the heart and calls on the natural bonds among the members of the family.

O meine Söhne! Feindlich ist die Welt
Und falsch gesinnt! Es liebt ein jeder nur
Sich selbst; unsicher, los und wandelbar
Sind alle Bande, die das leichte Glück
Geflochten—Laune löst, was Laune knüpfte—
Nur die *Natur* ist redlich! Sie allein
Liegt an dem ewgen Ankergrunde fest,
Wenn alles andre auf den sturmbewegten Wellen
Des Lebens unstet treibt—

(356–64)

The world is hostile, o my sons! and false
Of disposition. Each man loves himself

Alone; uncertain, loose, and changeable
Are all the bonds that Fortune ever wove, —
Caprice disjoins what by Caprice was joined, —
Nature alone is honest. She alone
Stands fast on the eternal anchor-bottom
When all things else upon the storm-tossed waves of life
Unsteadily go drifting.

(356–64)

In fact the strong emotional ties of love among members of the core family (in this instance the mother and the sons) seem to prevail over the negative emotions that resulted in civil war. Isabella suggests that the hatred between Manuel and Cesar can be broken because it went back to their childhood and therefore was not the decision of adults. This rationalization, of course, underestimates the ambivalence of these feelings and therefore the possibility of their reoccurrence as soon as a new object of desire comes into view that would renew the rivalry.

What remains unexplored in this celebration of harmonious union is the involvement of the mother as the underlying cause of the rivalry. As the agent of family diplomacy, she cannot see that the search for her affection was the mysterious, unexplored cause of the hatred in the first place. For this reason her words must remain conflicted. While she means to restore the law of the father in the public realm, her desire for reconciliation among her children is built on bonds of love.

In eures Vaters Gruft werft ihn hinab,
Den alten Haß der frühen Kinderzeit!
Der schönen Liebe sei das neue Leben,
Der Eintracht, der Versöhnung seis geweiht.

(429–32)

Into your father's tomb cast down the ancient
Hatred of your early childhood years!
To love let your new life be dedicated,
To harmony, to reconciliation.

(429–32)

Of course, the development of the action proves her wrong. As soon as the brothers realize that they are in love with the same woman, they fall back on their familiar pattern of rivalry and hatred. Therefore, the question has to be raised why there was a moment at all when they could love and respect each other. The answer has to do with another element of the plot Schiller criticism has for the most part treated as a conventional element, namely the fact that both brothers had independently discovered and fallen in love with their unknown sister before they met. The reconciliation was possible, I want to suggest, because the sons had shifted their desire from the mother to the sister. In other words, we are dealing with a displacement of the original Oedipal conflict. Since the father is already dead, the rivalry is carried out among the sons themselves who found another image for their original desire, that is, the sister. Hence the reason for the possibility of peace is also the reason for the later continuation of the hostility. The brothers cannot escape their own fixation.

In the critical literature, the figure of Isabella has been judged as a pragmatic, and to some extent manipulative, politician who wants to save the rule of her dynasty. There is no doubt that she means to bring back order to the city of Messina. But the exact nature of this order is rarely considered. While she invokes the name of the father, it is by no means certain that she simply wants to restore the order of the dead ruler. The textual evidence seems to point to a different direction, for the invocation of the family ties under the concept of nature [Natur] restructures the political order along the lines of feelings rather than decisions based on rational self-interest. Again, this means, as it did in Goethe's *Iphigenie,* that the structure of communication has to be transformed. Since the disorder of civil war is grounded in the personal animosity of the brothers, the political solution seems to lie in the overcoming of these feelings, as well. Isabella's understanding of the new order, I would argue, is significantly different from that of her dead husband. It would be a politics of personal bonds and love. Emotional transparency among members of the family appears to be at the center of this idea of a peaceful rule where the mother mediates between her sons. Thus it is not without significance that Isabella urges her sons to throw their mutual hatred into the open grave of the father.

Schiller's tragedy demonstrates, however, that this new order cannot materialize since Manuel and Cesar resume their antagonistic stance when they find out that they are in love with the same woman. The reason for the failure has to be carefully considered. At the psychological level, the tragic ending is motivated by the rigid and blind jealousy of the brothers. In the context of the logic of fate, the murder of Don Manuel is the unexpected but consistent fulfillment of the omen (for which no individual is responsible). In psychoanalytical terms, the Oedipal conflict, seemingly resolved by the end of the first act, returns in its displaced form in act II and radically undermines the plans of the mother. It is noteworthy that Isabella fails to persuade her son Cesar that in her role as his sister, Beatrice cannot be his lover or wife. The law of the father, which prohibits not only incest between mother and son but also marriage between sister and brother, is not respected. What ultimately happens after the murder of Don Manuel is a return to the old law of the father. Isabella realizes that her hopes for a new era of peace built on love and trust have been crushed.

> Da liegen meine Hoffnungen — Sie stirbt
> Im Keim, die junge Blume eures Friedens,
> Und keine schöne Früchte sollt ich schauen.
>
> (2437–38)

> There lie my hopes. And it has died a bud,
> That tender blossom of your harmony,
> And I shall not live to behold fair fruits.
>
> (2439–41)

Even her desperate attempt to embrace the murderous Don Cesar as the heir and ruler fails. For Don Cesar, a similar breakdown of hopes and aspirations occurs. His initial shock results from his mother declaring his dead brother to be the favorite son. Moreover, Beatrice does not show the hoped-for sympathy with his dilemma. In short, he realizes that he can neither be the favorite son nor the lover of Beatrice. This insight prepares him for the final step, namely his self-execution for the murder of Don Cesar. The realization of his guilt is the final turning point in his struggle to distance himself from mother and sister and accept solidarity with his dead brother.

> Nein, Bruder! Nicht dein Opfer will ich dir
> Entziehen — deine Stimme aus dem Sarg
> Ruft mächtger dringend als der Mutter Tränen
> Und mächtger als der Liebe Flehn —
>
> (2822–25)

No, Brother, I shall not deprive you of
Your sacrificial victim — From your coffin
Your voice more strongly calls than Mother's tears,
More strongly than the plea of love.

(2822–25)

Ultimately Cesar and Manuel will share the grave with the father, which had been left open after the ceremonial burial because of the warring among the brothers. The final lines of the chorus seal and affirm Cesar's decision and thereby the law of the father: "Das Leben ist der Güter höchstes *nicht*, / Der Übel größtes aber ist die *Schuld*" (2838–39). "Of all possessions life is not the highest, / The worst of evils is, however, guilt" (2841–42).

IV

While both Goethe and Schiller took the material for their plays from historically distant periods, they foregrounded a modern element, namely the centrality of the core family. What we observed in the case of *Iphigenie auf Tauris*, that is, its proximity to the modern domestic drama, can be extended to *Die Braut von Messina*. The feudal setting allows Schiller to enlarge domestic conflicts in which the nature of the family can be tested. This family, however, is not, as one might expect, the "ganze Haus" of the corporate society;[28] instead, the new family restricts itself to parents and children and, moreover, redefines its purpose in pedagogical terms. In this context the father functions primarily as the teacher and spiritual adviser of his children, while the mother is left with the task of primary care. The restructuring of the family, which occurred in the second half of the eighteenth century, shifted the expectations and the tasks of its members.[29] The more the family lost its traditional economic functions, the more it assumed nurturing and pedagogical functions, some of which became the prerogative of the father. In Gellert's novel *Das Leben der schwedischen Gräfin von G.*, for example, the education of the young heroine is taken over by a paternal figure as soon as she is old enough to receive formal instruction.[30] For the adolescent, as Lessing's plays demonstrate with great clarity, it is the father rather than the mother who becomes the central parental relation. Consequently, the mother is either absent (*Miß Sara Sampson, Nathan der*

Weise) or plays a minor and problematic role (*Emilia Galotti*). Unlike the love of the mother, which remains possessive, the love of the ideal father is oriented toward a final step of setting the adolescent free. The young person is ultimately encouraged to leave the family of origin. As Friedrich Kittler has pointed out, in Lessing's plays, the father assumes the function of cultural reproduction.[31] In this process, his spiritual nature (which manifests itself in his pedagogical concerns rather than his natural, biological character) is important. Thus, Nathan takes over the education of his stepdaughter Recha, leaving only the primary-care function to Daja, the surrogate mother. In the discourse of the Enlightenment, the preponderance of the spiritual father, who is not necessarily identical with the natural father, determines the ideal order of the family.

Around 1800, however, we witness a second transformation. As Kittler and Rüdiger Steinlein have argued,[32] the discourse about the internal structure of the nuclear family began to shift in such a way that now the mother is assigned the function of nurturing and educating the child. The network of interaction, especially its emotional side, is based on the interface between the mother and the small child, thus relegating the father to the margins. The mother-child dyad becomes the central axis because its prerational nature compensates for the losses that occurred in the child's experience when the members of the larger household became more and more excluded from interaction with the family. While the pedagogical discourse of the Enlightenment did not fully recognize these shifts and favored the father as the chosen educator, as can be gleaned from the children's literature of the late eighteenth century, the pedagogical ideas of the Romantic generation stressed the primary role of the mother.[33] The Romantic notion of education is mother-centered.

In the context of this social and cultural transformation, the classical plays of Goethe and Schiller deserve special attention. For one thing, they obviously do not fit neatly into the historical scheme developed by Kittler and Steinlein. It would be difficult to describe *Iphigenie* as mother-centered. In fact, there seems to be an avoidance of any serious exploration of Klytemnestra's fate. Iphigenie is much more interested in the well-being of her brother, the murderer of her mother, than in a discussion of her death. Goethe's play seems to continue, therefore, the tradition of Lessing's *Nathan,* where the resolution of the conflict lies in the hands of the spiritual father, who is distinct from the deceased biological father. Yet there is also

an important, even crucial, difference. Goethe's daughter-father relationship is decidedly more complex, for Iphigenie has to confront contrasting
father images: on the one hand, the murderous father in Agamemnon and,
on the other, the generous, benevolent father in Thoas. The process of education, however, is not controlled by Thoas; instead, it is Iphigenie who assumes the function of cultural reproduction. By transferring the moment of
agency from the father figure to the daughter, a revision of the law itself becomes possible. At the end of the drama, Thoas not only sets Iphigenie free,
thereby demonstrating that he has overcome his initial desire to possess her,
but he accepts and hence confirms a new formulation of the paternal law,
which is now grounded in bonds of love and mutual recognition among
the family members. To put it differently, the norms of the idealized core
family become universal laws.

One might possibly argue that Schiller's play is mother-centered. After
all, Isabella appears as the mediator between the feuding sons. But the
scheme miscarries because she ultimately fails in her new role as educator.
She cannot permanently inscribe the new moral and political order based
on feelings of love and recognition into her sons since she remains herself
a possessive mother who is unable to set the sons free. Through the attachment to the daughter, who replaces the function of the mother, Don Manuel
and Don Cesar stay fixated in their desire. Hence the old patrilinear order
reasserts itself after the murder of Don Manuel as the only law available to
Don Cesar. He dies in fulfillment of this law, rejecting both mother and sis-
ter/bride. Yet this ending does not contain the innovation we observed in
Goethe's *Iphigenie*. The tragic ending of *Die Braut von Messina* affirms, even
celebrates, the old paternal law, but it closes off the revisions that can be
recognized in Goethe's play. Schiller, it seems, chose a traditional resolution
to the conflict. One alternative would have been a drama in which Isabella
became the heroine who supplanted the law of the dead husband with a new
order based on familial bonds of love and recognition. Why did Schiller resist this recoding that the Romantics embraced? It appears that Schiller was
unwilling to radicalize the configuration to an extent that it would affirm
incestuous relationships, as Novalis did in Klingsohr's fairy tale in *Heinrich
von Ofterdingen*. In such a reconfiguration, the erotic desire would reach
an extrafamilial goal, if at all, only through the mediation of the desiring
and desired mother. This model, however, basically undermines the cultural reproduction as it was organized in a patrilinear order. Schiller was

not prepared to support such a discursive shift. It is worth noting, however, that *Die Braut von Messina* at least experiments with this constellation. Only in the last act is this solution firmly rejected in favor of the paternal law. The price of this return to a level of moral decisions, as it occurs when Don Cesar declares that he can no longer live after his murderous deed, is the loss of the utopian propensity that we find in the ending of Goethe's *Iphigenie auf Tauris*.

NOTES

1. See for instance Paul de Man, "Kant and Schiller," in *Aesthetic Ideology*, ed. Andrzei Warminsky (Minneapolis and London: University of Minnesota Press, 1996), 129–62.

2. See Jochen Hörisch, *Gott, Geld und Glück. Zur Logik der Liebe in den Bildungsromanen Goethes, Kellers und Thomas Manns* (Frankfurt am Main: Suhrkamp, 1983), 30–114; Todd Kontje, *Private Lives in the Public Sphere. The German Bildungsroman as Metafiction* (University Park: Pennsylvania State University Press, 1992), 51–78.

3. See among others Jürgen Habermas, *The Structural Transformation of the Public Sphere*, trans. Thomas Burger (Cambridge, Mass.: Massachusetts Institute of Technology Press, 1989); Michel Foucault, *Discipline and Punish. The Birth of the Prison*, trans. Alan Sheridan (New York: Vintage Books, 1979); Reinhart Koselleck, *Vergangene Zukunft. Zur Semantik geschichtlicher Zeiten* (Frankfurt am Main: Suhrkamp, 1979).

4. See Geoffrey Winthrop-Young, "Wissenschaft als Revolutionsbewältigung. Thesen zu Goethe und Lichtenberg," in *Geist und Gesellschaft. Zur deutschen Rezeption der Französischen Revolution*, ed. Eitel Timm (Munich: Wilhelm Fink, 1990), 70–81.

5. See Niklas Luhmann, "Theoriesubstitution in der Erziehungswissenschaft: Von der Philanthropie zum Neuhumanismus," in Luhmann, *Gesellschaftsstruktur und Semantik*, vol. 2 (Frankfurt am Main: Suhrkamp, 1993), 105–94.

6. See *Bürgerinnen und Bürger. Geschlechterverhältnisse im 19. Jahrhundert*, ed. Ute Frevert (Göttingen: Vandenhoeck & Ruprecht, 1988); Isabel V. Hull, *Sexuality, State, and Civil Society in Germany, 1700–1815* (Ithaca, N.Y. and London: Cornell University Press, 1996); Mary Murray, *The Law of the Father? Patriarchy in the Transition from Feudalism to Capitalism* (London and New York: Routledge, 1995).

7. See Lynn Hunt, *The Family Romance of the French Revolution* (Berkeley and Los Angeles: University of California Press, 1992).

8. Lynn Hunt, *The Family Romance*, 17–52 and 59–63.

9. See for instance Bernd Weyergraf, *Der skeptische Bürger. Wielands Schriften zur Französischen Revolution* (Stuttgart: Metzler, 1972); also Thomas P. Saine, *Black Bread — White Bread. German Intellectuals and the French Revolution* (Columbia, S.C.: Camden House, 1988); *The Internalized Revolution. German Reactions to the French Revolution, 1789–1989*, ed. Ehrhard Bahr and Thomas P. Saine (New York and London:

Garland, 1992); *The French Revolution and the Age of Goethe*, ed. Gerhart Hoffmeister (Hildesheim: G. Olms, 1989).

10. See Norbert Eke, *Signaturen der Revolution, Frankreich—Deutschland: deutsche Zeitgenossenschaft und deutsches Drama zur Französischen Revolution um 1800* (Munich: Wilhelm Fink, 1997).

11. See Friedrich Schiller, *Sämtliche Werke*, 7th edition, ed. Gerhard Fricke and Herbert G. Göpfert (Munich: Hanser, 1985), vol. 2, p. 1277. All Schiller quotations in German are from this edition. For the English quotations see: *Friedrich von Schiller*, trans. Charles E. Passage (New York: Frederick Ungar Publishing, 1962).

12. For Goethe's familiarity with Greek myth, see Humphrey Trevelyan, *Goethe and the Greeks* (Cambridge: Cambridge University Press, 1941); also Uwe Petersen, *Goethe und Euripides* (Heidelberg: Universitätsverlag Carl Winter, 1974).

13. Schiller, "Über den Gebrauch des Chors in der Tragödie," in Schiller, *Sämtliche Werke*, 2:815–23.

14. For an extensive and rigorous discussion of the modern subject, see Stanley Corngold, *The Fate of the Self. German Writers and French Theory* (New York: Columbia University Press, 1986).

15. See Käte Hamburger, *Von Sophokles zu Sartre. Griechische Dramenfiguren antik und modern* (Stuttgart: Kohlhammer, 1962), 95–120.

16. All German quotations from Goethe's *Iphigenie auf Tauris* refer to *Goethes Werke*, ed. Erich Trunz (Hamburger Ausgabe), vol. 5, ed. Liselotte Blumenthal and Eberhard Haufe, 10th edition (Munich: Beck, 1982). All the English quotations from Goethe's *Iphigenie in Tauris* refer to *Johann Wolfgang von Goethe—Verse Plays and Epic*, ed. Cyrus Hamelin and Frank Ryder (New York: Suhrkamp, 1987).

17. See Oskar Seidlin, "Goethe's 'Iphigenie' and the Human Ideal," in *Modern Language Quarterly* 10 (1949): 307–20; for a critique of this approach, see Theodor W. Adorno, "Zum Klassizismus von Goethe's Iphigenie," in Adorno, *Noten zur Literatur*, vol. 4 (Frankfurt am Main: Suhrkamp, 1974), 7–33.

18. For a more extensive discussion see the commentary in *Goethes Werke*, 5:422–29, especially 425.

19. This touches on the dialectical relationship between myth and enlightenment as Max Horkheimer and Theodor W. Adorno developed it in *Dialectic of Enlightenment* (1947); see the recent analysis by James Schmidt, "Language, Mythology and Enlightenment: Historical Notes on Horkheimer and Adorno's *Dialectic of Enlightenment*," *Social Research* 65 (Winter 1998): 807–38.

20. See Jacques Lacan, *Ecrits. A Selection*, trans. Alan Sheridan (New York and London: Norton, 1977); see also Lacan, *The Seminar. Book III. The Psychoses, 1955–56*, trans. Russell Grigg (New York and London: Norton, 1993); Lacan, *Le Séminaire, Livre IV*, ed. Jacques-Alain Miller (Paris: Seuil, 1994).

21. See for example the tightly and carefully argued interpretation of Gerhard Kluge, "Die Braut von Messina," in *Schillers Dramen. Neue Interpretationen*, ed. Walter Hinderer (Stuttgart: Reclam, 1979), 242–70.

22. See Karl S. Guthke, *Schillers Dramen. Idealismus und Skepsis* (Tübingen und Basel: Francke, 1994), 259–78.

23. For a full discussion of the concept of fate and its function in Schiller's play see Monika Ritzer, "Not und Schuld. Zur Funktion des 'antiken' Schicksalsbegriffs in Schillers 'Braut von Messina," in *Schiller heute,* ed. Hans-Jörg Knobloch and Helmut Koopmann (Tübingen: Stauffenburg, 1996), 131–50.

24. For a good discussion of Freud's theory of the Oedipus complex see John Munder Ross, *What Men Want. Mother, Fathers, and Manhood* (Cambridge, Mass. and London: Harvard University Press, 1994), 94–128.

25. Freud summarizes his understanding of the Oedipal triangle in his 1923 study "Das Ich und das Es," in Sigmund Freud, *Studienausgabe,* vol. 3, ed. Alexander Mitscherlich, Angela Richards, and James Strachey (Frankfurt am Main: S. Fischer, 1975), 273–330, especially 299–301.

26. For Example Ritzer, "Not und Schuld" and Kluge, "Die Braut von Messina."

27. Citations give the numbering of the verses of the Hanser edition (see note 11).

28. See Otto Brunner, "Das 'ganze Haus' und die alteuropäische Ökonomik," in Brunner, *Neue Wege der Sozialgeschichte* (Göttingen: Vandenhoeck & Rupprecht, 1956), 33–61.

29. See Jürgen Schlumbohm, *Kinderstuben. Wie Kinder zu Bauern, Bürgern, Aristokraten wurden 1700–1850* (Munich: dtv, 1983); Reinhard Sieder, *Sozialgeschichte der Familie* (Frankfurt am Main: Suhrkamp, 1987).

30. See Stephan K. Schindler, *Das Subjekt als Kind. Die Erfindung der Kindheit im Roman des 18. Jahrhunderts* (Berlin: Erich Schmidt, 1994), 39–100.

31. Friedrich A. Kittler, "'Erziehung ist Offenbarung'. Zur Struktur der Familie in Lessings Dramen," *Jahrbuch der deutschen Schiller Gesellschaft* 21 (1977): 111–37, especially 119.

32. Friedrich A. Kittler, "Über die Sozialisation Wilhelm Meisters," in *Dichtung als Sozialisationsspiel,* ed. Gerhard Kaiser and Friedrich Kittler (Göttingen: Vandenhoeck und Rupprecht, 1978), 13–124.; Rüdiger Steinlein, *Die domestizierte Phantasie. Studien zur Kinderliteratur, Kinderlektüre und Literaturpädagogik des 18. und frühen 19. Jahrhunderts* (Heidelberg: Universitätsverlag Carl Winter, 1987); see also Schindler, *Das Subjekt als Kind,* 9–38.

33. See Steinlein, *Die domestizierte Phantasie,* 137–263; Friedrich A. Kittler, *Aufschreibesysteme 1800/1900* (Munich: Wilhelm Fink, 1985), 31–75.

5 Allusions to and Inversions of Plato in Hölderlin's *Hyperion*

MARK W. ROCHE

The importance of Plato for German idealism cannot be overestimated. Whereas Kant's ethics, with its principle of noncontradiction, owes a great deal to Socrates, the influence of Plato is especially prominent in the reemergence of objective idealism, with its claim that nature is neither foreign to human consciousness nor the result of human consciousness, but the manifestation of an objective principle that constitutes both nature and human consciousness. Hölderlin believed in the existence of such objectivity, which represents not one sphere among others, but is itself the essence of all spheres—nature, consciousness, and intersubjectivity. Hölderlin was greatly influenced by Plato, but he did not simply represent Plato's positions in modernity, he reworked and revised them, especially in his novel *Hyperion.*[1] As with many cases of literary paternity, Hölderlin's relationship to Plato is marked by both appropriation and differentiation. Correspondingly, this paper has two parts: it discusses allusions to Plato in *Hyperion,* including a number of previously unrecognized allusions (I), and it analyzes the ways in which Hölderlin inverts some of Plato's positions in order to establish his own version of objective idealism (II).

I

"I believe that in the end we'll all say: sacred Plato, forgive us! You have been gravely wronged" (2:257).[2] Thus ends the preface to the penultimate version of *Hyperion.* What does Hölderlin mean with this prominent suggestion? In what way has modernity ignored Plato's wisdom? The preface opens with a reflection on the greatness of Greek antiquity, including its concept of beauty. Hölderlin redefines originality as depth of insight, not newness of creation: "I wouldn't wish in the least that it be original. Originality is for us novelty; and there is nothing dearer to me than what is as old as the world. / To me originality is sincerity, depth of heart and spirit. But nowadays one appears to want to know very little about this, at least in art" (2:255).[3] Hölderlin then develops his triadic notion of history: an original unity, "blissful unity, being, in the only true sense of the word," has been lost, and we must embrace this loss, if we are to achieve the higher state of reconstituting unity through consciousness. Our goal is "the peace of all peace, which is higher than all reason." Neither "knowledge" nor "action," the spheres of Kant's first and second critiques and the two modes Schleiermacher discusses in the second of his *Speeches on Religion,* will lead us there; knowledge and action are relegated to the sphere of infinite approximation. Beauty differs: "that infinite union, that being, in the only true sense of the word . . . is present—as beauty" (2:256–57). Hölderlin's paean to Plato follows.

For Hölderlin, poetry is not the creation of what is new; it is a recollection of what is already present. The contemplation of beauty awakens this recollection—both of originary unity and of the dissonance integral to a higher harmony. Not *poiesis* but *anamnesis* is the guiding force. It is for this reason as much as any other that Heidegger elevates Hölderlin in his critique of the *verum-factum* principle that dominates Western metaphysics: for Hölderlin, in contrast to much of the Western tradition, truth is not what is made. For Plato, as for Hölderlin, truth and beauty are not creations of the subject, but objective forces already present. They must be uncovered and recollected: like Heidegger after him, Hölderlin employs a concept of truth derived from the Greek *aletheia,* or unconcealment.[4] Both in the concept of originary "all-unity" and in his emphasis on narrative recollection, Hölderlin's character aligns himself with the Platonic concept of knowledge as recollection or *anamnesis.* Hyperion even evokes the Platonic concept of a "pre-Elysium," which is an equally mythic representation of preexisting, rather than subjectively created, truth.[5]

The Platonic doctrine of *anamnesis* suggests that there is truth (or knowledge) that precedes experience and is nonetheless not hypothetical. Ideas do not have their origin in experience; on the contrary, experience presupposes certain (eternal) ideas and itself strives to recognize them (cf. *Phaedo* 74ff). What the doctrine of *anamnesis* captures mythologically, Kant calls synthetic a priori knowledge. But where ideas have for Kant only regulative validity, for Plato and Hölderlin they have ontological valence: they are not chimeras of consciousness, but present in experience. Moreover, according to Hölderlin, what is eternally valid, what is to be recollected, is best grasped aesthetically.[6] Through divine possession, or through what Hölderlin likes to call intellectual intuition, the poet has an initial grasp of preexisting unity and eternal truth.

Because truth already exists, our task is to uncover its essence. Plato argues that we can be virtuous because humanity is potentially already virtuous; virtue as the essence of humanity is reached through reflection on this essence. In a similar vein, Hyperion receives from Adamas in letter four the invocation of his essence, through his name, in its parallel to the sun: "Be, like this! Adamas cried" (2:23), which is reinforced by Diotima in letter twenty-eight: "your namesake, the glorious Hyperion of the heavens, is in you" (2:83). This idea, also invoked by way of the concept of the "god in us," reaches back beyond the Stoics to the Platonic concept of a *daemon* (2:25).[7] Development for Plato and Hölderlin presupposes knowledge or recollection [*Erinnerung*] as a path into oneself, into one's essence, which is ideally an analogue of the higher sphere.[8]

Hölderlin's view of nature, which deviates from the subjective idealist view, is related to this evocation of Plato. For Hölderlin, as for the father of objective idealism, nature is not an extension of ourselves; it has, as a manifestation of objectivity, its own dignity and purposefulness and contains within itself the ultimate harmony sought by humanity; it is to be honored and embraced as an independent reflection of the absolute.[9] The "divine spirit that is particular to each of us and common to all" encompasses also the Logos of nature (2:162). Hyperion's hymns to nature in his second and sixtieth letters must be grasped from this framework, which harkens back not only to the Stoics, but also ultimately to Plato. Nature is not the product of subjective thinking, but is itself an independent and sacred entity ("sacred earth! . . . blessed nature!" [2:15]) containing within it the objective laws of beauty and reason, and it is capable of triggering recognition of the same.[10]

Most central in Hölderlin's reception of Plato in *Hyperion*, beyond the resurrection of *anamnesis* and the elevation of nature, is the integration of his theory of eros, evident in the name Diotima, which comes from the *Symposium*, and in allusions to the *Symposium*, as in Hyperion's reflection, "I came back to Smyrna like a drunk returning from a banquet [wie ein

Trunkener vom Gastmahl]" (2:29). It is also evident in two allusions to Aristophanes' myth of eros and in references, direct and indirect, to the definition of love as the child of plenty (*Poros*) and want (*Penia*). In addition, Hölderlin reflects on parallels between beauty, including artwork, and love, especially homoerotic love.

One of Plato's great achievements in the development of Greek philosophy is his ability to recognize unity and multiplicity not as two autonomous categories, but in their organic relation, as mutually connected. He offers us thereby an ontology that synthesizes the positive and the negative.[11] This unity behind all duality is especially prominent in Aristophanes' myth in the *Symposium*. Plato's concept of love, as told to us through Diotima and Socrates, suggests that both irrational and rational moments are integrated. The location of eros is in the soul, thus between the purely ideal noetic realm and nature, between the one and the many. Eros is not pure positivity—as Agathon suggests earlier in the dialogue—but a striving for the good and the beautiful. It belongs to a sphere between the two—being itself neither beautiful nor ugly—and so unites the two poles. Love is midway between wisdom and ignorance. This mediary status also captures the essence of humanity, which can be compared with both the sacred and the abysmal, as in the opening of Hyperion's tenth letter (2:51).

Hölderlin, like Plato, associates love with art. According to Plato's Diotima, both the initial catalyst for love and its ultimate telos is beauty. Hyperion, motivated by Diotima, acts precisely according to this structure. Moreover, for the Plato of the *Symposium*, art performs a mediating function; like eros, it has an in-between status, being both material and spiritual. Hölderlin, too, embraces both senses of mediation—from the gods to humans and between the ideal and the sensuous. Love not only integrates two diverse moments (the ideal and the sensuous), it is, if we read Aristophanes' myth symbolically, fully round (much like the perfect artwork). Aristophanes' myth is integrated into the novel at the conclusion of letter fifteen when it takes on a cosmic dimension (the earth strives to reunite with the sun) and in letter twenty-eight when Hyperion describes his burgeoning love for Diotima ("Never before had my spirit strained so fervently, so implacably against the chains that fate wrought for it, against the iron, inexorable law that kept it divorced, that would not let it be *one* soul with its adorable other half [nicht Eine Seele zu sein mit seiner liebenswürdigen Hälfte]" [2:80]). *Hyperion* has often been analyzed in the light of circular structures: the hero passes through a dialectic, with the synthesis involving a return to the origin; the narrator becomes conscious of himself, and the subject reflects on itself as an object; the novel ends with Hyperion's trip to Germany (the final letter) and begins with an account of his return to Greece (the first letter), so that on the story level, the final letter leads into the first. Even the name of the novel and its titular hero, with its allusion to the sun, evokes a circular image.[12]

In letter thirty, drawing on a quotation from Heraclitus in the *Symposium* (187a), Hyperion defines beauty as the unity of opposites or, more specifically, as the unity that is divided within itself, the *hen diapheron heauto*, which is also a classic idealist definition of love (2:92). The novel captures the unity of opposites throughout, not only on the narrative level, with the unity and diversity of the experiencing and the reflective Hyperion, but also as a dominant theme, involving the interplay of dissonance and harmony, of strife and reconciliation.

Central to the Platonic concept of love is its origin in wealth or plenty and poverty or want.[13] Hyperion refers to this dialectic when he shies away from it in an early passage, preferring to see in Diotima no lack whatsoever: "Let not your beauty age in the trials of the earth. For this is my joy, sweet life! that you carry within you the carefree heaven. You should not become needy, no, no! You should not see in yourself the poverty of love" (2:75). Hyperion, echoing Plato, writes: "What makes us poor amidst all wealth is that we cannot be alone, that the love in us, as long as we live, does not perish" (2:24). In another passage he embraces this concept of insufficiency or want by considering the untenability of its opposite: "Envy not the carefree, the wooden idols who are in want of nothing . . . who do not ask about rain and sunshine because they have nothing to cultivate" (2:48). The prose draft of the metric version is even more explicit: "when poverty united with abundance, there was love. Do you ask, when that was? Plato says: On the day Aphrodite was born" (2:208). Central to this dialectic is the idea that eros is characterized by its never reaching fulfillment or closure—so too *Hyperion*, with its concluding words, "More soon."[14]

Of interest for the integration of love and beauty is the elevation of homoerotic love. Beyond the question of physical attraction, at least two external reasons existed for the Greek elevation of homoerotic love. First, the mentoring relationship between the older and more active partner or lover, the *erastēs*, and the younger partner or beloved, the *erōmenos*, played a prominent role in helping future citizens develop intellectual and social virtues.[15] Second, in ancient Greece women tended not to be recognized for their intellect or as equals; such recognition is essential for the depth and symmetry of love.[16] But there may have been an additional moment. A dominant theory of the sexual act sees as its primary purpose procreation; thus, its end is instrumental and is driven by nature. A competing theory argues that the sexual act is primarily a physical analogue of the love relationship and an end in itself. The Greeks may have elevated homoerotic love — love without procreation, love outside of the *oikos* — not only for the reasons noted above, but also because of an emerging valuation of the concept of loving one particular individual as an end in itself.

The relationship between Hyperion and Alabanda is not exhausted by the hyperbolic rhetoric characteristic of eighteenth-century friendship. There are hints of a homoerotic relationship. Surprisingly, this has for the most part gone unnoticed.[17] Consider the following passages from letter seven. The first three might be grasped within the innocuous rhetoric of the age: "My horse flew to him like an arrow" (2:33); "Great one! I cried, wait and see! you shall never surpass me in love" (2:33); and "We became ever more intimate and happier together" (2:34). The cumulative effect of these passages, however, if not the following passage by itself, seems to suggest homoerotic, not to say homosexual, tendencies: "We came together like two brooks that pour forth from the mountain . . . in order to clear the way to each other, and to burst through until, now embracing and being embraced with equal force, they are united in *one* majestic stream, beginning the journey to the spacious sea [vereint in Einen majestätischen Strom, die Wanderung in's weite Meer beginnen]." After an account of the longings of each, Hyperion continues: "Wasn't it inevitable that the two youths should embrace one another in such joyous and tempestuous haste?" (2:35). And following a description of their reading Plato together, Hyperion continues with passages such as the following: "Alabanda flew to me, embraced me, and his kisses penetrated my soul" (2:36). The double entendres are unmistakable in a passage such as the following: "And yet I had been unspeakably happy with him, had so often sunk into his embraces, only to awaken with invincibility in my breast, had so often been hardened and purified in his fire, like steel!" (2:44). Finally, Hyperion speaks of their "days of betrothal together" (2:39), and when he is betrayed, he writes, "I felt like a bride who discovers that her betrothed is secretly living with a whore" (2:43). This is the same language Hyperion uses later in the letter to describe, in analogy to the Alabanda-Hyperion friendship, the Achilles-Patroclus friendship, which was seen in the post-Homeric era, for example, in Plato's *Symposium* (179e, 180a), as having an erotic dimension (2:44).[18]

The novel's simultaneous allusion to homoeroticism and veiling of it are underscored by the opening of the fourth letter: "Do you know how Plato and his Stella loved each other? / So I loved, so was I loved. Oh, I was a fortunate boy!" (2:19). In naming Plato's lover, Hölderlin avoids the Greek *Aster* or *Stern* in favor of the Latin *Stella*, which in German is a female name. Although the possessive pronoun should identify the gender of Plato's lover, this marker might easily be overlooked in the light of Stella's status as a female signifier. By employing the Latin term, Hölderlin seems to veil the gender to most of his readers, but the close reader and the student of antiquity will catch the homoerotic allusion, which is then deepened in Hyperion's later relationship with Alabanda.

Hyperion and Alabanda have the common purpose intrinsic to all love relationships; in this case, it is heroic longing.[19] The relationship, however, is also an end unto itself, a structure, as I have suggested, that is privileged in homoeroticism. An analogy exists with Hölderlin's concept of art: the idea of aesthetic education suggests that art serves a purpose, but the great artwork is also an end unto itself, a position that Hölderlin shares with Kant. The preface emphasizes the two Horatian moments of *prodesse* and *delectare*. Art, like love, contains this double moment, and like love, it is always incomplete. Thus, the novel ends with a reference to its fragmentary nature. By integrating Alabanda, through the double moment of erotic love, into his concept of art, Hyperion brings together in his writing not only his experience with Diotima, who essentially calls him to his artistry, but with Alabanda as well. We see in the novel not only the Socratic analogy between love and art but also an analogy between love and education. This is especially prominent in the fourth letter, which opens with the allusion to Plato and his lover and devotes itself almost entirely to the education of Hyperion through Adamas. According to Socrates, both love and education are characterized by a lack, by the striving for what they not yet are.[20] Education, not unlike love, is a contradiction, born of resource and need. For Socrates, education is consciousness of incompleteness and the desire for fulfillment. Like philosophy, love strives toward the good and the beautiful by overcoming its deficiencies. Each is a negation of negativity. Love and wisdom signal a reconstitution of original unity on a higher level. Here, too, is a recognition of truth as revealedness. Education, always incomplete, seeks originary unity. As further evidence of the parallel between education and love, note a passage such as the following where Hyperion uses the Platonic symbol of enlightenment in connection with love: "Yes! man is a sun, all-seeing, all-illuminating when he loves, and when he doesn't love, he is a dark residence, where a smoking lamp burns" (2:85).[21]

Hölderlin, elevating his own artistry, views Plato on behalf of Hyperion, not first and foremost as a philosopher, but as a poet on a level with Homer.[22] Not insignificantly, the fourth letter, which addresses the theme of aesthetic education, opens with Plato and closes with Homer. Clearly, the two are invoked as the great artists of Greek antiquity, the last and the first. The last comes first because the last seeks what is contained in the first, not vice versa.

II

Even as Hölderlin expresses his veneration for Plato, he also offers a different perspective on several fundamental questions. First, whereas for Plato art is merely the imitation of an imitation, two steps removed from the ideal, Hyperion, in his embrace of the sensuous moment, suggests that those who believe they have experienced "joy," but have not seen beauty, are themselves twice removed from light: "You have yet to see even the shadow of its shadow!" (2:60). For Hyperion, Diotima, the embodiment of beauty, is not removed from the ideal, but its fulfillment: "I have seen it *once,* the one thing my soul sought, and the perfection that we remove up there beyond the stars, that we put off until the end of time, I have felt it in its living presence. There it was, the highest, in this circle of human nature and things, it was there!" (2:61–62). This ideal is still present, if hidden: "it is now only more concealed in the world" (2:62). What Hyperion calls "the highest and the best" and that which is sought by others in "knowledge" or "action," in "the past," "the future," or the distant stars is beauty: "Do you know its name? the name of that which is one and is all? / Its name is beauty" (2:62). This echoes the conclusion of the penultimate preface, with its reference to Plato's *Phaedrus* and its idea that the higher reality is accessible through beauty.

Plato's view of art is complex. Though he is, as Hölderlin suggests, a great artist, and though Plato recognizes that the artist is capable of integrating truth, he sees that the artist, working instinctively rather than rationally, can also deliver untruths and can isolate pure form at the expense of substantial content. Because of its unconscious and unpredictable nature, art does not guarantee truth; truth is its chance product. Indeed, art contains much untruth.[23] This leads Plato, on the one hand, to dismiss art, and, on the other hand, to sublate it into his philosophy. Art guided by philosophy has its legitimacy. Similarly, Hölderlin sublates momentary enthusiasm into the greater stability of reflection—thus the essence not only of *Hyperion* but of Hölderlin's later reworkings of his earlier odes—and Hölderlin recognizes the untruth within art that must be sublated into a higher, more reflective whole (consider, for example, the positions of the Sophocles motto or of "Hyperion's Song of Fate" within the novel).[24] But Hölderlin also gives beauty a higher position as the source of all later reflection. Beauty has cosmic and ontological status insofar as it represents originary unity and harmony. Hölderlin extols beauty in contrast to a philosophy that elevates analysis [Verstand] and infinite approximation [Vernunft], thus the essence of his elevation of beauty and critique of contemporary philosophy in the thirtieth letter. Hölderlin shares with Plato a valuation of beauty and reflection, but he deviates from him when he endorses the artist as the carrier of beauty and embraces the sensuous and material moment within beauty.

Whereas Plato, not Socrates, would have us move upward on a heavenly ladder to contemplation of a purely idealized form of beauty, Hölderlin embraces the sensuous moment—image, language, appearance. Whereas Plato emphasized only the one movement, from the world of reality to that of the forms, Hölderlin aligns himself with the neo-Platonic tradition, which, beginning with Plotinus, stresses a complementary movement from the ideal to reality, expressed as emanation or radiance.[25] The idea that the ideal can be made sensuous was of course reinforced through the Christian idea of the incarnation. In contrast, Plato sees the human body as a prison,[26] a position invoked by the early Hyperion when he describes "the moments when we are set free, when the divine bursts open the dungeon . . . when it seems to us as if the unshackled spirit, its suffering and servitude forgotten, were returning triumphantly back into the halls of the sun" (2:61). The elevation of the sensuous also sets Hölderlin apart from his contemporary Hegel, who saw the sensuous as a sphere that must be left behind in the pure reflection of philosophy.

A bold inversion of Plato is evident in Hölderlin's short ode "Socrates und Alcibiades," where the original relationship is reversed: in the *Symposium,* Alcibiades loves Socrates, whose mind is focused on what transcends the physical; in Hölderlin, Socrates, the intellectual, turns to the figure of Alcibiades: "He who thinks most deeply, loves what is most alive [Wer das Tiefste gedacht, liebt das Lebendigste]" (1:205).[27] Indeed, Hölderlin's gesture is a double inversion, for not only does Hölderlin invert Plato, but the Greek philosopher had himself transformed the common image of a homosexual relationship initiated by the more mature partner.[28] Socrates is beyond this relationship and must resist the advances of the younger and less experienced Alcibiades, who of course had expected the more mature Socrates to initiate the relationship.[29] In *Hyperion,* Hölderlin does not simply reaffirm the traditional Greek image of homoeroticism, with its link to an educative relationship.[30] To be sure, Hyperion opens the fourth letter with an analogy between Plato and Adamas and Hyperion and Stella. This conforms to the traditional image of an asymmetrical, educative homoerotic relationship that may have symmetry as its goal, but is itself asymmetrical. The more pronounced homoerotic relationship in the novel, however, is between Hyperion and Alabanda. Hölderlin thus lays on to the traditional Greek structure the modern concept of symmetry. Hyperion and Alabanda love each other as equals. This represents an inversion of the most prominent paradigm of ancient Greek homoeroticism.

Plato's signature image is that of the cave. *Hyperion,* not surprisingly, is replete with allusions to the metaphor of light as the realm of truth and beauty. For Hölderlin, beauty is higher than everyday reality; it touches an essence, anticipates the ideal, and makes it once again present. This valuation is behind the idea of aesthetic education, which draws indirectly on the Platonic analogy between temperance (harmony of the soul), friendship (harmony between individuals), and justice (harmony in the state), suggesting that the harmony of art nurtures these virtues, which are in the end all one. In letter forty-five Hyperion elucidates the connection between Diotima's harmony and the harmony of the state ("our world is yours, too. / Yours, too, Diotima, for it is the copy of you. O you, with your Elysian repose, could we but create, what you are!" [2:127]), and already in letter twenty-six he invokes Harmodius and Aristogiton, who are celebrated in Plato's *Symposium* for their ideal friendship, which inspired them to free Athens from tyranny (2:72; cf. 182c).

Here, too, however, is a nuance of difference. Plato was the first intellectual to suffer what we might call the problem of the owl of Minerva. Plato, like Hegel after him, believed that philosophy arrived too late and could not change the world.[31] Spirit became dominant only in an age of decay when it was, tragically, too late to alter the course of events. For Hyperion, in contrast, insight into truth leads to change: thus, his mission as an educator. The language of Hyperion as educator is analogous to the language of the divine becoming human. Diotima again alludes to the essence of his name: "You must shine down, like the ray of the sun, descend, like the all-refreshing rain, into the land of mortality, you must illuminate, like Apollo, shake and enliven, like Jupiter, otherwise you are not worthy of your heaven" (2:99). Hölderlin's rejection of Plato's theorism derives from his prolepsis of nineteenth-century this-worldliness, as it would be represented by Feuerbach, Marx, and Nietzsche, among others.

Similar in a sense to Hölderlin's revision of Plato's concept of beauty is Hölderlin's reworking of Plato's concept of nature. Plato believes that nature has value because it is a reflection of the *Idea*. The *Timaeus*, central to the revival of the objective-idealist view of nature in Hölderlin's age and well known to the poet, explicates nature as following the model and essence of the Idea: the cosmos is a sensuously perceptible divinity, or "the sensible God" (92c). In a letter to Neuffer that alludes to the *Timaeus*, Hölderlin himself speaks of "the soul of the world" (3:102). Hölderlin, however, believes that nature has value because in nature the Idea is *real*. Immanence, not transcendence, is the dominant motif for the later thinker, who nonetheless holds to an integrative and organic, not a materialist or mechanical, paradigm of nature. In his letter to Neuffer, as in the concluding sentences of *Hyperion*, the world soul and nature are captured in the language of the heart and its arteries, with their unifying separation and return.[32]

We recognize Hölderlin's reevaluation of Plato also by studying the Christological references in the novel. As Mark Ogden has argued, Hölderlin's novel is characterized by a latent Christology, but Ogden has not recognized the extent to which Diotima's death is part of a (Christian) dialectic that embodies the moments of universality, particularity, and individuality. Plato's Diotima is characterized by stillness, the stillness of the pure forms.

Her greater mysteries teach a sublimation that culminates in contemplation of the immovable and eternal; ultimately she rejects life for intellectual vision. Hölderlin's Diotima undergoes significant (Christian) transformation, which allows her to embrace life. She is, if you will, an embodiment of Socratic, not Platonic, eros.

Why does Diotima die? On the superficial level of external causality, her death serves the plot: the death of Diotima and the departure of Alabanda free Hyperion from the spheres of love and heroism so that he can enter the sphere of poetry. But an immanent causality exists as well. First is the idea that God has assumed human shape. Diotima affirms human essence (God has become visible) not just by appearing in the world, but by passing away as well.

Second, an idea Hyperion internalizes in the course of his reflections is that death is an integral part of perfection: in death (or negativity) is divinity, for without death, and correspondingly the limits and possibilities of consciousness, divinity would be empty, barren, a waste.[33] This is both a revitalization of Plato's idea of the dialectic of opposites in the *Phaedo,* to which Hölderlin's novel alludes,[34] and an inversion of Plato's concept of the divine as removed from the vicissitudes and wants of humanity.[35] Hyperion's praise of Diotima as "free from want" and "divinely content" early in the novel (2:68) corresponds to Plato's vision of the deity in the *Timaeus,* where he speaks of "the self-sufficing and most perfect god."[36] But this concept is reevaluated in the course of the novel; the narrator deems such pure and timeless bliss empty: "I want nothing better than the gods. Must not everything suffer? And the more excellent, the more deeply! Does not sacred nature suffer? O my Divinity! That you could mourn, as you are blissful, for a long time I couldn't grasp that. But the bliss that does not suffer is sleep, and without death there is no life. Should you be eternal, like a child, and slumber, as does nothingness?" (2:164).

Third, and this reflection moves Hölderlin toward his great final hymns, Diotima has particularized divinity. She must die in order to release divinity from her particular person so that it can be transformed into spirit through Hyperion's narrative. Divinity is no longer localized in one person but available to a larger community, which encompasses all recipients of beauty. This idea will be more fully developed, first in *The Death of Empedocles* and then in the hymn "Patmos," but its seeds are already apparent in *Hyperion.*

The complexity of Hölderlin's relationship to Plato is clearest in his development of Diotima. Hölderlin's stress on Diotima's immanence, on the incarnation of divinity, would have been alien to Plato; here, the influence of Christianity and that of Spinoza are dominant. Nonetheless, the telos of Diotima is the death of her body as the transformation of her essence into spirit, a concept as Platonic as it is Christian.

III

Plato influenced Hölderlin in many ways during his writing of *Hyperion,* most prominently in his theory of objective idealism, with its recognition of preexisting truth and elevation of nature, and his theory of eros. Hölderlin integrates the former into his reflections on the triadic structure of history and his critique of the subjective idealism of Fichte, which draws as well on the writings of Spinoza.[37] Through Hyperion's accounts of education and beauty and his friendship and homoerotic relationship with Alabanda, we recognize elements of the Platonic eros, including the interconnections between art, education, and love. Despite the contemporary stress on a fragmentary, anti-organic Hölderlin, the poet, successful or not, was an integrative thinker, for whom the good, the true, and the beautiful were one.[38]

But Hölderlin does not merely represent Plato for the present. First, Hölderlin does not disparage art as twice-broken mimesis, but elevates it in the form of beauty as the origin and telos of all thought. Plato, too, elevated beauty in this way, but only after removing its sensuous dimensions. Hölderlin affirms along with the principle of sublimation the sensuous moment, and he recognizes along with the movement of human consciousness toward the absolute the complementary movement of the absolute into the world. This, too, colors Hyperion's view of nature. Like Plato, Hyperion sees in it a reflection of the ideal, but Hyperion in his pantheism affirms the reflection along with the Idea and in some moments even sees the reflection and the Idea as one and the same. Also moving beyond Plato, Hölderlin gives Diotima a Christian ontology: where Plato viewed Diotima as the disembodied spokesperson for the ideal forms, in Hölderlin's novel she becomes a Christ figure, who enters the world, giving particular shape to the universal, and passes away, releasing divinity from her particularity and allowing it to be reshaped for the community as art and spirit.

If aesthetic value, as Hölderlin suggests, is defined by the interplay of intellectual content and sensuous form, then reflection on the reception of Plato in Hölderlin's novel enlightens us not only with regard to intellectual-historical reception and inversion, it also brings into focus aspects of the work's aesthetic value. And it does so in a way that tells us not only what Hölderlin wanted to show, but why he wanted to do so, for Hölderlin, like Plato, philosopher and poet in one, wrote works that ask questions that have increasingly shifted from philosophy to art itself: what is the relationship of art to philosophy, and what are the intrinsic and extrinsic merits of the artwork? It speaks for Hölderlin that he is able to answer these questions in ways that exhibit neither the hubris of philosophy, with its claim that its sphere is in all respects superior to others, nor the despair common in contemporary art, with its never-ending search not for meaning but for the value of its own creation. Hölderlin's model of objective idealism freed him of both dangers, first by affirming the absolute in the world (and not just in spirit), and second, by recognizing that aesthetic merit is as objective as it is elusive.

NOTES

1. Much of Plato's influence on Hölderlin has been documented in critical editions, occasional references, and a few devoted studies. The most important study in English is R. B. Harrison, *Hölderlin and Greek Literature* (Oxford: Clarendon, 1975), 43–83, which, besides its references to earlier literature on the topic, focuses on the biographical development of Hölderlin's encounters with the Greeks, including Plato. Harrison cites numerous works besides *Hyperion,* but sees the novel as the most central text for Hölderlin's reception of Plato. Stephan Lampenscherf in his article, "'Heiliger Plato, vergieb . . .' Hölderlins 'Hyperion' oder Die neue Platonische Mythologie," *Hölderlin-Jahrbuch* 28 (1992–93): 128–51, also focuses on *Hyperion* and brings forth some interesting insights: the mediation of Plato through the writings of Carl Philipp Conz and the fictional travelogue of Abbé Barthélemy; analogies between Plato and Adamas and Stella and Hyperion; and Hyperion's embodiment of elements of eros, including his being awakened to love through beauty. Inversions of Plato do not play a role for Lampenscherf. Neither study integrates all the themes or passages I do, nor does either study relate the various themes to one another. If further evidence were needed for a closer examination of the topic, consider that several of the allusions I present below have not been recorded in the as yet most extensive critical apparatus to the novel, which was created by Jochen Schmidt in his comprehensive edition of Hölderlin (Friedrich Hölderlin, *Sämtliche Werke und Briefe,* ed. Jochen Schmidt. [Frankfurt am Main: Deutscher Klassiker Verlag, 1992–1994]). Note for example, overlooked allusions to the *Symposium* in letters 6, 15, and 28 or the missed

reference to Plato's mimesis doctrine in letter 13. Finally, for the most recent general discussion of Hölderlin's reception of Plato, without extensive reference to *Hyperion,* see Michael Franz, "'Platons frommer Garten.' Hölderlins Platonlektüre von Tübingen bis Jena," *Hölderlin-Jahrbuch* 28 (1992–1993): 111–27.

2. Hölderlin is cited, according to the Schmidt edition, as the edition most likely to be both in libraries and on scholars' private shelves. The translations from German are my own, although I consulted and benefited from the translation of *Hyperion* by Willard Trask (Friedrich Hölderlin, *Hyperion or the Hermit in Greece,* trans. Willard R. Trask [New York: Ungar, 1984]).

3. The passage anticipates Gottfried Keller's programmatic redefinition of originality in the preface to his *Stories of Zurich* as that which "deserves to be emulated" because of its excellence and uncommonness, "even if it is not something unprecedented and ultra-inventive" (Gottfried Keller, *Züricher Novellen.* [Frankfurt am Main: Insel, 1977], 21). These two authors, not normally linked, have in common an extraordinary respect for the accomplishments of their predecessors.

4. On Hölderlin's use of truth in the Greek sense of *aletheia,* or unconcealment, see for example, "Bread and Wine," v. 81–82 and "Germania," v. 17–18.

5. 2:80; see also 2:504; compare *Phaedo* 72e and *Meno* 85e.

6. See Hölderlin's letters to Schiller of 4 September 1795 and to Niethammer of 24 February 1796.

7. Compare, for example, *Phaedrus* 242b. Note in particular Hyperion's use of the concept in letter 56, "the god in us, the loving one" (2:147), with its allusion to the *Symposium* (195e).

8. Note Hegel's gloss on "Erinnerung" or recollection as "making oneself introspective, turning inward [Sich-innerlich-machen, Insichgehen]" in his discussion of Plato (G. W. F. Hegel, *Werke in zwanzig Bänden,* ed. Eva Moldenhauer and Karl Markus Michel [Frankfurt am Main: Suhrkamp, 1970], 19:44).

9. In the first great comprehensive study of Plato in German, Tennemann underscores the contemporary recognition of Plato as an objective idealist who recognizes a higher reason in both humanity and nature. See, for example, M. Wilhelm Gottlieb Tennemann, *System der Platonischen Philosophie,* 4 vols. (Leipzig: Barth, 1792–1795), 1:245 and 2:123–27.

10. In the *Phaedrus* (238d), Plato portrays Socrates—not unlike Hölderlin's later depiction of Hyperion—as being transfigured (divinely possessed) by his experience of nature.

11. See, above all, Hösle's magisterial account of Plato as the culmination of the logical development of Greek philosophy. Vittorio Hösle, *Wahrheit und Geschichte: Studien zur Struktur der Philosophiegeschichte unter paradigmatischer Analyse der Entwicklung von Parmenides bis Platon* (Stuttgart-Bad Cannstatt: Frommann-Holzboog, 1984).

12. On the novel's complex circularity (which is not without moments of both linearity and openness), see Lawrence Ryan, *Hölderlins Hyperion. Exzentrische Bahn und Dichterberuf* (Stuttgart: J. B. Metzler, 1965), Friedbert Aspetsberger, *Welteinheit und*

epische Gestaltung. Studien zur Ichform von Hölderlins Roman "Hyperion" (Munich: Wilhelm Fink, 1971), and especially Howard Gaskill, *Hölderlin's Hyperion.* (Durham: University of Durham, 1984), 50–65.

13. *Symposium* 203b–204c.

14. For commentary on this passage, see Mark William Roche, *Dynamic Stillness: Philosophical Conceptions of Ruhe in Schiller, Hölderlin, Büchner, and Heine* (Tübingen: Max Niemeyer, 1987), 106–7.

15. Eva Cantarella, *Bisexuality in the Ancient World,* trans. Cormac Cuilleanáin. (New Haven, Conn.: Yale University Press, 1992), 16.

16. Ibid., viii–ix.

17. The only exceptions I could find in the vast Hölderlin literature were, first, Derks's reference to *Hyperion* in a broad survey of homosexuality and German literature (Paul Derks, *Die Schande der heiligen Päderastie: Homosexualität und Öffentlichkeit in der deutschen Literatur 1750–1850* [Berlin: Winkel, 1990], 393–400) and, second, Bertaux's allusion to the novel within his highly speculative thesis of a homoerotic relationship between Hölderlin and Sinclair (Pierre Bertaux, "Hölderlin-Sinclair: 'ein treues Paar'"? *Homburg vor der Höhe in der deutschen Geistesgeschichte: Studien zum Freundeskreis um Hegel und Hölderlin,* ed. Christoph Jamme und Otto Pöggeler. [Stuttgart: Klett-Cotta, 1981], 189–93).

18. Note in this context also the following passage from *Hyperions Youth:* "Finally one spoke also of the many wonders of Greek friendship, of Achilles and Patroclus, of Dion and Plato, of all the lovers and loved ones, who ascended and perished, inseparable like the fraternal stars" (2:238).

19. The danger of this common bond is that heroism will turn into violence, and so the friendship between Hyperion and Alabanda eventually falls victim to one-sidedness. Hyperion, having learned from Alabanda both the advantages and disadvantages of the heroic, tempers this sphere with what Diotima teaches him of stillness. Compare Gregor Thurmair, *Einfalt und einfaches Leben. Der Motivbereich des Idyllischen im Werk Friedrich Hölderlins* (Munich: Wilhelm Fink, 1980) and Roche.

20. For a fuller account of the Socratic analogy between love and education, see Laszlo Versényi, *Socratic Humanism* (New Haven, Conn.: Yale University Press, 1963).

21. Compare letter 41: "Magnanimous one! Things have never gone as well for me, as when I felt the light of your love on me" (2:118).

22. Plato was known in the late eighteenth century for both his poetic genius and philosophical acumen, but the weight of Hölderlin's emphasis can be measured against the contemporary view of Plato in Tiedemann's study, which opens with a reflection on the proximity of "poetic genius and philosophical mind" (Dieterich Tiedemann, *Geist der spekulativen Philosophie,* vol. 2. [Marburg: Neue Akademische Buchhandlung, 1791], 63) but then leaves behind any additional references to Plato's poetic power and attends in the remaining 135 pages only to his philosophy. Similarly, Tennemann acknowledges Plato's poetic power, but rejects the idea that Plato is "more poet than philosopher" (1:150) and likewise devotes his study to Plato as a thinker.

23. For a discussion of Plato's view of art's potential untruth, with references to the dialogues, see Hösle 569–74.

24. Compare Roche 80–107, especially 96–98. In this context, see also Hölderlin's letter to his mother of 8 July 1799 and the following passage from "Reflections": "Only that is the truest truth, in which even error becomes truth, for truth posits error in the totality of its system, in its time and place. Truth is the light that illuminates itself and the night as well. This is also the highest poesy, in which even the unpoetic becomes poetic, for it is said at the right time and in the right place within the whole of the artwork" (2:521).

25. Compare Plotinus, for example, III:8.8, IV:8.5, V:1.3, V:1.5–7, V:2.1–2, V:4.1–2, VI:9.9.

26. For example, *Phaedrus* 250c, *Phaedo* 62b, *Cratylus* 400c.

27. For an earlier illustration of Hölderlin's inversion of Plato, whereby the poet integrates movement not only upward to the forms but also downward to reality — and with this, recognition of the absolute in the world, see "Hymn to Beauty." The theme continues to surface in the late works, for example, in "The Only One."

28. "The homosexual relationships that were conventionally approved by classical Greek society were strongly asymmetrical. A younger male was desired by an older, but did not himself desire the older; mutual desire between peers was not recognized" (K. J. Dover, "Greek Homosexuality and Initiation," *The Greeks and their Legacy: Collected Papers Volume II: Prose Literature, History, Society, Transmission, Influence* [New York: Blackwell, 1988], 118.)

29. *Symposium,* 217c; see also 183e–184e.

30. On the connections between pederasty and pedagogy in Greek antiquity, see especially Bernhard Sergent, *L'Homosexualité initiatique dans l'Europe ancienne* (Paris: Payot, 1986) and William Armstrong Percy III, *Pederasty and Pedagogy in Archaic Greece* (Urbana: University of Illinois Press, 1996).

31. For an analysis of Plato's view of philosophy as being too late, see Hösle 589–605.

32. In this letter Hölderlin writes of the "divine hours, when I returned from the bosom of blissful nature or from the grove of the plane trees by the Ilissus river, where I laid down among the students of Plato, watched the flight of the magnificent one, as he traversed the dark distances of the primeval world, or followed him dizzily into the deepness of the depths, to the most remote ends of the spiritual world, where the soul of the world sends its life into the thousand pulses of nature and to which the forces that have streamed out return after their immeasurable cycle" (3.102). At the end of *Hyperion* we read: "O soul! soul! beauty of the world! you indestructible one! you enchanting one! with your eternal youth! you are; what then is death and all the lamentations of men? — Ah! Those strange creatures have spoken many empty words. Yet from delight all comes, and all ends in peace. / Like the discord of lovers are the dissonances of the world. Reconciliation is present in the midst of strife, and all things that are parted find one another again. / The arteries separate and return to the heart, and all is one eternal, glowing life" (2:174–75).

33. On Hyperion's rejection of static divinity and his paradoxical recognition of incompletion as intrinsic to perfection, or the most desirable state, see Roche 63–119.

34. See Harrison.

35. Harrison (77–83) sees in Hölderlin's references to "aging and rejuvenation" (2:35) an allusion to the idea of the reciprocal generation of opposites in the *Phaedo*. Harrison stresses thereby the Platonic-Hölderlinian theme that death belongs to life, that everything is part of one big cycle. Lampenscherf, in contrast, argues that the passage refers to the myth of the reigns of Cronus and Zeus in the *Statesman*. Lampenscherf emphasizes the depravity of the age of Zeus, when divinity is absent, and the possibility of returning to the age of Cronus, an age of divinity and peace, which, however, is the result of divine not human action. Schmidt reads the passage as an allusion to the discussion of immortality and palingenesis in the *Meno* (2:996–97). He comments thereby on the theme of death and rebirth in nature and society. Each interpretation preserves elements of plausibility. Harrison's general suggestion of the importance of Plato's theory of the alternation of opposites for Hölderlin is not refuted even if one sides with Lampenscherf or Schmidt.

36. Timaeus 68e. Translation from Plato, *The Collected Dialogues including the Letters*, ed. Edith Hamilton and Huntington Cairns (Princeton, N.J.: Princeton University Press, 1978).

37. See Uvo Hölscher, "Hölderlins Umgang mit den Griechen," *Jenseits des Idealismus. Hölderlins letzte Homburger Jahre (1804–1806)*, ed. Christoph Jamme and Otto Pöggeler (Bonn: Bouvier), 326–27 and Margarethe Wegenast, *Hölderlins Spinoza-Rezeption und ihre Bedeutung für die Konzeption des "Hyperion."* (Tübingen: Max Niemeyer, 1990). In rightly elevating the influence of Spinoza, Wegenast nonetheless underestimates the influence of others, including Plato.

38. Consider in this context Hyperion's description of the ideal of Greek antiquity: "In the Olympus of the divinely beautiful, where out of eternally young springs, the true arises with all that is good" (2:108).

6 How Fireproof You Are: Father-Daughter Tales of Loss and Survival

KARIN SCHUTJER

As I considered writing about literary paternity, I became determined to tell a certain kind of story—one about a strong collaborative relationship between a father and daughter that would not end in tragedy or defeat. The challenge was finding the material for such an account. I looked first to the "Classical" German literary canon I knew best. Here, daughters seem decidedly secondary. As Gail Hart has argued concerning family politics in German bourgeois tragedy, female figures so often seem to show up only in order to be removed, and through their removal, to reinforce male bonds. I experimented with several conventional German literary topics, but grew increasingly frustrated.

What if I looked closer to home? Perhaps some contemporary American source would provide the model of father-daughter reciprocity I sought. But while it is obvious that father and daughter roles have evolved immensely over the last generation, many old cultural patterns die hard. Surveys indicate, for example, that American men generally prefer sons.[1] Such gender preference can color father-daughter relationships from the outset. One recent study vividly illustrates this point. Even in the first few days of the infant's life in the hospital, fathers were observed to respond more to the vocalizations of sons than daughters. These patterns continued at home. While fathers tended to hold girls more closely and snugly, they actively encouraged their boys' development: "In a play situation, fathers consistently stimulated their sons more than their daughters. Fathers touched their sons and visually stimulated them by showing them a toy more often than their daughters. Fathers even looked at their boys more often than their girls."[2] From infancy on, then, many girls must fight fiercely for full recognition from their fathers.

So what sort of account could convey both the troubled past and the evolving possibility of the father-daughter relationship? I realized finally that I needed to tell more than one story, to hold out more than one possible outcome. I therefore offer two. Both are stories of reading and writing. As a daughter enters this "literary" sphere, her struggle for paternal recognition becomes particularly acute. Through reading and writing, she moves into new communities, tries out new subjectivities, discovers a universe of traditions and possibilities. Since it is the father who still often stands as the gatekeeper to this public, linguistic realm beyond the family, his reception of his daughter at this juncture is of great consequence for her sense of self. The delicate drama of paternal recognition plays itself out not only between real fathers and their young daughters but also in all sorts of surrogate relationships throughout life.

The two stories I present here form a quite unconventional pair. I consider the relationship of Goethe, the paradigmatic father of German literature, to his literary, rather than literal, daughter Bettina Brentano von Arnim. But I precede it with a quite remarkable drama of father-daughter conflict and reconciliation, broadcast as an interview on Public Radio International's *This American Life* in 1998. Both accounts involve a crisis of differentiation as the daughter, as reader, discovers her own agency in relationship to her father. Both turn on the issue of the father's recognition of that separate agency. Yet they produce almost inverse models of subjectivity. The first account ends with differentiation but sustained connection; the second ends in a severed relationship, a fractured internalization of the other. My analysis of the dynamic of intersubjective recognition at work in these relationships is inspired by the psychoanalytic theories of Jessica Benjamin. I turn first to outline Benjamin's basic model.[3]

For Jessica Benjamin, recognition — indeed a mutual recognition — is the very key to healthy child development. She explicitly draws her model of mutual recognition from Hegel's master-slave dialectic. In brief, in attempting to experience one's own reality, one seeks affirmation from another. But in order for this external affirmation to be meaningful, one must recognize the other, too, as a subject, both like and unlike oneself. She further elaborates this model of mutual recognition through D. W. Winnicott's notion of destruction. Destruction is the mental negation through which the other emerges as separate. In a drive to assert omnipotence and affirm his or her own reality, the child (or adult) may fantasize about destroying the other. Yet when the other refuses to disappear, or indeed retaliate, the self rejoices in the survival of this stubborn measure of reality outside itself. Winnicott describes the response of the self toward its object, the other: "'Hullo object!' 'I destroyed you.' 'I love you.' 'You have value for me because of your survival of my destruction of you.'"[4] Through the drama of destruction, then, one replaces one's own, ultimately empty fantasy of omnipotence with the knowledge of a real other, capable of limiting oneself as well as affirming one's own autonomy.

Benjamin thus emphasizes the pleasure one takes in discovering the separate existence of other human beings. While traditional ego psychology views the other instrumentally, as a source of need gratification that one learns to internalize, Benjamin writes of "the joy and urgency of discovering the external, independent reality of another person."[5] The thrust of healthy maturation is therefore not merely internalizing the comfort one originally receives from without, but also sustaining connection to another subject who resists total assimilation, who remains outside the self. Where mutual recognition succeeds, there can emerge a pleasurable interdependence between self and other, where both identification and differentiation are in play.

In the accounts below, we witness the fragility of this essential developmental process as it plays itself out between father and daughter. The emergence of a healthy subjectivity depends on the response of a real other human being who lovingly persists through conflict. Mutual recognition (in Benjamin's model) is so precarious, then, precisely because it is not merely an internal psychic phenomenon: it takes two real people.[6]

Act four of the Father's Day edition of *This American Life* consists of an interview by host Ira Glass of *New Yorker* writer Lawrence Weschler and his articulate eleven-year-old daughter Sara.[7] Several years earlier, father and daughter had experienced a conflict, what Glass describes as "an odd breach of trust" as a consequence of their practice of reading together. Early on, a kind of dramatic play had evolved out of their story readings. Sara would interrupt, say, in the middle of *Little House on the Prairie* and insist the pages be turned back so she could prepare an Indian character to meet Laura. She might say: "Indian, now look, in a few pages you're going to meet Laura. You gotta understand: I know she's taking your land, but it's not her fault, she's just a kid." Her father would then take on the role of the character. "Who's that talking?!" the surprised Indian might reply.

One book in particular captured Sara's imagination, *The Borrowers* by Mary Norton. Norton's book describes a clan of four-inch-high people who live under the floorboards, eluding the sight of human beings and "borrowing" small objects left around, a stamp here, a pocketwatch there, to furnish their miniature homes. One day when she was seven, an exuberant Sara announced to her father that *they* had Borrowers living in *their* house.[8] With her own eyes, she had seen a tiny girl in a pink taffeta skirt in the basement. Sara began leaving behind small practical gifts, such as toothpicks, for the Borrowers to take. Every morning she would race to check whether the supplies were gone. Her father, observing her "disappointment verging on desolation" as the offerings remained untouched day after day, finally took the fateful step of pocketing them himself. With their disappearance, Sara was, according to her father, "transported with delight" and decided to leave a note for her little tenants. When her father secretly penned his own reply to the note under the pseudonym Annabellie, Sara was, in his words, "over the moon." Thus began an extended correspondence between Sara and her father in the guise of a four-inch girl.

What comes out clearly in the interview is just how much creative energy Weschler brought to his role as Annabellie. In his notes, for example, he dropped hints that put Sara on an elaborate genealogical trail linking Annabellie's family to the Borrower family in the book. Thus Sara quickly became emotionally and intellectually absorbed in this imaginary world, into which she soon introduced her friends as well. Indeed, this adventure, Weschler realized at some point, was "the main thing going on in her life." Yet despite his concern about his daughter's level of investment in the fantasy, he could never quite bring himself to end the game. He might send Annabellie's family on a vacation, but when Sara anxiously anticipated their return, he would indeed bring them back. The program's Web site includes a cut segment from the interview in which Weschler discusses an "epic letter" from Annabellie relating a grand battle with raccoons that served to explain why Sara had not heard from her friend for several weeks. Weschler explains ". . . in a way I was going and back and forth. I would cut it off cold turkey, and then I would kind of binge on the other side." "It's important to understand," he says, "that I was as consumed by this as Sara was, at a certain point."[9]

Meanwhile, Weschler kept hoping that Sara would make the association between this correspondence and the role playing they used to do when reading. Then perhaps she could simply take pleasure in the game. But his daughter did not make this association consciously, even when she recognized a similarity between Annabellie's writing and her father's, or noticed that both used the same kind of pen. Instead, after many months passed, it was the content of some of Annabellie's letters that at last tipped Sara off. She explains in the interview that at that time in her life she would occasionally exaggerate to her father about things she had seen or heard. When details of near encounters with the Borrowers that she recognized as her own embellishments showed up in Annabellie's letters, she realized something was wrong. Finally one day (she was now eight), Sara sought out her father, who was working in the basement and confronted him with her doubts. Her father describes the painful encounter:

LW: . . . And she began, her lips were trembling, her lower lip was trembling, and she looked at me very firmly, as she is quite capable of doing, and she said, "Daddy, I am going to ask you a question now and you have to tell the truth because it's a sin for daddies to lie to their daughters." And my heart just sank. And she said, "Daddy are you the one who's been writing Annabellie's notes?" And I looked at her and she looked at me and there was like silence for five or six seconds and then I said, "Um, you know it's kinda complicated, uh, can we talk. . . ." And she said, "Daddy, it's not complicated, it's simple. Are you the one?" And I said, "Well, can we talk about it later?" And she said, "No, just tell me, are you the one or not?" And I took a big breath and I said, "Yes, it is me." And she broke into . . ."

SARA: [inaudible . . .] crying. I was so sad.

LW: Oh God, she was sobbing, she started sobbing. It was easily the most wrenching thing that had happened in my parenthood up until that point. I mean I had totally blown it, I just felt total disaster and I was crying and she was crying and you know we were both kind of clutching each other and holding each other. And it was . . . we were really in a trap there, we were down the hole at that point, we were in big trouble. And Sara . . . and suddenly this kind of calm came over Sara's face. It was kind of like the sun rising in the morning, and her forehead stopped being furrowed. It became smooth. And she just looked at me and she said "Daddy, don't you realize you ruined *everything*, because there *are* Borrowers and you were taking the letters before they were able to get them."

The moment when Sara recovered, Weschler refers repeatedly to her as "saving us." He never fully explains the meaning of this "saving," offering at this juncture only that Sara had come up with an explanation she could tell her friends so that they might all laugh together about her crazy father. Yet the great import he attaches to the "saving" becomes clear when Glass asks him how he might handle the same situation differently if given the opportunity.

LW: [laughing] I mean, I'd like to say that had I to live it over again I wouldn't do it this way but I'm not so sure, because it was a . . . it started so naturally, and in the end, by the way, what I'd have to say is, probably the most poignant, closest, amazing moment I've had as a sing—
. . . you know, the moment I'll remember of a particular phase in my life is that: the holding onto each other in the basement, both of us crying, but . . . but Sara not running away and Sara saving us. And that kind of cemented our relationship in a really kind of wonderful way. So, uh, I mean I don't . . .

SARA: It might not end that way for everybody.

Sara indeed remains firm in her conviction that her father made a mistake. When asked what she would have done had she been the parent, she shows understanding for her father's dilemma, but concludes that she would not pick up the notes no matter how disappointed her child might be, because it is wrong to lead someone on. In a diary entry included on the Web page, Weschler quotes Sara on the day of the confrontation as saying: ". . . Daddy why couldn't you have just let it run its course, Daddy. Sometimes you have to just let things run their course."

Yet even as she insists upon her father's misstep, Sara emphasizes the bond between them. She cherishes the letters which she now knows are not from Annabellie, but from her father:

LW: When we pulled out the box last night of letters did it bring you pleasure to look at those letters?

SARA: Well actually I look at them a lot.

IRA GLASS: You look at them a lot? And what do you think when you look at them?

SARA: Well, I just think it was sort of, now looking back, it was sort of nice of him to do. That's because, when it was happening, I mean after I figured out it was him, I had asked him, well can we still sort of write to each other? We never really wrote to each other after that, but I just sort of thought after a while it was a nice thing and that even though maybe there was no Borrower writing to me there was, um . . . having my dad make up this whole family with me is just as special, or maybe almost as . . . as special as having actually been writing to a Borrower.

Sara ultimately agrees that the confrontation in the basement became a moment of special closeness, but adds, "I'm very close to my dad all the time."

This account of an "odd breach of trust" between Sara and her father seems to me very close to the delicate process of identification and differentiation that Benjamin describes. From the beginning, Sara's father shapes a rich reality for his daughter. If fathers typically serve as gatekeepers of the symbolic order, of the unyielding world outside the nursery, Sara's father also plays the role attributed to many mothers — of creating an environment that responds to the child's own imagination.[10] The linguistic, literary order Sara enters with her father is a realm of play. When Sara speaks to the books, the books speak back to her.

Yet this early relationship between father and child may, not surprisingly, still be based on something closer to omnipotence than mutual recognition. By animating the world around her according to her fantasies, Sara's father empowers his daughter's imagination, yet ultimately remains the author and source of his daughter's delight. Within this magic world, indeed both daughter and father can feel all-powerful: Sara as her imagination is gratified (the book talks back), her father as he creates a hermetic world in which his child's imagination is stimulated and sheltered. At this stage, Sara might not even distinguish clearly or consistently between her own imagination, her father's inventions, and a reality independent of them both. This could explain why she is so slow to realize that her father, and *not* Annabellie, wrote the letters, despite clues such as the handwriting and the pen.

There may be no sharp contradiction in her mind between her father's participation and the real existence of Annabellie. Reality may simply have the mark of her father on it.

A discrepancy emerges for Sara only as she discovers herself as a separate source of invention; she discovers that *her* embellishments of her experiences, which she had related to her father, began appearing in Annabellie's letters. In this way, she begins to discern her own creative contribution to a world that had appeared to emerge magically around her father. That Sara's undifferentiated fantasy relationship with her father comes to an end is thus a testimony to her developing sense of her own agency and self.

Yet both father and daughter have difficulty relinquishing this stage. In Sara's mind, her father's misstep is that he did not let things "run their course" because he could not face her pain and disappointment. He could not let go of a relationship in which he could make appearances conform to his child's imagination. He was, as he admits, "as consumed by this as Sara was."

Now the meaning of the "saving" becomes clear: Sara saved her father by not letting his overextended fantasy of control destroy her. When it became clear that her father not only did not really believe in the Borrowers, but had in fact also fabricated the family himself, Sara took ownership of her own belief, insisting that there *were* Borrowers—her father had just intercepted their mail. In this moment, as he watched her recover "like the sun rising in the morning," Weschler recognized his daughter's own strength and independence. The Web site includes a quotation from his diary entry on that day: "Sara walks in and confronts me in this astonishingly mature voice—the voice she will have on her best days thirty years from now—centered, level, serious, solemn." That is, Weschler perceived in Sara not his little girl, nor the sexualized young woman many fathers anticipate in their daughters, but a thirty-eight-year old woman, an adult at the height of her powers.

Clearly the survival was reciprocal: Sara's father was also not destroyed in her eyes when she exposed him as having deceived her. Rather he took her distress seriously, admitted the truth, hugged her, and even cried along with her. What she lost was an omnipotent father who could make reality match her imagination; what she gained was a fallible parent who had gone through great effort to help her create an imaginary world. The outcome of this drama of destruction and survival for Sara is that she continues to feel "close to my Dad all the time."

And yet Sara, with remarkable wisdom, notes that "It might not end that way for everybody." With this warning, Sara echoes Jessica Benjamin, whose book largely concerns how this relationship goes awry. According to Benjamin, one of the worst consequences of traditional family and social arrangements is the breakdown of mutual recognition between father and daughter. Within a social structure where the mother is still identified with a domestic sphere in which she is at once all-controlling and yet dependent on her child for her sense of self worth, the father quickly comes to represent escape and "a pathway of individuation" to both male and female children.[11] Through identification with the father, the child imagines his or her own agency, autonomy, and competence in the outside world. Yet as the study mentioned earlier suggests, at even the earliest stages of child development, fathers often fail to recognize their daughters as like themselves and indeed repel their identification. The result for many girls is not the sense of healthy interdependence that mutual recognition brings, but instead a polarized relationship between self and other in which the girl masochistically submits herself to an all-powerful father figure in order to share vicariously in his subjectivity. Power and agency remain concentrated in one end of the dyadic relationship rather than shared.

To this intersubjective and intrapsychic breakdown, Benjamin applies the psychoanalytic term "splitting," which "indicates a polarization, in which opposites — especially good and bad — can no longer be integrated; in which one side is devalued, the other idealized, and each is projected onto different objects."[12] Rather than see both herself and her father as simultaneously strong and weak, simultaneously independent and dependent, the girl sees herself as only weak, and only strong through her father or lover.

Such splits fracture Bettina von Arnim's relationship with Goethe, whom she views in her writings as her literary father and her source of spiritual development. In reconstructing this relationship, we have a more complicated set of documents with which to work: among them, an original correspondence between the two (1807–1811); Goethe's novel *Wilhelm Meister's Apprenticeship* (1795–96), which provides von Arnim with a model for their relationship; and von Arnim's fictionalized version of the correspondence,

Goethe's Correspondence with a Child (1835). In the original correspondence, Goethe's participation appears unsteady and at times half-hearted. In her literary version of the relationship, von Arnim creates a much more involved, responsive Goethe, whose painful abandonment of their friendship ultimately helps her—as if it were part of some benevolent strategy—to develop her own authorial subjectivity. (To distinguish the protagonist and author of letters and journal entries in this literary account from the historical woman Bettina von Arnim, I will refer to the character as "Bettine," as the name appears in the Goethe book.)

While Goethe's *letters* offer little examination of his relationship to her, Bettine takes Goethe's novel *Wilhelm Meister's Apprenticeship* as a source: his fictional characters Wilhelm and Mignon, Wilhelm's adopted daughter, offer Bettine a paradigm for her father-daughter relationship with Goethe. As Konstanze Bäumer has explored at length, allusions to Mignon, both explicit and implicit, abound in Bettine's Goethe book.[13] Clearly a chief attraction of this role for her is its promise of the kind of spiritual transfiguration [Verklärung] that Mignon undergoes in the novel. Throughout the book, Bettine expresses her longing to have, through Goethe, her flesh made spirit. I will look, then, at transfiguration as a trope for the father-daughter transaction.

We turn first to Goethe's novel. What is the nature and meaning here of Mignon's transfiguration? Certainly it involves a process of differentiation from Wilhelm. When the odd, orphaned little acrobat first attracts Wilhelm's attention, she clearly is linked in some way to the marionettes that were his favorite toys and theatrical inspiration as a child.[14] Thus Mignon, while mysterious and uncategorizable, seems in the beginning a being not wholly independent of Wilhelm's fantasy. Under his care, she seems to blossom and reveal herself. Meanwhile, in her strange movements and disjointed poetry, she provides him with an aesthetic stimulus that leads him to become more deeply engaged in the theater. Initially then, Wilhelm and his adoptive daughter seem to exist in an imaginative symbiosis, where she is at once both his muse and his creation.

Yet as Mignon emerges into adolescence, Wilhelm clearly begins to fear the force of her separate desire. In one episode, the truth of which is only revealed much later in the novel, Mignon plans to sneak into Wilhelm's bed, "without any further thought than a fond, peaceful nestling."[15] Yet she is devastated when she witnesses another female character, Philine, slipping into his room ahead of her, and Mignon suddenly bites Wilhelm in the arm as he approaches. The next morning he "is frightened" by her changed, more serious demeanor (HA 7:328; CW 9:199). Soon, despite her pleas to be allowed to remain with him, he sends her off to be educated by a female friend. Rather than face the strange changes in her, the fury and desire, Wilhelm in effect withdraws from Mignon and hands her off to others. With this withdrawal, Wilhelm fails the test of his daughter's aggression and desire. For Mignon, the path of a healthy differentiation has been blocked.

Now a strange, alternative psychic dynamic ensues. Separated from Wilhelm and given over to the care of Natalie, Mignon grows at once more sickly, more feminine and more spiritual. After playing the role of the angel at Christmastime, she refuses to wear anything but her white angel costume. She sings on her zither that she wishes to wear the white dress until she leaves the earth and no clothing "surrounds the transfigured body [den verklärten Leib]" (HA 7:516). At last, Mignon's weakened heart fails and she expires in Wilhelm's presence. Her body is artfully preserved and interred in the Hall of the Past, a funerary building that is itself a grand work of art. As she is lowered into the marble, a choir of youths sings: "The treasure now is well preserved, the beauteous image of the past. Unconsumed, in marble it rests; in your hearts it lives and works" (HA 7:578; CW 9:354). Mignon is memorialized and rendered into art.

Mignon's "transfiguration" is therefore as much a matter of her internalization within Wilhelm as her differentiation from him. Kathryn Edmunds has argued that mourning is the psychic process driving all of Wilhelm's strong attachments within the novel, including his relationship to Mignon, as he seeks to recover from the loss of his initial love object Mariane. Mourning is in effect internalization: "the process of restoring or recreating the lost object in the inner psychic world of the bereaved."[16] But Edmunds, drawing on the work of Melanie Klein, distinguishes from a true, integrative mourning, a false or manic mourning involving splitting and idealization of the lost other. Rather than integrate in one's memory the good and bad aspects of both oneself and the other, one creates an internal image of the other that is wholly good and idealized—and thus unstable. This false, splintered mourning is, according to Edmunds, ultimately the kind of mourning toward which Wilhelm tends.

If then we are to read Mignon's death in the novel as a fantasy of destruction—and Wilhelm indeed refers to her as "the child . . . that I killed"

(HA 7:545; CW 9:334)—the outcome of this process is quite unlike what Benjamin and Winnicott describe. In the course of her decline and demise, Mignon clearly emerges as separate from Wilhelm, but she does not survive this differentiation as a complex, externally real other for him. Instead the actual connection to her is severed, and she becomes an idealized internal object—an object of and for art. We can perhaps identify here then a drive opposite to the one that finds joy in discovering the real existence of the other, one that prefers loss and mourning because of the opportunity to shape and own the image of the other internally.

Clearly Goethe intends Wilhelm as an ironic figure, subject to our criticisms, yet Goethe may be simultaneously recognizing a tendency in himself to prefer separation and memory to sustained connection.[17] In the following passage from *Poetry and Truth*, Goethe acknowledges in himself an early preference for creation in solitude: "As I reflected on my natural gift and found that it was truly mine alone and that it could be neither furthered nor hindered by outside forces, I inclined toward making it the basis for my whole intellectual existence. . . . I felt very strongly that one could only produce something significant by isolating oneself. My works, which had found so much favor, were children of solitude."[18] In order to produce his literary "children of solitude," Goethe appears to have often broken connection with the real people—so often women—who were his inspiration.

How then does Bettine fare in her role as Mignon in the Goethe book? Does she seek a "transfiguration" at the price of such a break? Von Arnim's own identification with Mignon clearly stopped short of death or removal. Her brother Clemens quotes her response to her first reading of the novel: "only into death I could not follow [Mignon]."[19] In the Goethe book, Bettine describes a dream in which she dances in front of Goethe, as Mignon dances before Wilhelm. Dressed as an angel, she rises aloft where she sees that Goethe's eyes still follow her. But unlike Mignon whose apotheosis is her death, Bettine floats back down to earth into Goethe's arms.[20]

Bettine's longing to be transfigured into art, to have her flesh made spirit, amounts more simply to a desire to have Goethe lend weight and import to her words and actions, to recognize her as a poetic, spiritual being. At one point in the book, Goethe uses Bettine's letters as the source for poems, an exchange he calls "translation." Bettine is overjoyed that Goethe treats her offering "as if it were of ever so much worth." His hand renders her words immortal: "But I see with joy how you take me up into yourself; how you hold these simple flowers, which would fade in the evening, in the fire of immortality, and you give them back to me" (WB 2:117).[21]

But Bettine represents Goethe as not only the recipient and transformer of her naïve reflections but also as the origin of everything poetic in her. In a letter to Goethe's mother, she describes Goethe as her creator: ". . . I feel, that only through my love to *him* I am born in the spirit, that through *him* the world unlocks itself to me, where the sun shines to me, and the day divides from night" (WB 2:36–37; GCC 28). Her sense of connection to Goethe extends so far that after another dream about Goethe, she concludes that her happy fantasy must be an indication of *his* feelings: "From this dream I awoke today, full of joy, that you are kindly disposed to me. I believe that you take part in such dreams that in such moments you love; — whom else could I thank for this happy existence, if you did not give it to me?" (WB 2:118; GCC 98).

In the course of the Goethe book, Bettine's fantasy of perfect psychic symbiosis with Goethe turns out to be just that — her own fantasy driven by desires that originate in herself. The reader easily imagines Goethe's surprise at the force of his young correspondent's longings for, and indeed demands of, him. In describing a fantasy encounter, for example, she directs Goethe's imagination: "and [you] must kiss me; for that is what *my* imagination grants to yours" (WB 2:246; GCC 201). Indeed, he once seems to reproach her for the voraciousness of her imagination: "actually one cannot give you anything because you either create/procure [schaffen] everything for yourself or you take it" (WB 2:335).

The forcefulness of Bettine's imagination pushes the relationship into crisis. Like Wilhelm in the novel, Goethe eventually balks at his "daughter's" assertion of an independent desire, but does little to act as a real limit to her fantasies about him. Instead, he gradually withdraws and grows cold. Bettine begins to long for Goethe's deceased mother, who (unlike Goethe) never hesitated to counteract her feelings, both calming her and teaching her toughness toward herself (WB 2:239). Goethe at last falls into complete silence (the fight between Goethe's wife and von Arnim that is the cause of the actual break is left out of the book). Bettine feels self-disgust and remorse: "I feel now that it was not easy to endure me in my passionate behavior, indeed I cannot endure myself and with terror I turn from all the pain that this thought stirs up in me" (WB 2:411; GCC 337). She is left to believe that her overextended emotions have made the man she adored disappear. Rather than offer sustained resistance to Bettine's omnipotent fantasies, rather than chart out their real differences, Goethe lets the relationship collapse.

In Bettine's first letter to Goethe after the break, dated some six years later in 1817, she describes in great detail a scene of fiery destruction and expresses an exultant hope that *he* might survive, might show himself fireproof, just as she intends to survive for him. This seems very much the fantasy of destruction that Benjamin and Winnicott describe.

> The very day on which I had written this the theater took fire; I went to the place where thousands with me enjoyed this astonishing scene . . .
>
> The fire descended into the inner rooms, and from without frisked here and there on the edge of the building; the timber of the roof in an instant tumbled down, and it was splendid. Now I must also tell you, that meanwhile there was an exulting within me, I also was glowing; the earthly body consumed itself, and also the false splendor was consumed with it . . .
>
> In this other world, into which now I was raised by mind, I thought of you, whom so long already I had forsaken; your songs, which for a long time I had not sung, moved on my lips; I alone, perhaps, among those thousands who stood there shuddering and lamenting, felt in delightful solitary enthusiasm, *how fireproof you are;* a problem was resolved, better and clearer could the pain, which often in former times stirred within me, not be elucidated. Yes, it was good! — with this house a moldy building was burnt down, — so free and bright it grew in my soul, and my fatherland's air blew on me . . .
>
> Will you again reach me your hand over all this rubble; will you know me to be warm and loving to you to the end; then say one single word to me, but soon, for I am thirsty. (WB 2:412–13; GCC 338–39; italics mine)

Goethe rejects Bettine's plea, however, and remains silent. In Bettine's subsequent letter dated four years later, we see signs of the splitting that according to Benjamin can ensue when the other does not "survive." Bettine now addresses herself only to a memory of a loving Goethe: "It is with you I have to speak, not with him who has pushed me from him, who has not cared about tears and, miserly, has neither curse nor blessing to spend — before *him* thoughts recoil. With you, genius! protector and inflamer!" (WB 2:414; GCC 339).[22]

Now that she has cast off the "bad" Goethe who has abandoned her, Bettine moves to internalize and own through art her "good" Goethe; she starts designing a heroic marble statue of Goethe for the city of Frankfurt. The inscription she chooses "This flesh has become spirit" (WB 2:570) suggests an ironic twist to her dream of transfiguration. While Bettine places a figure of her alter-ego Mignon on the monument, the object of this apotheosis into spirit may not at last be herself or Mignon but Goethe. Just as Wilhelm trades the real Mignon for an idealized memory, Bettine, faced with Goethe's rejection, now replaces Goethe in the flesh with a heroic image. The "good" Goethe, whom she now artistically controls, can serve as an internal source of power and authority for her—albeit a necessarily unstable one.

In her "Diary," the last part of the Goethe book, Bettine suggests that her creation of the monument has brought about a reconciliation with Goethe. (In fact Goethe did accept occasional visits from von Arnim in the last years of his life, but never replied to any of her letters, nor certainly, developed into a reliable friend.) In the book, Bettine has Goethe, upon seeing the design for the first time, call it with approval "a transfigured product [verklärtes Erzeugnis] of my [Bettine's] love" (WB 2:568). I would argue that the *transfiguration* of love into art in this story stands rather for the *loss* of love, understood as a sustained mutual connection. The real other becomes supplanted by the work of art, Goethe's "child of solitude." While one can admire Bettine's resourcefulness and resilience, the tone of triumph at the end of her book seems premature if she is left, like her literary father, to create in isolation.[23]

One need not question the actual artistic accomplishments of Goethe or Bettina von Arnim to wish for a different model of literary paternity from the one that emerges through the Goethe book. A hopeful alternative to the breakdown between Goethe and Bettine is the relationship of Sara and her father. While Bettine mirrors Goethe's example of a splintered mourning for an other that did not survive, Sara and her father discover with elation their mutual survival. The story of Sara and Lawrence Weschler suggests the joy of a sustained relationship and holds out the promise of a less lonely, though not necessarily conflict-free, literary realm for both father and daughter.

NOTES

1. *Tragedy in Paradise: Family and Gender Politics in German Bourgeois Tragedy 1750–1850* (Columbia, S.C.: Camden House, 1996). "Both mothers and fathers prefer boys, not just in the United States and Britain, but in India, Brazil, and a variety of other countries as well. This preference is particularly strong in men; between three and four times as many men prefer boys as prefer girls." Ross D. Parke, *Fatherhood* (Cambridge, Mass.: Harvard University Press, 1996), 93. There is, however, some anecdotal evidence to suggest that this overall parental preference could be changing. In a cover story for the *New York Times Sunday Magazine,* Lisa Belkin reports that fertility clinics engaging in sex selection are seeing a much higher rate of request for daughters than for sons. Ronald J. Ericsson, who has licensed his sex selection method to twenty-eight American clinics, attributes this trend to "feminism" and the influence of mothers in fertility decisions: "Women are the driving force, and women want daughters," he says. Thus Belkin's evidence may not reflect a change in male preference. "Getting the Girl" *New York Times* (25 July 1999), Sunday late ed., sec. 2: 26ff.

2. Parke reports here on his own research (94).

3. Jessica Benjamin, *The Bonds of Love: Psychoanalysis, Feminism, and the Problem of Domination* (New York: Pantheon, 1988). I say "inspired," for my analysis here will not follow Benjamin's theory of developmental stages in all its detail.

4. Quoted in Benjamin, 38.

5. Benjamin, 44.

6. In this respect, Benjamin's model of mutual recognition may differ from Hegel's, since in Hegel the material status of the other is never entirely clear.

7. Episode 106, dated 19 June 1998, was made available as a Real Audio recording (copyright Saturday, 20 June 1998 by KCRW) through the program's archive on the Web site, www.thislife.org. All of my quotations from the interview are my transcriptions from this Internet recording. It is worth stressing that the radio segment is itself a work of art—an edited reconstruction rather than unmediated presentation of a conversation.

8. I gather from the context that this was her age when the correspondence began.

9. These and other supplementary notes to the interview appear at www.thislife. org/pages/iraborrow.html.

10. See Benjamin's description of mutuality in the mother's play with her young infant, 26–27.

11. Benjamin, 95. Benjamin is, however, careful not to present identification with the father as by itself a viable substitute for recognition of the mother: "For women, then, failures in the struggle for recognition cannot be fully repaired by using a male identification to revolt against the mother" (121). Indeed: "The search for the subject of desire—the ideal father—is part of a broader search for the constellation that provides not only the missing father but the reconciliation with the mother who acknowledges this desire . . ." (121). The father's rejection can in the meantime only hinder this search.

12. Benjamin, 65fn.

13. Konstanze Bäumer, *Bettine, Psyche, Mignon: Bettina von Arnim und Goethe* (Stuttgart: Akademischer Verlag, 1986), 118–44.

14. Helmut Ammerlahn, "Wilhelm Meisters Mignon—ein offenbares Rätsel: Name, Gestalt, Symbol, Wesen und Werden," *Deutsche Vierteljahrschrift* 42 (1968): 102–4.

15. Johann Wolfgang von Goethe, *Goethes Werke* [Hamburger Ausgabe], 14 vols. 1950–1968 ed. Erich Trunz (Munich: C. H. Beck, 1989), 7:523. Hereafter references to this edition will appear in the text parenthetically as "HA." Translation: Johann Wolfgang von Goethe, *Collected Works,* ed. Victor Lange, Eric Blackall, and Cyrus Hamlin. 12 vols. (New York: Suhrkamp, 1983–1989), 9:321. Hereafter references will appear parenthetically as "CW." Where not otherwise noted, translations are my own.

16. Kathryn Edmunds, "'Ich bin gebildet genug . . . um zu lieben und zu trauern': Wilhelm Meister's Apprenticeship in Mourning," *Germanic Review* 71:2 (1996): 84.

17. While one does not want to identify the historical figure Goethe too closely with his novel character Wilhelm, with the protagonist of his own autobiography, or certainly with the character Goethe in von Arnim's book, these various sources can help mutually interpret each other.

18. Quoted in Hart, 71.

19. Clemens Brentano, *Briefe,* 2 vols. (Nuremberg: Hans Carl, 1951), 1:296.

20. Bettine von Arnim, *Werke und Briefe,* 3 vols., ed. Walter Schmitz and Sibylle von Steinsdorff (Frankfurt am Main: Deutscher Klassiker Verlag, 1986), 2:98. Hereafter references to this edition will appear parenthetically in the text as "WB." On this passage, see also Bäumer, 142.

21. Translation based on: Bettina von Arnim, *Goethe's Correspondence with a Child* (Boston, Mass.: Ticknor and Fields, 1859), 97. Hereafter "GCC." I have made frequent alterations in translations for stylistic reasons. If not otherwise noted, translations are my own.

22. The term "inflamer" of course repeats the fire image we just saw in Bettine's description of the burning theater. In fact she uses the image of fire throughout the book to describe the force of love emanating from either Goethe or herself. Clearly, it is her fantasy that she and Goethe might ignite each other without consuming or annihilating.

23. One, however, can see this book, Bettine's first, as a preliminary stage in Bettine's development of an artistic intersubjectivity. It is here, according to Marjanne E. Goozé, she first establishes "the keynote of her style—the dialogic form." "Ja, ja, ich bet' ihn an": Nineteenth-century Women Writers and Goethe," *The Age of Goethe Today: Critical Reexamination and Literary Reflection,* ed. Gertrud Bauer Pickar and Sabine Cramer (Munich: Wilhelm Fink, 1990), 46.

PART III.
Literary Archaeologies (II):
Codes of Friendship and Paternity
in German Romanticism

7 Mediation and Domination: Paternity, Violence, and Art in Brentano's *Godwi*

JOHN LYON

For Stanley, with gratitude

It might seem misguided to discuss in a *Festschrift* devoted to paternity a novel that foregrounds maternity as obviously as does Clemens Brentano's *Godwi* (1801/1802), but a close analysis of the novel invites one to read it as concerned with the far-reaching influence of the father and the qualities he represents. The novel's subtitle, *The Stone Image of the Mother,*[1] underscores the prominent role of the mother in Brentano's first novel. The marble statue of the protagonist's deceased mother, a focal point of the estate and of the novel, embodies Godwi's yearned-for ideal of totality, for he states: "Everything was confining to me, except when I sat by that white image in the garden, then it seemed to me as if everything that I lacked was embraced in it" (174). The mother mediates her son's desire for totality— she promises liberation from all that confines him as well as compensation for lack and inadequacy. In Romantic writings, mothers typically function as an iconographical sign for the experience of inwardness and intimacy.[2] According to one critic, the desire for the mother corresponds to the desire for cosmic order, totality, and harmony, emblematic of the thought of this period.[3] Kittler, drawing on examples from Novalis, Brentano, Friedrich Schlegel, Tieck, Arnim, and Hoffmann, argues that in Romanticism a matrilinear order replaces the patrilinear order of the Middle Ages.[4]

Yet much Romantic scholarship, reading the mother as the mediator of the protagonist's ideal of totality, overlooks one crucial theoretical issue at the heart of Romanticism: the problem of mediation. In *Godwi*, Brentano posits the defining characteristic of Romantic art as biased or tainted mediation. He states: "Everything that stands as a mediator between our eye and a remote object to be seen, and brings the remote object closer, but simultaneously gives to it something of its own, is Romantic" and ". . . the Romantic is thus a telescope [Perspectiv], or much more the color of the glass and the distinguishing [Bestimmung] of the object through the form of the glass" (314). Romanticism instills a heightened awareness of artistic mediation, for in mediating our perceptions, it also colors and shapes them with its own particular interests.[5] This heightened awareness of mediation draws our attention not only to the mediated object, but also to that which mediates it. In this move from the mediated to the mediator, we recognize that although the mother is the focus of mediation, the father controls mediation. This is evident in the passage cited earlier, in which Godwi speaks of his mother's statue. Notice that Godwi relates not to his mother immediately, but instead to a statue of her commissioned by his father. The son experiences totality through his mother, but experiences his mother (who died in his infancy) only through the medium of art. Closer attention to this novel purportedly about mothers reveals paternity as a force more influential and sinister than maternity. Aesthetic mediation, if not all mediation, ultimately reveals itself as the domain and possession of the father. Thus, although Romantic art is maternally focused, it is at a deeper level subject to the strict command of the father.

Godwi inherits both his name and his estate from his father; on the estate sits a chapel-like structure that his father built to house the numerous artworks he commissioned. Godwi associates this structure itself and the artistic creations commissioned by his father with violence. Most of these artworks represent women who were objects of violence, and include women who were kidnapped, seduced, deceived, and deserted. The statue of his mother represents her shortly before her death (she drowned herself due to his father's deceit), and for Godwi the pain in the statue is evident; he describes it as follows: "[She] cannot cry, for the eyes / And the tears are stone. / Cannot sigh, cannot breathe, / and nearly resounds with pain. / Alas, the entire image wants to explode from painful forces" (171). Just as Godwi projects a notion of totality onto this statue, so, too, does he project onto it physical and emotional pain.

Godwi learns from his father that art and violence are inseparable. This is evident not only in the subject matter of the artworks, but also in his father's relation to the artist. One of Godwi's earliest childhood memories recalls:

"In my childhood this church lay before me as an unbearable secret, and I always shuddered when my father went in with one of the strange [fremden] artists, and came out again alone, as if he had murdered him" (389). Young Godwi's concept of paternity becomes entangled with both aesthetics and violence—his father is both commissioner of the artwork and murderer of the artist. This paternal violence encourages similar acts on the part of the son, but as I will demonstrate, it also inhibits the son from becoming a father himself. In other words, for Brentano, paternity perpetuates violence and art rather than genetic material and a family name.

Brentano's association of paternity, violence, and aesthetics is most striking when Godwi explains his father's motivation for commissioning these works of art: "My father's eccentricity [Bisarrerie] was the beautiful eccentricity to make beautiful the evil that can never be made good; his idea was that good is in time and beauty is in space and the possibility of compensation for a depraved youth would be to give it form in one's more mature years. He said, every action becomes a memorial that condemns me, and that I can never overturn, but I can compel this stone to become a beautiful image of the act that it marks" (390). Godwi's father makes an apparently Kantian distinction between ethics and aesthetics: moral concerns do not encumber pure beauty, for beauty is exclusively formal. Yet the closer one examines this, the less it looks like Kant, for where Kant would abstract from this form a purposiveness and a supposed general agreement among perceivers, and from that deduce both a *sensus communis* in humans as well as a higher principle, even a higher being,[6] Godwi's father relies on beauty to excuse himself from all higher principles and all connections to community. He wishes to sublimate his moral guilt into aesthetic production and thus avoid the pain or responsibility of restitution or reparation ("that can never be made good"). Art, for the father, is a purely private phenomenon—Godwi notes that his father built the chapel that houses his art "in a condition of the greatest secrecy and concealment . . . and only for himself alone" (389)[7]—void of all connections to others, to higher principles, higher beings, and to morals.

Yet in pressing beauty into his service, the father must force ("compel") the artistic medium to be beautiful (artistic production becomes fundamentally violent). Art, for Godwi's father, is not a moral escape from violence, but is rather an amoral representation and aestheticizing of it. In fact, for Godwi's father, beauty is only a secondary consideration in art, as the following passage indicates: "My father . . . did not want the beautiful in art, he wanted only its power. It should serve him by giving in all ways [auf alle Arten] the same impression that he wanted. It should present on all sides of him something that he would have liked to have forgotten and was never able to forget, in spite of his unattainable wish" (321). The father desires not beauty, but rather a singular, powerful impression from art. In other words, for the father, art mediates the past in its multiple manifestations ("in all ways"), yet this mediation should produce an identical impression ("the same impression that he wanted [denselben Eindruck, den er wollte]") in all observers. And, as Godwi's father tells the reader, violence is the only means by which he can remember his past: "I have done all sorts of things, had many friends, spent much money, loved many maidens, lost many eternities, and that is all past, nothing remains but the scar, and that pains me whenever the weather changes" (458). All that remains of his wild, younger years is a metaphorical scar, a symbol of wounding and physical violence, such that recollection is intimately linked with pain. In other words, reminding himself of the past is not only a reminder of past violence, but also an act of violence itself, causing pain in himself as observer. Thus the impression he hopes to generate with art is neither moral nor educational, for it is precisely such forces that the father avoids by turning to art. I argue that art is a constant reminder not only of the father's guilt but also of his power, of the violence he perpetrates, and of the pain he can endure. Art involves the observer only insofar as the observer is willing to acquiesce to the violent power of the father. The reception of art is not democratic, where individuals are allowed the freedom to develop their own impressions; rather it is totalitarian, where the father controls all responses and forces them into a uniform reaction.[8]

In a novel combining textual representation of several nontextual art forms (sculpture, painting, architecture, music, drama, etc.[9]), the reader must rely wholly on Maria's (the male narrator's) description of these artworks. Yet Maria reads and depicts these works as if under the direction of Godwi's father, focusing on his own impressions rather than on the work of art itself. For example, when Godwi shows Maria a painting of Annonciata Wellner (a young woman who was kidnapped and seduced and later went insane), Maria pours forth a stream of impressions that culminate in "Pain, Pain! burning desire, who will break for you the seal of the heart, and to whom are you sent?" (392). Godwi interrupts him and covers the picture, stating "It was enough, dear Maria, the painter fulfilled his obligation, and you were well on the way to observing the impression of the image on you and not the image itself" (392). Godwi identifies his father's desired mode of artistic reception—one in which the violence and pain associated with art overwhelm the observer—and thus implicitly accuses Maria of falling subject to his father's desire to represent violence and pain. To borrow Brentano's metaphor cited earlier, the impression that the lens creates is so powerful that one no longer sees the object it mediates.

Therefore I agree with critics such as Bernd Reifenberg who identify the father's main artistic impulse as follows: ". . . he differentiates things from each other, destroys their coherence and preserves them in their independence [Eigenständigkeit]."[10] The father reifies, even petrifies, instances of violence and fragmentation. Yet I disagree with Reifenberg who posits this impulse as a contrasting pole to the "all-unity of Nature, that is the presumed authenticity of motherly-womanly discourse and sensation,"[11] for this suggests a balanced polarity between maternal totality and paternal fragmentation. Instead, I view this relationship as unbalanced: the father's fragmentation does not counterbalance the mother's authentic totality, for the father mediates the mother's totality through a representation of violence against her. The impression of totality and authenticity that the mother's statue presents is an intentional construct by the father and was created to elicit a response that ultimately reminds the viewer of the father's disruptive and destructive power. The Romantic ideal of the mother is grounded in paternal violence and control.

One might read the father's activities through a Freudian lens and assert that his actions represent efforts to control the mother and to interrupt the child's desire for her. Yet such a reading assumes a stable, bourgeois family structure. The novel justifies no such assumption. On the contrary, for Brentano, paternity dismantles such a model. At one point in the novel, Godwi Sr.[12] states: "I would find it quite agreeable to have a wife and a child, but to desire the wife of one's father or of one's own, bores me, and stealing is forbidden" (459). Brentano undermines here the basic premise of the Freudian Oedipal triangle,[13] for not only does the father not desire the mother, but also the father (as son) does not desire his own mother. As the narrator gradually unravels the intricate web of relationships in the course of the novel, the reader soon realizes that there are few examples of a traditional family structure.[14]

This is clearest toward the end of the novel, where Godwi relates the reunion and reconciliation of his father with Joseph (also known as Werdo Senne), from whom he had taken Marie (Godwi's mother). Werdo and Godwi Sr. join Molly Hodefield, with whom Godwi Sr. had fathered Godwi's half brother Karl, to travel to Italy, and with them travel Werdo's daughter Otilie (whose mother had died many years earlier), her husband Franzesko Fiormonti, and Franzesko's son from an earlier relationship, Eusebio. Godwi describes this "procession to Italy" as follows: "At the front [an der Spitze] flew Eusebio, behind him Franzesko and Otilie, and behind these my father with old Joseph, but between them Molly von Hodefield, in a pyramid-like manner, just as storks fly . . ." (483). This "family" creates a pyramid, a form with apparent stability, and the comparison with storks, the mythical bringers of children, suggests this as a familial model. Yet this form does not rely on the stability of bourgeois familial structures, for nowhere in this "pyramid" do we find a father-mother-child relationship — one member is always absent, either the child (for example with Godwi Sr. and Molly) or the mother (with Werdo and Otilie Senne or Franzesko Fiormonti and Eusebio). The father, however, is always present, whether as Godwi Sr., Werdo, or Franzesko. Male figures — here Godwi Sr., Werdo, and Eusebio — form the "points" of this pyramid; they ground it and give it stability. For Brentano, the father and his son literally form the family; the mother is either absent (as are the mothers of Otilie, Franzesko, and Eusebio) or simply fills in the spaces along the lines defined by the male figures (as do Molly and Otilie). Brentano thus posits a family structure in which mothers are significant only insofar as they adapt to a form that the father determines.

This drive away from the personal and individual and toward the formal typifies the father's role in *Godwi*. For example, Godwi observes that his father directs his desire against all human relations and toward abstractions: "Hence he was very unhappy, because he yearned for love and friendship, but not for people" (464). For the father, people become simply means to an end; they mediate his desired ideals. "Friendship" and "love" are thus ideals void of correlates in the world of experience. In fact, we learn that forms and representation, as violent as they may be, threaten the father less than actual interpersonal relations. In the first volume of the novel, we read of Godwi's extensive travels and we learn from his half brother Karl Römer why his father not only allows but also funds these travels. Although he misses his son deeply and feels concerned that Godwi might not love him, Godwi's father also tells Römer: ". . . a secret lies over [Godwi's] childhood, and it would kill me, if I had seen him around me for much longer" (33). We learn later that this secret is Godwi Sr.'s deceit of Godwi's mother, which led to her death, the moment that his father preserved in the stone statue. In other words, although the statue reminds Godwi Sr. repeatedly of his guilt, he does not feel as threatened by it as he does by his son's presence. The father can represent images of violence because, although they have aesthetic impact and force, they do not threaten him and do not demand active and dynamic involvement of him. Paternity for Brentano entails fleeing personal relationships and moral responsibility.

Yet how can this practice of paternity perpetuate itself? In *Godwi*, it perpetuates itself on the formal and abstract level, but it cannot perpetuate itself biologically. Godwi, like his father, has a rather wild youth and exploits numerous women without much concern for their well-being, and he, too, makes an artistic representation of one of them. However, unlike his father, he himself has no children. The form of paternity represented in this novel inhibits offspring from becoming parents; instead, this type of paternity maintains the infantile status of its offspring.[15]

Throughout the novel, we find instances where Godwi either loves an ideal instead of a person or shuns personal interaction and responsibility altogether. For example, when Godwi first meets the Countess of G (disguised as a man), he tells her: "Well, I would very much like to love and be loved, without necessity and fear, without apprehensions and toil, for I fear nothing more than affection. You cannot imagine a more sworn enemy of the sentimental world . . ." (489). The resonance with the description of his father cited earlier ("he yearned for love and friendship, but not for people") is unmistakable. Godwi desires love, but shies away from the realities of interpersonal relationships and of intimacy and tenderness. The result is that Godwi is incapable of establishing an enduring relationship with any woman; even Violette, whom he deserts but later rescues, dies shortly after their reunion. Godwi is incapable of establishing even basic familial relationships, for when Godwi sees the "family" reunion of his father, Molly, Werdo, Franzesko, Otilie, and Eusebio, he remarks: "People were never so wonderfully united as these were, but I felt that I did not belong to them" (482). Godwi recognizes a unique, even fairy-tale-like connection ("wonderfully connected") in this family, yet his only impression is that he does not belong to them. Apparantly Godwi has learned from his father to seek ideals of love and relationship in representation rather than in reality. Since Godwi claims to find complete fulfillment only in a statue of his mother, one must assume that the world of empirical reality estranges and distances him. Like his father, Godwi finds a relationship to a stone statue far superior to one with an actual human being.

In fact, Godwi portrays his own disposition in terms of two statues: the statue of his mother and the statue of Violette that he commissioned. He states: "The path seems long from the monument of a mother to that of a prostitute; it isn't, but nonetheless it constitutes my disposition [Gemüth]" (463). Rather than discuss the relation of the mother figure to the prostitute,[16] I conclude by focusing on Godwi's relationship to their stone images. It will become evident that Godwi, like his father, constructs representational art as an expression of violence and as a means of distancing himself from interpersonal relationships.[17]

Godwi first meets the subject of the statue, Violette, when he begins a torrid affair with her mother, the Countess of G. Violette falls in love with Godwi, but he only pities her at the time without returning her affection. Godwi eventually ends his affair with the Countess, fearing that the experience of free love was becoming too confining.[18] He knows that in leaving the Countess, he also leaves Violette to a lifestyle that will destroy her.[19] Indeed, the Countess opens up "the free tent of her pleasure" (556–57) during the Napoleonic wars and enlists Violette's assistance; by the time Godwi finds Violette again, she has wasted away and is near death. Godwi and Violette join together briefly ("No priest united us, but nor did life; it was love alone . . ." [558]), but she dies after a very short time. Godwi memorializes her with a statue of her apotheosis in which a god-like figure with a lyre in one hand and a flying swan pressed against his breast pulls her up to him by the hair.

The reader learns of the statue from Maria, who quickly slips from a description of the statue itself into — as earlier — the impression the statue has on him. He writes: "In the middle of the image, where the hand entwines itself in her locks, his lust and his love, which had surged up with the maiden, die, and his pride and his grandeur, that floats down from the head of the soaring genius, dissolves, and opens up like a wound, that gives unity to the whole, and in which they both beautifully interpenetrate [in der sich beide schön durchdringen] and it is beautiful how the swan nestles against this wound, and soothes the pain of the spectacle" (362). Maria sees a wound in this statue. As Marlies Janz rightly points out, this wound is not actually on the statue, but is projected there by Maria.[20] Maria thus again perceives in the paternally determined mode: he allows himself to be overwhelmed by the impression of the statue and envisions a wound. Precisely this wound, this mark of physical violence, gives the statue unity. Maria goes so far as to associate this wound with beauty in describing how the swan alleviates the pain of the wound. Maria thus sees in Godwi's statue a constellation of beauty and violence, similar to that which Godwi saw in the statue his father constructed.

Maria's attempts to mediate this wound to the reader continue as he describes with an extended metaphor "where one would find the image in life" (362). He speaks in the second person, stating that if "you" walk through beautiful gardens on a spring evening, find a sleeping woman there, overcome your inhibitions, and begin to disrobe her, and then attempt to remove the hand that covers her breast:

> . . . if the beautiful, pleasing breast then speaks to you with the bloody lips of an open wound . . . if all your pleasure sinks into this wound, as into her grave, and seeking for help you pull down the robe from the entire beautiful body and look upward from the painful wound, towards the head, to draw in prayer [Gebet zu holen], and down over the enchantments of the beautiful body, with the dream of earthly rapture, to soothe your pain, . . . and if you must return to this wound eternally until all of this runs together in it, and pleasure and pain and grandeur blossom from the wound — then you have the complete impression of the image, then you stand before Violette's monument, and if you turn, and step into the narrow, dark house to those people who you are used to calling "yours," then you feel what you feel when you turn away from the image. (363)

In this disturbing aestheticizing and eroticizing of violence — of male voyeurism and potential rape — the father's impact on both Godwi and Maria becomes most acutely apparent. This passage abounds with typical romantic tropes, the conflation of the erotic and the religious ("to draw in prayer, and down over the enchantments of the beautiful body"),[21] the invocation of the grave in connection with desire ("if all your pleasure sinks into this wound, as into her grave"),[22] the conflation of "pleasure," "pain," and "grandeur,"[23] and the organic language ("blossom") associated with this wound. In the sense that the passage enacts Maria's mediation of his impression of the statue to the reader, it is quintessentially Romantic, at least according to Brentano's definition cited earlier.

The problem with this quintessential Romanticism becomes evident in the last phrases, in which Maria demonstrates that the impression of Violette's statue is so overwhelming that, like the statue of Godwi's mother, it promises a totality unattainable in empirical reality. For Maria, all personal and familial relations are merely impoverished alternatives to the totality of art. The house where one lives is "narrow" and "dark," and one's family becomes people associated with you only because you call them yours, not because of a common emotional or biological bond. The impression made by Godwi's statue of Violette is similar to the one Godwi's father's artworks produce: the conflation of beauty, eros, and violence evokes a desire for totality in art and encourages a turning away from human relationships.

As Maria's impression of Violette's statue resonates in so many ways with Godwi's impression of his mother's statue, it seems clear that both Maria and Godwi perceive life similarly and also that Godwi has inherited from his father the tendency to conflate beauty and violence in representational art while simultaneously having inherited the yearning to flee genuine relationships for the sake of aesthetic ideals. Godwi's desire for totality in art corresponds to his inability to sustain interpersonal relationships in the empirical world. Paternity, as presented in *Godwi,* uses the mediation of art both to enforce paternal power and to evade moral responsibility. The extremes to which paternal mediation exerts itself inhibit its own perpetuation and thus ensure its own demise. The result is a Romanticism that turns against itself, subverting the totality associated with the mother through the fragmentation and violence associated with the father's mediation.

NOTES

1. *Das steinerne Bild der Mutter.* All translations are mine, unless indicated otherwise. Parenthetical page references cite Clemens Brentano, *Godwi oder das steinerne Bild der Mutter,* ed. Werner Bellmann, vol. 16 of *Clemens Brentano. Sämtliche Werke und Briefe,* ed. Behrens, Frühwald, and Lüders (Stuttgart: Verlag W. Kohlhammer, 1978).

2. Hannalore Schlaffer, "Mutterbilder, Marmorbilder: Die Mythisierung der Liebe in der Romantik," *Germanisch-Romanische Monatsschrift* Neue Folge 36.3 (1986): 305.

3. Heide Christina Eilert, "Clemens Brentano: *Godwi* (1800/1802)," in *Romane und Erzählungen der deutschen Romantic,* ed. Paul Michael Lützeler (Stuttgart: Reclam, 1981), 131.

4. "The All-Mother, who eternally gives birth, intensifies sensations, and produces incest-phantasms, takes the place of the symbolic father, who divided into genders and generations." Friedrich Kittler, "Der Dichter, Die Mutter, das Kind. Zur romantischen Erfindung der Sexualität," in *Romantik in Deutschland. Ein interdisziplinäres Symposion,* ed. Richard Brinkmann. (Stuttgart: J. B. Metzler, 1978), 105.

5. Note that Brentano's definition of Romanticism is much broader than, for example, Friedrich Schlegel's, who in the *Dialogue on Poetry* defines romantic art as that, "which presents a sentimental theme in a fantastic form." Friedrich Schlegel, *Dialogue on Poetry and Literary Aphorisms,* trans. Ernst Behler and Roman Struc (University Park: The Pennsylvania State University Press, 1968), 98. Schlegel is likewise aware of the significance of mediation, but unlike Brentano, prescribes both form and content.

6. See Kant's *Critique of Judgment,* for example, §40 "On Taste as a Kind of *sensus communis,*" and § 90 "On What Kind of Assent There Is in a Teleological Proof of the Existence of God." Immanuel Kant, *Critique of Judgment,* trans. Werner S. Pluhar (Indianapolis, Ind.: Hackett, 1987).

7. Note, however, that Godwi's father places the statue of his deceased wife in plain view. For art that claims to be private and personal, it has an almost exhibitionist quality about it. For example, we learn early in the second volume of the novel that the people of the nearby town are quite familiar with the sculpture on the estate — that it is anything but private (280).

8. Compare Janz: "The artworks should judge him, but only insofar as his attitude of submission confirms to him that he is master of the situation." Marlies Janz, *Marmorbilder: Weiblichkeit und Tod bei Clemens Brentano und Hugo von Hofmannsthal* (Königstein/Ts.: Athenäum, 1986), 23.

9. See Eugene Reed's "The Union of the Arts in Brentano's Godwi," *The Germanic Review* 29.2 (1954): 102–18 for a discussion of textual and nontextual art, as well as Ingrid Mittenzwei's "Kunst als Thema des frühen Brentano," in *Clemens Brentano. Beiträge des Kolloquiums im Freien Deutschen Hochstift,* ed. Detlev Lüders (Tübingen: Max Niemeyer, 1978), 192–215, and Ursula Regener's "Arabesker *Godwi:* Immanente Kunsttheorie und Gestaltreflexion in Brentanos Roman," *MLN* 103.3 (1988): 588–607 for the theoretical significance of art in the novel.

10. Bernd Reifenberg, *Die "schöne Ordnung" in Clemens Brentanos Godwi und Ponce de Leon* (Göttingen: Vandenhoeck & Ruprecht, 1990), 132. Janz makes a similar observation: "The work of the fathers is represented as the gravedigging of one's own life. The lords of creation produce nothing but the reproduction of their own finitude: the pile of rubble next to their own grave" (29).

11. Reifenberg, 132.

12. Since Godwi and his father share the same name, I refer to the novel's protagonist as Godwi and to his father as Godwi Sr.

13. In *An Outline of Psycho-Analysis,* Freud describes the Oedipus complex as the child's sexual desire for the mother, which the father prohibits. The child's "early awakened masculinity seeks to take his father's place with her; his father has hitherto in any case been an envied model to the boy." Sigmund Freud, *An Outline of Psycho-analysis,* trans. James Strachey. (New York: Norton, 1969), 46. Implicit in this model is a family where both father and mother are present, and where both father and son desire the mother. Neither the former nor the latter conditions obtain in *Godwi,* for Godwi Sr. does not desire his wife, and Godwi Jr. does not have a mother to desire.

14. Rolf Spinnler's insightful analysis compares *Godwi* to the "Bildungsroman" genre, insofar as this genre represents the process of socialization. Spinnler notes that: "Brentano's novel contains implicitly the basic model of a pathologically developing process of socialization, which is told in always new variations, and he traces this pathology back to deficiencies in the early childhood socialization within the family, to damaged families that can no longer correctly perceive their pedagogical function." Rolf Spinnler, *Clemens Brentano oder Die Schwierigkeit, naiv zu sein* (Frankfurt am Main: Verlag Anton Hain, 1990), 58.

15. Spinnler notes that in this failure to relinquish childhood, *Godwi* cannot fulfill the project of the "Bildungsroman" and that this motivates Brentano after this novel to turn to the genre of the "Märchen" [fairy tale], which privileges childhood rather than adult life (Spinnler, 23–24).

16. For further analysis of these issues, see Hannalore Schlaffer's "Mutterbilder, Marmorbilder," Marlies Janz's *Marmorbilder,* and Rolf Nägele's *Die Muttersymbolik bei Clemens Brentano* (Winterthur: P. G. Keller, 1959).

17. Janz notes: "The petrified women of *Godwi,* the monument of the mother and of Violette, symbolize the silencing of the female body through patriarchal violence, but simultaneously the seductive power of female images, whose promise of happiness appears to lie beyond all possibility of realization and thus appears to be linked to death" (43).

18. "Free love is beneficent, but a constrained unruliness that bridles me with licentiousness [*mit Zügellosigkeit zügelt*] is most pernicious of all and everything good is ruined by it" (552).

19. "The Countess may have been however she wanted to be, but together with her child, she was bad" (542).

20. ". . . the statue of Violette does not have a wound, rather the wound 'appears' to Maria" (Janz, 44).

21. See Gabriele Brandstetter, *Erotik und Religiosität* (Munich: Wilhelm Fink, 1986). One example in Romantic literature is in Bonaventura's *Die Nachtwachen von Bonaventura,* trans. Gerald Gillespie (Austin: University of Texas Press, 1971): "People chased me a few times from churches because I laughed there, and just as often from houses of pleasure because I wanted to pray in them" (111–12).

22. See, for example, the experience at the grave in the third of Novalis's "Hymns

to the Night:" "There the earthly splendor fled and my sadness with it—misery [*Weh-mut*] flowed into a new, unplumbed world." Novalis, *Hymns to the Night,* trans. Dick Higgins (New Paltz, N.Y.: McPherson, 1984), 17.

23. Recall, for example, a similar conflation in the fourth of Novalis's "Hymns to the Night:" "I float over there, / And each pain / Is somehow a sting / Of delight" (21).

8 Old Father Jupiter: On Kleist's Drama *Amphitryon*

GERHARD KURZ

Translated by Eric Jarosinski

I

Kleist's drama *Amphitryon* was published in Dresden in 1807 by his friend Adam Müller and first performed in 1899. The complete title reads *Heinrich von Kleist's Amphitryon, ein Lustspiel nach Molière.* Written during Kleist's French internment, it was the first work to appear under his name. (*Die Familie Schroffenstein* was published in 1803 without mention of the author.) It is thought that Kleist worked on the *Amphitryon* material beginning in 1803, with the main impetus for the project coming from his acquaintance Johann Daniel Falk, whose adaptation *Amphitryon, Lustspiel in fünf Aufzügen* had appeared in 1804.[1]

Contemporary critics highly praised the piece. Friedrich von Gentz, for example, read it with "complete admiration." He had only one complaint: the use of the expletive "Saupelz."[2] Already the first reviewers understood the drama from the perspective of the epoch-defining discussion about the divisions between classical antiquity and modernity, classicism and Romanticism, and French and German culture.[3] Paving the way for this reception was Adam Müller's preface to the play, in which he characterized Kleist's work as overcoming the "frivolity of Molière's Amphitryon" through German "meaning" and as forming a bridge between antiquity and the modernity: "This *Amphitryon* strikes me as neither a classical nor a modern adaptation; likewise, the author does not demand any crudely mechanical connection between the two. Instead, he attempts to realize a certain poetic actuality. When this is some day achieved, classical antiquity and modernity—as subordinate to this poetic present as they may be—will exist in harmony, much as Goethe had projected" (1929).[4] Müller's preface surely must have irritated Goethe, who in his 1805 treatise *Winckelmann* had newly separated antiquity from Christian modernity. After reading *Amphitryon,* he wrote in his diary: "I read and was astounded, as if by the strangest sign of the times." He objected to the "Christian construance of the fable," the "overshadowing" of Alcmene by Maria.[5]

Indeed, Kleist truly had translated ancient mythology into the terms of Christianity. Through numerous allusions to, and quotations from, scripture, the mythological procreation of a divine child by a god and an earthly mother is equated with God's coming to earth as man.[6] There are, for instance, allusions to Maria's Immaculate Conception and to the Annunciation when Jupiter proclaims: "To you there shall be born / a son, and Hercules his name" (3.2.83). From Christian religion come such terms as revelation, devil, sinner, saint, hermitage, idol, creation, God, and father. As Jupiter once remarks: "Isn't all that we see happening around us here a miracle?" (2.5.50). Amphitryon curses in a manner both ancient and Christian: "Lightning, hell, the devil!" (3.11.78).

Goethe also emphasized the radical ways in which Kleist's drama, belonging to its time, treats the problem of perception and self-certainty, and thereby also of religious certainty: "The significance of classical antiquity's treatment of Amphitryon involved the confusion of the senses, the conflict between the senses and conviction. . . . Molière emphasizes the distinction between spouse and lover, which is actually an object of the intellect, the wit, and gentle reading of the world. . . . The contemporary Kleist takes as his starting point the emotional confusion of the main characters."[7] Already in the first reviews an interpretive stance was taking shape that still holds today; the drama was read as if it were called *Alcmene.* As Uvo Hölscher recently put it: "The traditional comedy of Amphitryon has instead become a drama of Alcmene."[8] There is of course good reason for this reading. Consider, for instance, the play's conclusion: Kleist has Alcmene speak the last word, "Ach!" which had already fascinated the play's first audiences. In the adaptations by Plautus and Molière, however, Alcmene does not even appear in the last act. Still, there are also good reasons to take the title character seriously.[9] Only at the outset of Kleist's play is Amphitryon the coarse husband who demands his marital rights. This is how Molière, too, has him appear. At the end of Kleist's play, however, he is no longer the hollow cad that Jupiter makes him out to be in front of Alcmene. He, too, is a tragic figure, and he alone perceives Alcmene's unhappiness—"Lord of all / my life! Unhappy woman!"—and remains convinced of her virtue, even after she ridicules his body (3.2.77). "Every word she utters / is the truth—not gold ten times refined / is truer" (3.2.81). Amphitryon's last word is not paid to glory or to Jupiter, but rather to Alcmene!

I will now approach this drama as if it were experimentally entitled *Jupiter or Gott!* My thesis is that Kleist's "contemporary" drama does not present God's power, but instead his powerlessness under the conditions of modernity—it is the drama of a twilight of the gods or of God. In this regard, I view Jupiter as a tragic figure. To the extent that he is tragic, he no longer is a god. The drama's concluding "Ach!" is spoken not only by Alcmene, but also by Amphitryon, Jupiter, and, not to be forgotten, by Sosia as well. In brief, my analysis asks what Mercury's jovial Christian-classical formulation "old father Jupiter [alter Vater Jupiter]" actually signifies within the context of the drama (3.2.60). In Greek mythology, Zeus is considered the father of the Gods, and in Christianity, God is considered the father. This is not the only image of God or Zeus, but one that is significant and, in the Old Testament, dominant.[10]

II

Most frequently, commentary on the play has focused on Alcmene's "emotional confusion," a line of inquiry still pursued today. Broadly speaking, there are two main interpretive positions regarding the relations between mortals and the gods in the play.[11] On the one side, Müller-Seidel, Gadamer, Ryan, and others view the gods as an absolute, transcendent power, in line with classical and Christian conceptions of God.[12] The gods have descended to earth to punish humans for their wrongdoing. As evidence of this, it is noted that Alcmene ascribes Jupiter's arrival to her having worshipped her husband as "her idol" (2.5.47). A variation on this argument (for example, Jauß and Michelsen) views Jupiter as a zealous, awful god, as an "evil demon," who drives man into delusion much like Descartes' evil genius.[13] Following conceptions of God prevalent in German idealism, still another variation (Stierle) depicts Jupiter as a tragic god, who longs to shed his omnipotence and come into contact with humans on their own terms.[14]

By contrast, the second position reads the drama as staging a human rebellion against the authority of the gods. Wittkowski makes this argument the most strongly.[15] Among other things, he bases his argument on the scene in which Jupiter informs Alcmene that a god appeared to her in their night of passion, and she will love him so that she will have to weep if he returns to Olympia without allowing her to follow. To that Alcmene replies:

No, never think that, my Amphitryon.
If I could turn back time one single day,
I'd bolt my closet shut against all gods
and heroes, yes, I would—

(2.5.54)

Jupiter's response, "Damn the deluded hope that tempted me down here!" entails a repudiation of God. In choosing between the love of God and that of man, Alcmene decides in favor of human love. It is often overlooked, however, that Alcmene's decision in favor of Amphitryon is a decision for her "image" of Amphitryon. As his words indicate, she would lock herself in her "cell" not only to shut out Jupiter, but also the real Amphitryon. After all, Amphitryon is himself a hero. He is a descendent of Perseus, the son of Zeus and of a king's daughter. Even those who adhere to this interpretive position assume that although the god loses his game, his divine power remains untouched. As far as I can determine, only Arthur Henkel, Jochen Schmidt, and, most recently, Hans-Jürgen Schrader have expressed doubt about these positions and pointed to the fact that the drama demythologizes the myth.[16] With my analysis, I wish to add to their reading.[17] Along with Goethe, I read the play as a "contemporary" or "current [gegenwärtiges]" drama, as a drama about the "aging" of religion.

III

Kleist's drama *Following Molière* stands in a long tradition of a literary recycling of the Amphitryon myth.[18] Homer was the first to mention it, and Pindar likewise assumes an acquaintance with the material. In Benjamin Hederich's *Gründliche Mythologisches Lexikon* of 1770, the myth is recorded in a version of the Hesiod School (the so-called Shield of Herakles) as follows:

> Amphitryon, the grandson of Perseus, had helped the King of Mikinai against the robberly teleboans. In exchange, he received Alcmene, the princess, as his wife. Alcmene follows Amphitryon to Thebes, when he has to leave Mikinai due to the murder of her father. Yet Amphitryon will not have the marriage take place until he has avenged the murder of Alcmene's brothers. He therefore leads his army into battle against Pterelas, King of the teleboans.
>
> In the meantime, however, Alcmene has caught the eye of Zeus. During the night he assumes the shape of Amphitryon and sleeps with her. In the same night Amphitryon returns, seeking the consumation of the engagement. Impregnated both by the god and the hero, she gives birth to twin sons. To Zeus, she bears Herakles; to Amphitryon, Iphicles.

The dramatic versions range from Sophocles (not preserved) to Plautus, from Molière and Kleist to Giraudoux and Peter Hacks. In Homer's version, a son is born, part human and part god. According to the Hesiod School there are two sons, one human and one a god. Following Uvo Hölscher, this division illustrates an act of rationalization of a numinous occurence.[19] In both Molière and Kleist, the coupling of a god with a human again results in one son. In Kleist's drama, Amphitryon demands, as a sort of restitution from Jupiter, *one* child:

> What you did for Tyndareus, do for
> Amphitryon too: bestow a son on him
> as great as are the two Tyndarides.
> (3.11.83)

This comparison, to be sure, brings about the possibility of a doubling of the child itself, for the Tyndarides are the twins Castor and Pollux.

The plot structure and character constellation is typical of mythology — the *dieu à femmes* Jupiter, the confusion of the wife, the horned husband — these generate a classic love triangle situation and readily lend themselves to mythological comedy. Incidentally, the courting Jupiter also plays a role in Kleist's *Das Käthchen von Heilbronn*. There, in a secular variant of the Jupiter-Alcmene model, the emperor fathers a child with a bourgeois woman. In the love scene, Jupiter "rises in the east with his glittering light" (V.2410–11).

In the history of the reception of the Amphitryon myth, which, according to Jauß, is one of the "richest among all basic mythological motifs,"[20] some versions focus on the doubling and the confusion, some on the relationship between Jupiter and Alcmene, and some on the miraculous birth. All of these versions, however, share a common trajectory traced by the question of the possibility and assertion of personal identity.

In the Amphitryon myth, personal identity is doubly split: in the connection of the human to the godly and in the figure of redoubling. "They've doubled you," says Sosia to Amphitryon (2.2.34). Or, as an army general comments: "No eye / can tell apart two creatures so exactly / like each other" (3.5.66). In this regard, the myth contains not only a comic but also a tragic potential. Kleist's drama exploits both possibilities. Like *Der zerbrochne Krug, Amphitryon* is simultaneously a comedy and a tragedy.[21] With its motif of the redoubling or confusion of identities, this myth strongly resonated with Kleist. It appears, for instance, in Agnes and Ottokar's clothes-swapping scene in *Die Familie Schroffenstein,* in *Der Findling* (Nicolo and Colino), in *Michael Kohlhaas* (Elisabeth and the gypsy), and in *Das Käthchen von Heilbronn* (Käthchen and Kunigunde). Considering this long line of Romantic *Doppelgänger,* one can speak of an epoch-defining interest in such redoublings and *Doppelgänger.*[22]

In his examination of the social function of Greek tragedy, René Girard interprets the character of the *Doppelgänger* as the expression of a social crisis in which differences between people are lost, and with them, their personal identity.[23] The self has the terrifying experience that it is also something else, or that it is split and encounters itself as something foreign.

The theater provides one way of confronting this threat through its cathartic play with masks and roles. With a kind of aesthetically sublimated terror, wearing masks and playing roles, even to the point of identification—"Sean Connery is James Bond"—allow for the possibility of the redoubled self, the divided self, the loss of the self, and the transformation of the self. This, too, is why Kleist's play is called *A Comedy after Molière.* The double meaning of the preposition "after [nach]" has long been noted. The preposition indicates, first of all, a comedy in imitation of Molière's. In this way the drama itself ironically becomes that which it is about, namely a redoubling. It is also "after" Molière in the same way that Jupiter takes after

Amphitryon and Mercury after Sosia, just as the dramatic action of Sosia and Charis doubles that of Amphitryon and Alcmene. Hence also the conspicuous description in Molière's cast of characters, "Jupiter, sous la forme d'Amphitryon," and, in Kleist's, "Jupiter, in the shape of Amphitryon."

That roles are being played is indicated throughout the play by the use of terms such as "play [Stück]" — also "Heldenstück," "Freundschaftsstück," and "Höllenstück" — as well as "scene" and "role."

The confusion that has seized humans in Molière's play also torments Kleist's Jupiter, who exclaims "Damn the deluded hope that tempted me down here!" (2.11.85). To be sure, Jupiter, unlike Alcmene, does not lose confidence in his self or his perceptions, but he does lose his power. While Molière still grants Jupiter the role of a feudal lord, Kleist has the god abdicate completely. It is in a state of powerlessness that he must learn of Alcmene's choice for the love of man above that of the god. He, the lover, is her "God." This resignation is in accordance with Christian theological teaching of God's becoming man. His desire to be loved as God in the figure of Amphitryon, that is, to appear as God in Amphitryon, is deflected by Alcmene's love for the mortal Amphitryon, no matter how much she depicts him as a god. Sosia comments on this utterly tragicomic game with the question: "Since the world began, did you ever hear of such a thing?" (1.2.13). Similarly, the "miracle" of God's becoming man is parodied in the game between Sosia and Charis.

Szondi and subsequently Jauß have written that in comparison to Molière, Kleist downplays the social circumstances of the comedy in favor of the problems of identity and perception.[24] While Molière's dialogue between Mercury and Sosia reads:

"Qui va la? — Moi. — Qui, moi?" (309)

Kleist renders it as:

"Halt! Who goes there? — Me. — Me? What me, man?" (1.2.7)

Mercury's question is impossible to answer, because as opposed to a person or a thing, about which one can ask what kind of person or what kind of thing, the I is an indexical pronoun that cannot be specified. Simply answering the question would lead to a division of the I. It is just this question that leads to Alcmene. To her love for Amphitryon, one may pose the question: "Which Amphitryon?"

Between Mercury and Sosia, and later between Jupiter and Alcmene, as well as between Alcmene and Amphitryon, a battle for the "fortress" of consciousness takes place, in which not only the other's name but also the entire I is stolen and robbed (3.10.75). As a result, Sosia and Amphitryon are "de-Sosialated" and "de-Amphitryonitized" by their doubles (3.2.77).

All certainty of the I is systematically destroyed. While at the outset, Sosia retreats to the certainty of "I am, because I am" — a biblical allusion to the "I am that I am" of God's name,[25] which Jupiter with objective irony turns into "Yes, it was me. But it's no matter who it was" (2.5.46) — he loses not only this self-affirmation, but also that of his own name and body.[26] Yet the bodily pain from Mercury's blows restores his sense of self, together with his name.

The loss of Alcmene's identity is even more radical. She calls into question the singularity of her own name, the image of her body in the mirror, and her sense of self. She acquires her sense of herself in and through the other, her lover. She would rather be mistaken in herself than in him. But it is exactly in her amorous cognition that she will be mistaken, and has, in fact, already erred. The Amphitryon of their night of passion was actually not Amphitryon. Struck by the strange initial on the diadem, a "J" for Jupiter, instead of an "A" for Amphitryon or Alcmene, she realizes that she has deluded herself:

Oh Charis! As soon mistake myself,
I would! As soon imagine I'm a Persian
or a Parthian, in spite of that profoundest feeling,
sucked in with my mother's milk, which tells
me I am I, Alcmene. Look, this hand,
Does it belong to me? This bosom? My
reflection in the mirror? He would have had
to be stranger to me than my own self!
Put out my eye, still I would hear him; take touch away
I'd breathe his presence in; take all my senses,
every one, but only leave my heart,
that bell — its note is all I need to find
him out, wherever, in the world.

(2.4.43)

Alcmene's "innermost feeling" misled her. She decides, as if trivially, for the more beautiful, yet false Amphitryon.

The redoublings and divisions of the I, the "wish-wash" of identities, as Amphitryon calls them, are not depicted in the play simply as actions of the gods, but rather as those planned and carried out by mortals. The appearance of gods in the form of humans appears as a realization, personification, or in any case, a continuation of the roles that the mortal actors are already playing.

The connection between role playing and problems of identity is evident already in the exposition.[27] Sosia enters and plays a role, namely himself and Alcmene, who then receives him. Incidentally, he begins his depiction of Alcmene with the interjection that Alcmene will utter at the play's conclusion: "Ach!"

To the extent that Sosia plays himself and Alcmene, he plays himself as an other:

> And now it's time, my friend, to give some thought
> to your commission.
>
> . . . .
>
> If you practiced up your part beforehand,
> What do you think? Right Sosia, what a good idea!
> (1.1.4)

In a way much like judge Adam in *Der zerbrochene Krug*, he comments on his acting with a pleasure for language and the role: "What a fellow I am, hear my silver tongue!" (1.1.4). "A plague on me if I know where I get my wit!" (1.1.5). The subsequent entrance of Mercury in the form of Sosia divides into two the role that Sosia had been playing on his own.

Amphitryon's redoubling is likewise prepared, namely in Alcmene's love for him. For her, Amphitryon unites two roles within himself, "both" (1.5.20) the husband to whom she must "pay" the "debt" of her love, and the lover, whom she freely loves (2.5.54). She allows Jupiter to bring her to the point of separating husband from lover in the figure of Amphitryon. She loves Amphitryon not just as himself, but also as the "son of the gods." Just like Penthesilia loves Achiles, the Marquise of O. loves the Duke, the Prince of Homburg loves the "image of glory and happiness,"[28] or Elvire loves the "image" of the young knight in *Der Findling*, so she loves her "image" of

Amphitryon.²⁹ In this "image" or "portrait" she has already deified the real
Amphitryon:

> I might have thought he was
> a portrait of himself, a painting by a master's
> hand showing him exactly as
> he is, yet transfigured, like a god!
> Standing there he seemed, I don't know what,
> a dream; unspeakable the bliss I felt,
> whose like I'd never known before, when he,
> Pharissa's conqueror, radiant
> as if with Heaven's glory, appeared to me.
> Amphitryon it was, the son of the gods!
> I would have asked him if he had descended
> from the stars, except he seemed in my eyes
> already—starborn, from the skies.
>
> (2.4.44)

To this Charis comments, ambiguously: "It was imagination, dear—love's
way of seeing things" (2.5.44). What love sees is the "portrait" that it creates.
Because Alcmene loves her "portrait" or "image" of Amphitryon, when she
decides between the two Amphitryons, who resemble each other as if they
were two "drops of water," she chooses the wrong one.

This delusion [Einbildung], this deification, is equated in the drama with
a loving and aesthetic act of Alcmene, in which she divides the flesh-and-
blood Amphitryon from a "painting . . . showing him exactly as he is," that
is, an image *after* Amphitryon. She perceives the real-life Amphitryon only
as an image. At the same time, her choice of words betrays the fact that in
his rendering [Verzeichnen] as a god, there is included a human imperfec-
tion.³⁰ The verb *verzeichnen* can assume several meanings: among them to
enter, to write down, to characterize, to display pictorially, or to illustrate
in an incorrect, distorted, or unrealistic manner. Throughout the drama,
there are repeated reminders of the aesthetic influence on the characters'
perception of the world through *Verzeichnen,* in all its valences. A complex
associational field thereby arises, consisting of terms such as *zeichnen, verzeichnen, auszeichnen, ziehen,* and *Zug.* (*Zug* means a movement or a form;
asthetically, it can refer to a certain style, or a *Kunstgriff;* the term can also

mean a move, such as in a game of chess. The word also appears in the term *Namenszug* [monogram or initial], which appears on the diadem).

Alcmene's words shed light on the scene of Jupiter's "arrival." While spinning yarn in her cell, she dreams about Amphitryon and his battle. Yet she does not dream about "him," Amphitryon, but instead about "it." She repeats this pronoun twice. Amphitryon's request had set the stage:

> AMPHITRYON. No, later on will do. As I just said,
> I'd like to hear, before I go indoors,
> your account of my homecoming yesterday.
> ALCMENE. It's quickly told. The dark had come, I sat
> inside my closet at the wheel, the humming
> of the spindle lulled me off into the field,
> among armed warriors, when I heard a loud
> exulting shout from from the direction of the farther gate.
> AMPHITRYON. Who was shouting?
> ALCMENE.   Our people.
> AMPHITRYON.   And?
> ALCMENE. And promptly I forgot it, for even in
> my dreams it never crossed my mind what pure
> joy the gods in all their graciousness
> had destined for me. But just as I took up
> the thread again, a tremor ran through all
> my limbs —
>
>   (2.2.35)

This picking up of the thread, which in this context also refers to Alcmene's dreaming about Amphitryon, is placed in direct connection with the arrival of the god. Hence, Amphitryon will later speak of the "web" that he wishes to tear apart (2.2.37). Jupiter appears [erscheint] to Alcmene now during "nightfall" (2.2.31). The "appearance [Erscheinung]" of Jupiter in the form of Amphitryon materializes or personifies Alcmene's delusion or imaginary construction [Einbildungen] of love.

With this questioning of the certainty of perception or of the I, Kleist is clearly reacting to contemporary philosophy. In a letter dated 1801, Kleist addresses the "newer, so-called Kantian philosophy" and states as its result: "We cannot determine if what we call truth, truly is truth, or if it only seems that way to us" (23 March 1801).[31] Perception and cognition are biased and are necessarily dependent upon perspective. What we perceive is something that we consider to be something, an "appearance [Erscheinung]," a "portrait [Bild]," and we make, for ourselves, something of this object of our perception. Related to this is Kant's concept of *Erscheinung*, by which he clearly does not mean *Schein*, but rather the object of possible experience. In Kleist, the meaning of *Erscheinung* changes to that of "revelation" (2.5.51), to apperance as the production of semblance, as "delusion." Everything that happens in the drama is insistently related to the perspective of subjective perception and validity. The formulation "Es gilt [it is valid]" (rendered in context in the English translation as "What does it matter?" [2.10.75] and "Agreed" [3.2.79]) takes on the meaning both of an arrangement as well as a description of the perception of reality. This perspective is indicated throughout by use of the pronouns "me" and "you" (the German datives "mir" and "dir"). Amphitryon is Amphitryon to Alcmene; he is *her* Amphitryon. Everything that approaches her, says Jupiter, is Amphitryon. Jupiter has to submit himself to this truth claim and cannot flee from it:

JUPITER.   But now suppose
    I were, for you, the god — ?
ALCMENE.   Suppose that you —
    my head is spinning! — were, for me, the god?
    Should I go down before you in the dust, or shouldn't
    I? The god — it's you, it's you?
JUPITER.   For you
    to say. Myself, I am Amphitryon.
ALCMENE. Amphitryon —
JUPITER.   For you, Amphitryon,
    oh yes.
                                        (2.5.55)

Charis also speaks this way:

"What a scene that was!" (2.3.38)

As the drama is enacted through the character of Alcmene, the identity of being [Sein] and validity [Geltung] falls apart and completes the portrait as a *Verzeichnung*, a distortion, or a delusion. For this reason, Jupiter attempts to hold Alcmene to the Old Testament commandment against making likenesses of God.[32] Jupiter accuses Alcmene of actually having paid homage, when praising him, to Amphitryon:

JUPITER.   Yes,
    you flung yourself down on your face—but *why?*
    I'll tell you why—in the lightning's bright electric
    flourish you read a well-known letter.

. . . .

ALCMENE.
    Am I supposed to pray to marble
    walls? Well, I need features I can see
    if I'm not to think of him.

                                        (2.5.52)

The force of validity in perception and feeling is also the reason that Alcmene snubs Jupiter in his desire to be loved as he is, rather than as a collection of "all those mad ideas [Wahn] / they entertain about him" (2.5.54).

For the experience of the power of validity, the word "Vorfall [incident]" or "Fall" ["fall or eventuality]" is used, with its resonance with the German word *Sündenfall* [the fall of man]. He would dwell in detachment from a world in which God determines the being of each thing, bestowing upon each one its name,[33] through an anthropocentric world in which for only validities are valid ("nur noch Geltungen gelten") to the subjects.

IV

The dialogues between Alcmene and Jupiter involve not only the question of the identity of Amphitryon and Alcmene, and the identity of being and validity, they also raise the question of the power and privileges of the paternal god, that is, of the power of religion itself. These dialogues are asymmetrical.

For the spectator/listener/reader, Jupiter speaks at many points as Jupiter himself. Already in the nocturnal love scene he calls himself a "god." Even at these moments, however, Alcmene believes him to be Amphitryon, to the point that she denies her eventual acknowledgment of the god and clings to her image of Amphitryon. Even long before this, she chooses formulations that, in Jupiter's words, have "more significance" than she may think (1.4.20). Yet the reader's or spectator's doubts about whether she really knows what she is actually saying increase in the course of the dialogues. Similar to the Marquise of O., her consciousness limits her knowledge of her own formulations. An example can be found already when she first addresses the real Amphitryon after her armorous night with Jupiter: "Heavens, it's Amphitryon!" ["O Gott! Amphitryon!]") (2.2.30). Similarly, in their night of passion, Jupiter called himself "a god" (2.2.36). The interjection is simultaneously an address, as it is in her exclamation: "Now you and I must separate, oh god, forever!" (2.5.47). The urgency of her request is issued against her knowledge:

Oh my dear husband, please
do tell me, was it you or not? Speak, it
was you, it was!

(2.5.46)

Ambiguous, too, is her strange exclamation: "Oh, lost soul!" (2.5.49). That is her reaction to Amphitryon, who in her eyes has committed sacrilege with his disclosure that it was Jupiter who appeared to her. With this, she also reacts to Jupiter, whose attempt to become human is now negated. Amphitryon uses the word "lose," in that he speaks of "miracles" that are "appearances in this world from another [die sich / aus einer anderen Welt hieher verlieren]" (literally, "which lose themselves to here from another world") (2.2.34). Alcmene realizes that the separation of lover from husband during that night could be a "crime." She will not "blurt out" this secret, however (1.4.19).[34] Her revealing exclamation is reminiscent of Lessing's Emilia Galotti: "He himself! He!" (2.5.50).

Needing love, Jupiter has appeared to Alcmene in the form of Amphitryon in order to be loved as "him," himself, instead of as a delusioniary image. He tries repeatedly to get Alcmene to confess her love to him.[35] In the critical literature, most recently by Jauß in his incisive essay, this has been understood as a test of Alcmene. These are not tests, however, but rather Jupiter's powerless attempts at seduction to save his power and rights. In this sense they are attempts ("Versuche") and seductions ("Versuchungen"). In these attempts too, the validity of traditional theological models is staged.

In the first seduction, he attempts to sway Alcmene to differentiate between her husband and her lover. To the husband is ascribed the "law of all the world," marital duty—and to the lover, "love" (2.5.55). Such formulations allude not only to Molière's courtly comedy, but also to the difference between the Old ("law") and New ("love") Testaments. Alcmene accepts this division, commenting: "Yes, / all right—I don't know what to say!" (1.5.20). Jupiter fails to bring her any further, however, because for her Amphitryon is "both" at once (1.5.20).

The next attempt at seduction consists in the transformation of the initial "A" on the diadem (Amphitryon, Alcmene) into a "J" (Jupiter). This change sends Alcmene into deep despair. She now loses her certainty. In order to pull her out of this despair, Jupiter must level the differentiation between lover and husband that he had earlier forced upon her.

> JUPITER. for nothing
> not Amphitryon is ever able
> to come near you.
> ALCMENE.   Oh my dear husband, please
> do tell me, was it you or not? Speak, it
> was you, it was!
> JUPITER.   Yes, it was me. But it's
> no matter who it was. I beg you: make
> an effort to be calm, for everything you saw,
> you thought, you touched, you felt was me—and who
> else should it be?
>
> (2.5.46)

Jupiter presents himself as an omnipotent god, yet he must admit that he fooled Alcmene and himself:

> ALCMENE.   How shamefully
> deceived I was!
> JUPITER.   *He* was deceived, my idol! His wicked
> swindle took *him* in, not you, not your
> unerring feeling! When he imagined it was you
> he wound his arms around, all the while
> you lay upon Amphitryon's beloved
> breast, and when he dreamt he kissed your lips,
> your lips were pressed tight to Amphitryon's.
> Oh, he has got a sting, let me assure

you, planted in his fevered bosom all
the skill the gods possess can't pull out.

(2.5.47)

In this scene, Jupiter, the all-powerful god, undertakes a blasphemous transformation into an utterly earthly being; he addresses Alcmene as "the wife
I hold in reverence" and as "my idol" (2.5.47). In order to restrain Alcmene
from the final "despair," Jupiter reveals that it was "Zeus himself" who
visited her. He must admit that he deceived her and stole Amphitryon's
"features" (2.5.50–51).

But this time, too, Alcmene does not react as he would have wished.
Jupiter presents himself as a merciful god and portrays Alcmene's honor in
words more befitting to a glory-seeking commander such as Amphitryon.
However, Alcmene cannot envy Jupiter's chosen ones, such as Callisto and
Leda. She begins to anger Jupiter greatly as she instead speaks of the "pain"
he has inflicted upon her, and later cries, "Oh, I'd be so frightened!" (2.5.53).

He now stylizes himself as a punishing and vengeful god. His descent
to man, portrayed earlier as an act of mercy, is now to be understood as a
penalty. Jupiter wishes to punish Alcmene, because she practiced idolatry,
in that she did not worship Jupiter himself on the altar, but instead Amphitryon, the lover, in the figure of Jupiter. With that, Jupiter demands what
he had previously denounced: love as debt and duty. He wants to force her
"to think him" (not to think of him)—a strange, helpless formulation, as
if god were only a product of thought. According to traditional theological
doctrine, God cannot be reached as God through the necessarily limited
and limiting process of thought because he is an absolute essence above all
thought.[36] Jupiter justifies his right to love with a pantheistic argument:

JUPITER.   Is he a being who exists
for you? His glorious handiwork, the world—
do you have eyes for it? Do you see him in the sunset
glow that lights up the hushed underwoods?
Do you hear him in the pleasant noise of waters
and the nightingale's voluptuous chorusing?
Don't the mountains towering up to heaven
announce him to you all in vain, in vain
the cataract plunges from the steep to shatter
on the rocks below? When the sun aloft

in his great temple sends his beams abroad,
when through Creation beats a pulse of joy
and all things hymn his praise, don't you
descend into the mine shaft of your heart
to adore your idol?

(2.5.51)

This pantheistic argument, however, is thoroughly compromised by his intention and by contradiction when he states that he descended in order to seek revenge from Alcmene.

Alcmene promises him that she will distinguish between Amphitryon and Jupiter, though rather casually: "Fine, good—you'll see how satisfied you'll be with me" (2.5.53). In the first hour of each dawn she will think only of Jupiter, but after that she will forget him. "Reverence" is due to "the father"—"love" to man (2.5.55).

Consequently, Jupiter presents himself as a transcendent god with an eternal countenance, that is, as anything but human. He prophesizes that Alcmene will love this god unlike she has previously loved any man. She will weep if not allowed to follow him back to the Olymp.

Alcmene again denies herself, responding: "No, never think that, my Amphitryon" (2.5.54). She would prefer that this day had not come about at all:

If I could turn back time one single day,
I'd bolt my closet shut against all gods
and heroes, yes, I would—

JUPITER.   You would? You really
would?

ALCMENE. Indeed I would, oh gladly.

JUPITER [aside].
Damn the deluded hope that tempted me
down here!

It is hence a delusion for a god to wish to be loved as a man.

Now Jupiter attempts another trick; he pleads for sympathy with a lonely Olympian:

Olympus too, Alcmene, without love,
is desolate!

Here, he stylizes himself as a father by addressing Alcmene as "my pious child" whose duties include "sola[cing]" his "stupendous being" (2.5.54). Earlier, he frivolously addresses her as "You darling child!" (1.5.20). Jupiter once again admonishes his creation to "pay back" her "debt" with a single smile (2.5.54–55). The love he desires is not portrayed as love, however, but instead as narcissistic self-reflection:

> what he longs
> for is to see himself reflected in a living
> soul, his own image mirrored in a tear
> of ecstasy."
>
> $$(2.5.54)^{37}$$

With that the drama puts the Old Testament passage "And God created man in his image"[38] under suspicion of having been issued by a narcissistic god, just as Alcmene's love is suspected of being narcissistic. But again Alcmene refuses: Jupiter is deserving of reverence, but Amphitryon of love.

In the form of hypothetical formulations, he resigns himself to Alcmene's perception and, as a last resort, reveals his identity: "But now suppose *I* were, for you, the god—?" (2.5.55). In posing this question, however, he has already disempowered himself as an all-mighty, pantheistic, or transcendent god. By posing this question, he no longer is a god, but is instead only considered to be [gilt als] one. This last attempt does in fact lead Alcmene to the final realization that it is Jupiter who stands before her. Likewise, it brings on sorrow that her feelings betrayed her, that she, as a narcissist, loved *her image* of Amphitryon.

JUPITER. . . .
> But now suppose
> *I* am the god embracing you, and lo,
> Amphitryon appears—your heart, what would
> it say to that?

ALCMENE.   You were the god embracing
> me, and lo, Amphitryon appeared?—
> I'd be so very sad, oh so dejected,
> and wish that he could be the god and you
> would go on being my Amphitryon
> forever, as you are.

JUPITER.   My creature whom
I worship! In whom I am so blessed—in blessing,
blessed!

(2.5.56)

Still, Jupiter deludes himself yet again. Employing a hypothetical formulation, Alcmene says that she would rather cling to her illusion, to her image
of Amphitryon, than to love the god as a god, that "you would go on being
my Amphitryon forever, as you are." She does not say, "that you remain
the Amphitryon that you are." In this love triangle, the god must assume
the role of the betrayed husband. Alcmene remains true to her likeness of
Amphitryon when she publicly identifies the false one, Jupiter. At the conclusion, Jupiter must accept his defeat:

Your husband, Lord Amphitryon,
and *no one else* has ever been allowed
within the precincts of your soul—
and I wish the world to know it.

(3.2.77)

Alcmene remains faithful to the imaginary construction [Einbildungen] of
her love, while failing the real Amphitryon. Her *Verzeichnung* into what is
godly, wronged Amphitryon, the man. She calls to the heavens for protection against Jupiter and faints into Amphitryon's arms. As reparation and
reconciliation, Jupiter announces the birth of Hercules. This happy ending is, however, clouded with black irony. It is not just Alcmene's "Ach!"
which makes this reconciliation a forced one. The annunciation of Hercules, with its blasphemous allusions to the Annunciation of Jesus, ends in
the pronouncement of an apotheosis, but does so with an image of death:
the pyramid. Especially in European architecture around 1800, the pyramid was used as the form of monuments for fallen heroes.[39] The deeds of
the mythical Hercules can also be understood as a pyramid to heaven. His
death upon a funeral pyre freed him from terrible suffering, something the
audience knows. As Jupiter remarks:

And when the pyramid
is built at last, grazing with its top
the Empyrean's cloudy fringe, heavenwards

he'll mount its steps and on Olympus I'll
receive him then, a god.

(3.2.84)

The departure of the ancient-Christian father of the gods is described with
one phrase, a phrase with which Alcmene knowingly and unknowingly
characterized God's becoming man: a losing of oneself. The stage direction
reads: "He loses himself in the clouds." According to this stage direction,
the "Olympians" belong to a world or a setting that is no more: "He disappears into the clouds, which meanwhile have opened overhead to disclose Olympus and the Olympians reclining at their ease upon its summit."
(3.11. 84)

NOTES

1. See Helmut Sembdner, "Kleist und Falk. Zur Enstehungsgeschichte von Kleists
Amphitryon," in *Jahrbuch der deutschen Schillergesellschaft* 13 (1969): 361–95.

2. Letter to Adam Müller, 16 March 1807, in *Heinrich von Kleist. Lebensspuren,* ed.
Helmut Sembdner (Frankfurt am Main: Insel, 1977), 135–36.

3. See especially the review by August Klingemann in the *Zeitung für die elegante
Welt,* ebd., 139–40. Klingemann views the play as a Romantic interpretation of an ancient myth. For him, Romanticism appears in the predominance of reflection and the
integration of Christian motifs. For further Kleist reviews, see *Berliner Kleist-Blätter*
4 (1991): 53–64.

4. Heinrich von Kleist, *Sämtliche Werke und Briefe,* 2 vols., ed. Helmut Sembdner,
fifth ed. (Munich: Hanser, 1970). Translations follow Heinrich von Kleist, *Five Plays,*
trans. Martin Greenberg (New Haven, Conn.: Yale University Press, 1988).

5. Kleist, *Lebensspuren,* 144–45.

6. For more on this biblical-classical synchronicity, see also Uvo Hölscher, "Gott
und Gatte. Zum Hintergrund der Amphitryon-Komödie," in *Kleist-Jahrbuch* (1991):
115ff.

7. Kleist, *Lebensspuren,* 144.

8. Hölscher, "Gott und Gatte," 110.

9. See the analysis by Norbert Oellers, "'Kann auch so tief ein Mensch erniedrigt
werden?' Warum Amphitryon? Warum 'ein Lustspiel'?" in *Heinrich von Kleist,* ed.
Heinz Ludwig Arnold, Text + Kritik, Sonderband (Munich: Edition Text und Kritik, 1993), 72–82. See also Hans Robert Jauß, "Poetik und Problematik von Identität und Rolle in der Geschichte des Amphitryon," in *Identität,* ed. Odo Marquard
and Karlheinz Stierle, Poetik und Hermeneutik VIII (Munich: Fink, 1979), 240. Also
see Michael Neumann, "Genius malignus Jupiter oder Alkmenes Descartes-Krise," in
Kleist-Jahrbuch (1994): 141–55.

10. See further the essays in Hubertus Tellenbach, ed., *Das Vaterbild im Abendland I* (Stuttgart: Kohlhammer, 1978); the entry "Vatername Gottes" in *Religion in Geschichte und Gegenwart*, 3. Aufl. (Tübingen: Mohr, 1962), 6:1232–35. On the same topic, also see the excellent essay by Hans-Jürgen Schrader, "Der Christengott in alten Kleidern. Zur Dogmenkritik in Kleists Amphitryon," in *Antiquitates Renatae. Festschrift für Renate Böschenstein*, ed. V. Ehrich-Haefeli et.al. (Würzburg: Königshausen und Neumann, 1998), 191–207.

11. For more detailed description of the postions taken in current research, see Karl-Heinz Wegener, *Amphitryon im Spiegel der Kleistliteratur* (Frankfurt am Main: Lang, 1979); Bernd Fischer, "Wo steht Kleist im *Amphitryon?*" in *Studia Neophilologica* 56 (1984): 61ff.; Thomas Wichmann, *Heinrich von Kleist*, Sammlung Metzler 240 (Stuttgart: J. B. Metzler, 1988), 89ff. Future discussions of the concept of feeling should now be based on the excellent study by Stanley Corngold, *Complex Pleasures: Forms of Feeling in German Literature* (Stanford, Calif.: Stanford University Press, 1998).

12. Walter Müller-Seidel, "Die Vermischung des Komischen mit dem Tragischen in Kleists Lustspiel Amphitryon," in *Jahrbuch der deutschen Schillergesellschaft* 5 (1961): 118–35; Hans-Georg Gadamer, "Der Gott des innersten Gefühls," in *Neue Rundschau* 72 (1961): 340–49; see also Lawrence Ryan, "Amphitryon: doch ein Lustspielstoff?" in *Kleist und Frankreich*, ed. Walter Müller-Seidel (Berlin: Schmidt, 1969), 83–121.

13. Jauß, "Poetik und Problematik von Identität," 234ff; Peter Michelsen, "Umnachtung durch das Licht. Zu Kleists Amphitryon," in *Kleist-Jahrbuch* (1996): 123–39.

14. Karlheinz Stierle, "Amphitryon," in *Interpretationen. Kleists Dramen*, ed. Walter Hinderer (Stuttgart: Reclam, 1997), 33–74.

15. Wolfgang Wittkowski, *Heinrich von Kleists Amphitryon* (Berlin: de Gruyter, 1978), and his "Goethe and Kleist. Autonome Humanität und religiöse Autorität zwischen Unbewußtsein und Bewußtsein in *Iphigenie, Amphitryon, Penthesilea*," in *Goethe im Kontext*, ed. Wolfgang Wittkowski (Tübingen: Niemeyer, 1984), 205–29.

16. See Arthur Henkel, "Erwägung zur Szene II, 5 in Kleists *Amphitryon*," in *Festschrift für Friedrich Beißner*, ed. Ulrich Gaier and Werner Volke. (Bebenhausen, 1974), 147–64; Jochen Schmidt, *Heinrich von Kleist. Studien zu seiner poetischen Verfahrensweise* (Tübingen: Niemeyer, 1974), 161ff., 225ff. Schrader, "Der Christengott in alten Kleidern," 204ff.

17. See also the discussion of Michelsen's lecture, "Umnachtung durch das Licht," 140ff.

18. See Orjan Lindenberger, *The Transformations of Amphitryon* (Stockholm: Almqvist and Wiksell, 1956); Peter Szondi, forward to: *Amphitryon. Plautus, Molière, Dryden, Kleist, Giraudoux, Kaiser* (Munich, 1964), 7–29. Wittkowski, *Heinrich von Kleists Amphitryon*, 26–50; Jauß, "Poetik und Problematik," 214ff.; Max Kunze, Dieter Metzler, and Volker Riedel (eds.), *Amphitryon. Ein griechisches Motiv in der europäischen Literatur und auf dem Theater* (Münster: LIT, 1993); Marie MacLean, "The Heirs of Amphitryon: Social Fathers and Natural Fathers," in *New Literary History* 26 (1995): 787–807. On the question of literary paternity, compare Stanley Corngold's reflec-

tions, "Nietzsche, Kafka, and Literary Paternity," in *Nietzsche and Jewish Culture,* ed. Jacob Golomb (London and New York: Routledge, 1996), 137–57.

19. Hölscher, "Gott und Gatte," 111–12.

20. Jauß, "Poetik und Problematik," 213.

21. See Ingeborg Harms, *Zwei Spiele Kleists um Trauer und Lust: "Die Familie Schroffenstein" und "Der zerbrochene Krug"* (Munich: Fink, 1990).

22. See Schmidt, *Heinrich von Kleist,* 179ff.

23. See René Girard, *La Violence et le sacré* (Paris: Grasset, 1972), especially 201ff.; on the motif of the double, see also Jean-Pierre Vernant, *Mythe et pensée chez les Grecs* 1965 (Paris: La Découverte, 1988), 325ff. Vernant is interested primarily in the function of the "double" as conduit between the living and the dead, the visible and the invisible.

24. See Szondi, forward to: *Amphitryon;* also "'Amphitryon.' Kleists 'Lustspiel nach Molière,'" in *Euphorion* 55 (1961): 249–59. Both essays are also in Szondi's *Schriften II.* (Frankfurt am Main: Suhrkamp, 1978), 155–98.

25. Exodus 3.14.

26. See Hendrik Birus, "'Ich bin der ich bin.' Über die Echos eines Namens (Ex. 3, 13–15)," in *Juden in der deutschen Literatur,* ed. Stéphanie Moses and Albrecht Schöne (Frankfurt am Main: Suhrkamp, 1986), 25–53.

27. See in particular John Walker, "Und was, wenn Offenbarung uns nicht wird: Kleist's Kantkrise and Theatrical Revelation in Amphitryon," in *Oxford German Studies* 22 (1993): 100–101, and Volker Nölle, "Verspielte Identität. Eine expositorische 'Theaterprobe' in Kleists Lustspiel *Amphitryon,*" in *Kleist-Jahrbuch* (1993): 160–80.

28. *Der Prinz von Homburg,* V.72.

29. For the epistemological significance of the "Bild" in Kleist, see Kurz, "'Gott befohlen.' Kleists Dialog *Über das Marionettentheater* und der *Mythos vom Sündenfall des Bewußtseins,*" in *Kleist-Jahrbuch* (1981/82): 264–77.

30. See also *Prinz Friedrich von Homburg,* V.778.

31. On this much discussed "crisis," also see: Werner Frick, "Kleists 'Wissenschaft,'" in *Kleist-Jahrbuch* (1997): 216ff.

32. Exodus 20.3.

33. See Genesis 1.1.

34. See Johannes Endres, *Das "depotenzierte" Subjekt. Zur Geschichte und Funktion des Komischen bei Heinrich von Kleist* (Würzburg: Königshausen und Neumann, 1996), 183–84.

35. See Jauß, "Poetik und Problematik," 241ff.; Wegener, *Amphitryon,* 171ff.

36. See Philippians 4.7.

37. See also 3.2.83:

> Zeus wishes you to know, Amphitryon,
> that he has been well pleased by his reception
> in your house.

38. Genesis 1.27.

39. See the reproductions in Winfried Nerdinger, Kaul Jan Philipp and Hans-Peter Schwarz (eds.), *Revolutionsarchitektur. Ein Aspekt der europäischen Architektur um 1800* (Munich: Hirmer, 1990), 19, 39, 186. The announcement of Hercules' birth is no "life saver for a positive interpretation," Fischer "Wo steht Kleist im *Amphitryon?*" 67.

9 Two Lovers, Three Friends

JOCHEN HÖRISCH

Translated by Eric Jarosinski

Hollin and Oduardo arrived at school the same day and took an immediate liking to each other. They managed to have the rector assign them to the same shared room, which they occupied together until leaving for the university. The former was superior to the latter in age, wealth, and talent; this superiority was accepted as natural, however, and did not damage their friendship. Everything one does at school they did together: they did their homework together, secretly fried potatoes for each other, fought with their rivals at other schools together, and secretly kept a fine suit, which they took turns wearing at the variety or the coffee house; everyone at school knew them as Castor and Pollux. Oduardo, who had spent some hard years with his father, a doctor in G., had consequently attained more awareness, caution, and cleverness. He became a sort of benevolent caretaker for Hollin and saved him from countless foolish acts. In all other respects, they became so much like each other [lebten sie so in einander über] that the teachers had trouble telling their handwriting apart.

Thus writes Achim von Arnim in his 1810 novel *Armut, Reichtum, Schuld und Buße der Gräfin Delores*.[1] The title, this passage, and the text as a whole generate their allure by testing boundaries and deeming them crossable (among others, the borders between poverty and wealth, guilt and punishment, happiness and sorrow, life and death, and life and reading). The boundary Arnim's novel subjects to the most rigorous test is that of dividing friendship from love. It is perhaps superfluous to point out that Arnim thus transforms autobiographical moments into literature: namely, his cultically stylized friendship to Clemens Brentano, which began in 1801, and his equally stylized love for Bettina, whom he first met in 1802.

"Draw a distinction": differentiate between love and friendship. Arnim and many of his contemporaries around 1800 had obvious difficulty with this.[2] Already in the opening passage of the novel, with its explicit theme of friendship, the key word "love [Liebe]" manages to slip in: "Hollin and Oduardo arrived at school the same day" and "took an immediate liking to each other [gewannen einander sogleich lieb]." This moment is followed by turns of phrase that invite clearly erotic, even conjugal, associations: "They managed to have the rector assign them to the same shared room, which they occupied together until leaving for the university." Their connection is so close that they even assume the female role for the other and play cook for each other when they "secretly [!] fried potatoes for each other." Further, a passage filled with erotic words and symbols makes clear that the symbiosis between Hollin and Odoardo has not only friendly but also erotic qualities. "In all other respects," we read, "they became so much like each other [sie lebten so in einander über], that the teachers had trouble telling their handwriting apart."

The text makes no secret of the fact that in Germany around 1800 the distinction between a man's love for a woman and his friendship to another man is not yet the conceptual compass of emotional relationships between those who are close in age. Despite the efforts of Matthias Claudius's essay "Von der Freundschaft" to separate friendship from intimacy, a confusion about the two concepts prevails and, by extension, a confusion in overall orientation. Ever since Beethoven's musical sealing of Schiller's pathos-filled verses on friendship, only one thing could be said for certain: anyone capable of neither friendship nor love gets short shrift, unless he preempts this fate by first stealing himself away. To put it more elegantly: those capable of neither friendship nor love are excluded, or exclude themselves, from social ties of all kinds.

Wem der große Wurf gelungen,
    Eines Freundes Freund zu sein;
Wer ein holdes Weib errungen,
    Mische seinen Jubel ein!
Ja—wer auch nur eine Seele
    Sein nennt auf dem Erdenrund!

Und wers nie gekonnt, der stehle
   Weinend sich aus diesem Bund!

Whoever has had the great success
Of being a friend's friend;
Whoever has won a lovely wife,
Share in his jubilation!
Yes, even who has only one soul
On this earth to call his own!
And he who could not attain this joy,
   He, weeping, steal himself away from this union!

Thus not an exclusive "or," but an inclusive one. One must have a relation either of a close friendship or of love; having both at once is even better; and having neither a friend nor a wife to call one's own is tantamount to social exclusion. It would not be difficult to name another of the many examples of the ways in which love and friendship were not clearly distinguished from each other around 1800. Hölderlin, for one, begins what he calls his 1804 "Night Songs," the last collection of poems that he was still capable of publishing himself, with the note: "Dedicated to love and friendship, Frankfurt/M. 1804."

Here again, an inclusive "and" appears instead of an exclusive "or." Evidently, the combination of the four terms "love," "friendship," "man," and "woman" is not adequately exhausted by the commonly sanctioned compounds "heterosexual love" and "same-sex friendship." After all, the possibility also remains open for same-sex love and friendship with the opposite sex. Of these four combinations, which are capable of being placed in a chiastic chart and as such have a clear layout, it is the last that has had the least chance of being poetically represented in modern European literature. If the friendship between a young man and a young woman is ennobled through literary presentation at all, it is usually only to illustrate the failure to transgress the border between friendship and the erotic (as, for example, in Goethe's novella about the strange neighbor's children, Fontane's novel *Schach von Wuthenow*, or Thomas Mann's early tales).

The second version of *Hollins Liebesleben*, quoted at the outset, appeared as an addition to Arnim's *Delores* novel on Easter 1810, that is, eight years after its separate initial publication. Goethe responded to Arnim's early publication, as well as to many other "Romantic" stories about Eduarde and Odoardo, with a grandiose and quite serious satire, his 1809 novel *Elective Affinities.*[3] The plot is well-known: Eduard, a wealthy baron in his best years, invites an old friend to his castle for an extended stay. He does so despite the quiet reservations of his wife, with whom the guest falls in love. Likewise, Eduard himself falls passionately in love with his wife's orphaned niece, whom she had invited as a countermove to the visit of her husband's friend. It is strange and noteworthy, incidentally, that despite the great passion the young beauty stirs among men—such as the servant, the architect, the count, and her cousin's fiancée—nothing flares between Ottilie and the captain. Their relationship is that of a perfect nonrelationship, touched neither by love nor friendship (and similarly, not even by dislike or hatred).

The constellation of Eduard and Ottilie is rather different. It begins as a relationship between the most distant of relatives, quickly skips the friendship phase, and, just as rapidly, assumes the most passionate dimensions. The scene in which Eduard does not so much declare his love to Ottilie as tell her to her face (or rather, to her hand) that she loves him, has a trigger: in copying the papers of her "friend," she had, in an act of perfect mimicry, assumed Eduard's handwriting:

> Though he was pleased that she was doing something for him it distressed him keenly that he was not able to see her at once. His impatience increased by the minute. He paced up and down in the big drawing-room, tried all manner of things but could concentrate on nothing. What he wanted was to see her, and see her alone, before Charlotte came back with the Captain. It grew dark, the candles were lit.
>
> At last she came in, radiantly lovable. The feeling that she had done something for her friend had enhanced her whole being beyond itself. She laid down the original and the copy on the table in front of Eduard. "Shall we compare?" she said with a smile. Eduard did not know what to reply. He looked at her, he looked at the copy. The first pages were written with the greatest care, in a delicate female hand; then the writing seemed to change, to become easier and freer; but how great was his astonishment when he ran his eyes over the final pages. "In heaven's name!" he cried. "What is this? That is my handwriting." He looked at Ottilie, and again at the pages. Especially the ending was exactly as if he had written it himself. Ottilie said nothing, but she was looking into

his eyes with the greatest satisfaction. Eduard raised his arms. "You love me!" he cried. "Ottilie, you love me!" And they held one another in a tight embrace. It would not have been possible to say who first seized hold of the other.[4]

The second version of Arnim's earlier text is an obvious reaction to this scene. Only here is the motif of the characters becoming each other, illustrated by their nearly identical handwriting, stressed from the beginning. The first version, by contrast, downplays the significance of one's respective individual handwriting. As Hollin writes to Odoardo: "You are right, more than handwriting or a *Stirnmesser* [as the Grimms' dictionary explains, 'Lavater's physiological measuring device for determining one's character based on the size of the forehead,' J. H.], the books we love reveal more of our inner, secret side."[5] In the second version, which ties the loving friendship between Hollin and Odoardo so intimately to the motif of their shared handwriting, Arnim reacts to *Elective Affinities* and thus, by extension, to Goethe's response to Romantic conceptions of Odoardo's loves and friendships. It is a defensive battle mounted against a newly prevailing conception of love and friendship. To put it plainly, what Goethe includes under the heading of "love" is what Arnim hopes to subsume still under the heading of "friendship." Being incapable of distinguishing between two persons and their handwriting because they have grown so intertwined ("ineinander über leben") — that is the criterion either for friendship (Arnim) or for love (Goethe).

Goethe wins, Arnim loses. Or in the sober words of Niklas Luhmann, who, in his seminal book *Love as Passion*, argues — based on a wealth of historical, semantic, and literary material — in support of the suspicion that "in the valorization of sexuality . . . the competition between 'love' and 'friendship,' too, becomes decisive as a basic formula for a coding of intimacy. Love wins."[6] That love wins in the long run had become evident in European literature already long before 1800. Consider, for instance, the examples of Petrarch and Dante. Yet these are also texts that not only value love over friendship, but simultaneously thematize the unobtainability of the deified lover. It is just this motif of unrealizable love that Cervantes ironizes in the character of Dulcinea. Love, as a literary genre, is to be rated higher than friendship — but at the price that it is a love of letters [Letternliebe].

Shakespeare's work is marked by a turn away from this highly literary and therefore unrealistic order of love. Shakespeare renders, *sit venia verbo,* love literarily real. It can fail tragically (as in *Romeo and Juliet*) or succeed in spite of all imaginable errors and confusion (as in *A Mid-Summer Night's Dream*). Almost regularly, however, one encounters in Shakespearean texts the motif of the precarious struggle between friendship and love. This is the case, paradigmatically in *The Merchant of Venice.* The friendship between Antonio and Bassanio clearly bears homoerotic traces, which helps explain Antonio's melancholy when Bassanio, his closest friend, turns toward a woman. His turning toward her, however, also stands to be revised. After all, as Bassanio says to Antonio at the end of the drama: "Antonio, I am married to a wife / Which is as dear to me as life itself; / But life itself, my wife, and all the world, / Are not with me esteem'd above thy life: / I would lose all, ay, sacrifice them all, / Here to this devil, to deliver you" (4.1). Bassanio's wife is present at this declaration of love for the friend—as a judge, disguised in men's clothing. Her commentary is of remarkable sobriety: "Your wife would give you little thanks for that, / If she were by to hear you make the offer."

The ring episode allegorically illustrates the seriousness of Bassanio's offer. He parts with his recently obtained wedding ring upon the judge's prodding, handing it over to a man, who, luckily, turns out to be a woman, his wife. Here, too, the maxim holds true: *amor vincit.* Yet this victory is highly precarious, and it is a triumphant procession that reaches Germany quite late. Shakespeare's German contemporaries, the poets of the baroque, continue to adhere for the most part to the higher valuation of friendship. The German reception of Shakespeare does not commence until the end of the eighteenth century, with translations by Wieland, and later by Schlegel and Tieck, compensating, with its vigor, for its belatedness. The German reception of Shakespeare likely played a decisive role in the delayed triumph of *amor* in Germany. For good reason, Wagner's musical drama *Tristan and Isolde* is considered an almost unsurpassable celebration of ecstatic love. Yet even in this work there is the strong undercurrent of a friendship that must first be overcome.

The stammering of those whose lives have become intertwined [ineinander über lebenden]," Tristan and Isolde, the lovers who cannot survive ("überleben") their own ecstatic love, symbolizes the triumphant victory of love over friendship: "I, not Tristan, I, Isolde . . . Thus we would die, to remain inseperable." Wagner's construction of love's triumph over friendship is remarkably radical. Through his love for Isolde, Tristan betrays the clearly intimate, even homoerotic, pact of friendship with Melot and Kurwenal.[7] Now fallen for Isolde, Tristan says of his relationship to Melot: "My friend was the one, / Who loved me true and dearly." This is how Tristan, in love with Isolde, characterizes his own relation to Melot, who, in turn, simply calls him a "traitor." Melot "was" Tristan's friend, with whom, as Isolde complains, "the men all get along." In turning away from the ties of friendship in order to accept the ties of love, the most ecstatic of all lovers conforms, to Melot's dismay, to the law of regularity. Anyone in nineteenth-century Europe still wishing to adhere to the connection of intimacy and friendship can only find refuge in the subculture of men's societies. And yet, these are not even true subcultures (think, for example, of the fencing fraternities, the *Wandervögel*, or the clubs), in that they often facilitate what is called an entrance into the ruling classes. Still, this has no effect on the predominant semantic paradigm, according to which intimacy in the nineteenth century is exclusively ascribed to love and, increasingly, fiercely denied friendship.

Already in the first version of Arnim's novel, Hollin, who has fallen in love with Maria, tries to make clear to his friend Odoardo that this is and must be the case. He insists "that love has to grant joyfully everything that it can give which friendship cannot"—that is, intimacy.[8] Odoardo reacts to this by remaining Hollin's best friend, yet he also makes two new friends. What one of them, Roland, tells him, he feels compelled immediately to pass on to his Ur-friend. Roland "told me that, when he first fully enjoyed a girl's love, he called out within himself: 'Is that all!'"[9] Yet this hint is not heard. Hollin, responding to Odoardo, denies his friend—much like Tristan saying to his Ur-friend Melot and King Marke: "What you would ask about, / you can never experience the authority to talk about matters of love"—the competency to talk about matters of love: "You can't understand, Odoardo, if you've never felt the mysterious pulsating of blood when near your female lover."[10] Odoardo's retort: "Though I do not quite understand you anymore, I feel that you have not become a stranger to me."[11]

These friends of the early Romantic period remain friends, unlike Wagner's late Romantic male friends (even though one of them falls madly in love). However, once intimacy is denied friendship and ascribed to love instead, friendship itself undergoes deep transformations. The most important one can be put bluntly: love becomes exclusive, friendship inclusive.

The guiding ideal conception of love must follow the code "you, and no one else." "Is there still," we read, "another Maria? Impossible, in all the heavens, no!"[12] In such emphatic tropes, of course, there is always automatically a touch of irony. Hollin surely must know that there are other Marias "in all the heavens." And even on Earth, one can encounter other Marias in addition to the beloved Maria. It is no accident that Hollin takes part in a performance of *Maria Stuart*. Still, there remains the *deificatio* of the one beloved Maria (in the Petrarchian tradition): you and no one else. Thus when Hollin encounters the "degeneration of modern femininity"[13] in the form of a young, rich widow, he must respond to the Countess Irene's overtures with a "friendly" rejection: "I spoke with her in a friendly way, as if with a sister. . . . Touched, I told her that another possessed my heart, but my friendship was hers. She kissed me."

Correspondences: all of this is written by a man to a male friend. "Friendship," we read, "also has its secrets."[14] Among the open secrets of friendship is the fact that a correspondence between men does not break off once their intercourse with a female lover commences. This paradigm can be found to the point of boredom in German literature around 1800. Be it Werther or Lucinde's lover, Hollin or Hyperion, Franz Sternbald or Godwi and *tutti quanti:* a man always writes to a male friend about his passionate love for a woman. That is, he lets him take part in his love via correspondence, but only via correspondence. In his tale "The Judgment," even Kafka is indebted to this model — and he brings it to a head. The fiancé finds himself in a "special relation of correspondence" with his friend:

> As a result Georg merely contented himself with writing to his friend of such unimportant events as randomly collect in one's mind at random when one is idly reflecting on a Sunday. His sole aim was not to disturb the picture of the home town which his friend had presumably built up during the long interval and had come to accept. Thus it happened that three times on three quite widely separated letters Georg had announced the engagement of some indifferent man to some equally indifferent girl, until quite contrary to his intentions his friend began to develop an interest in this notable occurrence.
>
> However, Georg greatly preferred to write to him about things like these than confess that he had himself become engaged, a month ago, to a Fraulein Frieda Brandenfeld, a girl from a well-to-do family. He

often talked to his fiancée of this friend of his, and of the special relationship which he had with him owing to their correspondence. "So he won't be coming to our wedding," said she, "and yet I have a right to get to know all your friends." "I don't want to disturb him," Georg replied, "don't misunderstand me, he probably would come, at least I think so, but he would feel awkward and at a disadvantage, perhaps even envious of me, at all events he would be dissatisfied, and with no prospect of ever ridding himself of his dissatisfaction he'd have to go back again alone. Alone—do you realize what that means?" "Yes, but may he not hear about our wedding in some other way?" "I can't prevent that, certainly, but it's unlikely if you consider the circumstances." "If you've got friends like that, Georg, you should never had got engaged." "Well, we're both of us to blame there; but I wouldn't have it any other way now." And when, breathing faster under his kisses, she still objected: "All the same, it does upset me," he thought it really couldn't do any harm to tell his friend the whole story. "That's how I'm made and he must just take me as I am," he said to himself, "I can't fashion myself into a different kind of person who might perhaps make him a more suitable friend."

And he did in fact report to his friend as follows, in the long letter which he wrote that Sunday morning, about the engagement that had taken place: "I have saved up my best news for the end. I have become engaged to a Fraulein Frieda Brandenfeld, a girl from a well-to-do family which only settled here some time after you left, so that you are unlikely to know them. There will be opportunity later of giving you further details about my fiancée."[15]

It is indeed a "special relation of correspondence," this epistolary intercourse with a friend about the intercourse with a woman and the suspicion that something might be wrong with this intercourse. Even Kafka fundamentally perpetuates (and fundamentally undoes—how could it be otherwise in Kafka?) the differentiational scheme, established around 1800, between friendship and love. A new relationship between exclusion and inclusion opens up. Love becomes exclusive and anticommunicative (great love cannot be had without the *topos* of the unspeakable), while friendship becomes inclusive and remains communicative.[16] Concretely, this means that love is conceptualized in polemic counterdistinction to the economy of the mistress, following the ideal schema of a *folie à deux*. Friendship, however, becomes ever more frequently a bond among three people: "Please grant me the wish of becoming the third member of your union [Ich sei, gewährt mir die Bitte, in Eurem Bund der Dritte]." After all, even Odoardo reports to Hollin that he has found a new pair of friends. Three friends, this model quickly becomes popular: *The Three Musketeers, Three Men in a Boat, Die Drei von der Tankstelle* (The Three From the Gas Station) as well as many children's and young people's books with titles such as "Drei Freunde auf großer Fahrt" (Three Friends on a Great Journey). These all testify to the molding influence of the three-person model of friendship, which distances itself from the two-person model of love in the epoch following the triumph of love over friendship.

Arnim's Ur-friend Brentano observes with remarkable clarity in his "wild" novel, *Godwi,* that new borders are drawn in order to immediately have their permeability put to the test. Has "enamored frienship" in fact been shattered by the "general affectation of love" that, with *Werther,* exploded like a supernova? This is one of the questions posed by the novel, a text fully devoted to the incestous primal paradigm of conceptual wildness. Brentano's prose confronts the new exclusive cult of love with words as harsh as those he employs for an amorous friendship:

> The general affectation of love is, incidentally, the work of a *Complimenteur,* as Philander von Sittewald translates it; a compli menteur, a complete liar.
>
> The enamored friendship is, however, nothing other than either pitiful, sweet weakness, and complete unmanliness, or delusion. I am confident that the friend, who lies long in my arms is either unconscious, deathly ill, wounded, etc., or else he must think that I am some beautiful girl or a secret, unobtainable lover, in whose arms he would so like to lie so peacefully and free.
>
> If then I should tolerate it that a friend should do such a thing, then I am doing it out of sympathy. I let him think of his girl, and if possible, I also think of one myself.
>
> The essence of actual friendship is thereby disturbed, as it exists not in substitution, intense involvement, and permeation, but rather in mere sociability.[17]

The temptation to counter spurts of empathy with spurts of sobriety is irresistible. But this work of sobering has its own analytical power. It ac-

knowledges the social and semantic transformation that we can characterize either emphatically or in all sobriety. Friendship becomes "mere sociability." And sociability includes more than just two people. That means,
however, that friendship threatens to become, owing to the sociability that
inhabits it, inflationary and thus ceases to be friendship. Brentano himself
raises this objection when he writes: "Haber interrupted me here, saying,
'In my opinion, mere sociability is not friendship by far. I know many so-
ciable people who are incapable of an actual warm friendship that emanates
truly from the soul. They do not possess the urge to hold their friend in an
embrace, heart to heart, eye to eye, lip to lip; to share pulse, vision, breath,
and voice.'"

The terms used here to describe couplings, however, are actually no
longer available for the characterization of friendships. Evidently, they are
already taken—by the register of love. Thus, all that is left for friendship
are ironic, saracastic, even cynical perspectives. Looking back at the differentiation between the love of two and the friendship or sociability of three,
one may turn to Oscar Wilde's *Dorian Gray:*

"Poor Lady Brandon! You are hard on her, Harry!" said Hallward, list-
lessly.

"My dear fellow, she tried to found a *salon,* and only succeeded in
opening a restaurant. How could I admire her? But tell me, what did she
say about Mr. Dorian Gray?"

"Oh, something like, 'Charming boy—poor dear mother and I absolutely inseperable. Quite forget what he does—afraid he doesn't do anything—oh, yes, plays the piano—or is it the violin, dear Mr. Gray?'
Neither of us could help laughing, and we became friends at once."

"Laughter is not at all a bad beginning for a friendship, and it is far
the best ending for one," said the young lord, plucking another daisy.

Hallward shook his head. "You don't understand what friendship is,
Harry," he murmured—"or what enmity is, for that matter. You like
every one; that is to say, you are indifferent to every one."

"How horribly unjust of you!" cried Lord Henry, tilting his hat back,
and looking up at the little clouds that, like raveled skeins of glossy white
silk, were drifting across the hollowed turquoise of the summer sky.
"Yes; horribly unjust of you. I make a great difference between people. I
choose my friends for their good looks, my acquaintances for their good

characters, and my enemies for their good intellects. A man cannot be too careful in the choice of his enemies. I have not got one who is a fool. They are all men of some intellectual power, and consequently they all appreciate me. Is that very vain of me? I think it is rather vain."[18]

One only has to compare these sentences by Wilde to Hartley Coleridge's 1833 poem "To a Friend," which, from a historico-semantic perspective, fights rear-guard battles in order to highlight how the conceptions of friendship have shifted.

When we were idlers with the loitering rills,
The need of human love we little noted:
Our love was nature; and the peace that floated
On the white mist, and dwelt upon the hills,
To sweet accord subdued our wayward wills:
One soul was ours, one mind, one heart devoted,
That, wisely doating, ask'd not why it doated,
And ours the unknown joy, which knowing kills.
But now I find how dear thou wert to me;
That man is more than half of nature's treasure,
Of that fair Beauty which no eye can see,
Of that sweet music which no ear can measure;
And now the streams may sing for others' pleasure,
The hills sleep on in their eternity.[19]

Gone are the days in which one could still orient oneself according to binary terms such as love and friendship. There is much that indicates that, today, these two terms have lost their competing powers because they have become pluralized within themselves. In societies that characterize themselves as postmodern, one will no longer be able to talk of any *one* binding conception of love, or of any *one* culturally dominant understanding of friendship: rather, *mille plateaux,* n-variations, an incomprehensibe number of combinations that no chiasmic chart can accommodate. That is the stuff that new literary mixtures of love and friendship are made of. A paradigmatic example is Thomas Meinecke's novel *Tomboy.*[20] What remains, however, is the promise of literature to thematize "the unknown joy, which knowing kills" in such a way that even the known, described, and dedicated pleasure remains pleasure.

Because this is so, there also exists the pleasure of the text with which one is befriended and/or which one loves. Festschriften are meant to, and should, pay tribute to such lovers of texts. Hamann writes:

In the temple of learning, there truly is an idol, not lacking in high priests and Levites, whose image bears the inscription *philosophical history*. Stanley and Brucker have given us colossal creations, just as peculiar and incomplete as the image of beauty that a Greek assembled out of the allure of all beautiful creatures, which appeared to him either by intention or by coincidence. These are masterpieces, which are always gladly admired and sought by studied experts of the arts. They are, however, silently ridiculed by the learned as fantastic growths and chimeras, or else are imitated out of boredom in theatrical illustrations.

Because Stanley is British, and Brucker is Swabian, both have earned their fame by ridding the audience of its boredom. The audience also [deserves] to be praised for the generosity with which it has overlooked the unequal failings of these national authors.[21]

NOTES

1. Achim von Arnim, *Romane und Erzählungen — Auf Grund der Erstdrucke*, ed. W. Migge, vol. 1 (Munich: Hanser, 1962), 93. Unless indicated otherwise, translations of German texts are the translator's.

2. That this differentiation was difficult may well have something to do with the argument that "the entire eighteenth century is marked by the effort to transform the code for intimacy from love to 'inner' friendship." (N. Luhmann, *Liebe als Passion — Zur Codierung von Intimität* [Frankfurt/M.: Suhrkamp, 1982] 102). In making this assertion, Luhmann follows Albert Salomon's study "Der Freundshcaftskult des 18. Jahrhunderts in Deutschland — Versuch zur Soziologie einer Lebensform," *Zeitschrift für Soziologie* 8(1979):279–308; He also follows the classic study by F. H. Tenbruck, "Freundschaft — Ein Beitrag zu einer Soziologie der persönlichen Beziehungen," *Kölner Zeitschrift für Soziologie und Sozialpsychologie* 16(1964):341–456.

3. See also Gabrielle Bersier, *Goethes Rätselparodie der Romantik — Eine neue Lesart der "Wahlverwandtschaften"* (Tübingen: Niemeyer, 1997).

4. Goethe, *Elective Affinities*, trans. David Constantine (Oxford: Oxford University Press, 1994) 81.

5. Achim von Arnim, *Hollins Liebeleben — Roman* (1802), in *Arnim: Werke in einem Band*, ed. W. Migge (Munich: Hanser, 1971), 15.

6. N. Luhmann, *Liebe als Passion*, 147.

7. See also J. Hörisch, *Gott, Geld und Glück — Zur Logik der Liebe in den Bildungsromanen Goethes, Kellers und Thomas Manns* (Frankfurt/M.: Suhrkamp, 1983) (Chapter 5: "Ver-rückte Liebe in Wagners 'Tristan und Isolde'").

8. Ibid., 16.

9. Ibid., 19.

10. Ibid., 26.

11. Ibid., 35.

12. Ibid., 36.

13. Ibid., 17.

14. Ibid., 32.

15. Franz Kafka, "The Judgement," in *The Problem of the Judgment. Eleven Approaches to Kafka's Story,* ed. Angel Flores, trans. Malcolm Pasley (New York: Gordian Press, 1977), 3–4.

16. Claudia Schmölder's analysis points in a different direction: "How is the talkativeness of love different from that of friendship? The French, and above all Mademoiselle de Scudéry of the seventeenth century, believed that loved opened one's heart to everything and every subject—friendship was thought of as more modest. Or to paraphrase Else Lasker-Schüler: love is royal, whereas friendship is Indian." (Claudia Schmölders, "Lieben auf jüdisch und deutsch—Vermutungen zur Ideengeschichte," *Merkur* 596 [November 1998]: 1039).

17. C. Brentano, *Godwi, Werke,* ed. F. Kremp, vol. 2. (Munich: Hanser, 1964), 238.

18. Oscar Wilde, *The Picture of Dorian Gray,* ed. Donald L. Lawler (New York: Norton, 1988), 12–13.

19. Hartley Coleridge, "To a Friend," in his *Poems 1833* (Oxford: Woodstock, 1990), 1.

20. Thomas Meinecke, *Tomboy* (Frankfurt am Main: Suhrkamp, 1989).

21. J. G. Hamann, *Sokratische Denkwürdigkeiten für die lange Weile des Publicums . . . ,* ed. S. A. Joergensen (Stuttgart: Reclam, 1968), 18.

PART IV.

Languages of Friendship
and Sexual Identity

10 The Love That Is Called Friendship and the Rise of Sexual Identity

ROBERT TOBIN

In the eighteenth century, Western Europe witnessed a cult of friend-ship that left literary traces admittedly difficult to understand at the end of the twentieth century. As Michel Foucault stated in an interview with Bob Gallagher and Alexander Wilson,[1] the emergence of homosexual iden-tity coincided with the breakdown of the cult of friendship; Foucault sub-sequently locates the actual "birth" of the homosexual in 1870.[2] Because of this sexual history, readers are cautioned not to project an excessive amount of a modern homosexual identity into the texts of eighteenth-century friendship. Eve Kosofsky Sedgwick, however, wittily parodies the approach of many readers who are anxious not to project their own fan-tasies onto such texts: "Passionate language of same-sex attraction was ex-tremely common during whatever time period is under discussion — and therefore must have been completely meaningless."[3] The cautious approach that Sedgwick critiques misreads a fundamental aspect of the literature of friendship. Because the homosexual identity did not exist in the concrete form that was to emerge in the following century, same-sex desire ambigu-ously infused a broad range of texts that, after the emergence of clear sexual identities, would have been less likely to be filled with erotic tension. Thus, contrary to the prevailing critical assumption that modern readers are likely to project sexuality into eighteenth-century friendships because of moder-nity's awareness of the categories of homosexuality and heterosexuality, it is actually the case that the current categories of sexuality make it hard for modern readers to understand the great extent to which same-sex eroticism permeated eighteenth-century friendship. Modern friendships are asexual, by virtue of the categories of friend and lover, heterosexual and homo-sexual; because of the lack of such categories, eighteenth-century friend-ships were erotic.

While it might seem that this discussion is a primarily historical one, about the nature of friendships in the eighteenth century, it is in fact more important and relevant to literature than anything else. Much of the evidence concerning friendships from this time period comes from such literary authors as Gleim, Schiller, and Jean Paul. The friendships themselves flourished most extensively in epistolary form. Recipients shared letters with like-minded associates; it was not surprising when they were published. In his letters on friendship, the eighteenth-century poet Nikolaus Dietrich Giseke mentions the devotion of the weekly journal *Der Jüngling* (*The Youth*) from Leipzig as early as 1747 to the theme of friendship, underscoring the importance of textual documents for the construction of friendship within other textual documents.[4] In Giseke's letters the equation of "friend" and "poet" further connects the theme of friendship and literature; he hopes that, if "a poet or friend" visits the area in which he is residing, he will be able to detect some of the spirit that he has left behind.[5] As poets, these men construct their relationship verbally, primarily in letters.

An early example of this kind of epistolary friendship with a fine literary legacy was the fervent correspondence between Pope, Arbuthnot, and Swift, which appeared in 1737. It became such a landmark of model friendship that Jean Paul celebrated it in his novel *Siebenkäs*.[6] As Jean Paul's narrator reflects on the intimacy between his two male protagonists, Siebenkäs and Leibgeber, he compares their relationship with that of the English writers: "Why should I constantly repress the old feeling welling forth in me that you have reawakened so powerfully and with which in my youthful years the friendship between Swift, Arbuthnot, and Pope refreshed and penetrated me, so to speak furtively and yet so strongly?"[7] The narrator assumes that a community will form around the appreciation of this male bonding: "And won't many others, like me, have warmed themselves and taken courage at the sight of the touchingly calm love of these manly hearts for each other?" (495). The verb translated as "to take courage" is "sich ermannen," which, with its root "Mann," suggests that this community will be an all-male one. Thus male friendship, transfigured into literature by master letter writers, inspires, within a novel written over sixty years later, further male friendship. The imbrication of literature and friendship is complete.

Other writers concur with Jean Paul's belief that textual descriptions of friendship help engender friendship, and they therefore encourage a kind of literary promiscuity. Friends spend a great deal of time describing their friends to each other. In his *Vertrauliche Briefe* (*Confidential Letters*), which were not so confidential as to preclude publication, Giseke describes to his old friends a new friend, who is so sensitive that he cries when he reads Voltaire: this friend "hasn't found a true friend, has no hope of finding one either, and despairs for that reason."[8] The connection to one friend strengthens connections to other friends. Similarly, the Swiss historian Johannes von Müller, a passionate devotee of the cause of friendship, not only expresses his friendships in letters, he encourages others to join in the construction of friendships with descriptions of friends. In a letter dated 21 August 1804, he wants to hear more about the friend of a friend: "I share with you the delicate bond that you have with your friend, Mr. von Stansky. Tell me more about him, describe him more exactly to me."[9] Friendship not only arises out of the textual relationship between two letter writers, it also creates material about which to write, strengthening other textual bonds of friendship.

Being primarily a literary phenomenon, eighteenth-century friendship opened itself up to all the complexities of interpretation that literature raises. The confusion caused by the cult of friendship is understandable. At times, the declarations of love among men in eighteenth-century Germany were so fervent as to indicate either an extraordinary acceptance of same-sex eroticism or a use of language radically different from the current one. The "marriages" between poets are a case in point. Johann Wilhelm Ludwig Gleim, the high priest of the German cult of friendship, who was famous for the "friendship temple" in his garden in Halberstadt,[10] expressed the desire to be in a relationship similar to marriage with Johann Georg Jacobi. Jacobi, on the other hand, wrote to Jean Paul that he felt that friends should love each other exactly as wives love their husbands. The dramatist of the Storm and Stress, Jakob Michael Lenz, wrote an essay entitled *Unsere Ehe* (*Our Marriage*), in which he compared his relationship with Goethe to that of a marriage. In his fiery letter of 7 January 1805, Heinrich von Kleist declares his love for Ernst von Pfuel with the request that two authors live together, as man and wife. What these men meant with these metaphors of marriage is unclear from a late twentieth-century perspective. It might seem that the only characteristic distinguishing the married couple from the unmarried couple is the ability to have religiously sanctioned sex. On the other hand, perhaps there were other features to married life that struck these poets as desirable when they expressed their wish to marry each other.[11]

Gleim's outlook on eros and friendship suggests how closely associated the two concepts were in the eighteenth century. When Christoph Martin Wieland expressed in a letter concern regarding the novelist Heinse's "priapism," Gleim responded that many claimed that "German youth first heard of Greek love from Wieland himself and then began to keep Ganymedes,"[12] pointing to the importance of literature in constructing paradigms of sexuality and friendship. His tone is lighthearted, and if any moralism is involved, it is a censure of Wieland's new prudishness. Gleim's lack of defensiveness with regard to same-sex desire is remarkable in a poet who celebrates a love between members of the same sex. The most famous document of this friendship was the correspondence between Gleim and Jacobi in the years 1767–68. Gleim filled his letters with such eyebrow-raising, gender-bending effusions as the following declaration of love to Jacobi:

> I would like to be a girl:
> He would marry me;
> He wouldn't lack for friends,
> Nor for love, nor for wine:
> I would like to be his girl![13]

Admittedly, Gleim, who has devoted his life to the study of friendship, is more cautious in his theoretical distinctions, differentiating between love and friendship. He argues that the latter is superior, in that it fills the soul entirely. Whereas one can be unfaithful in love, one can't be unfaithful in friendship. Reflecting on Jacobi's numerous affairs with women, Gleim reverses his opinion on his own gender, announcing: "O how happy I am, how fortunate, that I'm not a girl, for then it would be possible that my Jacobi would be unfaithful to me."[14] Given the context, this reversal of opinion seems to be more a concession to Jacobi's womanizing than an effort to remove sensuality from same-sex friendship.

Indeed, the very lack of a difference between same-sex friendship and love between men and women so enthused Jacobi that he could write to Jean Paul that friends should love each other as wives love their husbands (Dietrich); once again, textual documents connect Jean Paul, writing at the end of the century, to the great friends of previous generations. Jacobi's remark to Jean Paul shows how desirous he is of uniting the phenomena of love and friendship; he makes the claim just as strongly in his letter dated 24 August 1767 to Gleim: "Yes, my dearest friend, friendship is not far from

love. At your departure, I felt everything that a lover can feel, not except-
ing even the small circumstances that are so interesting for him."[15] Unless
Jacobi assumes that a lover does not have any sensual experiences in relation
to his beloved, he must be asserting a certain sensuality in the friendship
between men.

Significantly, the correspondence between Gleim and Jacobi was scan-
dalous in its day. Gleim's friend, the poet Anne Luise Karsch, censored him
mildly with the reproach: "there are too many kisses for this love to be able
to escape libel, suspicion and mockery."[16] Thus it is not modernity alone
that finds the expressions of love in the cult of friendship ambiguous. Instead, the eighteenth century was becoming deeply concerned with the diffuse eroticism found in the writings of friendship.

One of the last to write unabashedly in the mode of friendship was the
Swiss historian Johannes von Müller. In a classic example of how one is
usually *not* supposed to read documents of the cult of friendship, *The Gay
Book of Days* gives an entry to Johannes von Müller, near such luminar-
ies as J. Edgar Hoover, Joe Orton, Sherlock Holmes, and Francis Poulenc.[17]
This publication, which bears the subtitle "An Evocatively Illustrated Who's
Who of Who Is, Was, May Have Been, Probably Was, and Almost Certainly
Seems to Have Been Gay During the Past 5,000 Years" would seem most unlikely to have an interest in a Swiss historian of the late eighteenth century.
Its reason for including Müller is the beauty of his letters to Charles von
Bonstetten, "love letters, among the loveliest every penned" (18). A closer
look at the Müller case justifies *The Gay Book of Days* by revealing that the
ambiguity that allows the book to include Müller was just as present by the
end of the eighteenth century as it is in the twentieth.

In the foreword to the *Biographische Denkwürdigkeiten* (*Biographical
Memorabilia*), the editor of Müller's collected works, a relative named Johann Georg Müller, describes the meeting between the older Müller and
Bonstetten as follows: "At that moment the lightning struck that sparked
a quickly moving, all-encompassing fire, that friendship whose documents
Friederike Brun, the Danish muse, worthy of the same sentiments, brought
to the eyes of the public; a friendship of the strictest, purest virtue, in every
other way the same as those ancient Greek friendships that brought forth
the best and greatest things" (4:viii–ix). Interestingly, Johann Georg Müller
has no interest in defending the Greek friendships with regard to their strict
and pure virtue: Johannes von Müller's friendship is "in every other way"

similar to the Greek friendships. Johann Georg Müller does feel the need to defend the purity of the letters that Brun published without the permission of Johannes von Müller. In fact, many at the time doubted the purity of those letters, for which reason Müller had to defend himself, although he insisted that he would never take back the sentiments expressed in the letters. Reflecting on the scandal provoked by Bruns's publication of the letters, Müller writes to Gleim, whose own letters had scandalized the country, "What I said about my intimate love to you, what I said in general . . . I am proud of, I won't hide it" (17:204). The denial by both the Müllers of an impure content in Johannes von Müller's letters indicates precisely that the sexuality of letters was a debatable point in the late eighteenth century.

Both Paul Derks and Simon Richter have written about the Batthyani scandal, which damaged Müller's reputation almost irreparably. One of Müller's students faked letters from a putative "Count Batthyani," who, like Müller, was unmarried, looking for a friend, loved antiquities, and otherwise seemed to be Müller's "type." In the course of the correspondence, Müller's student slipped requests for money into the letters. By the time the fraud was detected, Müller was ruined financially, mortified socially, and had to leave Vienna. The social mortification came about because these letters, filled as they were with the discourse of friendship, were as sexually suspect at the end of the eighteenth century as they are at the end of the twentieth.

Prior to the Batthyani affair, Müller had another encounter with a man that also instructively underscores the eroticism of eighteenth-century friendship. In 1797, Müller met a Marquis and fell for him with a passion that bears all the mark of falling in love. He writes about their meeting to his brother:

> It was the coming together of two people determined for each other by eternity, and I cannot say which of the two felt it first and most warmly; just as little could I say that I thought in this moment of his extraordinary charm, which wins all hearts for him, or of the rich and fine culture of his mind, his wide knowledge, his honest, sensitive, religious heart; indeed I discovered these perfections for the most part later, but the harmony of the whole transported me, I felt that I would be his and he mine, before I knew why. (6:123)

Although these flowery passages seem like love at first sight, they could still be interpreted as a kind of chaste friendship. The next letter that Müller writes to his brother attempts to force just such a sexless interpretation:

> I had previously poured out my heart to you regarding my friend, and then it occurred to me to wonder whether you, accustomed to feeling more quietly, might not find my youthful fire (for I feel I am not over 25!) crazy, whether you might not *discuss* with a witty remark the tender bloom that rejoices my heart, whether you would treat everything in the friendly way that otherwise characterizes you; and this disturbed me especially because I would be responsible for it: for Ch[ilesien], although Italian, and although 13 years my junior, and although poet, and although he loves me uncommonly, would however not have written the way I did, and disapproved when I showed it to him. . . . (6:127).

In hastening to endorse an asexual interpretation of the friendship, Müller is underlining the confusion that is possible between erotic relationships and friendships. Both the Marquis and Müller's brother would not have used the same language in describing this friendship, presumably because such language was already erotically suspect. Thus interpreting these passages is confusing not only for twentieth-century readers, but also for eighteenth-century ones. Müller was willingly entering a linguistically suspect arena when he indulged in his flowery declarations of love.

These issues of interpretation appear in the more traditional literary genres, as well as in published letters. Many of Friedrich Schiller's writings are infused with intense male bonding that has recurrently allowed for queer interpretations. Hammer finds in Schiller's writings "intermale relationships so passionate that they interrupt and violate the standard circuit of male homosocial bonding."[18] Schiller's ode "Friendship" (1782) demonstrates his interest in the phenomenon of same-sex intimacies, as does the play that Hammer deals with most intensely, *Wallenstein* (begun in 1797 and published in 1800), "the dramatic creation most overtly concerned with manhood, homosocial bonds" (161). Although (or perhaps because) the play concentrates on the masculine arena, it displays friendships of the kind that the poets wrote about in their letters to each other. Wallenstein admits to taking on the feminine role in his care and love for Max:

I myself was your female nurse, I was not ashamed
Of small services, I tended you
With a woman's bustling care.[19]

He does this all because of his love for Max: "you I *loved*" (l. 2157). Passages like this have provoked a steady stream of queer appropriations of these texts throughout the twentieth century. In *Wallenstein,* Schiller is content to allow the sexual ambiguity to sit, unresolved.

A short story by Schiller, *Spiel des Schicksals* (*Play of Fate*) thematizes the haziness of the boundaries between friendship and erotics. In this story, a prince is quite taken with a young man named G*, "the very image of blooming health and Herculean strength" (5:36). Explicitly, the prince is not interested solely in G*'s mind, but also finds his body attractive: "If the prince was entranced by the mind of his young companion, this seductive exterior irresistibly transported his sensuality" (5:36). The relationship blurs the boundary between friendship and love: "Equality of age, harmony of inclinations and character established quickly a relationship between them that possessed all the strength of friendship and all the fire and turbulence of passionate love" (5:36–37). In the course of time, a count, Josef Martinego, manages to insinuate himself into the good graces of the prince. In order to have the prince all to himself, the count urges the prince to indulge in unnamed "vices." Knowing that "nothing is more entitled to a bolder intimacy than the co-knowledge of secretly held weaknesses, the Count awakens passions in the Prince that had until now still slumbered": "He carried him away to such excesses as permit the fewest witnesses and accessories" (5:39). Derks argues convincingly that these unnamed, secret vices are very probably sexual; the fact that the prince subsequently has a string of other male "favorites" allows one to presume that the vices are homosexual in nature. In this story, Schiller clearly meditates on the vagaries of friendship and its proximity to vice.

Like *Wallenstein,* Schiller's *Don Carlos* was picked up by early twentieth-century writers as a text dealing with male-male desire—most famously by Thomas Mann, whose Tonio Kröger uses the play as a way of getting to know Hans Hansen. The play is a network of male-male desire. Tonio Kröger concentrates on the king's love for Posa, while other readers from the beginning of the twentieth century concentrated on the love between Posa and Don Carlos. Referring to the sacrifices that Don Carlos makes for Posa, one writer from the early homosexual rights movement laments dramatically that "already now in our materialistic, egotistical time, boys and youths who let themselves be beaten bloody for their beloved friend as Schiller reports of Don Carlos, are becoming rare."[20] However, not only twentieth-century readers find such possibilities in the text. In 1788 Schiller himself had to answer the argument that the play presents "passionate friendship" as a viable alternative to "passionate love": "You claimed recently to have found evidence in *Don Carlos* that *passionate friendship* could be just as moving a subject for tragedy as *passionate love*" (2:230). While Schiller denies this argument, his discussion of the issue underscores the many possible interpretations that the eighteenth century gave to accounts of friendship in literature.

While Schiller denies the relevance of passionate friendship to *Don Carlos,* he admits that he is interested in handling precisely this theme in another work, *Die Malteser* (*The Maltese*). In *Die Malteser* it becomes clear that the distinction between "passionate friendship" and "passionate love" is subtle indeed. The work, which is linked with *Don Carlos* in that it treats the all-male knightly order to which Carlos's friend Posa belongs, was to feature two characters, Crequi and St. Priest, who were to be lover and beloved. Although in his notes Schiller dutifully assures the reader that this love is "pure," he also refuses to desensualize it: "Their love is of the purest beauty, but it is nonetheless necessary not to take from it the sensual character which grounds it in nature. It may and must be felt that it is a transference of sexual love, a surrogate of the same, and an effect of nature" (3:172). This emphasis on the sexual in the relationship between the two men recurs repeatedly in his notes. Clarifying Crequi's love for St. Priest, Schiller writes, "His passion is true sexual love and makes itself known through a concern for little things, through raging jealousy, through sensual adoration of the figure, through other symptoms" (3:173). The actors are even encouraged to show their love so far that the audience is suspicious: "The lover may demonstrate his tenderness so blatantly, although it could appear to be suspicious" (3:171–72). Once again, it is not the case that only modern eyes find reason for suspicion in this text: Schiller fully expected his contemporaries to confront issues of same-sex desire within the context of friendship. And why should eighteenth-century readers have regarded passionate friendship as significantly different from passionate love if it was to exhibit all the symptoms of that love? In all probability, the directness with which Schiller phrased this question made it impossible for him to finish the drama.

Jean Paul is another author whose accounts of friendship have always lent themselves to queer interpretation. His novel *Siebenkäs,* for instance, is filled with male-male kisses and embraces. Even the narrator gets into the action, occasionally interrupting his narrative in order to lament tearfully the absence of friends of Jean Paul's, such as for instance Gleim. There are warrior scenes in which young male friends lie intertwined with each other: "they lay clinging to each other on the waves of life, like two ship-wrecked brothers, who swim in the cold waves, embraced and embracing, and hold nothing more than the heart of which they are dying" (713). Elsewhere, a similarly masochistically tinged, homoerotic fantasy appears: "Finally the smoke rolled apart over the two bloody people, who lay in each other's wounded arms, it was two sublime friends, who had sacrificed everything for each other, themselves first, but not their fatherland. 'Lay your wounds on mine, beloved!—Now we can be reconciled again; you have sacrificed me to the fatherland and I you.—Give me your heart again, before it bleeds to death.—Ah! We can die together!'" (679). Jean Paul further draws on anthropological reports of his time to invoke utopias where male partnerships are blessed, like Tahiti, where the men "exchange names as well as hearts with their [male] beloveds" (474), and the Balkans, where male-male partnerships are blessed like marriages between men and women. In these visions, Jean Paul erases the boundaries between same-sex friendship and heterosexual love, and allows for ambiguous interpretations.

The ambiguity surrounding friendship in the eighteenth century made it appropriate for literature, which by its nature encourages multiple interpretations and always seeks to free itself from the tyranny of specific meanings. Jean Paul's ambiguity runs against the current of his time, however, which was distinguishing increasingly strictly between sexual and nonsexual friendship. Of course, none of the writings from the earlier parts of the eighteenth century actively promoted sexual friendship. Indeed, sexual friendship was clearly tabu, as Giseke's description of friendship as "couragous in love and pure in intention" indicates.[21] Giseke's poem "Schreiben über die Zärtlichkeit der Freundschaft" ("Treatise on the Tenderness of Friendship"), which documents some of the rules for friendship in the earlier part of the eighteenth century, is filled with embraces and declarations of love, yet it does insist on the purity of friendship: ". . . Too proud for coarser drives / He devotes himself exclusively to friendly love."[22] A major goal of friendship is to keep the friend on the straight and narrow, pointing out his failings to him and encouraging him to pursue the good. While such a conceptualization of friendship might seem a bit dry and explain the relative obscurity of Giseke, the very presence of these admonishing remarks indicates that even a very religious man like Giseke could envision a more sexual kind of friendship. Similarly, Adelung's dictionary defines friendship both as occurring between members of the same sex and as explicitly asexual: "reciprocal love of two people, without a difference of sex and without any intention of satisfaction of sensual desires."[23] In an era in which homosexuality was still undefined, it is surprising that the lexicographer found it necessary to confirm that a laudable relationship between members of the same sex had no intention of satisfying sexual desires. Clearly, it was possible in the eighteenth century to conduct a friendship in a way that led some people to believe that the intentions of one or both sides were less than honorable.

Much of the earliest discussion of same-sex relationships took place in the context of the study of antiquity. Classicists were trying to come to terms with descriptions of intense male-male friendships in the texts of ancient Greece and gradually came to the conclusion that these relationships had a certain level of eroticism. Johann Georg Hamann, for instance, reached his conclusion on the sensuality of all friendship in his *Sokratische Denkwürdigkeiten* (*Socratic Memorabilia*), published in 1759: "One cannot feel a lively friendship without sensuality."[24] But while Hamann was open to the possibility that modern friendships were like Greek friendships and that both shared a common sensuality, the aesthetician Friedrich Wilhelm Basileus Ramdohr is more typical of the end of the eighteenth century when he tries in 1798 to distinguish rigorously between Greek friendships and Greek love. He concludes that the love documented in ancient Greek texts was in fact not friendship: "It therefore cannot be maintained that the love of youths, as it was approved by the morals of the time of the Socratic School, was friendship. It was rather a tenderness based on sexual sympathy and even on bodily drives."[25] Ramdohr does attempt to preserve the dignity and honor of some of the ancient Greeks by denying that this love was entirely carnal: "On the other hand, it was also not—as others have maintained—the consequence of coarse physical desire. This only crept in and occasionally took the upper hand" (3:150). His willingness to concede that coarse bodily love did intrude occasionally and sometimes take over makes his defence a qualified one at best. In any case, he insists that "a confusion between love and friendship is never found in Xenophon and Plato" (3:152). Ramdohr feels that his own era has been much more lax about this distinction than the ancient world: "There hasn't been an appropriate differentiation between friendship and sexual tenderness, at least not until now. It has been said: Friendship is a weaker degree of love! But what is love here? And what constitutes its strength? Is there not the word of a friend who said to the other: your love was more to me than the love of women!" (1:208). The ancient tradition, which had been used by Hamann to plumb the depths of sexuality within friendship, was now employed to disengage sexuality from friendship.

In the course of distinguishing friendship from sexual relations between members of the same sex, Ramdohr helps establish a new sexuality. In order to distinguish true friendship from sexually tinged relationships between members of the same sex, Ramdohr calls for a "semiotics, doctrine of signs for differentiation of friendship from sexual tenderness" (1:229). The circumstance that both partners in a friendship might belong to the same sex is only "an ambiguous sign for distinguishing friendship from sexual tenderness" (1:229) because members of the same sex could in fact have a sexual relationship with each other: "On the other hand there are enough cases in which so-called male friends and female friends felt true sexual tenderness for each other" (1:231). He has "countless" examples of this happening (2:104). Ramdohr explains such relationships by asserting that bodily sex is only loosely related to a person's actual gender. A relationship could therefore consist of a masculine woman and a feminine man, as well as a number of other possible combinations: "men can live in domesticity happily together with men, women with women, or finally men with women—in every relationship of this sort, one is always in word and deed the leading, ruling one, the other always the one who acquiesces but profits" (1:174). With this alternative interpretation of the household, Ramdohr is on the verge of identifying people by their sexual orientation. The consequence of removing sexuality from friendship is the creation of the homosexual.

Ramdohr has not received the credit that he is due for conceptualizing a category of people who love members of their own sex (or, as he would put it, people who love people who have the same bodily sex as they do). He believes that such people have an essential urge that comes from the origins of their being: "Desires that are based on the original construction and development of our being do not deserve reproach and their striving for union cannot be attributed to the goal of satisfaction of an unnatural desire" (3:205). Since these desires are based on a natural urge, they should not be criticized. For this reason he admonishes those who criticize Winckelmann or other art connoisseurs who are peculiarly susceptible to this kind of desire: "Shame on him who suspects something shameful here. It happened unselfconsciously, it happened publicly, as evidence for the involuntary movement of sexual sympathy, which was probably unknown to the enthusiast himself" (2:134). Indeed, this desire should never be considered a perversion or even an error: "In no people in the world can one consider the desires for union of such bodies that according to external characteristics belong to one sex, but in their organization actually stand in the harmonious relationship of the more delicate organization to the stronger, for a mere degeneration of sensuality or a confusion of nature" (3:137). Thus, although Ramdohr does not have the vocabulary of "homosexual" to work with, he is part of the project of establishing a category of person whose essential being prepares him or her to love exclusively and sexually members of his or her own sex. And while such a move is on one level liberating and clearly antimoralistic, it also comes at a cost: the cost of desexualizing friendship.

A generation later, Heinrich Hössli critiques, develops, and cements Ramdohr's observations. Horrified by an 1817 murder in which the thirty-two-year-old lawyer Dr. Franz Desgouttes had killed his beloved roommate, the twenty-two-year-old Daniel Hemmeler, Heinrich Hössli commissioned a novelistic treatment of the subject from the Swiss writer Heinrich Zschokke. Hössli, who wanted to delve sympathetically into the realm of male-male love, was unsatisfied with Zschokke's treatment, finding it too moralistic. For this reason, he wrote his own account, a two-volume treatise defending male-male love, published 1836–38. Long before Foucauldians might expect it, Hössli is arguing for a type of man who is characterized by a sexual orientation toward other men: "there is a certain man-loving, purely humane type of male person."[26] He concludes his book on a similar note: "Masculine love . . . is its own special certain type, just a twig of the general sexual life, which can just as little become a native love for the other sex, as that kind of love could conversely ever intentionally restructure itself as the other" (2:319).

Hössli and his era are clearly moving toward seeing sexuality as more than an act, but as a major determinant in identity. One of Hössli's sources, a certain J. H. Schmid, points out that the "concept of sexuality is no longer determined exclusively by sexual organs, but rather by the entire organism" (1:302). Indeed, the entire personality is based on sexuality according to Hössli

> The roots of the love, however, with the research of whose nature we are concerned here, was and is sexual love (we are not speaking here merely of the sexual drive), because this sexual love involuntarily desires, searches for, and needs a male being, precisely because of his sex, and not a female being, again precisely because of her sex—for what alone speaks to us, grabs us, excites us, carries us away, attracts us, takes us in possession, completes us, perfects us, that says which love is in us. (2:348)

This is an early document for the importance of sexuality as a fundamental of the psychology of that new creature called "man" that Foucault asserts is less than two centuries old.[27]

In this new creature, the sexual orientation of those who love their own sex is natural and as unchangeable as that of those who love the other sex: "The large and general part that loves the other sex can never have the nature of those who do not love the other sex, and those who love their own sex cannot become lovers of the other sex" (2:5). Like Ramdohr, Hössli is determined to distinguish "masculine love" from "the love of souls" or friendship. Working with the Greeks, he points out that their male love affairs always contained a lover and a beloved, whereas friendship was reciprocal and not directional in its nature. Friendship seems to take a while to develop, being intellectual and emotional, whereas "sexual love" had its "roots in the corporeal" (2:223). Like Ramdohr, Hössli depicts same-sex love with a minimum of moralizing and helps establish a category that is waiting for the identity-based terminology of the second half of the nineteenth century. At the same time, however, he helps close down the possibility of a sexually diffuse friendship that thrived on a generalized eroticism.

With the arrival of an increasingly well-defined state of being that would become known as "homosexuality," it becomes impossible for men to make the kind of declarations of love to each other that was more common among the poets of the eighteenth century. Already Giseke was concerned that

"there are only a few left who can love nobly."[28] Like many later thinkers on the subject, Giseke is convinced that friendship is an old and dying
art. Müller also insisted that the "moderns" failed to understand his notion
of friendship. Writing to the fictional "Batthyani," he underscores how few
people understand the thought of friendship: "Often the thought of friendship, which so few today completely grasp, uplifts my heart." The tone
is similar when he writes to Gleim defending his earlier declarations of
friendship. Müller anticipates the twentieth century in claiming that modern readers don't understand the textual friendship of the eighteenth century. While perhaps these "misunderstandings" are less serious than Giseke
and Müller claim, it is certainly true that by the end of the eighteenth century, characters in literature increasingly steer clear of effusive declarations
of love lest they be marked as a specific type of lover of men. The expulsion of sex from friendship begins to create modern heterosexuals, as well
as modern homosexuals.

Schiller provides an excellent example of this process. While his sexually ambiguous *Don Carlos* was written mainly in the 1780s, he makes much
more clear the sexual boundaries of *Wilhelm Tell,* which appeared in 1803
and was the last work he completed. Although Schiller pays hommage in
Wilhelm Tell to "a reliable man / Johannes Müller . . . von Schaffhausen" (ll.
2947–48), he avoids all the sexual complexities that were associated with
Müller. Like Schiller's other works, *Wilhelm Tell* is still all about men and
patriarchy, but it clearly posits that patriarchy is heterosexual. Again and
again, the men bond over their control over women. In the opening scenes,
Baumgarten defends his actions against Wolfenschießen, "the violator of my
honor and my wife" (l. 82). As Baumgarten tries to convince the ferryman
to take him across the river despite a dangerous storm, his supporters point
out that he is "a father of a family, with wife and children!" (l. 133). The ferryman points out that he, too, has "wife and children at home" (l. 115). Once
Tell agrees to take upon the heroic task of transporting Baumgarten across
the lake, he asks the shepherd to console his wife (ll. 158–59). When the
patriots decide to stand up for their rights, these rights are clearly marked as
fatherly and husbandly: Stauffacher exclaims, "We stand for our land / We
stand for our wives, our children!" (ll. 1286–87). The latter part of the exclamation, about wives and children, becomes the refrain that the entire crowd
repeats (l. 1288), which suggests that the domestic relationship to wife and
children is even more important to these men than their patriotism. Thus

the struggle for freedom is inextricably linked with patriarchal power in Schiller's representation. But while this power had seemed infused with the possibility of male-male love in his earlier works, such ambiguities are completely ruled out in *Wilhelm Tell,* which makes clear the heterosexuality of its characters.

While most of the descendents of the erotic participants of the eighteenth-century friendship cult become clearly attached to wives and children, others seem to be more explicitly lovers of men. Out of the ashes of the cult of friendship comes the character constellation that will draw upon itself the name "homosexual." As the incendiary force of friendship disappeared, sexual identity began to make its appearance. Initially these characters are in fact specifically modeled on the cult of friendship. When Johannes Friedel describes in his anonymously published *Briefe über die Galanterien von Berlin auf einer Reise gesammelt von einem österreichischen Offizier* (*Letters on the Galantries of Berlin, Collected on a Trip by an Austrian Officer* [1782]) a small circle of "the warm," men who love men, he admits that he at first had not recognized them as what they were because he thought they were just close friends: "I assumed all these scenes took place in the tone of friendship, true masculine sympathy of the soul's mood. And observing from the side, I admired the small group of cordial friends."[29] It is worth reemphasizing that as long as friendship was a potent force in society, people found it hard to distinguish between legitimate and erotic friendship. This possible confusion is an example of what Luhmann refers to in a footnote as "the difficult question of homosexuality as a secret mortgage on the concept of friendship."[30] In part because of these anxieties, the paneroticism of eighteenth-century friendship gave way to clearer definitions of homosexuality and heterosexuality.

In this era, some of the first literary depictions of men who love men show up. *Ein Jahr in Arkadien: Kyllenion* (*A Year in Arcadia: Kyllenion*), published in 1805 by August, Duke of Sachsen-Gotha and Altenburg, is perhaps the earliest homoerotic novel in the German tradition. It depicts the love between a nobleman and a shepherd: "Alexis the splendid and Julanthiskos, the no less dear."[31] They see each other at a dance, appreciate each other's beauty, and even dance with each other. Julanthiskos is completely smitten with the prince, but Alexis, in the whirl of his social life, only toys with the shepherd boy's affections. After other romances are brought to a conclusion, Julanthiskos chances upon his beloved Alexis, lying wounded and covered with blood in the forest: "as they slept mouth on mouth on the soft moss in a Kyllenian cave, the youths were finally found by Alexis's slaves" (79). The rest is history: "Alexis the saved was no longer ungrateful and Julanthisko the finder was no longer unhappy" (79). The two go on to live together, like all the other lovers in the story. In keeping with its aristocratic pedigree, *Kyllenion* conservatively holds on to the traditions of the erotic friendships, refusing to create a rigorous boundary between nonerotic and erotic friendships. All of the pairs in the novella, regardless of whether they consist exclusively of men or of men and women, are friends intellectually, emotionally, and physically. One would not be able to distinguish between the friendship that obtains between the men and women and the friendship between Julanthiskos and Alexis. The only aspect that gives it a sharper, more modern edge is the openness with which it suggests a permanent physical relationship between the two men.

August von Platen provides a compelling example of a poet using the accoutrements of friendship to reach a notion of something like sexual identity. According to his autobiographical writings, Platen, who lived from 1796 to 1835, dealt intensively with issues of love and friendship during the years of his adolescence and his young adulthood, from approximately 1806 to 1818. He indicates that he began with a desire for love, but was restricted by his knowledge of friendship only: "I wanted love; but I had until then only felt the desire for friendship . . . my first inclination was for a man. I may not add that I didn't have any conception of unplatonic love."[32] The complicated negation of the final sentence stutteringly admits his desires for a carnal relationship with another man, although he later claims that he "had in those days no idea that a punishable relationship could exist between two men" (65). Despite his claim that he "ignored the possibility that sensual pleasure could play a role in this" (65), Platen describes attempting to use friendship in order to achieve the goals of marriage: "I became accustomed to wasting my hopes and dreams of love on people of my own sex and sought to achieve in their friendship that goal that the lover seeks in marriage" (61). Arguably, "that goal," the one goal that distinguishes marriage from a friendship, is sexual satisfaction. Nonetheless, Platen strives to bring "true friendship" and "pure love" together in order to satisfy his inclinations (61). Friendship continues to interest him enough that he would like to write "an academic treatment on friendship among men" (90), but he nonetheless seems to reach a point where friendship doesn't bother him as much as it did: "The fight in my breast between love and friendship has been calmed" (92). While it might seem that Platen is able to rehabilitate the eighteenth-century notion of an ambiguously erotic friendship, in fact the reconciliation that he effects between friendship and love has a much more strident and self-assured ring to it: "I don't need to be ashamed of what my own conscious considers good," he asserts about the kinds of friendships that he would like to have (92). At times, he seems to broach the possibility of a natural orientation toward members of his own sex: "But what should make me tremble the most is that my inclinations are oriented far more toward my own sex than they are toward the feminine sex. Can I change what is not my doing?" (102). Half a century prior to Foucault's "birth of the homosexual," a certain type of natural sexual identity was being constructed out of the ruins of friendship.

The Swiss author Heinrich Zschokke's novella *Der Eros*, from 1821,[33] portrays even more clearly the emergence of someone whose identity is shaped by his love of members of his own sex. Commissioned by Hössli, who then rejected it, Zschokke's work deserves attention as a document in the creation of modern sexual identities. In the novella, news of a terrible murder similar to the Desgouttes case that so preoccupied Hössli sparks a discussion concerning friendship and love. Referring to same-sex friendship, one character opines that it is "the most unsuspicious love of souls" (219). Reflecting on such friendships in ancient Greece, another character, Holmar, argues that the male-male love that took place then could not be classified as friendship or as love today: "I can give it neither the name of love, nor that of friendship, because we associate completely different conceptions with such names" (226). He posits a time when there was a kind of middle way between love and friendship, something like the erotic friendship with which the poets of the eighteenth century had experimented. For Holmar, timeless emotions like "love" and "friendship" turn out to have culturally particular histories. Specifically, in his society—nineteenth-century central Europe—notions of love and friendship have become polarized so that there can be no overlap between them.

Arguing for a return to a less restrictive range of emotional possibilities, Holmar believes that all early peoples had friendships of the kind that existed in ancient Greece (227). He concedes that sometimes "among dissolute souls the holy fire of Eros probably now and then inflamed the depraved desires of bestiality" (228), admitting the nearness of this love to erotic love. While he does in fact generally strive to preserve the "purity" of this love, Zsochkke views it as "a natural drive, like the reciprocal inclination for each other of the sexes, or like the instinct of the mother and the infant" (232). While all young, virile, natural societies exhibit such love (227), decadent, unnatural, more civilized ones penalize it, forcing the young man who loves other men into a frightening and criminal subculture (235). For such a man "his existence was his crime," according to Holmar, who continues: "he had to become a murderer because he had disintegrated into the most irreconcilable conflict within himself and with the whole world, he had to disintegrate, he who in more humane time periods would have made himself and others happy" (221). In depicting the crisis of friendship, Zschokke also sets the stage for a personal identity, based in nature, corrupted by society, that is characterized by the love of members of one's own sex.

As sexuality becomes more and more clearly excluded from notions of friendship, friendship itself becomes increasingly less provocative, suggesting that it was the potential for sex that had made friendship so enticing in the eighteenth century. If there were men who clearly love men and men who did not love men, the ambiguity and complexity of friendship in the eighteenth century became much less troubling. One merely had to determine whether the friends were "just friends" or "more than friends." For this reason perhaps, Sigismund Wiese's drama *Die Freunde. Trauerspiel in 3 Akten* (*The Friends. Tragedy in 3 Acts*)[34] did not cause the scandal that the collections of letters written by Gleim and others half a century earlier had. Although, as its title suggests, the play is as concerned with friendship, it did not draw upon itself accusations of immorality. Like the earlier works cited, it is filled with references to such famous pairs of friends as Jonathan and David, Achilles and Patrocles, and Orestes and Pylades. As one character looks for his beloved friend in the captured enemy lines, his assistant compares his desire to heterosexual love:

If ever a child of humanity
Searched with hotter ardor for his beloved woman
As you examine the rows of Frenchmen,
I'm no child of woman. Tell me
Are you in love, is she hiding in men's clothes?

(15)

When Philipp responds that he can't find "him," his assistant reacts with horror to the pronoun: "Him? Not her? Dear Philipp, what's that?" (15). There is a kind of emancipatory rhetoric in the play, but it never aroused censure, because by this point "friendship" was no longer considered an erotic category. One might think that a document endorsing passionate male-male friendship would create a scandal in the nineteenth century when the conventions of the cult of friendship were long gone. In fact, although eighteenth-century texts endorsing passionate friendship were controversial, despite the existence of a recognized discourse on friendship, the nineteenth-century text drew no attention to itself—because friendship had lost its erotic charge with the emergence of new sexual identities.

While the tradition of ambiguously erotic friendships was not gone for good—Walt Whitman, with his paeons to the societally beneficial adhesiveness of male bonding, would revitalize it at the end of the nineteenth century, both for the masculinists around the early homosexual rights publication *Der Eigene* (*The Exceptional*) and for the newly liberal Thomas Mann of the 1920s[35]—it lost considerable currency at the beginning of the nineteenth century. In the first decades of the nineteenth century, it was simply not interesting to portray erotic friendships between members of the same sex. Poets no longer offered to marry each other, and their characters stopped kissing members of their own sex—unless those characters were marked as having a specific identity surrounding that sexual urge. With the rise of such clearly marked sexual deviations, friendship became asexual, whereas it had been infused with a subtle eroticism. Sexuality became, in Sedgwick's terms, "minoritizing," rather than "majoritizing." Contrary to the assumptions of many modern critics, then, who argue that modern readers confuse friendship and love, thereby projecting too much eroticism into eighteenth-century friendships, friendship in the eighteenth century was far more erotic than modern friendship. Precisely because modern readers have learned from late eighteenth-century writers to distinguish so precisely between love and friendship, modern friendship lacks the erotics of that earlier era.

NOTES

1. "Michel Foucault: An Interview," *Edinburgh Review* (1986): 52–59.

2. *The History of Sexuality. Volume 1: An Introduction,* trans. Robert Hurley (New York: Random House, 1980), 43.

3. *The Epistemology of the Closet* (Berkeley: University of California Press, 1990), 52.

4. Fritz Brüggemann and Helmut Pautian, eds., *Der Aufbruch der Gefühlskultur in den fünfziger Jahren*, vol. 7 of *Deutsche Literatur. Reihe Aufklärung* (Darmstadt: Wissenschaftliche Buchgesellschaft, 1966), 64.

5. Brüggemann, *Der Aufbruch*, 62.

6. Ibid., 54; Giseke, incidentally, also cites Pope in his discussion of friendship.

7. Jean Paul [= Johann Paul Friedrich Richter], *Jean Paul. Werke in drei Bänden*, vol. 1 (Munich: Hanser, 1969), 495.

8. Brüggemann, *Der Aufbruch*, 63.

9. Johannes von Müller, *Sämtliche Werke*, (Tübingen: Cotta, 1811–1815), 17:274.

10. Paul Derks, *"Die Schande der heiligen Päderastie": Homosexualität und Öffentlichkeit in der deutschen Literatur 1750–1850* (Berlin: Rosa Winkel, 1990), 587.

11. Luhmann points out that marriage was also undergoing a change in eighteenth-century Germany, and public moralists were for the first time calling upon men to be friends with their wives. At the same time that the poets are attempting to restructure their friendships along the lines of marriage, others are attempting to recast marriage along the lines of friendship. It becomes impossible to determine which institution is copying which.

12. Derks, *"Die Schande,"* 234.

13. Hans Dietrich [= Hans Dietrich Hellbach], *Die Freundesliebe in der deutschen Literatur*. Nachdruck der Ausgabe Leipzig 1931. Homosexualität und Literatur, 9 (Berlin: Rosa Winkel, 1996), 30.

14. Brüggemann, *Der Aufbruch*, 204.

15. Ibid., 202.

16. Simon Richter, "Winckelmann's Progeny: Homosocial Networking in the Eighteenth Century," in *Outing Goethe and His Age*, ed. Alice Kuzniar (Stanford, Calif.: Stanford University Press, 1996), 36.

17. Martin Greif, *The Gay Book of Days* (Secaucus, N.J.: Mainstreet Press, 1982), 17–18.

18. Stephanie Barbe Hammer, "Schiller, Time and Again," *German Quarterly* 62.2 (1994): 155.

19. Friedrich Schiller, *Sämtliche Werke*, 5 vols, eds. Gerhard Fricke and Herbert G. Göpfert (Munich: Hanser, 1965), ll.2149–51.

20. Harry Oosterhuis, ed., *Homosexuality and Male Bonding in Pre-Nazi Germany: the Youth Movement, the Gay Movement, and Male Bonding Before Hitler's Rise. Original Transcript from "Der Eigene," the First Gay Journal in the World*, trans. Hubert Kennedy (New York: Harrington Park, 1991), 171.

21. Brüggemann, *Der Aufbruch*, 46.

22. Ibid., 45.

23. Johann Christoph Adelung, *Grammatisch-kritisches Wörterbuch der Hochdeutschen Mundart* (Vienna: Pichler, 1807), 2:285.

24. *Sämtliche Werke*, ed. Josef Nadler, vol. 2 (Vienna: Herder, 1950), 68.

25. *Venus Urania: Ueber die Natur der Liebe, über ihre Veredlung und Verschönerung,* 3 parts (Leipzig: Goschen, 1798), 3:150.

26. *Eros. Die Männerliebe der Griechen,* 3 vols. (Berlin: Rosa Winkel, 1996), 1:264.

27. *The Order of Things: An Archeology of the Human Sciences* (New York: Pantheon, 1970), xxiii.

28. Brüggemann, *Der Aufbruch,* 52.

29. Edited by Sonja Schnitzler (Berlin: Eulenspiegel, 1987), 138.

30. Niklas Luhmann, *Liebe als Passion: Zur Codierung von Intimität* (Frankfurt am Main: Suhrkamp, 1994), 147.

31. August Herzog von Sachsen-Gotha, *Ein Jahr in Arkadien. Kyllenion. Nachdruck der Ausgabe von 1805,* ed. Paul Derks (Berlin: Rosa Winkel, 1985), 106.

32. August von Platen, *Memorandum meines Lebens,* ed. Gert Mattenklott and Hansgeorg Schmidt-Bergmann (Frankfurt am Main: Insel, 1996), 49.

33. Reprinted in Hössli, vol. 3. 201–56.

34. *Drei Dramen,* (Leipzig: Brockhaus, 1836).

35. See Walter Grünzweig, *Constructing the German Walt Whitman* (Iowa City: University of Iowa Press, 1995).

11 Of National Poets and Their Female Companions

HERMAN RAPAPORT

Das Denken ist fast wie ein Mitdichten.
—Martin Heidegger, "Hölderlins Hymne 'Andenken'"

Among the central issues in German idealism to which contemporary German philosophers like Dieter Henrich and Manfred Frank have been returning is the so-called original insight of Johann Gottlieb Fichte, which concluded that the self cannot be understood apart from its being self-posited or self-asserted. Fichte, of course, was well aware that the act of self-assertion explicitly raised questions of self-presentation, self-construction, self-reflexion, self-objectification, and self-transcendence, in other words, a battery of problems that organize themselves under the general rubric of "posure." Fichte himself put the question of positing, or posure, in an almost Heideggerian way when he wrote, "Thus the first question would be: how does the self exist for itself? The first postulate: Think of yourself, frame the concept of yourself; and notice how you do it." However, emphasis upon enframing was quickly subsumed by reflection theory. "Everyone who does no more than this [pose the question of the self] will find that in the thinking of this concept [one's] activity as an intelligence reverts into itself and makes itself its own object."[1]

In *Einführung in die frühromantische Ästhetik: Vorlesungen,* Manfred Frank provides some detailed historical accounts of how the German idealists developed the question of positing. He notices, for example, that Novalis had already begun to question positing of the self in terms of the relationship between being and reflection in the following citation. "Das Wesen der Identität läßt sich nur in einem Scheinsatz aufstellen."[2] Yet, if the question of identity and being is mediated by the posure of reflexive representations, for Novalis there nevertheless was a transcendental and unifying notion of Being that was not to be questioned in the same sense that, in reflection, a certain feeling unified and stabilized the subject's "Vertrautheit mit dem Selbst." No doubt, Manfred Frank's probing into the relationship between ontology and reflection theory is a historical follow-up to Martin Heidegger's late essay, "Kants These über das Sein" (1962), which aggressively reconceptualizes self-positing by means of citing passages in Kant's *Critique of Pure Reason* that provide an opportunity to question the subject-object relation that reflection theory presupposes.

Heidegger argues that already in Kant there may be an awareness that the object cannot be divorced from the question of the difference between Being and beings and that thinking is not, in fact, grounded in the "Ich-Subjekt," but is posited or posed in relation to how Being is positioned; thinking is in no way to be considered entirely independent of Being, but quite to the contrary, must be understood in terms of how Being is posited, posed, or positioned with respect to how subjects apprehend objects. Whereas the subject-object relation takes priority in much of reflection theory, Heidegger argues that, in fact, this relation is only the consequence of an ontological orientation or positioning that shows itself more or less explicitly from time to time in Kant's writings. Fundamental to Heidegger's analysis is the insight that Being may not be a fixed category that is identical to itself, nor posited or positioned in a determinate manner with respect to what Kant, in the *Critique of Pure Reason,* called "Sein und Denken." Whereas reflection theory drove Kant, Fichte, Schelling, and Hegel toward a dialectical mode of analysis, Heidegger's ontological considerations offer the possibility that the "Ich-Subjekt" can be thought of within a structure that does not give priority to the dialectical circularity of the reflection model developed in, say, Fichte's "Deduction of Presentation," which, as Jean Hippolyte tells us, was fundamental to Hegel's *Phenomenology of Spirit.*

Indeed it was Edmund Husserl who had already attacked the Kantian comprehension of "Sein und Denken." In *Ideas 1,* Husserl argued that the positing of intentionality—an already existing attitude presupposing the experience of something perceived as "there" or "on hand"—can be negated or called into question. Methodologically one can simply "parenthesize it." In so doing, Husserl suggested that one could interrogate the question of being, which may well be foundational for an understanding of how intentionality (but more generally, consciousness) is posited. Husserl spoke of this parenthesis, or epochê, as a means to acquire "a new region of being never before delimited in its own peculiarity."[3] But Heidegger, who was quite aware of Husserl's critique, thought that this "new region" should not be thought of as proper to consciousness, intentionality, or of the object, but as a place [Ort] cleared by Being. In the essay on Kant, Heidegger calls this place an *Ortsnetz*, a network, or more colloquially, telephone exchange. Oddly, it is in terms of such a telecommunications system that "das Sein als Position gehört." In short, the *Ortsnetz* (as opposed to the Kantian faculties) is the manifold of open relationships in the world, as such, within which we have to rethink Kantian reflection, and particularly as it concerns a subjectivity that in Heidegger has been exteriorized or drawn out of the self.

It is in this sense that the following passage on reflection radicalizes Kant. Indeed, Heidegger focuses on a reflective movement back to the "Ich-Subjekt" that breaks with the circularity of Kantian reflection thanks to the intercession of the *Ortsnetz im Ort des Seins*, which I translate as "telecommunications network in the neighborhood of Being." "Die Betrachtung geht nicht mehr geradezu auf das Objekt der Erfahrung, sie beugt sich zurück auf das erfahrende Subjekt, ist Reflexion. Kant spricht von 'Überlegung.' Achtet nun die Reflexion auf diejenigen Zustände und Verhältnisse des Vorstellens, dadurch überhaupt die Umgrenzung des Seins des Seienden möglich wird, dann ist die Reflexion auf das Ortsnetz im Ort des Seins eine transzendentale Reflexion. [Reflection is a way of thinking that is not directed immediately on the object of experience, but arches back to the experiencing subject. Kant speaks of "deliberation." Provided that reflection heeds the situations and conditions of presentation, through which above all the delimitation of the Being of beings would be made possible, reflection would be transcendental in terms of a communications network in the neighborhood of Being.]"[4]

No doubt, one could read this back into Heidegger's own writing on poetry. For example, one could begin to explore how a term like *Gespräch* is mediated by a conception closer to the *Ortsnetz* than, say, mere conversation or dialogue. In fact, I imagine that this kind of radical interpretation of *Gespräch* is what the philosopher Véronique Fóti had in mind when she translates the term into English as "destinal interlocution." In *Heidegger and the Poets*, Fóti purposely avoids the word "conversation" because it does not reflect the openness or indetermination of Being that is fundamental to its Heideggerian call. In short, the term interlocution is used to denote something other than dialogue, or to put it another way, speculative reflection. Thanks to an interlocution, as opposed to mere dialogue, the poet achieves a subjectivity of the *Ortsnetz*, a tele-communication, which suggests that there is always more than one subjectivity on the line. Hence the interlocution with Being takes into account a subjectivity that is by no means solitary, but, rather, is brought into relation with Being by means of an other [Mitsein]. Indeed, Heidegger himself pointed to this potential in poetry when he said of Hölderlin's hymn "Andenken," "das Denken ist fast wie ein Mitdichten."

In terms of Dorothy Wordsworth and Suzette Gontard—the respective female companions of William Wordsworth and Friedrich Hölderlin—this remark broaches questions of how the poet's self-positing may be internally divided or shared with an other who is the poet's friend or companion. In particular, it raises the question of how a self-positing can be conceptualized from the standpoint of a "destinal interlocution," which I take to be a fateful speaking given or destined alongside that of the poet in which is manifest a positing, positioning, or posure that is not self-identical or present to itself and, as such, cannot be constituted or objectified through self-reflection per se. Such positing or posure would not be totalizable or unifiable, but characterized by a rupture, which I would like to call a caesura of difference that preserves an alterity even as it denies separability. It is this caesura that we will see figured in the abysses of the poets and their companions.

I

In May of 1800, Dorothy Wordsworth began *The Grasmere Journal*, a text influential for her brother's most important lyrics. In her first entry, May 1800, Dorothy Wordsworth addresses the departure of her brother on a trip, which will separate them for some days. "My heart was so full that I could hardly speak to W. when I gave him a farewell kiss," she wrote.

I sate a long time upon a stone at the margin of the lake, and after a flood of tears my heart was easier. The lake looked to me I knew not why dull and melancholy, the weltering on the shores seemed a heavy sound. I walked as long as I could amongst the stones of the shore. The wood rich in flowers. A beautiful yellow, palish yellow flower, that looked thick round and double, and smelt very sweet—I supposed it was a ranunculus — Crowfoot, the grassy-leaved Rabbit-toothed white flower, strawberries, Geranium — scentless violet, anemones two kinds, orchises, primroses. The heckberry very beautiful as a low shrub. The crab coming out. Met a blind man driving a very large beautiful Bull and a cow — he walked with two sticks.

There are no gods in the passage, no longing for Ancient Greece, no commemorative greetings, no heroes, and moreover, no national poet. Instead the sister, having bade the poet farewell, sits behind by the margin of the lake where one day she will see a raft of daffodils flashing beneath the darkness of thunder. And though her mood has clearly altered the aspect of the landscape, it is clear that she is concentrating so strongly that she has forgotten herself at that moment she encounters the melancholy and dullness of the water. Yet given this withdrawal of nature into dullness, she does not make depressive pronouncements such as the following, which can be found in Hölderlin's *Hyperion:* "es gibt ein Vergessen alles Dasein, ein Verstummen unsers Wesens [there is a forgetting of all being, a mutilation of our essence]." The extrapolation from particularized moments of experience to the destiny of historical epochs is simply not made. Instead we are told the wood is rich in flowers and that the heckberry is very beautiful. In place of a meeting with a demigod, Dorothy encounters a blind man driving a large bull and cow. The blind man is treated as if the most remarkable thing about him were the two beautiful animals with which he seems so out of place. If there is nothing mythic about this blind man, there isn't anything ordinary about him either. And Dorothy Wordsworth will come back to such wanderers in a place called Rydale, because without explicitly making the connection, she has unselfconsciously associated her brother's journey with the wanderings of destitute people.

"At Rydale," she writes,

a woman of the village, stout and well dressed, begged a halfpenny — she had never she said done it before, but these hard times! — Arrived at home with a bad head-ach, set some slips of privet. The evening cold, had a fire — my face now flame-coloured. It is nine o'clock. I shall soon got to bed. A young woman begged at the door — she had come from Manchester on Sunday morn with two shillings and a slip of paper which she supposed a Bank note — it was a cheat. She had buried her husband

and three children within a year and a half—All in one grave—burying very dear—paupers all put in one place—20 shillings paid for as much ground as will bury a man—a stone to be put over it or the right will be lost—11/6 each time the ground is opened. Oh! that I had a letter from William![5]

As far as history is concerned, the two beggar women exemplify a world in decline. As such, they reflect a condition of being that is threatening to Dorothy Wordsworth. The first woman is still well dressed and is at the beginning of what will be her ruin; the second woman is beyond what one would ordinarily consider ill fate. She had buried her husband and three children in the same grave and may not be able to pay for the cost of a stone with which to ensure the plot's sanctity. Narratively positioned between these two female figures is Dorothy herself, who arrived at home with a bad headache and who, with steadfast heart, plants some slips of privet. The evening is cold, and she builds a fire. And only then, for the slightest moment, does she come into appearance with the phrase, "my face now flame-coloured." That, of course, is the extent of her Cartesian awakening, her figuring the self as a being-in-the-world. "I burn, therefore I am." One wonders: is it around nine o'clock that the second beggar woman has come to the door? Or does the memory of the beggar woman and her dead only occur to her just then? It's as if the flames had consumed time, as if in the moment of self-awareness time got slightly derailed. In that moment where she has figured herself, one suspects that where there should have been a moment, an abyss had opened in which the difference and identity between Dorothy and the unfortunates on the road undergoes disequilibrium, a kind of vertigo, which is only arrested by recollecting the poet, her brother. "Oh! that I had a letter from William!"[6]

This line, of course, has the status of a lost object whose absence has only been temporarily forgotten or displaced only to return without warning to stabilize the abyss where thoughts are swirling, as well as to mark the painful break around which the entire day's events have been circulating. In the *Grasmere Journals,* such a lapse or failure to remember is not uncommon. It is noticeable in terms of small temporal slippages, narrative inconsistencies, sudden fade-outs, and the force of displaced recollections that mark openings or abysses of disequilibrium in which the temporality of everyday life is disturbed. We should not be surprised, therefore, that the sudden exclamation that Dorothy would like a letter from her brother is not only expressed *aprés coup*, but is, at the same time, irrationally premature. After all, William has just left some seven or eight hours earlier from the moment at which the wish is narratively introduced. Arriving both too late and too soon, the remark intensifies even as it stabilizes the very disequilibrium it addresses. This is further troubled because the wish for a letter or word from the poet immediately follows remarks about the reopening of mass graves and the deaths of husbands and children, suggesting further that we're still in some kind of opening, caesura, or abyss.

Coincidentally, in the same year and month, May 1800, a banker's wife, Susette Gontard, is writing the German poet, Friedrich Hölderlin in Homberg. Hölderlin, who is no longer a tutor living in the Gontard household, is still in love with this passionate young woman with the Athenian profile. "Are you returning?" she writes to him in her last letter dated Thursday morning, May 1800.

> The whole region is silent and deserted without you and I am in such agony. How will I be able to keep to myself those strong feelings for you if you don't come back? And should you return, it will also be difficult to maintain my balance and not experience even more violent feelings. Promise me you will not come back and that you will leave peacefully; deprived of this certitude, I will perpetually remain in a tense and disturbed state at my window every morning. And in the end we will be calm again, therefore pursue your way with confidence and let us be happy even in the depths of our pain and hope that it will ever ever be so for us since we want the affirmation of the perfect nobility of our feelings . . . Adieu! Adieu! Blessings . . . be with you.[7]

Here again we notice a text by a woman whose love is illicit to the poet, and a poet who is not just any poet, but a national poet, though, as in the case of William Wordsworth, at a time before his significance as such has been definitively established. Moreover, in both instances, we notice how the writing is meant to calm what is clearly a very emotional and agitated state of mind, which follows upon the poet's departure. Like Dorothy Wordsworth's journal entry, Gontard's letter to Hölderlin correlates mood to place—the silent and deserted country—and proceeds with a number of rather abrupt shifts marked by contrary desires: the desire for him to be with her and the desire for him to go away. Deprived of the certitude of knowing he is gone forever, she says she will always be anxious. Yet in the end they will both find peace. In their despair they will find happiness. Nobility of feeling will be achieved and, in the end, she even anticipates that calm nobility of mind as she blesses the poet, even to the point of anointing him in an act so selfless and giving, that the entire letter undergoes an enormous sea change reminiscent of various moments in *Hyperion*, which, Gontard tells Hölderlin elsewhere, she admires, even though her nervous temperament isn't well suited to the reading of serious literature. What is quite noticeable as well is that just as Dorothy Wordsworth's journal approaches the kind of natural and social observations associated with the poetry of her brother, Gontard's letters are reminiscent of the dialectics of the philosophical circles in which Hölderlin moved. For example, the dialectics of nearness and distance suggested in the letter ends in an elevated and noble resolution in which the poet receives benediction or sanctification. Her letters also invoke philosophical terminology as in the following example in which she argues that her spirit and soul are mirrored in his. "Mein Geist, meine Seele spiegeln sich in Dir, Du giebst was sich geben läßt, in so schöner Form, als ich es nie könnte. [My spirit, my soul are mirrored in you; you give what can be given in so beautiful a form as I never could.]" Nowhere in Dorothy Wordsworth's journals do we hear such relatively elevated language. Conversely, nowhere in Gontard's letters are we given any sense of the immediate experiences through which the passions are at once dampened and intensified. Indeed, Gontard herself points out that despite the fact that the passion of Hölderlin's letters have given her the idea to start a diary, she is so agitated that she can never find the right words to express herself: "Ich bin nur so wenig ungestöhrt, wenn ich es verstohlen tun muß, ist eine Art von Angst in mir, die mich hindert die rechten Worte zu finden, so oft werde ich aus meinen Gedanken gerissen und werde dann leicht verdrüßlich, doch, will ich es versuchen, und jede ruhige Minute nutzen, nur mußt Du auf keinen Zusammenhang rechnen [I am but so agitated, and when writing in secret I feel an anxiety which keeps me from finding the right words, so often am I cut off from my thought and then easily irritated; however, I will attempt it and use every quiet moment, but you must not count on any coherence]" (12 March 1799). If one thinks of Hölderlin's later poetry, especially, these words strike an uncannily sympathetic accord between the poet and his beloved, as if her attitude about writing had disclosed something essential about the destiny of his poems. To put this a bit more sharply, I would like to say that this destinal anticipation is not just relayed by means of Gontard's empathic appropriation of certain German idealist manners of philosophical expression, but is given or destined by means of what is "so wenig ungestöhrt," that is to say, of a disequilibrium of mind that has its abysses or rifts.

Gontard frequently broaches these abysses, for example, in a letter of early fall 1798 when she tells Hölderlin that her mind is always elsewhere and that she cannot stabilize her thoughts. "When I want to dream," she says, "even my phantasy won't serve me." And "when I want to read, my thoughts stay still." She says she feels apathetic, beside herself, unable to express the right words. Courage and activity fail her. All of these feelings relate to a moment analogous to that in the *Grasmere Journals,* the departure of the poet. Gontard writes, "I have often regretted having advised you, at the moment of our separation, to distance yourself in another place." And she tells the poet that she did not understand what feeling had compelled her to do that. "I believe, though, that it was fear, of the whole sensation of our love, which became too intense for me in this powerful break [Ich glaube aber, es war die Furcht, vor der ganzen Empfindung unserer Liebe, die zu laut in mir wurde bei diesem gewaltigen Riß]." This is the break, encouraged by Gontard, that, unpredictably, has opened as an abyss in her being that cannot be stabilized, despite her meticulous instructions about how Hölderlin is supposed to secretly make his way to her bedroom, as if these elaborate rituals could somehow compensate for the *Riß* that has opened. It is a *Riß* that Gontard tries to figure even as her text holds it back in disequilibrium as part of an experience that is properly speaking hers and which sets her apart from Hölderlin, the poet, who is so often being pushed away by these abysses, these lapses, in which Gontard says she cannot pose herself in relation to him. Yet, in the very holding back of these abysses by not only Gontard, but by Dorothy Wordsworth, who so carefully hides them as so many secrets in the seams of her sentences, there is, nevertheless, a destinal or fateful effect of these abysses that is perceptible in the poetry of Gontard's and Wordsworth's companions.

II

How, then, do these abysses in being figure in the poetry of poets who only much later will be strongly identified within their respective cultures as national poets? If we turn to Martin Heidegger's examination of Hölderlin in the 1934 seminar on *Germanien,* we will immediately notice that he considers language. "Das Gedicht ist Sprache. Aber wer spricht nun eigentlich im Gedicht?"[8] Throughout Heidegger's various seminars on Hölderlin during the 1930s and early 1940s, the main strategy is to jettison authorial and formalist readings while allowing the words to speak poetically in ways that further philosophical thinking about man's relation to the world and to the divine.

Central to Heidegger's thinking is a notion of openness, of which the *Abgrund* or "abyss" is but one. If poetry is speech, who or what is speaking? Not Hölderlin, simply, but according to Heidegger, language itself, which keeps shifting levels and introducing new voices and tonalities whose sources are concealed. In *Germanien,* for example, the stanzas are not all spoken by the same subject, and the "I" who announces itself for the last time in line twenty-nine cannot, according to Heidegger, be considered the origin or source for the poem. For "dieses Sprachgefüge ist in sich ein *Wirbel,* der uns irgendwohin reißt."[9] That is, the speaking is constellated such that it delimits a tourbillon or whirling movement that rips and pulls us — sweeps us away — in some unspecified direction. In *Germanien* this disequilibrium drags us to no one else than the virgin woman, the mother of all things who is said to be the upholder of an abyss. This abyss is a particularly odd one that I want to exploit in that if one looks at drafts A and B of *Germanien,* one notices that the phrase "und den abgrund trägt" is missing from the B manuscript. Heidegger himself makes quite a bit of this, and in the Hamburger translation, one notices that in the German, the phrase is left out, while in the translation it is supplied. Hamburger too sees that in Hölderlin's B manuscript the abyss has been evacuated or emptied in the place of its having been posited in the A manuscript, which is to say, the abyss has literally fallen into itself and disappeared. Hence it could be said to be present in its very absence.

Die Mutter ist von allem, [und den abgrund trägt]
Die Verborgene sonst genannt von Menschen,

So ist von Lieben und Leiden
Und voll von Ahnungen dir
Une voll von Frieden der Busen.[10]

The Mother of all things, [upholder of the abyss,]
Whom men at other times call the Concealed,
Now full of loves and sorrows
And full of presentiments
And full of peace is your bosom.[11]

In these lines, particularly, an allusion to Diotima—Hölderlin's name for
Susette Gontard—is made with respect to the notion of concealment. In all
of the poems entitled "Diotima," it is quite explicit that Diotima is in decline and that she is becoming increasingly concealed in the earth. "Deine
Sonne, die schönere Zeit, ist untergegangen [Your sun, of a lovelier time,
has descended]." This is why she blooms "verschlossen," concealed, in a
fallen world that cannot fully sustain her. In Germanien, the traces of this
Diotima survive in that other feminine presence, the upholder of the abyss.
Like that abyss, however, she is both appropriated and expropriated by the
poem, gathered and dissipated. Indeed such an appropriation and expropriation could be said to be the destiny of other texts that are always being
held in reserve, outside the poem, namely, the letters of Susette Gontard
with their numerous small breakdowns and intimate shocks. We could put
this another way by saying that thematically encrypted in her apotheosis
in Germanien, is an abyss into which she disappears, though it is an abyss
that is itself a sublation of those abysses of her prose that have been destined to take on national significance with respect, in this case, to a poem
about the fatherland and its people. This codetermination of companion
texts, held in reserve outside the poem, that nevertheless achieve their destiny within the poem bears on what Heidegger calls Gespräch, or "destinal
interlocution." In the case of Hölderlin and Gontard, this interlocution is
precisely that of how the woman's disequilibrium has been put at the dis-
posal of the poet even as it has been held back within her experience as a
woman (not to say, within her writings, which were prejudicially deemed,
at the time, to be of lesser significance because of her gender). Yet, it is in
the everydayness of her experiences that a certain comportment has been
disclosed that involves the construction of an Abgrund, a zone of disequi-

librium where the figure of the poet is posed or posited as a figure that cannot stabilize or hold together the *Wirbel* that is sweeping the text away from its moorings or supports—the stable relationships of everyday life. At the same time, these texts are engaged in a destinal interlocution where the *Abgrund* of female experience will not only require itself to be divinized or spiritualized by the poet, but much more radically, will also require that such experience become a codetermining force of disruption or rupture within a national poetry *as yet to come,* say, in the twentieth century. And this poetry that will not only speak to the piety of the fatherland, but by extension, to the *calling into Being* of that fatherland's people as a distinctively German people. It is here, of course, that turning from the private relationship between poet and female companion—their destinal cohabitation—to that of the public relationship between poet and a national people, or *Volk,* occurs by means of a destinal interlocution, or *Ortsnetz im Ort des Seins,* from which women's writings are not to be so easily excluded (as for example, by Heidegger himself who does not consider the possibility of a fateful significance of Gontard's writings for the destiny of the German people).

For it is in the writing of Susette Gontard that something is concealed, reserved, held back, or set aside, a disequilibrium in which the self has lost itself in the transport of conflicting moods, motivations, desires, fantasies, or somatic symptoms, which point to a hole, gap, or rupture that cannot be repaired by any ecstasy whatsoever, least of all, Gontard's brief ecstasies with Hölderlin in her bedroom. It is in this woman's letters, then, that we see to what extent a destructive tear is guarded or vouchsafed for the sake of a destinal interlocution through which she gives herself over to the destinal arrival of a national poet, a giving or positing that holds something back that cannot be posed. It is in that positing/nonpositing by the poet's companion that a destructive poetic rupturing becomes visible—the tornado or *Wirbel*—through which the fatherland as homeland of Being is posed as the proper place [*Ort*] for a national German identity, though, of course, this place is precisely what the destinal interlocution has called into question as something that is essentialistically posed or posited by the poet(s).

In the case of the Wordsworths, where we might think an English temperament avoids the sort of nationalistic political horizon imaginable in the case of Hölderlin, it has to be said that something not entirely dissimilar is at work. If we look at the famous poem "Lines, Composed a Few Miles above

Tintern Abbey on Visiting the Banks of the Wye During a Tour. July 13, 1798," we see that William has rendered his sister divine and that she has been put in the role of a spiritual guide and, in anticipating the keen poetic perceptions of the *Grasmere Journals,* of a muse. Yet, as in the journals, there is temporal distortion as well, for William has fast forwarded their lives to such an extent that he is recovering the present companionship with his sister from an undetermined future point, from whose perspective the walk with Dorothy by the Wye River is itself but a stabilizing moment whose purpose is to assuage the violence of an abyss — the approach of death that will inevitably sunder one from the other. Hence the walk a few miles above Tintern Abbey will be posed or set up by William for Dorothy as a remembrance that pays homage to her from the perspective of the future anterior, a temporal perspective, which, when compared to the present, delimits a very curious caesura that in rendering the sister divine also points to the evanescence or the forgetableness of the moment that is supposed to be salvific, as if that moment were swallowed up into itself in the very same way that the abyss in Hölderlin's *Germanien* disappears into its own absence. In fact, it is this disappearance, or fading of the scene within a temporality of the future anterior, that makes the closing lines of "Tintern Abbey" extremely emotional and brings them quite close to the Diotima poems of Hölderlin, where the very flowering of Diotima characterizes the decline of her sun. Like Diotima, William's sister is made sacred or recovered, even as from the future anterior she is destroyed or lost in advance. And the abyss, which delimits this recovery and loss, is that within which a figure is constructed and dismantled, or in Heidegger's terms, appropriated and expropriated. But, of course, it is this division or difference between appropriation and expropriation that we see reflected in the everyday events of the sister herself, events that are already recorded in the *Alfoxden Journal* of the year 1798, the very same year the poem "Tintern Abbey" was composed in tranquility.

It is in this journal that Virginia Woolf was especially sensitive to Dorothy's reticence or holding back. Commenting on the passage about having received Mary Wollstonecraft's biography, Woolf notices that there is no comment about Wollstonecraft's life as such, just a caesura. And yet a day later, "an unconscious comment" is dropped. "Quaint waterfalls about, about which Nature was very successfully striving to make beautiful what art had deformed — ruins, hermitages, etc. etc. In spite of all these things,

the dell romantic and beautiful, though everywhere planted with unnatural-
ized trees. Happily we cannot shape the huge hills, or carve out the valleys
according to our fancy."[12] Whereas Wollstonecraft wanted to dramatically
revolutionize the world, Dorothy Wordsworth argues for a *conservation* or
abiding relation wherein the attention to the minute details of the landscape
discloses the *Abgrund* or abyss, and this is in fact revolutionary in a different way from Mary Wollstonecraft's fulgurations; for the abysses of Dorothy
Wordsworth are in fact the destabilizing codeterminants of a destiny that
will work itself through in the poetry of her brother, an *Ortsnetz im Ort
des Seins* that brings the countryside of England into the place of Being as
homeland, or perhaps even fatherland (the land of words-of-worth), to a
people who are called into assembly by an intimate company. In their place
she accepts the com-posure of brother and sister, a com-posure or conversation that for all its correspondences resists intersubjectivity. As such
they are not posited in terms of a Fichtean reflection theory wherein the
subject's striving toward determination through the positing of the self in
relation to an object is to be occupied or taken over, merely, by an other.
Rather, Dorothy and William Wordsworth reflect what in the context of
"Andenken" Heidegger calls "der Zurückbleibende," the ones who in staying back have achieved a com-posure that enables them to encounter their
land as "fatherlandish" — not subject to the feminist challenge of one like
Wollstonecraft — and to hear the call of its holiness as a call to "das Eigene."
Yet, as in the context of Heidegger, this "Eigene" is nothing but the staying
back of the poet and of the poetic word that keeps to itself as interlocution
rather than conversation: the silence in which the truth is concealed and
disclosed, a truth that is the truth in art.

Toward the end of *The Prelude*, William Wordsworth points us in the
right direction when he speaks of a humbler destiny in contrast to the revelation of a divine spirit on the peak of Mount Snowdon. "A humbler destiny
have we retraced, / And told of lapse and hesitating choice, / And backward
wanderings along thorny ways." It is in this humbler destiny with its lapses,
hesitating choices, and backward wanderings that the holding back of the
sister comes to appearance as the "trait" of the national poet, if not that
of the fatherland itself. In that sense, the sister is the trait without which
the fatherland could not disclose itself as Being, or what Heidegger in the
context of Hölderlin calls the holy. That this trait is destined in the interlocution between sister and brother speaks to the divisibility and noncoin-

cidence that persists even in the disclosure of the natural world as "das Eigene," a natural world that will come to be identified more and more strongly with nation. On Wednesday, 2 October 1800, Dorothy Wordsworth wrote in her journal: "A fine morning—a showery night. The lake still in the morning—in the forenoon flashing light from the beams of the sun, as it was ruffled by the wind. We corrected the last sheet."

Post-Script

In an essay entitled "Sauf le Nom," Jacques Derrida cites the following lines of Angelus Silesius's *Cherubinic Wanderer*: "Friend, let this be enough; if you wish to read beyond, / Go and become yourself the writ and yourself the essence." Commenting on these lines, Derrida writes, "The friend, who is male rather than female, is asked, recommended, enjoined, prescribed to render himself, by reading, beyond reading; beyond at least the legibility of what is currently readable, beyond the final signature—and for that reason to write." Derrida's point is that the friend is at once pre-scribed and rendered by the poet's reading and simultaneously situated "beyond the final signature." Both Susette Gontard and Dorothy Wordsworth, in my view, are situated in precisely this way as friends whose own writings fall outside the writing of national poets despite the fact that they are, as Silesius might put it, "the writ" and "the essence." Derrida summarizes this as follows:

> Not to write this or that that falls outside his writing as a note, a *nota bene* or a *post-scriptum* letting writing in its turn fall behind the written, but for the friend himself to become the written or Writing, to become the essence that writing will have created. (No) more place, starting from there, beyond, but nothing more is told us beyond, for a *post-scriptum.*
>
> The *post-scriptum* will be the debt or the duty. It will have to, it should, be reabsorbed into a writing that would be nothing other than the essence that would be nothing other than the being-friend or the becoming-friend of the other. The friend will only become what he is, to wit, the friend, he will only have become the friend at the moment when he will have read that, which is to say, when he will have read beyond—to wit, when he will have gone, and one goes there, beyond, to give oneself up, only by becoming writing through writing. The be-

coming [Werden], the becoming-friend, the becoming-writing, and the essence [Wesen] would be the same here.[13]

My account of the poets and their female companions adds a biographical dimension to Jacques Derrida's claims about friendship, in which the presence of the friend is always already prescribed as arche-trace or, more precisely, arche-voice.[14] That the friend is writ is something I have attempted to show in terms of how the female companions are themselves what one might call the "post-scriptum" or PS of the text—what in earlier writings Derrida was calling the supplement, in this case, a supplement that precedes or comes in advance of a national poetry. That the relation between the poet and the friend escapes a binding or tangible connection is, of course, why one necessarily speaks of a caesura wherein there is both a turning toward and turning away from an other. Indeed it is because of the undecidable logic of this caesura that the post-scriptum calls to us from "beyond the ear," an unheard-of intimacy. Here, of course, one encounters the peculiar possibility that a national poetry will come to pass, not because a poet was necessarily attuned to a people or *Volk,* but because the poet participated in what we could call an "unheard-of intimacy" with a woman that escapes objectification as a concrete relation. What comes to pass in this unheard of intimacy, however, is the destinality of an interlocution that expresses itself over time (that is, historically) as the recognition of a national poet whose work is "fatherlandish" to the extent that it grounds the destinal interlocution by means of asserting a male poetic voice that is heard by others *as if* it were the voice of a people or nation.

Derrida has alerted us to the fact that in terms of a Heideggerian understanding of *Mitsein,* one is always going to encounter what Heidegger himself called *Kampf.* "*Kampf* belongs to the very structure of Dasein. It belongs to its historical structure and thus, this must also be explicitly stated, to the subjectivity of the historical subject."[15] In our context, this *Kampf* obviously relates to the question of gender and the prioritization of a male voice. No doubt, we can think of this as reflecting a subjectivity that is itself the consequence of a national *Kampf* or interlocution that implicitly or unconsciously organizes itself around an idea of there being a fatherland—a national *paysage* grounded in terms of the priority of a man's poetic voice, that is to say, a voice that determines the writ of the female companion to be post-scriptive, despite its essential significance as a voice that makes legible a determining caesura without which a certain poetry could not have come to pass. In the case of the Wordsworths, this is evident in the relation between Dorothy's *Grasmere Journals* and William's *The Prelude*. In the case of Hölderlin, the *Kampf* can be detected in the subsuming of Gontard's turbulence within the lyricism of works like *Germania*.

In *Being and Time*, Heidegger asks, "To what extent and on the basis of what ontological conditions does historiality belong, as an essential constitution, to the subjectivity of the 'historial' subject?"[16] If the prioritization of the fatherlandish voice of the national poet could be said to fulfill those metaphysically oriented ontological conditions upon which historiality depends, is it not, in fact, the case that this fatherlandish voice is always already constituted by the caesura of an interlocution to which a female voice is quite essential? After all, is it not to this post-scriptum that the fatherlandish is largely indebted, insofar as the writ of the female companions is an engendering of something other than themselves? In "Sauf le Nom," Derrida thinks of this sort of engendering in terms of a logical breakdown between the possible and the impossible, since a becoming-self engenders a becoming-other if not a becoming-nothing that is, strictly speaking, impossible even if it is inevitable. This surplus "introduces an absolute heterogeneity in the order and in the modality of the possible. The possibility of the impossible, of the 'more impossible' that as such is also possible ('more impossible than the impossible'), marks an absolute interruption in the regime of the possible that nonetheless remains, if this can be said, in place" (43). That the trace or trait of this possibility/impossibility may exceed hearing or is, strictly speaking, beyond the ear points to the peculiarity of a destinal interlocution that characterizes the fate of a poetry that over considerable time will be recognized as having national significance. That reflection theory will eventually install itself at the very point when the two genders face off over the question of who speaks for a people is inevitable, something that feminists exemplify more often than not. Important for us, however, has been the prehistory of this *Kampf* in terms of a caesura and *Mitdichten* that undermines conceptions of self-positing upon which a nationalized battle of the sexes is necessarily founded.

NOTES
1. Fichte, *The Science of Knowledge* (London: Cambridge, 1982), 33.
2. (Frankfurt am Main: Suhrkamp, 1989), 251.

3. Edmund Husserl, *Ideas Pertaining to A Pure Phenomenology,* trans. F. Kersten (The Hague: Nijhoff, 1982), 63.

4. "Kants These über das Sein," in *Wegmarken* (Frankfurt am Main: Klostermann, 1967), 300.

5. Dorothy Wordsworth, *The Grasmere Journals* (Oxford: Oxford University Press, 1991), 1–2. The entry I've quoted is the first to appear in the journals.

6. Dorothy Wordsworth, *The Grasmere Journals,* 15–16.

7. All entries from the letters appear in Adolf Beck, ed., *Hölderlins Diotima Susette Gontard: Gedichte—Briefe—Zeugniss* (Frankfurt am Main: Insel, 1980), 32–90.

8. *Hölderlins Hymnen "Germanien" und "Der Rhein,"* in *Gesamtausgabe,* vol. 39 (Frankfurt am Main: Klostermann, 1980), 45.

9. Heidegger, *Hölderlins Hymnen,* 45.

10. See Hölderlin, *Sämtliche Werke,* vol.2, ed. F. Beissner (Stuttgart: Kohlhammer, 1951), 739 for complete variants.

11. Friedrich Hölderlin, "Germania," in *Poems and Fragments: A Bilingual Edition,* trans. Michael Hamburger (London: Cambridge, 1980), 400–401.

12. Virginia Woolf, *The Second Common Reader* (New York: Harcourt Brace, 1960), 149.

13. Jacques Derrida, *Sauf le nom* (Stanford, Calif.: Stanford University Press, 1995), 41–42.

14. Also see J. Derrida, "Heidegger's Ear: Philopolemology," in *Reading Heidegger,* ed. John Sallis (Bloomington: University of Indiana, 1993), 174.

Dasein's opening to its ownmost potentiality-for-being, as hearing the voice of the other as friend, is absolutely originary. This opening does not come under a psychology, a sociology, an anthropology, an ethics, or a politics, etc. The voice of the other friend, of the other as friend, the ear that I prick up to it, is the condition of my own proper being. But this voice nevertheless defines the figure of an originary sharing [*partage*] and an originary belonging, of a *Mitteilen* or of everything that is, as Heidegger says in this passage, "shared" (*geteilt*) with the other in the *Mitsein* of discourse, of address and response.

15. Ibid., 177.

16. Quoted in Derrida, "Heidegger's Ear: Philopolemology," 177.

12 Between *Aufbruch* and *Secessio:* Images of Friendship among Germans, Jews, and Gays

JOHN NEUBAUER

Der Mensch wird am Du zum Ich.
—Martin Buber, *Ich und Du*[1]

1998

Writing these first words, I am distracted by music blasting from the closing boat parade of the Amsterdam Gay Games, which displays the motto: friendship.

1983

I made my first public appearance as professor of comparative literature in Amsterdam by opening a conference on literature and homoeroticism entitled "Vriendjespolitiek," a sarcastic reference to backroom politicking (old boys' network). I had no idea what to say. In the end I saved myself with Thomas Mann's 1922 speech *Von deutscher Republik,* his coming out in defense of the Weimar Republic and homosexuality. A few months later I sat in a committee to judge a dissertation on the role of adolescent readings in the formation of homosexuals. Page Grubb's "You got it from all those Books" includes a study of Mann's *Tod in Venedig,* as well as an analysis of questionnaires returned by members of Amsterdam's gay community.[2] I appear in the old Lutheran church for the defense in (borrowed) cap and gown; the audience consists mostly of friendly gay leather jackets.

1922

Were there "friendly gay leather jackets" in the academic audience when Thomas Mann gave his lecture *Von deutscher Republik* in Berlin? The published text reports only about "extended unrests" and about hostile scraping of feet on the ground. Anticipating this hostility, he tried to make his ideas palatable to conservatives: he urged his audience to reclaim the Republic from aggressive Jew boys ("scharfe Judenjungen");[3] he extensively quoted Novalis to reach the neo-Romantics; and he suggested connections between male bonding in the youth movement, the state, and the war[4] on the one hand and Walt Whitman's homoeroticism on the other.

Mann skillfully strengthened these tenuous connections by appealing to popular publications by Hans Blüher that his young audience was likely to know and respect. Blüher's three-volume history of the *Wandervogel* caused a sensation in 1912 by claiming that this first organization of the youth movement was propelled by homoerotic bonding and that the later ejection of homosexuals from the movement was to be understood in terms of Freud's theory: the leaders who persecuted the homosexuals were "weak" inverts who projected their self-hatred upon others.[5] Blüher's second book, *Die Rolle der Erotik in der männlichen Gesellschaft*, extended his theory of male bonding to a great variety of other organizations, above all to the state, which he proclaimed to be the homoerotic counterpart to the heterosexual family.[6]

Mann referred to Blüher in his 1922 lecture (without naming him) by remarking: "eros as statesman, even as state creator, is an image familiar to us from ancient days and intelligently advocated anew today" (2:48). But whereas three years earlier he found Blüher's lecture on *Deutsches Reich, Judentum, Sozialismus* "excellent" and "almost word for word" spoken from his soul,"[7] he now qualified the praise by adding that it made no sense to ascribe libidinal energy only to monarchy and its restoration.[8] The qualification indicates that both Blüher and Mann changed their ideological position between 1919 and 1922: in 1919, Mann was still the Prussian-German conservative of his *Betrachtungen*,[9] while Blüher thought that temporarily the best political system for Germans was a democratic republic and he said soothing words about socialism.[10] By 1922 the tables had turned: Mann came to defend the Republic, whereas Blüher published *Secessio judaica,* a highly disturbing book that needs reconsideration, however painful this may be.[11]

Blüher predicted that the German Reich would rise from its ashes, whereas the Jews would disappear from the country. Although he considered some Jews as noble and great, and although he sneered at Teutonic, *völkisch,* and "vulgar" anti-Semitism, he regarded the impact of Jewish thinking upon Germans as "corruptive." Such were the theories of Einstein[12] or Freud (23–24), and above all, socialism and Marxism, which promulgated internationalism and class struggle at the expense of class-transcending nationalism. "Jewish socialism," the product of a race without nation, derived politics from economics and denied the primacy of the nationhood (32–33): "One cannot follow the Jewish and the German way simultaneously. All nations listening to the Jewish voice are lost" (36). Zionism was welcome because it revived Jewish nationalism and turned against the "mimicry" of assimilation. Believing that Jewish mimicry was most quickly disappearing in Germany, Blüher predicted that his country will be spared of "the inevitable *Weltpogrom*": "Germany alone will flinch from murder" (57).

But *Secessio* went beyond Zionism, for Blüher's argument constantly slipped from diagnosis into prescription. He demanded that Jews be forbidden to serve as German officers or judges, and he opposed German-Jewish marriages (38). *Secessio judaica* meant dislodging the Jews from the host nations onto which they had grafted themselves (21). To recognize *sine ira et studio* the historical necessity of the secession was theoretically founded (and hence not "vulgar") anti-Semitism: "Whoever calls a Jew a Jew is an anti-Semite" (41). Jews had no right to say "we Germans" (42) even if they had bravely fought for the fatherland, for as a group they represented defeatism: "Prussians and heroism belong together; Jews and the spirit of defeat belong together" (49). The Weimar Republic was for Blüher a senseless antihistorical construct [geschichtswidriges Gebilde] because it originated from a Jewish spirit: "Its ideal is the well-being of all [Allgemeinheit], and this 'all' is the Jewish substitute for the state. The German Republic is therefore a typical Jew-product without historical honor" (52).

It would be easy to dismiss *Secessio judaica* as proto-Nazi "hate literature," but we should resist the temptation, for it is an uncanny amalgam of blindness and insight. Kafka, for one, understood it this way when on

16 June 1922 he started in his diary a reply he was unable to finish. The problem, he noted, was not only "Blüher's philosophical and visionary power," but that responses had to counter the suspicion "of wanting ironically to dismiss the ideas of this book." What Kafka could not dismiss ironically was surely the inevitability of the Jewish *secessio*—an idea that, tragically, so many assimilationist German Jews did indeed dismiss.

The problem with Blüher's book is not that it stated the necessity of the *secessio,* or even that it made a colossal blunder in predicting that no pogrom would occur in Germany. Rather, it failed by mixing prescription into the diagnosis and taking a duplicitous position with respect to the Jews: it claimed to make dispassionate observations about historical inevitabilities, but resorted time and again to venomous and "vulgar" anti-Semitic ideas. Once more, Kafka brilliantly perceived the ethical conundrum: "He calls himself an anti-Semite without hatred, *sine ira et studio,* and he really is that; yet he easily awakens the suspicion, almost with every remark, that he is an enemy of the Jews, whether out of happy hatred or unhappy love."[13]

Whether Blüher was an "enemy of the Jews," and if so, whether he was motivated by "happy hatred" or "unhappy love" are complicated psychological and personal questions that texts, which are linguistically and inherently ambiguous, are unlikely to answer unequivocally. Nevertheless, whatever the vagaries of language, in real life we must answer such questions if we are to distinguish between friends and foes, and if, as historians, we wish to use in some sense the past in coping with the future. I shall then attempt to sketch an answer to the questions that Kafka, with good reasons, left open by filling the gaps and resolving the ambiguities of *Secessio judaica* with biographical information. I shall try to understand his both philo- and anti-Semitic stance by looking at his friendship with Jews. More concretely, I suggest that he was motivated by an "unhappy love" and that the mechanism behind his notion of *secessio* was a version of the construct that he himself had set up to explain the ostracizing of the homosexuals in the *Wandervogel.* Purging Germany of the Jews was modeled (unconsciously?) after the purging of the *Wandervogel* of homosexuals: just as the leaders of that youth organization ejected homosexuals to resolve their own inner conflict, so too, Blüher developed his anti-Semitism to suppress his homoerotic attraction to certain Jewish men. *Secessio judaica* was a tragicomic personal farewell to his "unhappily beloved ones."

1919

Blüher's Munich lecture was in good measure philo-Semitic. According to the prefatory note to the published text, the lecture was occasioned by an internal dispute of the *Freideutsche Jugend* in Berlin and designed to prepare the ground for the upcoming national assembly. Attempting to mediate between right-wing chauvinists and the heavily Jewish left wing, Blüher called upon his audience in Berlin, Hamburg, Hannover, and Munich to remain loyal to the idea of the expired Reich, so that Germans, "now the pariah of the world," would not have to disperse like the Jews in diaspora and cease to exist as a nation. If the idea of the Reich matured to become one of life's "final matters," it could become what Zion was for the Jews. Jews and Germans had comparable fates.[14] Although the disappearance of the historic Jewish state had led to a fatal weakening of male bonding so that the heterosexual family had to assure racial survival for a long time, Zionism revived male friendship and opened new hopes for reestablishing the state. And this, Blüher proposed, was a shining example for his German audience, now also threatened with the loss of its national identity.

But this admiration for the exemplary rise of national consciousness among Jews was coupled to another, much more negative view of the Jews in the lecture's final harangue against the left: the socialist party was disloyal to the Reich (25), and socialism was basically a Jewish idea (22): "The spirit is always both conservative and revolutionary. The true creators and pillars of culture have always been related to the idea of the priest or the king. But priestly and royal human beings have no place on the left; they are mere empty constructions there. Hence I say to you: *freideutsche* youth beware of the left! Distrust the men of the Enlightenment, the freethinker; beware the benefactors of humanity [*Menschheitsbeglücker*] who never as yet succeeded in making anybody happy; distrust the *Zivilisationsliterat*, the tribunes of the people, the busybodies, the men of progress and the reformer who cannot reform even himself" (28–29). In Blüher's 1953 autobiography, the ambiguities and contradictions of the 1919 lecture are flattened into an equally brilliant but pompous and one-dimensional attack on Weimar, which would have shocked Mann had he come to read it—and not only because it is unkind to him:

Certain segments of the youth movement joined the communists, and people repeatedly assumed that I did so too, for, according to a strange conception, *Geist* was leftist. Others again had diametrically opposite ideas about me. Parts of the refluent army had settled at the time in Munich, either to study or to engage in literary and political nuisance. In short, I was expected to take a definitive position, for I was not expected to take a wavering attitude, such as Thomas Mann took. He also stayed in Munich, and wanting to avoid injustice he found everywhere and in everything something good. I have therefore made my position known in the lecture "Deutsches Reich, Judentum und Sozialismus," and I calmed hereby the mood and gave people direction. The lecture in the Steinickesaal, which I had delivered already in Leipzig, Berlin and Münster, was a great success and had to be repeated. I wasn't quite so a-political after all; but there is a difference between defending one's fatherland and espousing vague ideas about reforming mankind. All the good-looking youth — mostly in uniform, racially and individually superb in appearance — gathered around me at the time, while all the long-haired, ill-kempt rabble piled up on the other side: the literati with profound humanity-gaze, *freideutsche* by-products of the type that was loafing around then.[15]

1915

Blüher's account of his 1919 Munich lecture suggests a homoerotic attachment to racially and physically "superior" men in uniform. Indeed, he fought the infamous law against homosexuality earlier by arguing that a certain type of homosexual, the *Männerheld* [male hero], was a physically and mentally superior and healthy masculine specimen.[16] Yet his case for homosexuality was based on educational, artistic, and cultural values, and his most vigorous public defenses of inversion date from the first war years when he was most deeply attached to Jewish intellectuals: in *Rolle der Erotik*, he claimed that the spiritual type closest to him was overwhelmingly represented by Jews (1:212), and his autobiography recalls that he had been in such an "intensely philo-Semitic disposition" and so strongly "attached to Jewish people" that his father "started to frown."[17]

Blüher's theoretical and personal problems with Jews can in good measure be traced to his fascination with and attraction to the brilliant young men around the short lived and now all but forgotten left-wing journal of the *Freie Studentenschaft* called *Der Aufbruch*. The editorial staff included, next to Blüher, a galaxy of future celebrities: the writers Kurt Hiller, Rudolf Leonhard, and Alfred Wolfenstein, the future philosopher of science Hans Reichenbach, as well as his brother Bernhard, and the anarchist writer and political activist Gustav Landauer. Martin Buber was linked to the group through his close friendship with Landauer. Editor in chief was a student called Ernst Joël, president of the social committee in the *Freie Studentenschaft*,[18] who was also the founder and moving spirit of a shelter [*Siedlungsheim*] that the *Studentenschaft* ran in Charlottenburg for workers and the poor.

The central themes in *Der Aufbruch* were opposition to the comradery of the beer halls and the war, and affirmation of a socially engaged homoerotic male friendship. They link Ernst Joël's "Brief an einen Freund" (21–23), Landauer's Whitman translations (25–31), Blüher's "Was ist Antifeminismus?,"[19] and Joël's "Von deutschen Hochschulen" (44–55). In Alfred Wolfenstein's programmatic poem "Kameraden!" (20–21), the "call for Friendship [Ruf nach Freundschaft]" was to replace the blood relationship to family and the heterosexual desire of the street.

The first issue of *Der Aufbruch* appeared at the end of July 1915 and came through unscathed; the following double issue (August/September 1915) brought disaster. Bernhard Reichenbach's poem "Anti-Barbarus" (66–68) was severely censored, and Joël's satire on the torch parade of the Berlin students for the Swedish queen led to his expulsion from the university by the rector, Ulrich von Wilamowitz, who also accused him of tolerating "homosexual obscenities" in the publication. Blüher protested in an open letter, comparing Wilamowitz's treatment of Joël with his famous attack on Nietzsche's *Geburt der Tragödie* and subsequently resigned from the university.[20] Landauer drafted a protest to the lower house of the Parliament, but apparently did not send it off.[21]

While Joël's expulsion temporarily cemented the friendship between the editors, plans for a Free Academy eroded it. Buber (supported by Landauer), Joël, and Leonhard all had their plans.[22] The participation of women became a major stumbling block when Blüher accused the feminists in "Was ist Antifeminismus"[23] of attempting to infiltrate homosocial organizations like the youth movement and the university, which, in his view, had traditionally provided political and spiritual leadership. Antifeminism was a "will to the purity of male bonding."[24] Joël agreed: in his eyes, a community of higher learning could only consist of (male) teachers and young men. Unlike Leonhard, he was unwilling to admit women, even if that meant that the plan, so dear to his heart, would fail.[25] But Landauer, who participated in the editorial board in good measure because he found Blüher interesting,[26] was irritated by antifeminism. Unaware that Joël sided with Blüher, he wrote to him on 24 December 1915: "I remained a stranger to some of your intimates and helpers; others, like Mr. Hiller and even Mr. Blüher I reject. I say 'even' because I find him very attractive and I look at his work with genuine participation. But we enter distinct paths. I want to wait patiently his further developments and conquests, and I will contribute to this according to my strength. I say therefore nothing final about our differences. But the given must be my point of departure. Thus, for instance, I can only say, as a symptom, that the article 'Was ist Antifeminismus' would never have appeared in the *Socialist* [Landauer's own journal] without unleashing a polemic in which I myself would have participated."[27] As Landauer explained in letters to Blüher (26 February 1916) and Buber (3 March 1916), he unconditionally opposed the exclusion of women; he regarded their equal rights and spiritual equality as self-evident. Blüher finally proposed in *Der bürgerliche und geistige Antifeminismus*[28] something like a compromise. He envisioned a "gothic" and a "dionysian" wing for the Academy (18). In the gothic wing, women had no place (19–20); in the dionysian one, male eros was to have a hegemonic position (21), but (the cleverest and most feminine) women would be granted a subordinate role—as long as they accepted the supremacy of male bonding and rejected feminism (22–23). Hardly a proposal to persuade Landauer!

The Free Academy never got off the ground, and the friends went their own ways. Buber moved to the vicinity of Frankfurt in March 1916; Joël matriculated at the University of Heidelberg; Hiller launched the pacifist-revolutionary *Aktivismus* movement and the yearbook *Das Ziel;* and Blüher started to court conservative, reactionary, and nationalist circles, which slowly but inexorably pushed him to abandon his former Jewish friends.

Let us follow then the strategies that Blüher followed in seceding from Hiller, Joël, Landauer, and Buber. Hiller, who was Blüher's closest ally in fighting for gay emancipation, represents the most revealing and drastic case. In his first public announcement about his break with Hiller, a concluding note in his collected essays (1919), Blüher declared that he was greatly enriched through his association with Hiller, one of the most intelligent minds in Germany. He fondly recalled their visionary talks and plans for a *Bund der Geistigen,* a union of intellectuals and artists.[29] Indeed, Blüher wrote several contributions for Hiller's *Das Ziel* in 1915 and 1916; by 1918 he claimed that the so-called *Bund* was held together only "by the bookbinder's work."[30] The falling out had surely more than one reason. When in early 1916 Joël openly attacked Hiller and left, Blüher was torn between two of his intimate friends and hesitated. The Blüher Archives in the Staatsbibliothek of Berlin preserve a long letter from 3 April 1916 to Joël, which sings high praises of Hiller and most sharply condemns Joël for his treachery. But next to Hiller's grateful acknowledgment of the defense (14 June 1916), there is also an emotionally charged letter by him from 2 December 1917, which shows that Blüher later reversed himself and also left the *Bund.* Hiller bewailed that the Judas in Blüher destroyed everything that he considered in him beautiful, great, and even holy, yet he could not refrain from wooing him: "Find your way back to me! I cannot come to you; I am sure of my case and I consider my system good and clear . . . How unfortunate this break! You have a mind that only a few have; our movement loses something when it loses you."

Hiller's pathos indicates the homoerotic attractions and jealousies in matters of politics and philosophy. What interests me here is not so much the precise psychological mechanism of the triangular (or polygonal) relation, but resultant arguments and ideologies. In the mentioned long letter of 3 April 1916, Blüher criticized Joël for calling Hiller a *Literat,* and he accused him of playing up to the bourgeois anti-Semites and right wingers: "you would undoubtedly turn anti-Semitic against Hiller if you were not a Jew yourself." Ironically, Blüher came to adopt precisely the attitude he found so objectionable in Joël: from 1917 onward, Hiller became for him — together with Maximilian Harden, Siegfried Jacobsohn, Arnold Zweig, and Kurt Tucholsky — the prototypical Jewish literator. The words of 1919, which keenly try to avoid the charge of anti-Semitism, ominously foreshadow his later stance: "My friendship with some of the most important living Jews, to which I attach the highest value, protects me from the possibility of falling prey to gross and cheap anti-Semitism. Yet the thinking of some Jewish literati, which occasionally produces some quite useful results, is for this very reason undeniably inadequate for seizing and animating the heart of the species that grew here between the North Sea and the Alps. Very different spiritual forces are needed for this, which the Jewish literati cannot muster, in spite of their intense endeavors."[31] Indeed, the 1919 lecture on *Deutsches Reich, Judentum und Sozialismus* distinguished Buber and the other admired Zionists from secular and assimilationist abstract thinkers like Freud and Einstein on the one hand, and on the other hand, from social activists, reformers, socialists, liberals, and progressivists who dedicated themselves to the task of transforming humanity. The last group, to which Hiller belonged, was to blame for the anti-Semitism and Germany's postwar ills. The Jews produced an excess of the *Tschandala* (a fashionable term at the time, also used by Thomas Mann and others, for inferior human beings). These Nietzschean slave mentalities produced a special philosophy of ressentiment, which concealed itself behind the noble ideas of liberalism, progressivism, Enlightenment, belief in science, and rationalism.[32] Germans, Blüher warned, had better keep their distance from ideologies that Jews of this type were trying to force upon them, and he specifically cautioned against "the last flowering of the Jewish literati culture, the so called Activism movement," which carried on its banner these "insufferable ideals for making mankind happy," though it was basically only a "matter of the ghetto."[33] It must be added that Hiller never responded venomously and continued to show warmth and admiration for Blüher even after the war.

Blüher's *secessio* from Landauer seems to have been less violent, although this impression may simply be due to the absence of extant letters between Blüher and Landauer from 1917 onward. In their absence we have to rely on Blüher's autobiography, which actually devotes more space to Landauer than to any other figure in Blüher's adult life.[34] Blüher unconditionally admired Landauer's serenity, integrity, and spirituality; his *Aufruf zum Sozialismus* was among the few pieces of socialist theorizing he found palatable. Although he considered it utopian and politically ineffective — in Blüher's eyes anarchist Jews were bound to misunderstand the state[35] — he admired its quasi-mysticism, its denial that economics had primacy, and its opposition to Marxism. Under Landauer's spell, Blüher even abandoned for a moment his Nietzschean elitism and turned against the hubris of the intellectuals. In "Hybris bei den Geistigen," published in the last issue of *Der Aufbruch,* he advocated a descent of the spirit into the *Volk,* a "socialization of the spirit" [*Sozialisierung des Geistes*] by means of male bonding: "for the male bond captures and domesticates the hubris of those that are superior; it transmits the spirit downward and brings about an equalization of castes."[36] It was Landauer's translation of Whitman that must have inspired this affirmation of a Whitmanian democratic homoeroticism, which anticipates Thomas Mann's *Von Deutscher Republik.*

Blüher's autobiography shows several traces of Landauer's homoerotic spell over Blüher and of Blüher's jealousy of both male and female rivals. Thus he tells us that confronted with proponents of the "final solution" he would point to Landauer's photo and ask whether his guest would want to subject this man to Hitler's methods. Without fail, the handsome, spiritual face would achieve what nothing else could: the visitor's "Arian worldview" would begin to crumble.[37] Blüher boasts that Landauer always addressed him when important matters were discussed at *Der Aufbruch*,[38] and he contests that Landauer finally "rejected" him.[39] As to Landauer's wife, the poetess Hedwig Lachmann: she disliked Blüher for his antifeminism and was such a disturbing presence when the two men discussed matters of the state that they had to move to Blüher's place in order to continue in a "genuine atmosphere of male bonding" (393–97). Landauer wrote to Hedwig, according to Blüher, some of the most beautiful German love letters, but once they were married, he opened an amorous correspondence with another woman (390ff.).

In the next years the relation cooled, in part because Landauer consistently opposed the war, and Blüher came to believe that he wished for Germany's defeat.[40] At their final meeting, in September 1918, Blüher apparently attempted to dissuade Landauer from going to Munich, where things started to boil, but Landauer saw hope in chaos and left, together with Buber (398–99). Their subsequent correspondence (399) is no longer extant.

Blüher recalls that during his lecture tour in January 1919 he saw Landauer (with Buber) on the streets of Munich in a fur jacket and high fur cap; "he looked like the incarnation of the old Kropotkin" whose history of the French revolution Landauer had translated (400). But Blüher now avoided talking to Landauer. According to his autobiography, he was now on the side of the racially well-bred officers, Landauer's future murderers, whereas Landauer associated with the long-haired and ill-kempt "riff-raff," "Tschandala-Jews" like Erich Mühsam, who was, Blüher adds with a tinge of jealousy, Landauer's Thou-friend (400). And yet in those very days, Blü-her would still recommend Landauer's *Aufruf zum Sozialismus* to Thomas Mann, who duly read it on 21, 22, and 23 February 1919.

Less than three months later, on 1 May 1919, Landauer was brutally murdered in his jail cell by right-wing officers. We do not know what Blüher's immediate reaction was, but the revision of a remark in *Secessio judaica* indicates the trend of his later attitude. In the original edition of 1922 he still wrote: "The murder of Gustav Landauer weighs on Germany's account of liabilities. This deed will be a heavier burden to carry than the Versailles peace treaty."[41] It is a sad comment on Blüher's civil courage that in the third edition, which came out in 1933, just after Hitler came to power, we read: "The murder of Gustav Landauer burdens Germany only as much as the death of Archimedes had burdened Rome."

Blüher's autobiography says nothing about Joël's expulsion from the University of Berlin, about Blüher's defense of him, and about the quarrels between Blüher, Hiller, and Joël. Joël is mentioned only as one of Blüher's less famous Jewish acquaintances, who killed himself in 1919 because he did not want to endure "Germany's disgrace [*die Schmach Deutschlands*]."[42] But what does "Germany's disgrace" mean here? In Blüher's autobiography, within his later right-wing and Prussian ideology, "disgrace" consistently refers to Germany's defeat in World War I, brought about by internal, mostly Jewish opponents of the war who stabbed the military "in the back [*Dolchstoß*]." As we have seen, Blüher had broached this topic already in his 1919 lecture. Joël's protest suicide would thus exonerate him from the charge that Blüher (and others) leveled against the Jews, namely that they wanted and furthered Germany's war defeat: Joël became so to speak a victim of the *Dolchstoß*.

But this cenotaph for a German-Jewish martyr is spurious, for he did not commit suicide: in 1919 he was a student of medicine in Rostock, in the 1920s a physician working with the children of the Berlin poor, in 1928 he contributed to the festschrift for Buber's fiftieth birthday[43] and participated in Benjamin's experiments with hashish.[44] Only on 15 August 1929 did the shocked Buber report to Franz Rosenzweig that this "noblest face of the German youth movement" had died a few days earlier.[45]

Could Blüher have been ignorant that his erstwhile friend lived another ten years in the very city where Blüher lived? How did Joël's suicide slip into Blüher's otherwise factually reliable autobiography? Joël's letter to Buber from Rostock, dated 1 July 1920, may provide a clue. Landauer's death deeply depressed him, and he reproached himself for having been disloyal to the man who was apparently something like a spiritual leader for him. In Rostock, he felt more isolated than ever; he was disgusted by the students, who appeared to him "worse" and "more securely in the saddle" than ever. He was so revolted by the mean and undignified behavior that the Germans showed in defeat that he seriously entertained the idea of eventually emigrating.[46]

It is highly unlikely that Blüher came to know the content of this letter (which was published only after his death), hence we cannot assume that he adopted the meaning that Joël attached to "disgrace." Joël found Landauer's murder and the German responses to the defeat disgraceful, whereas in Blüher's autobiography, disgrace refers to the allegedly Jewish sabotage of Germany's war effort. In short, Blüher consciously or unconsciously "kills off" the Joël who persisted in the oppositional position he assumed during the war, preserving only the transfigured image of a German patriot.

Ironically, Blüher treated the most outspoken hawk among his Jewish friends, the one that Landauer called *Kriegsbuber* (something like "war boy Buber"), most ignobly. It seems that neither Buber's move to southern Germany in 1916, nor the publication of *Secessio judaica,* nor even Blüher's later anti-Semitic publications brought to an end the relationship. Indeed, Buber reports in a conversation with Werner Kraft on 11 May 1956 that once in the twenties he saved Blüher, upon the latter's own request, from suicide.[47] Did Blüher displace his own, never-mentioned suicide with Joël's never-occurred one? Be it as it may, Blüher's heavily anti-Semitic *Die Erhebung Israels gegen die christlichen Güter* (1931), "finished off" Buber differently. The crucial passage occurs in an appendix to a remark in the text that liberal and enlightened Christians follow Buber and their ilk in criticizing the Christian notion of grace. Buber is thus one of those who "corrupt" Christianity and Germany. The appendix purportedly intends to rectify Buber's image, for "it is actually inadmissible to attack such an important and thoroughly pure man as Martin Buber on the basis of a passage in a letter, and to suppress the rest."[48] Yet the introductory critique of *Völkisch* anti-Semitism quickly switches to a defamatory attack on Buber: "It goes without saying that Martin Buber, together with Gustav Landauer and other, less happy manifestations of Jewdom, had supported those circles that later paralyzed the resistance of our nation against the enemy and forced it to capitulate.

What else could he have done as a Jew, especially once the Balfour Declaration about Palestine existed?" (200). The accusation that he (and the Jews in general) was against Germany's war efforts and among those that forced it to capitulate deeply hurt Buber. On 14 February 1933, just two weeks after Hitler came to power, he reported to Ernst Simon that nothing happened to him as yet, but in view of what "nationalistic literati like Hans Blüher" wrote about his alleged attitude during the war, he was prepared for the worst. He added, with precise reference to the just quoted passage, "although it is untrue, I did, of course, not dispute it."[49] By an irony of fate, the Nazis found Blüher's disdain for Völkisch and "vulgar" anti-Semitism unpalatable. His publications were taken out of circulation, and for the next twelve years he worked on a philosophical treatise, *Die Achse der Natur,*[50] that he considered his magnum opus. After the war he unsuccessfully solicited the help of Thomas Mann and other luminaries to get it published and finally had to be content with a minor publisher. Neither *Die Achse der Natur* nor the *Werke und Tage* became the success he hoped for. Blüher became a relic of the past.

1953

Buber escaped to Israel in 1938 and got a chance to demand a rectification from Blüher after the war, when the tables had turned. He did not respond to the complementary copy of *Die Achse der Natur,* but when Blüher congratulated him on his seventy-fifth birthday in 1953,[51] he copied into his response the twenty-year-old annotations from his copy of *Die Erhebung Israels* (preserved in the Buber Archives at the University of Jerusalem), contesting Blüher's allegations line by line (3:337–40). Blüher was taken aback, remained silent for a year, and then, in a long, undated letter, he complained that Buber unjustly accused him of having been a Nazi and a vulgar anti-Semite (3:369–73).[52] Buber wisely responded on 3 April 1954: "No, Hans Blüher, I have never regarded you as a 'vulgar' anti-Semite. But, since you apparently have not noticed it yourself, I thought I ought to make you aware that what you have said publicly on the matter in highly critical times and in a highly erroneous manner has factually furthered the case of the most vulgar form of anti-Semitism" (3:374). Blüher's response, dated 20 December 1954, is a both moving and psychologically complex attempt to satisfy Blüher's need to set things in order before Christmas and his approaching death. The renewed relationship was to be based on an intellectual-spiritual bonding on the margins of and in opposition to politics: upon hearing that Buber was under severe attacks in Israel because of his dovish attitude with respect to the Arabs, Blüher declared that he treasured the relationship (he did not dare calling it friendship) with Buber infinitely more than those with Heuss (at that time the president of Germany) or any other CDU (Christlich-Demokratische Union) leader [sic]: "my relation to you is important, those to others are not" (3:388). There is, of course, a bit of the braggadocio in the belittling of the contacts with German political celebrities, which was to show that Blüher still had important connections ("I have friends high up but I love you most"), yet Blüher's final wooing was surely genuine, for it was coupled to the painful admission that he used to believe "a bit" in race (3:388).

The author of *Ich und Du* responded on 19 January 1955 with words directed as much at us as at Blüher:

I cannot reject an initiative like yours, especially because I never felt animosity towards you; I welcome your proposal to reestablish our contacts. . . . What "broader circles" most blame me for is: first that I have stood since 1917 for a cooperation with the Arabs (until 1947 in the form of a binational state and since Israel's victory over the seven aggressor states in the form of a mid-Eastern federation of people) and have been at the spearhead of actions leading in this direction. Secondly (as you surely know from my frequently reprinted 1953 speech in the Pauluskirche) that I have been and will be hardly less emphatically against the confounding of the German people with the murderous bands of the gas-chamber organization. . . . Generalization seems to me the primary injustice . . . not only with respect to the fictions of "race" but also against the realities of people. (3:389–90)

Epilogue

The wisdom of Buber's last quoted letter may have reached Blüher too late, for he died on 4 February 1955. Its message to us is so obvious and relevant that commentaries could only trivialize it. Indeed, I shall resist the temptation of leading my story to a grand moral conclusion. The story, pieced together from personal and historical events, could, of course, be concluded with yet other dates (1956?, 1967?, 1989?, 1999?), but as a token of friendship I prefer keeping it open. Like friendships, which come about serendipitously and remain fragile, my constructed story is tentative. I had no clear strategy when I set out to trace history from the moment of writing to some turbulent years earlier this century. Looking back at my own rather lengthy process of writing, I recognize in the unplanned process a resistance to certainties and conclusions. Though I have entertained a few hypotheses, I have no grand psychological or sociological thesis concerning Blüher's friendship with Jews. But my shuttling backward and forward in time expresses, perhaps, an unpremeditated wish to understand what happened not as inevitable but contingent, not as fateful but unfortunate, and above all, not as a matter of blood.

NOTES

1. Martin Buber, *Ich und Du* (Berlin: Schocken, 1922), 36.
2. "You got it from all those Books: A Study of Gay Reading" (Diss. University of Amsterdam, 1984).
3. Thomas Mann, *Reden und Aufsätze*, 2 vols. (Frankfurt am Main: Fischer, 1965), 25–26; see also 39.
4. Mann, *Bluts- und Todeskameradschaft*, vol. 2 of *Reden und Aufsätze*, 48.
5. Hans Blüher, *Wandervogel. Geschichte einer Jugendbewegung*, 1912, 3 vols. (Frankfurt am Main: dipa, 1976); see John Neubauer, "Sigmund Freud und Hans Blüher in bisher unveröffentlichten Briefen," *Psyche* 50 (1996): 123–48.
6. Hans Blüher, *Die Rolle der Erotik in der männlichen Gesellschaft*, 2 vols. (Jena: Diederichs, 1917–1919).
7. Diary entry on 11 February 1919, made after Mann attended Blüher's lecture. Reading the published text on September 11, Mann still found it "excellent." Two days later he delved into the second volume of *Die Rolle der Erotik*. He found it "one-sided but true" and concluded that his own *Betrachtungen* were undoubtedly an expression of his own sexual inversion. His deeply self-revelatory letter to Carl Maria Weber of 4 July 1920 is indebted to Blüher's ideas. Mann, *Tagebücher 1918–1921*, ed. Peter de Mendelssohn (Frankfurt am Main: Fischer, 1979). For a more detailed discussion, see Neubauer, "Am Scheideweg: Thomas Mann und Hans Blüher, München 1919, mit einem unveröffentlichten Brief Blühers an Mann," in *Poesie als Auftrag. Festschrift für Alexander von Bormann*, ed. Dagmar Ottmann and Markus Symmank (Würzburg: Königshausen & Neumann, 2001), 171–83.
8. Mann, *Reden und Aufsätze*, 2:48.
9. Mann, *Betrachtungen eines Unpolitischen*, 1918 (Frankfurt am Main: Fischer, 1956).

10. Hans Blüher, *Deutsches Reich, Judentum und Sozialismus* (Munich: Steinicke, 1919), 27.

11. Mann was still riveted ("sehr gefesselt") by Blüher's *Die Aristie des Jesus von Nazareth* when he read it in July 1921. He never mentions *Secessio judaica* and may not have read it.

12. Hans Blüher, *Secessio Judaica. Philosophische Grundlegung der historischen Situation des Judentums und der antisemitischen Bewegung* (Potsdam: Weißer Ritter, 1922). Reprint: (Bremen: Facsimile-Verlag/Versand, 1982), 56.

13. *Diaries 1914–1923* (New York: Schocken, 1965), 231.

14. Blüher, *Deutsches Reich*, 8.

15. Blüher, *Werke und Tage* (Munich: List, 1953), 399–400.

16. See Neubauer, "Sigmund Freud."

17. Blüher, *Werke und Tage*, 361.

18. The editors met in the apartment that Joël shared with Walter Benjamin, who became the president of the *Studentenschaft* in May 1914. Benjamin then "declared war" on Joël "on all fronts," but the two got along well when they met again in the late twenties. Walter Benjamin, *Gesammelte Briefe*, ed. Christoph Gödde and Henri Lonitz, 3 vols. (Frankfurt am Main: Suhrkamp, 1995–1997), 1:212 and 3:323.

19. "Was ist Antifeminismus?" *Der Aufbruch* 1/Heft 2–3 (1915): 39–44.

20. Hans Blüher, *Ulrich von Wilamowitz und der deutsche Geist. 1871/1915. Ein Kampfschrift gegen Verrätertum am Geist* (Selbstverlag, 1916) and (Prien: Kampmann, 1920); and "In Sachen der Freiheit der Akademie. An das Rektorat der Universität," in *Gesammelte Aufsätze* (Jena: Diederichs, 1919), 74–77, 109.

21. Gustav Landauer, *Sein Lebensgang in Briefen*, 2 vols., ed. Martin Buber (Frankfurt am Main: Rütten & Loening, 1929), 108–9, 112, 125–27.

22. Ibid., 125–26.

23. *Der Aufbruch*, 39.

24. Ibid., 42.

25. Letter to Buber, 11 March 1916 in Martin Buber, *Briefwechsel aus sieben Jahrzehnten*, ed. Grete Schaeder, 3 vols. (Heidelberg: Lambert Schneider, 1972–1975) 420–21.

26. Landauer, *Sein Lebensgang*, 65.

27. Ibid., 114.

28. Hans Blüher, *Der bürgerliche und der geistige Antifeminismus* (Berlin: Selbstverlag, 1916).

29. Blüher, *Gesammelte Aufsätze*, 105.

30. Blüher, "Der Bund der Geistigen," *Tätiger Geist* (vol. 2 of *Ziel*) (1917–1918): 12–50.

31. Blüher, *Gesammelte Aufsätze*, 108.

32. Blüher, *Deutsches Reich*, 21.

33. Ibid., 22.

34. Blüher, *Werke und Tage*, 375–403.

35. Blüher, *Deutsches Reich*, 27.

36. "Die Hybris bei den Geistigen," *Der Aufbruch* 1/4 (1915): 93–95. Quoted from *Gemsammelte Aufsätze*, 6.

37. Blüher, *Werke und Tage*, 376–37.

38. Ibid., 393.

39. See Landauer's above letter of 24 December 1915 to Joël.

40. Blüher, *Werke und Tage*, 388–89, 397.

41. Hans Blüher, *Secessio Judaica*, 57.

42. Blüher, *Werke und Tage*, 36; the sentence is not in the 1920 version: *Werke und Tage*, vol. 1 (Jena: Diederichs, 1920).

43. Buber, *Briefwechsel*, 2:8–9.

44. See the "Haschisch Protokolle," 11 May 1928, in Walter Benjamin, *Gesammelte Schriften*, ed. Rolf Tiedemann and Hermann Schweppenhäuser, 7 vols. (Frankfurt am Main: Suhrkamp, 1978–1989), 6:771–79. The editors of Benjamin's works suggest that Joël could also be the author of the later protocols, but by that time Joël was no longer alive.

45. Buber, *Briefwechsel*, 2:339.

46. Ibid., 2:50–51.

47. Werner Kraft, *Gespräche mit Martin Buber* (Munich: Kösel, 1966), 26.

48. Blüher, *Die Erhebung Israels gegen die christlichen Güter* (Hamburg: Hanseatische Verlaganstalt, 1931), 199.

49. Buber, *Briefwechsel*, 2:465.

50. *Die Achse der Natur* (Hamburg-Bergerdorf: Strom, 1949).

51. Buber, *Briefwechsel*, 3:335.

52. The Blüher Archives preserve an undated and unpublished draft fragment (box 10), in which Blüher excuses himself for an angry letter (obviously the one just mentioned) that he wrote under the influence of an "intimate advisor." But Blüher still justifies his former displeasure by remarking that they had several oral and written contacts (!) after the publication of *Die Erhebung* and Buber never contested the allegations. He adds: "Well, in view of my approaching death this is past." The editors of Buber's correspondence were apparently not aware of this fragment, though in connection with Blüher's undated letter (3:369–73) they report as information received from the Blüher Archives that Blüher, who was already fatally ill, underwent a crisis upon receiving Buber's letter of 13 March 1953 (Buber, *Briefwechsel*, 3:373).

13 Women's Comedy and Its
Intellectual Fathers: Marx as
the Answer to Freud

GAIL FINNEY

At a time when socialism has all but vanished from the global stage,
it remains instructive to study its representation on the dramatic stage,
since the practice of socialism and its ideological underpinnings in Marxist
theory have been enormously influential for the theater of the past century.
Perhaps foremost in this heritage is Bertolt Brecht, whose epic theater is
avowedly indebted to the dramatist's training in Marxist theory and whose
own impact on twentieth-century drama has been profound.

Among some of the more interesting heirs of Brechtian theory and practice are contemporary women playwrights whose work integrates this influence with feminist and psychoanalytic thought that might at first glance
seem unsuited to such a linkage. Possibly even more surprising is the blending of these heterogeneous ideologies within the comic mode.

I would like to exemplify the effectiveness of such an innovative combination of intellectual and cultural influences through a comparison of the
comic dramas *Cloud Nine* (premiered 1979) by the British playwright Caryl
Churchill (b. 1938) and *George Sand* (premiered 1988) by the German writer
Ginka Steinwachs (b. 1942). My analysis will illuminate the ways in which
the two writers employ antirealist techniques in order to call critical attention to the sexual, economic, and social practices that have been buttressed
by the aesthetics of realist theater in the West.

Although psychoanalytic theory is an important influence on both Churchill and Steinwachs, these plays contain a strong indictment of Freud's
views on female sexuality and femininity. To put it simply and to announce
my argument in advance, for both writers the answer to Freud is Marx: in
place of Freud's thought, which rests on a hierarchy of gender as equated

with sex, they advocate pluralism in terms of gender and sex, and egalitarianism in terms of class and race. Although Marx's writings do not focus on matters of sex, gender, and aesthetics, for Churchill and Steinwachs the economic egalitarianism he advocates goes hand in hand with sexual and aesthetic pluralism. In other words, although the debt of the two playwrights to their intellectual fathers is considerable, as I will show, the one father—Freud—is largely rejected while the other—Marx—is embraced.

Like so much drama, Churchill's *Cloud Nine* focuses on a family and on the complexities of the relationships between its members. We watch as the family father Clive carries on with a Mrs. Saunders behind the back of his wife Betty, who, while on the surface is extremely conventional and subservient to her husband, falls for his friend, the explorer Harry Bagley. The young children of Clive and Betty, Victoria and Edward, are cared for by a governess called Ellen.

But this is no typical British family, and no typical play. The first act is set in a British colony in Africa during the Victorian era, the second act in London in the present, although the characters have aged only twenty-five years. Even more striking is Churchill's use of cross-casting: in Act I, Betty is played by a man and the family's black servant Joshua by a white man, in each case embodying the figures who shape their behavior and self-image; the nine-year-old Edward is played by a woman (as Churchill writes, "within the English tradition of women playing boys,"[1] but he is also a budding homosexual); and the two-year-old Victoria is played by a dummy, reflecting the way she, as a young girl, is being raised. In the second act, all characters are played by actors of their own sex except Cathy, the daughter of Victoria's friend Lin, in a move that according to Churchill simply represents a reversal of Edward's earlier casting, although further reason could be found in her fondness for violence and weapons. Although considered radical and daring at the time of its premiere in 1979, Churchill's *Cloud Nine* has during the past twenty years become firmly situated in the canon of twentieth-century theater, if not canonized; Susan Carlson calls it "one of the most widely known comedies by a contemporary British woman."[2]

One character who is decidedly not cross-cast, but rather completely at home in his natural identity, is Clive. As one whose job is to look after Her Majesty's domains, he functions as a virtual personification of the British colonial presence in Africa. His representative function is made clear in his exhortation to his son Edward: "Through our father we love our Queen and our God, Edward. Do you understand? It is something men understand" (*CN*, I:43). At the outset of the play, with the Union Jack flying high, Clive and his family sing a song of praise to Queen Victoria, the large empire over which she rules, and the forces of war that keep it safe. For Clive, British imperialism is a "high ideal" (*CN*, II:111). Yet Clive is cruelly domineering and patronizing to blacks and women alike.

Clive's similar treatment of blacks and women intimates a parallel between colonialism and male-female relations in the Victorian era. This parallel becomes explicit when we compare remarks he makes to his mistress Caroline Saunders and his wife Betty with statements made to his friend Harry Bagley, the explorer. Clive tells Caroline Saunders, "You are dark like this continent" (*CN*, I:23), and exclaims to his wife Betty that "Women can be treacherous and evil. They are darker and more dangerous than men" and that "We must resist this dark female lust, Betty, or it will swallow us up" (*CN*, I:44–45); talking to Harry Bagley, he refers to the "natives," whom he also calls "savages" (*CN*, I:18), as his enemy: "there is something dangerous. Implacable. This whole continent is my enemy. I am pitching my whole mind and will and reason and spirit against it to tame it, and I sometimes feel it will break over me and swallow me up" (*CN*, I:43–44).

There is no mistaking the comic effect that lines like these are intended to produce in contemporary audiences. Yet the parallel Clive's discourse draws between the murky, untamed dangers of female sexuality and the dark, primitive hostility of the colonized blacks in Africa, both threatening to "swallow him up," can scarcely help but evoke the infamous metaphor conceived by an actual Victorian personage, Sigmund Freud: "the sexual life of adult women is a 'dark continent' for psychology" (with the phrase "dark continent" left in English in the German original).[3] Sander Gilman describes this expression as a "phrase with which [Freud] tied female sexuality to the image of contemporary colonialism and thus to the exoticism and pathology of the Other."[4]

Because the allusion to Freudian thinking is so unmistakable, the sexual, economic, and racial imperialism under attack in *Cloud Nine* can be illuminated by a capsule rehearsal of Freud's views on femininity and female sexuality. Prominent among the characteristics he associates with women is dependence, in particular on their fathers: "the number of women who remain till a late age tenderly dependent on a paternal object, or indeed on their real father, is very great."[5] (The analogy to the British colonizer, paternalistically assuming the white man's burden vis-à-vis the childlike, benighted natives, is not difficult to recognize.) Similarly, Freud dissociates women from the sphere of work and civilization, since he views them as intellectually inferior due to "the inhibition of thought necessitated by sexual suppression";[6] rather, "Women represent the interests of the family and of sexual life. The work of civilization has become increasingly the business of men, it confronts them with ever more difficult tasks and compels them to carry out instinctual sublimations of which women are little capable."[7]

Also notable in Freud's conception of femininity are women's paltry sense of justice and their secretiveness and insincerity.[8] Interestingly, he associates women with both narcissism and masochism; for him the narcissistic woman is "the type of female most frequently met with, which is probably the purest and truest one" — and yet: "The suppression of women's aggressiveness which is prescribed for them constitutionally and imposed on them socially favours the development of powerful masochistic impulses, which succeed, as we know, in binding erotically the destructive trends which have been diverted inwards."[9]

Woman, according to Freud, is truly a multifaceted being. Little wonder, then, that she is more prone to hysteria (psychosomatic illness), the condition that plagued so many of Freud's earliest Jewish female patients in Vienna, whose maladies have been preserved in the *Studies on Hysteria* written by himself and his colleague Josef Breuer (vol. II of *SE*). And given the picture he paints of femininity, little wonder that he assumes that women long to be men — the feeling that has famously come to be known as "penis envy": "The wish to get the longed-for penis eventually in spite of everything may contribute to the motives that drive a mature woman to analysis, and what she may reasonably expect from analysis — a capacity, for instance, to carry on an intellectual profession — may often be recognized as a sublimated modification of this repressed wish."[10]

What all this comes down to is that Freud, as he repeats from his earliest writings on the subject to his last — from his statement in *Three Essays on the Theory of Sexuality* (1905) that the erotic life of women is "still veiled in an impenetrable obscurity" to his characterization of the nature of femininity as a "riddle" in "Femininity" (1933)[11] — is baffled by women. In the latter essay, which is the written version of an undelivered lecture, he continues addressing his imagined audience as follows: "Nor will *you* have escaped worrying over this problem — those of you who are men; to those of you who are women this will not apply — you are yourselves the problem" (113). One of Freud's most frequently quoted statements is his description to Marie Bonaparte of "the great question that has never been answered and which I have not yet been able to answer, despite my thirty years of research into the feminine soul": "What does a woman want? [Was will das Weib?]."[12]

In short, women are as darkly impenetrable to Freud as the native inhabitants of Africa are to Churchill's Clive. But what is clear about patriarchy and imperialism is the bipolar nature of their ideology: they are both based on clear-cut, hierarchical differences — between white and black, male and female, normal and abnormal, powerful and weak, wealthy and impoverished. By contrast, what Churchill advocates instead is an egalitarian pluralism, a multiplicity of views and ways of being in the world.

This position is perhaps most evident in the sphere of sexuality. Whereas Clive's attitude toward homosexuality is clear from his reaction to Harry's sexual overture to him — "The most revolting perversion. Rome fell, Harry, and this sin can destroy an empire" (*CN*, I:52), other characters embrace a homosexual or bisexual way of life. In the second act, Victoria's friend Lin, a divorced single mother, persuades Victoria, who is married with a young son, to enter into a sexual relationship with her, and Edward has a boyfriend called Gerry. When Victoria and Edward have difficulties with their respective partners, they both move in with Lin. The play's most graphic expression of pluralistic sexuality is put into the mouth of Edward, who, lamenting that he is sick of men, says, "I think I'm a lesbian" (*CN*, II:92);[13] he later reveals that he sleeps in the same bed as his sister and her lover Lin. In *Cloud Nine*, no one form of sexuality — heterosexuality, homosexuality, or bisexuality — is placed above the others as the norm; no one form has hegemony; all can coexist. Indeed, pluralistic sexuality provides the key to the meaning of the play's title. The song "Cloud Nine," sung in Act II during a scene between Gerry and the Edward character from Act I, includes the following stanzas:

Smoked some dope on the playground swings
Higher and higher on true love's wings
He said Be mine and you're on Cloud 9.

Twentyfive years on the same Cloud 9.

Who did she meet on her first blind date?
The guys were no surprise but the lady was great
They were women in love, they were on Cloud 9.

(*CN*, II:99–100)

The title metaphor hence contains associations with transgression—such as drugs and homosexuality—yet Churchill encourages us to look carefully at the social code that regards these activities as transgressions.

The larger ramifications of the play's statements about sexuality are made explicit by Victoria, who tells Lin, "You can't separate fucking and economics" (*CN*, II:96). The linkage between sexual and economic exploitation reprises the theme of colonialism that dominates Act I, where the institutions of imperialism and conventional familial and sexual constellations are simultaneously undermined through their connection by Harry Bagley, celebrating "the empire—the family—the married state to which I have always aspired" (*CN*, I:60), since by this point the audience knows that he is a sexually voracious homosexual and pederast. The survival of imperialism in the present and its often disastrous repercussions continue to be critiqued in Act II, in the news that Lin's brother has been killed in the army in Belfast and the recurring nightmares she has as a result.

More broadly, Churchill's attention to economic oppression reflects the influence of Marxism on her intellectual formation. Her conception of an ideal society—"decentralized, nonauthoritarian, communist, nonsexist"— reflects the typical characterization of her as a "socialist-feminist intellectual."[14] The Joint Stock Theatre Group, the collective with which Churchill worked between 1976 and its closing in 1989 and which produced *Cloud Nine*, was socialist in orientation. Given its source, Clive's lament at the end of the play that Africa is presumably to be communist can be read as a statement in support of that doctrine. Yet the ideology that the play ultimately seems to advocate is less one of doctrinaire Marxism than of simple egalitarianism, free from binary power relationships between oppressor and oppressed, exploiter and exploited. The best exemplification of this ideology is found in the domestic situation featured in Act II, in which Lin and Victoria work and Edward stays home with their children, an arrangement that breaks with conventional, hierarchical gender and sex roles and that manages to provide for all of them.

So what do these ideological issues have to do with comedy? In fact,

Cloud Nine abounds in comedy, both verbal humor and comic situations. Much of the humor stems from the dramatic irony created by the gap between the actual status of the actors, visible to the audience, and the roles they are assigned by other characters. For example, early in the play Clive announces, "My son is young. I'm doing all I can / To teach him to grow up to be a man," to which Edward—who we recall is played by a woman— responds, "What father wants I'd dearly like to be. / I find it rather hard as you can see" (*CN*, I:4); the humor is of course magnified by the incongruous use of rhyming couplets in iambic pentameter. Somewhat in the same vein of sex-gender slippage, when Clive, Harry, and Edward play catch, Edward misses the ball, thus demonstrating the lack of athletic ability that he associates with the female characters. When Clive and Betty talk to their young daughter Victoria (played by a dummy) and she does not respond, Clive observes, "Not very chatty tonight are we?" (*CN*, I:12). Later Betty remarks that "Victoria was a pretty child just like a little doll—" (*CN*, II:70). Humor is also created by an incongruity between characters' expectations of other characters and the actual language or behavior of those characters, as when the governess Ellen tells her employer Betty that she does not like children (*CN*, I:50). The exaggerated nature of the amorous language Ellen uses in trying to seduce Betty is rendered all the more grotesque by Ellen's marriage to Harry Bagley.

This wedding between a male homosexual and a lesbian, the event with which the first act closes, functions as an ironic inversion of one of the most stalwart conventions of comic drama, an inversion magnified by the indication in the stage directions that Joshua raises his gun to shoot Clive while he is making a toast to the happy couple. This thwarting of comic convention links Churchill to other women writers of comedy, particularly in recent decades. Work is increasingly being done on the ways in which women, who for so long participated in comic drama mainly as the object of men's humor, adapt the comic mode to their purposes today.

To indicate just a few traits viewed as characteristic of women's comedy, process comes to take precedence over resolution so that the "happy ending" is deemphasized (indeed, since the end of a comic drama in the male tradition has so frequently been marriage, a resolution that often meant the end of a woman's autonomy, from the female perspective this ending was not necessarily a happy one). The pluralism and multiplicity of vision that I have been discussing in thematic terms with regard to Churchill are evident formally as well; comedy by women often eschews linearity and conventional laws of time and space in favor of simultaneity and heterogeneity.[15] Churchill's break with these laws in *Cloud Nine* has been mentioned—the fact that Act I is set in a British colony in Africa during Victorian times and Act II in London in 1979, while the characters have aged only twenty-five years. Similarly, the play's conclusion stands in clear contrast to the conventional comic ending: in lieu of a wedding, the Betty character of Act I embraces the Betty of Act II, symbolizing the fact that Betty, who has left Clive, gotten a job, and found a place of her own, has finally come to accept who she is.

To an even greater degree than Churchill's *Cloud Nine*, Ginka Steinwachs's play *George Sand* represents a pluralistic, twentieth-century response to a hierarchical, nineteenth-century conception of gender, sexuality, and the social structures that support them. In the play, a series of scenes depict the adventures of the historical Sand—writer, feminist, revolutionary, lover of many famous men and women, and explorer who crossed the Alps alone and on foot—from the early 1830s until 1876, paying special attention to her husband, her lovers, her children, her divorce trial, her role in the Revolution of 1848, and her death. This summary, however, makes the play sound like a nineteenth-century realist novel, and it is anything but that. It could best be described as a happening or a comic extravaganza, roaming freely through time and space, moving without clear transitions from nineteenth-century Paris to Majorca, Venice, and the banks of the Nile; and interweaving dream, hallucination, and reality. Nevertheless the objects of Steinwachs's critique are recognizable, and even more vividly than in *Cloud Nine,* Marxist inspiration colors comic vision.

In economic terms, the primary target of Steinwachs's attack is not imperialism, as in *Cloud Nine,* but the commodification of art and the artist. George, eavesdropping on the art scene in Paris, describes it as "the hubbub of literature on the stock exchange of the art market . . . where value and lack of value are represented as currency."[16] Even this most down-to-earth setting betrays Steinwachs's fondness for surrealism (she wrote her dissertation at the École Normale in Paris on André Breton): predatory crocodiles infest the literary marketplace as the Seine becomes the Nile. The most pervasive symbol in the play for the relationship between art and commerce is the Nineteenth-Century Opera Express of Art, a train engineered by Gustave Flaubert and stoked by Honoré de Balzac; as Katrin Sieg points out,

"The image of the literary machine as a train is a visual pun on the word *Kohle* as 'coals' and 'money.'"[17] Stendhal and Victor Hugo are passengers on the train, as is George Sand.

As a woman artist, Sand is doubly commodified. The status of women as commodities is noted by Marx in *Capital*:

It is plain that commodities cannot go to market and make exchanges of their own account. We must, therefore, have recourse to their guardians, who are also their owners. Commodities are things, and therefore without power of resistance against man. If they are wanting in docility he can use force; in other words, he can take possession of them.

In the 12th century, so renowned for its piety, they included amongst commodities some very delicate things. Thus a French poet of the period enumerates amongst the goods to be found in the market of Landit, not only clothing, shoes, leather, agricultural implements, &c., but also *"femmes folles de leur corps"* [wanton women].[18]

The introduction of Marxist thought is not inappropriate, since Steinwachs, like Churchill, studied Marxism. As we will see, much in *George Sand* reflects this training.

The answer of Steinwachs's Sand, as of the actual Sand, to her double commodification—as both artist and woman—is to adopt male dress and habits. Her notorious male attire and the cigars she smokes are not intended merely to be provocative but to help her win some of the rights and freedoms that men in her society enjoy. Sand's trousers function as a crucial symbol in Steinwachs's play. When George rides her horse into the men's shop to request a pair of pants, the salesmen assume that they are for her husband. When she clarifies her wish, the manager responds, "we don't make trousers for women . . . we now live in a world which has been perfectly tailored to the needs of men, whose privileges no one can touch" (*GS*, II:297). Sand's response is to crack her riding crop and exclaim, "I AM THIS NO ONE, I require them immediately—" (*GS*, II:298), a quotation from Gotthold E. Lessing's "Seventeenth Letter Concerning the Newest Literature" of 16 February 1759, his famous polemic against the early eighteenth-century German theater critic Johann C. Gottsched for advocating the wholesale and, in Lessing's opinion, unimaginative imitation of French dramatic models. Just as Lessing distinguishes himself from the critical consensus of his day by standing up to the authority of Gottsched, so does Sand's challenge to male privilege set her apart from her peers. Given its incongruity in this context, however, the quotation from Lessing seems intended above all as an attack on rules and regulations in general, whether aesthetic conventions or gender barriers.

Steinwachs ironically highlights George's titanic status by evoking a parallel to the life of the greatest hero in German neoclassical drama: as she gallops through Paris following the scene in the shop, she proclaims, "here is where I want to live, become a human being" (GS, II:298), echoing the famous lines spoken by Goethe's Faust as he walks among the townspeople on Easter day after overcoming a period of suicidal depression, "I'm human here, here I can be!"[19]

George's offer of "my horse for a pair of pants" (GS, II:295 and passim) makes explicit the relationship between gender and material worth to which Steinwachs is calling attention; as George declares, "George Sand . . . proudly presents the fashion of women's trousers on economic grounds" (GS, II:300). Her masculine attire symbolizes her "completely insidious hope" to be able to live by means of her own writing (GS, II:300) (as the historical Sand largely succeeded in doing). As we later learn, her pose is at least partially successful: she trades regularly at the men's shop and is a female member of the Jockey Club.

In the scene "G(e)orge of Fontainebleau," George's trousers become a graphic symbol of her ability to negotiate between different worlds. As she is poised spread-eagled over a gorge, the stage directions specify that her right leg represents the institution of marriage, the church, the military, and the fatherland, while her left leg represents free love, anarchy, debauchery, and excess; her left leg is associated with her lover Jules Sandeau, a journalist who calls her a woman in motion, whereas her right leg is associated with her husband the baron, who insists that she is a woman of standing. In fact she is both these things, as the play's subtitle indicates — "A Woman in Motion, the Woman of Standing" — and in this scene George not only alternates between balancing herself on one leg and then the other, but decides that she will divide the year between time spent writing with Sandeau and time spent with her family. This quality of fluidity, of negotiation across categories of gender, sexual mores, and professions, links the character George Sand to her creator; as Mona Winter writes, "[Ginka Steinwachs] explores her anatomy and invents limits that do not limit."[20]

George's alternation between the two "legs" of liberal and conservative values, facilitated by the trousers she wears, or her adoption of a masculine pose, can be read as emblematic of the dialectical vision that informs much of the play. I have mentioned Steinwachs's Marxist training, and her dialectical vision in *George Sand* can be illuminated through reference to his work.

Marx's concept of the dialectic is indebted to the thought of Hegel. Marx critiques much in Hegel's philosophy, insofar as Hegel is an idealist and views the family and civil society as products of the idea of the state, whereas Marx, a materialist, sees these institutions as concrete realities and as the initiators of the state.[21] Similarly, in the afterword to the second German edition of *Capital*, Marx writes of the need to "discover the rational kernel within the the mystical shell" of Hegelian dialectic (vol. 35 of *Collected Works*, 19). Yet Marx recognizes that Hegel was the first to present the "general form of working [of the dialectic] in a comprehensive and conscious manner" (19), and much in Marx's conception of the dialectic reflects Hegel's influence.

With regard to Steinwachs's play, the fact that George Sand does not rest on either of her "legs" exclusively, but rather adapts facets of the ways of life represented by both is analogous to the process of sublation [*Aufhebung*] in the Hegelian-Marxist dialectic; although dialectical categories typically represent polar opposites, often reflecting laws of nature or of human beings, there exists a unity in the conflict between the two such that negating the second term leads to a new, synthetic entity that contains features of both opposites. For Marx, the notion of the dialectic is useful in talking about the contradictions of capitalism, the oppositions and conflicting forces that make up capitalism and its modes of production. With reference to the economically driven progress of history, in Marxist theory the dialectical tensions within capitalism and between capitalism and socialism would lead, in Marx's expectation, to the eventual triumph of the latter. Ira Gollobin offers a useful summary of the function of dialectical categories for Marx:

In *Capital*, the dialectical categories are like guideposts, spokes that in a variety of ways helped guide Marx from the periphery of reality toward its hub, the innermost features: for example, in differentiating *objective* reality from *subjective* fancy and basing himself on an *objective* approach; in finding that commodities — seemingly simple and well-understood entities—had a hidden *essence* behind their *appearance;* in tracing the *forms* of exchange from barter to the use of money as a universal equivalent and the *content* of each *form;* in delineating the production of *absolute* and of *relative* surplus-value; in ferreting out, in the welter of seemingly purely fortuitous economic occurrences, those that are *contingent* and those that are *necessary;* in determining the *particular* and the *general* in various economic relations.[22]

Not only does *George Sand* embrace a dialectical vision, its rhetoric points up the critique of the class system—a central element of Marxist thought—that helped inspire the revolution of 1848 in which the actual Sand took part and of which the Sand of Steinwachs is characterized as the "VIRTUAL MOTHER" (*GS,* XI:330): "THE BAD THING IS THAT THE EMPIRICAL CONDITION OF THE FRENCH BOURGEOISIE CANNOT YET ALLOW THE BIRTH OF THE SPIRIT OF EGALITARIAN JUSTICE IN PRODUCTION- AND CONSUMPTION-BASED PARTNERSHIPS. EXPLOITATION OF WORKERS. UNDERPRIVILEGED CRAFTSMEN. SOCIETY WOULD RATHER BE UNCHRISTIAN THAN SOCIAL . . . HERE THE COARSE MATERIALS OF THE POOR MASSES—THERE THE FINE FABRICS OF THE RULING CLASSES" (*GS,* XI:330).

Steinwachs's portrayal of this revolution as propelled by ideas that were increasingly coming to be associated with Marx is intensified by the fact that the text describes the revolution of 1848 as preparation for the Paris Commune of 1870–71 and the October Revolution in Russia. Likewise in the political arena, the dialectical vision attributed to Sand is split between her children: her daughter Solange, true heir to her father, speaks in favor of the need for military might to protect the interests of the proprietors' class and refers to the people as "MERDE," whereas George's son Maurice supports the proletariat and talks of a "DREAM PEOPLE FOR A DREAM REPUBLIC" (*GS,* XI:336).

As in Churchill's *Cloud Nine,* the pluralistic nature of Steinwachs's vision is expressed on a sexual level as well. Neither heterosexuality nor homosexuality nor bisexuality is advocated as the "proper" way to live; in the play's view each sexual orientation has a right to exist, and they coexist side by side. This position is manifested most extensively in the title character, who, like her historical model, counts not only Sandeau, Alfred de Musset, Frederic Chopin, the sculptor Alexandre Manceau, and other men among her lovers, but also Marie Dorval, an actress at the Comédie Française. An indirect, playful reference to Sand's bisexuality can be read in the reference in the scene of the divorce trial to "THE TWO-WORLD-THEORY OF HOMOLULU AND HETOROGONIA [sic] IN PHILOSOPHY" (GS, X:322).[23] As in Cloud Nine, sexual transgressiveness is linked here with other illicit pleasures; in the erotic scene between George and Marie, the two smoke marijuana onstage, appropriately enough, at a table with a statue of Baudelaire and the inscription "PARADIS ARTIFICIELS" (GS, IV:311).

As the stage directions tell us, the women's resulting state of intoxication "stimulates a production of the oral theater"; Marie later refers to the "palatetheater of the mouth" (GS, IV:312, 314). These important concepts in Steinwachs's aesthetic are elucidated by her brief essay "The Theater as Oral Institution" (1979), which includes the following passage:

> The theater as oral institution is oral. Orality in the Freud-Lacanian theory of the libidinal stages denotes a regression to the first and lowest of three (among which there are two higher) stages. All progress is regressive. . . . That indirectly attests progressivity to the theatoral theater. An oasis in the desert, I*d* capital I italic d, liquifidates a l(M)anguage as dessiccated [sic] as frozen assets. Articulatory relishing of words. In every instance, wallowing precedes swallowing. Babblebanquets, speechfeasts. (Translated and quoted by Sieg, 183)

Steinwachs's oral theater exploits multiple possibilites of the mouth—as the organ that transmits verbal language; as a polyfunctional sexual organ, capable of experiencing erotic pleasure of numerous kinds with both sexes; and as the agent of culinary and intoxicative pleasure.

Her aesthetic can be seen as an extension of Brecht's notion of "culinary theater," a term that he used for the most part pejoratively: he endeavored to create theater that would not simply be enjoyed and consumed by audiences, but that would be received intellectually and provoke critical thought that would ideally lead to social reform. Steinwachs has a similar intention, but views oral pleasure—of multiple kinds—as a means of achieving it.

In the short production of the oral theater within Steinwachs's play, the realms of sexual and aesthetic pleasure merge in the dialogue of the drug-intoxicated George and Marie, as the denotative meaning of language is subordinated to the sensual sounds and suggestive power of words. The overall effect, as with George's negotiation between two genders and two sexual orientations, is one of fluidity and simultaneity in which contradictions can coexist, one in which boundaries — whether established by social convention or by rational, lucid thought — are erased.

Steinwachs's concept of theater as an oral institution is clearly meant as part of her critique of the aesthetic doctrines of German classical theater, most overtly, of Schiller's 1784 essay "The Stage Considered as a Moral Institution [Die Schaubühne als eine moralische Anstalt betrachtet]." For Steinwachs, Schiller's sense of the theater's primary function as didactic robs it of its potential to give pleasure. As the passage cited above indicates, Steinwachs's oral theater instead invokes another German-language thinker, Freud, whose "Three Essays on the Theory of Sexuality" (1905) postulate three phases of development in infantile sexuality, the oral, anal, and phallic stages, each referring to the part of the body on which the infant's erotic interest is focused. Steinwachs's indebtedness to the Freudian belief that oral pleasure is primal is reflected also in her essay "The Palatetheater of the Mouth" (1983), in which she writes, "In talking of body language . . . it is sometimes forgotten that the language of the mouth or mouth language is n o t m e r e l y a n o t h e r, but rather the first of all gestural languages, p r e c e d i n g t h o s e o f h a n d a n d f o o t, o f u p p e r b o d y a n d l o w e r b o d y."[24] The influence of Freud on Steinwachs is evident as well in her published dissertation, *Mythologie des Surrealismus oder die Rückverwandlung von Kultur in Natur* (1971), one chapter of which uses Freud's theories of dream interpretation to elucidate Breton's concept of automatic writing.

When it comes to adult female sexuality, however, Steinwachs, like Churchill, distances herself from Freudian thought. The play's pluralistic attitude toward gender and sexual orientation, manifested above all in George's alternation between feminine and masculine roles and between heterosexualty and homosexuality, flies in the face of Freudian views on these matters. As we have seen, Freud's views are resolutely hierarchical, defining gender according to biological sex (men are to behave in a "masculine" fashion, women in a "feminine" fashion) and positing the male as the norm and the female as the deviation from it. Further overt jabs at Freudian conceptions of human sexuality include the stage directions to the first scene, a dream scenario, "SIGMUND FREUD INTERPRETS THE BREATHLESS DREAM-IMAGE AS FOLLOWS: SEXUAL INTERCOURSE ON THE RISE" (GS, I:290) — in view of the play's portrayal of lesbian sexuality, surely an ironic observation. In like manner, the language of an attorney at George's divorce trial can be read as a virtual parody of Freudian thinking on sexuality and gender roles, which can be seen to represent the views of most of his contemporaries in nineteenth-century Europe: "WOMEN IN DRAG WHO PURSUE THE MUSE, WOMEN ARTISTS WITH AMBITIOUS VIEWS, are and will always be an abomination to us, the BLACK PANTHERS of the FRACTION of THE BLACK PANTHERS in the GOVERNMENT. long live the PHALLUS. long live the PHALLUS. down with the mannish women. fear our malice. genital supremacy" (GS, X:325–326). George's response to this tirade constitutes a further attack on Freudian views, "down with the MYTH OF VAGINAL ORGASM, with the male-dominated imagination of the cunt" (GS, X:326).

The aesthetic pluralism reflected in Steinwachs's concept of theater as oral institution is evident in virtually every facet of the style of George Sand. Although Churchill breaks with laws of logical temporality in the transition from the first act of Cloud Nine to the second, in moving from Victorian times to 1979 while retaining the same characters, yet presenting them as only twenty-five years older, she maintains temporal consistency within each act. By contrast, much of George Sand jumps around freely between time periods and levels of reality. While most of the play is set in nineteenth-century France, references to contemporary European and American culture are interwoven into the text. Allusions to radical politics, such as the activity of the Black Panthers, are found along with references to icons of popular culture like MGM; both high literature—for example, the German author Botho Strauss—and popular literature—Bonjour Tristesse—are invoked. The play even contains evidence of Steinwachs's studies of literary and cultural theory, including references to Walter Benjamin, to the "transition from the raw to the cooked" (GS, IV:310), to Deleuze and Guattari, and others. Not only do we encounter Balzac, characters from his novels make an appearance as well.

One of the best illustrations of the heterogeneous, simultaneously satiric and surreal quality of much of the play can be found in a passage from the stage directions for the scene of George's divorce trial:

The GRANDVILLEORCHESTRA of rhinos, with the support of four green-monkeys as tambour-majorettes, conducted by a capuchin monkey, play the march. one, two, three, four, turn left, the ORCHESTRA turns from the courtroom of the STAGE into the auditorium of the THEATER. the three presiding asses from the gray fraternity occupy the court desk. in front of it, the attorneys confront each other. MAITRE THIOT DE VARENNES holds the lion of the salons, CASIMIR BARON DUDEVANT, on a leash; MAITRE MICHEL EVERARD DE BOURGES holds GEORGE SAND the lioness on his leash. an anticipatory scratching spreads through the audience of gapers and apes. (*GS*, X:322)

Linguistically, as well (and of course orthographically), the play is strikingly heterogeneous, punning freely and abundantly; inserting Latin phrases from the Catholic mass into the initial dream scene set in the atelier of the sculptor and lover of Sand, Alexandre Manceau; alternating between various languages in a seemingly random fashion; and filled with neologisms. Most of these devices are humorous, yet as should be apparent by now, the play does not move toward a conventional comic resolution. As in the case of Betty in *Cloud Nine*, the title character of this play progresses not toward marriage but away from it, becoming divorced in the course of the action. Although the historical George Sand was the first woman in European history to win back her premarital property in a divorce trial (Sieg, 187), the play does not end on a note of triumph. While the penultimate scene presents what could become a happy ending in its depiction of a class-free utopia where the needs of everyone are taken care of, Steinwachs undercuts this vision by calling attention to the greed and avid consumption that infects even the workers now that they have achieved the goal of the revolution. Most strikingly, the figure called HISTORY, portrayed as a "gracious virgin with flowing hair," "takes one step forward and two steps back" (*GS*, XI:338). And the final scene of the play, in which Sand dies and her lover Manceau shoots himself at her bedside, thwarts comic convention even more emphatically.

Both Churchill and Steinwachs, like so many other contemporary women writers of comic drama, resist or reject outright the conventions of a mode in which resolution has typically depended on tying up loose ends by tying down female characters, metaphorically speaking. Both *Cloud Nine* and *George Sand* advocate political and economic egalitarianism as well as an aesthetic and sexual pluralism that embraces contradiction and multiple possibilities, showing that similarities in their intellectual formation—

above all the influence of their intellectual father Karl Marx—constitute a more decisive factor for their work than do their differing nationalities.

In the end, the vision of the playful, whimsical Steinwachs appears darker than that of Churchill, who concludes her play on a forward-looking note as Betty achieves autonomy and self-awareness. Yet a haunting line repeated several times in the course of *George Sand* suggests that Steinwachs is not without hope for progress and reform: "THE THEATER FLIES AHEAD. we must follow it" (*GS*, XI:331 and passim) (an allusion to Ariane Mnouchkine's film about Molière). An interesting paradox emerges here. In her invocation of the theater's function as a model, Steinwachs echoes precisely the aesthetic against which her doctrine of the theater as oral institution reacted: Schiller's notion of the stage as a moral, didactic institution. Perhaps her thought is even more dialectical than she recognizes.

NOTES

1. Caryl Churchill, *Cloud Nine* (*CN*) (1979; New York: Routledge, 1991), Introduction, viii; subsequent quotations will be cited parenthetically in the text by act and page number.

2. Carlson, *Women and Comedy: Rewriting the British Theatrical Tradition* (Ann Arbor: University of Michigan Press, 1991), 189. Numerous studies have explored the potential of cross-casting and cross-dressing as a subversive device. These include Sue-Ellen Case, "Toward a Butch-Femme Aesthetic," in *Making a Spectacle: Feminist Essays on Contemporary Women's Theatre*, ed. Lynda Hart (Ann Arbor: University of Michigan Press, 1989), 282–99; Marjorie Garber, *Vested Interests: Cross-Dressing and Cultural Anxiety* (New York: Routledge, 1992); Jill Dolan, *Presence and Desire: Essays on Gender, Sexuality, Performance* (Ann Arbor: University of Michigan Press, 1993); and *The Politics and Poetics of Camp*, ed. Moe Meyer (London: Routledge, 1994). The subversive effect of cross-casting in *Cloud Nine* is questioned by James M. Harding, "Cloud Cover: (Re)Dressing Desire and Comfortable Subversions in Caryl Churchill's *Cloud Nine*," *PMLA* 113 (March 1998): 258–72, who argues that Churchill's cross-casting and other aspects of the play's staging can even serve to reinforce oppressive stereotypes; his analysis is not germane to mine, however, which is based on the written text of the play.

3. Freud, "The Question of Lay Analysis," vol. XX of *The Standard Edition of the Complete Psychological Works of Sigmund Freud*, trans. and ed. James Strachey et al. (London: Hogarth, 1955), 212; references to this edition will hereafter be cited by volume and page number to *SE*.

4. Gilman, *Difference and Pathology: Stereotypes of Sexuality, Race, and Madness* (Ithaca, N.Y.: Cornell University Press, 1985), 107.

5. Freud, "Femininity," *SE* XXII:119.

6. Freud, "'Civilized' Sexual Morality and Modern Nervous Illness," *SE* IX:199.

7. Freud, *Civilization and Its Discontents, SE* XXI:103.

8. Freud, "Femininity," *SE* XXII:134; *Three Essays on the Theory of Sexuality, SE* VII:151.

9. Freud, "On Narcissism: An Introduction," *SE* XIV:88; "Femininity," *SE* XXII:116.

10. Freud, "Femininity," *SE* XXII:125.

11. Freud, *Three Essays on the Theory of Sexuality, SE* VII:151; "Femininity," *SE* XXII:113.

12. Quoted by Ernest Jones, *The Life and Work of Sigmund Freud,* ed. and abr. Lionel Trilling and Steven Marcus (New York: Basic Books, 1961), 377.

13. Anne Hermann characterizes this statement as the "most transgressive moment in the play" as well as the "most parodic"; "Travesty and Transgression: Transvestism in Shakespeare, Brecht, and Churchill," in *Performing Feminisms: Feminist Critical Theory and Theatre,* ed. Sue-Ellen Case (Baltimore, Md.: Johns Hopkins University Press, 1990), 312.

14. Quoted from an interview with Judith Thurman, *Ms.,* May 1982: 54, as cited by Austin E. Quigley, "Stereotype and Prototype: Character in the Plays of Caryl Churchill," in *Feminine Focus: The New Women Playwrights,* ed. Enoch Brater (New York: Oxford University Press, 1989), 27; second quotation from Janelle Reinelt, "Caryl Churchill and the Politics of Style," in *The Cambridge Companion to Modern British Playwrights,* ed. Reinelt and Elaine Aston (Cambridge: Cambridge University Press, 2000), 175.

15. On women's comedy, see for example Regina Barreca, ed., *Last Laughs: Perspectives on Women and Comedy* (New York: Gordon and Breach, 1988); Barreca, *They Used to Call Me Snow White . . . But I Drifted: Women's Strategic Use of Humor* (New York: Viking, 1991); Barreca, ed., *New Perspectives on Women and Comedy* (Philadelphia: Gordon and Breach, 1992); Barreca, *Untamed and Unabashed: Essays on Women and Humor in British Literature* (Detroit: Wayne State University Press, 1994); Carlson, *Women and Comedy.*

16. Ginka Steinwachs, *George Sand (GS),* trans. Jamie Owen Daniel and Katrin Sieg, with Sue-Ellen Case, in *The Divided Home/Land: Contemporary German Women's Plays,* ed. Sue-Ellen Case (Ann Arbor: University of Michigan Press, 1992), 299; subsequent quotations will be given parenthetically in the text by scene and page number.

17. Sieg, *Exiles, Eccentrics, Activists: Women in Contemporary German Theater* (Ann Arbor: University of Michigan Press, 1994), 191; subsequently cited in the text.

18. Karl Marx, *Capital, Vol. I,* in Karl Marx and Friedrich Engels, vol. 35 of *Collected Works,* trans. Richard Dixon et al. (New York: International Publishers, 1996), 94–95; subsequently cited in the text.

19. Johann Wolfgang von Goethe, *Faust, Part I,* trans. Peter Salm (New York: Bantam, 1985), 59.

20. Winter, "Universell und hyperschnell: G.S. galoppiert durch die Theater-

geschichte," in *ein mund von welt: ginka steinwachs,* ed. Sonia Nowoselsky-Müller (Bremen: Zeichen + Spuren, 1989), 44; translation mine.

21. Marx, *Contribution to the Critique of Hegel's Philosophy of Law,* in vol. 3 of Marx/Engels, *Collected Works* (New York: International Publishers, 1975), 7–9.

22. Gollobin, *Dialectical Materialism: Its Laws, Categories, and Practice* (New York: Petras Press, 1986), 299.

23. In a piece entitled "Europa," Steinwachs characterizes George Sand as "hermaphroditic"; in *Nach Europa: Texte zu einem Mythos,* ed. Sabine Groenewold (Hamburg: Europäische Verlagsanstalt, 1993), 24.

24. Steinwachs, "das gaumentheater des mundes," in *ein mund von welt,* 92; translation mine.

PART V.

Simulations of Friendship and Paternity, Claims of Responsibility: The Case of Hannah Arendt

14 Friendship and Responsibility: Arendt to Auden

DAVID HALLIBURTON

Throughout her life, Hannah Arendt championed friendship and responsibility; and though she left no single work devoted entirely to the subject, her writings testify to her ongoing fascination with both. To sort out their significance, the discussion that follows will take up the interrelated themes of neighbor, brother, member, and comrade; friend versus enemy; friendship and ethics; the concept of responsibility; the relation of guilt to responsibility; and the "family man." The discussion will close with a section in praise of the guiding themes.

Fraternity and Friendship

Friendship must be distinguished from fraternity. To start with the obvious: in a slogan like "liberty, quality, and fraternity," the concluding term carries distinctly familial overtones; the problem is that the family is at best a minor player in Arendt's discursive arena. It is not that she discounts the historical or biological significance of the family. Her key concept of natality, the capacity for new beginnings that characterizes human being-in-the-world, explicitly takes for granted the existence of parents. Such existence falls, however, within the condition of necessity: although the newborn, at the moment of conception, had to have had a mother and a father, what finally matters is that the new arrival enjoys a certain creative freedom on entering the world. If Arendt rarely mentions family roles, it is because she is concerned not with biological origination but with the consequences for labor, work, and action that are constituted, in principle, by natality. The family, for its part, remains within the purview of the household, from which one infers that condition of fraternity, of being a brother, remains there, too. For being a brother implies existing in an essentially private way. A friend, by contrast, knows no such condition, but chooses freely to bond with another in the world even as that other so chooses.

Neighbor, Brother, Member, and Comrade

Love and Saint Augustine, the dissertation Arendt wrote for Karl Jaspers, elucidates the intertwining of neighbor, brother, and member. Remembering their sinful deeds as factors in an integral community history, human beings, insofar as they are redeemed in Christ, venture new interpretation of that past. Only in this way can they sustain the interdependence of past sinfulness and present existence; and here the role of neighbor enters: "Only in this reinterpretation can the pre-existing past continue independently, beside the newly . . . experienced being. Thus, it is only from this pre-existence that the neighbor derives his specific relevance. The neighbor is the constant reminder of one's own sin. . . ."[1]

Put a little differently, love of neighbor expresses the mutuality of one person to another in past sinfulness: "The reason one should love one's neighbor is that the neighbor is fundamentally one's equal and both share the same sinful past."[2] Transcendence of such a state occurs when I recognize in the other the same revealed grace that has been visited in equal measure upon me. Eventually, if such transcendence is to develop into a higher state of being and blessing, human beings must undergo estrangement from the world, must build up among themselves that state of institutionalized solidarity we call the city of God. Here mutual love reigns as faith, dissolving one's obligations to the prior world and rendering one ontically "explicit": "When I attain the explicitness of my own being by faith, the other person's being becomes explicit as well, in equality. Only then will the other become my brother ('brother' for neighbor and 'brotherly love' are terms found throughout Augustine's writings)."[3]

At this point, the individual as neighbor and brother assumes, within the context of a spiritual polity, the fuller identity of membership. "The community of Christ is understood as a body containing all individual members within itself. . . . The individual has ceased to be anything but a member, and his entire being lies in the connections of all members in Christ."[4] Such a collectivity, positive in itself, functions as a defense against menace brought on by the shared past of sin so that "the concrete impulse of neighborly love arises from the thought of one's own peril."[5]

Arendt's portrayal of Christian membership helps us understand its culminative nature, the complexities of Augustine's reflections, and the way in which, within his imagined community, individual freedom to decide is decisively limited. "What was once necessary by generation has now become a danger involving a decision, one way or the other, about him — the individual."[6] Now the individual may, in attempting to save one's neighbor and fellow member, imitate Christ, but in so doing the individual does not, on Augustine's account, choose freely. "Mutual love lacks the element of choice; we cannot choose our 'beloved.' Since the neighbor is in our same situation, he is already there before any choices can be made."[7]

Finally, the concept of friendship figures prominently in the Christian trinity. Faced with the mystery of the Father, Son, and Holy Ghost, Augustine finds an explanatory analogue in the everyday world.

> The paradigm for a mutually predicated relationship of independent "substances" is *friendship:* two men who are friends can be said to be "independent substances" insofar as they are related to themselves; they are friends only relatively to each other. A pair of friends forms a unity, a One, insofar and as long as they are friends; the moment the friendship ceases they are again two "substances," independent of each other. . . . This is the way of the Holy Trinity: God remains One while related only to Himself but He is three in the unity with Son and Holy Ghost.[8]

The paradigm of friendship has the virtue of circumventing familiar dichotomies and hierarchies, such as body and soul, or good and evil. As a mode of mutuality, it has the further virtue of positing in friendship an essential *equality.* Given that God has created human nature in his own image, Augustine understandably looks into that nature for the relationship of mutual predication, which is friendship. In Arendt's words, "since it is precisely man's mind that distinguishes him from all other creatures, the three-in-one is likely to be found in the structure of the mind,"[9] that is, in being, knowing, and willing.

Friend and Enemy

By contrast, familiars of the secular world, especially in its modern phase, set a high value on freedom as opportunity; this is nowhere more the case than in political liberalism, with its commitment to the sovereignty of the individual and "free" moral choice. It was partly to address the short-comings of the latter that a "decisionist" debate arose in Germany follow-ing the First World War, a debate in which Carl Schmitt's *The Concept of the Political* is one central text (and the focus of numerous revisionist read-ings of Schmitt's extensive corpus) and Heidegger's *Being and Time* (though a very different book in many ways) is another. In the latter, resoluteness [Entschlossenheit] is prized as the fitting attitude of anyone desiring, or de-ciding, to exist authentically. Not a few critics, including Leo Strauss,[10] have been troubled by the lack of concreteness in the concept, in particular, the failure to establish norms for choosing this over that: for *what,* finally, is one to be resolute? Is such freedom more than a blank check? Similar ob-jections may be raised against Schmitt who, less "vague" than Heidegger, is "clear" in a more reductive way. Thus he states bluntly: "The specific po-litical distinction to which political actions and motives can be reduced is that between friend and enemy."[11]

The enemy is more "other" than most of the social actors described thus far: he is not the civic brother, not the neighbor, not the friend. He is, how-ever, or can be, the member or the comrade; it may be noted that Schmitt joined the National Socialist Party in May 1933, at the same time as Hei-degger. Schmitt's friend-enemy antinomy aims at a sort of universality of camaraderie within the political. At the same time, the antinomy has about it an immediacy and almost visceral heat.

The distinction of friend and enemy denotes the utmost degree of in-tensity of a union or separation. It can exist theoretically and practically, without having simultaneously to draw upon all those moral, aesthetic, economic, or other distinctions. The political enemy need not appear as an economic competitor, and it may even be advantageous to engage with him in business transactions. But he is, nevertheless, the other, the stranger; and it is sufficient for his nature that he is, in a specifically in-tense way, existentially something different and alien. . . . [12]

Schmitt's enemy clearly dominates the foreground of discussion. It is this figure that incites the jurist's imagination, while other roles hover, as it were, in the background. Given this inequity, how is any organization or person to decide precisely who the friend and the enemy actually are? The answer, such as it is, is contextual and at the same time utterly indeterminate; only the specifics of a situation, one must infer, can provide anything like reliable guidelines.

> Only the actual participants can correctly recognize, understand, and judge the concrete situation and settle the extreme case of conflict. Each participant is in a position to judge whether the adversary intends to negate his opponent's way of life and therefore may be repulsed or fought in order to preserve one's own form of existence. Emotionally the enemy is easily treated as being evil and ugly, because every distinction, most of all the political, as the strongest and most intense of the distinctions and categorizations, draws upon other distinctions for support.[13]

The only means by which to judge a given situation accurately is to be a participant within it—a disarmingly abstract way of arriving at a concrete decision, it seems to me. Historically, moral and political philosophers have looked for some Archimedean point of leverage for gaining a sharable perspective on a given social or ethical situation. Without some such reference point, what is to prevent a disinterested "external" observer from transferring the mean traits of the enemy, as here depicted, to the friend? The answer is, apparently, nothing: ". . . the morally evil, aesthetically ugly or economically damaging need not necessarily be the enemy; the morally good, aesthetically beautiful, and economically profitable need not necessarily become the friend in the specifically political sense of the word." All such distinctions, to Schmitt's way of thinking, are entirely dependent on circumstances and may be multiplied ad nauseam. What remains the same and publicly manifest is the friend-dichotomy antinomy per se: "Thereby the inherently objective nature and autonomy of the poetical becomes evident by virtue of its being able to treat, distinguish, and comprehend the "friend-enemy antithesis independently of other antitheses."[14] Schmitt is as prepossessed by the appeal of the enemy as Cicero is by the appeal of the friend, but the latter has decided to defend friendship as the supreme human value; and even when a given friendship goes bad, he does not allow

that either of the partners could ever become an enemy: "what has happened is just a termination of friendship and not a declaration of war. For
if a man has been your friend, it is the most discreditable thing in the world
to let him become your enemy."[15]

Friendship and Ethics

Arendt, for her part, does not follow this deviation from the broad Aristotelian view of friendship sketched out in the *Ethics*. In the latter, as in
Arendt's essay on Lessing (to which I will turn below), the enemy is hardly
theorized at all. Arendt, like Aristotle, seeks out what is positive and concrete, not what is abstract and merely possible. Friendship, as it exists in
the world, is an observable social phenomenon helping to provide cohesion
among the constituents of any given people or polity. Now, with Schmitt,
we could abstract a group of enemies opposed to my group of friends. But
the former cannot be opposed to each other: they must in fact be friends to
one another, and enemies only to us. What is there in such an enemy but
the possibility of a friendship turned against another friendship? Could a
political theory formed on such principles be anything but occasionalist?

In the second book of the *Ethics*, friendship stands, positively, for community:

> Brothers and comrades go shares in everything, other friends share this
> or that part of their possessions and to a greater or less extent accord-
> ing to the warmth of their friendship. . . . And with an intensification of
> friendship there naturally goes an increase in the sense of obligation be-
> tween the friends, because the same persons are involved and their obli-
> gations of friendship are co-extensive with their obligations in justice.[16]

Finally, Aristotle anticipates Augustine in seeing all who are thus obliged
as what amounts to civic members: "But all associations may be regarded
as parts of the association we call the state. Thus when people associate in
their travels it is to secure some advantage. . . . Well, political societies too
are believed to have been originally formed, and to continue in being, for
the advantage of the citizens."[17]

In her essay "On Humanity in Dark Times," Arendt takes a point of departure for her discussion of friendship from the ancients, which for her

means always the ancient Greeks, who "thought friends indispensable to human life, indeed that a life without friends was not really worth living."[18] Postponing specifically political perspectives, Arendt emphasizes the affective, suggesting that a shared joy is the highest joy; she also notes the modern emphasis on friendship as a function of intimacy. It is a function, however, that raises more difficulties than it solves. For, with Rousseau, the modern individual is so alienated from the greater world that

> he can truly reveal himself only in privacy and in the intimacy of face-to-face encounters. Thus it is hard for us to understand the political relevance of friendship. When, for example, we read in Aristotle that friendship among citizens is one of the fundamental requirements for the well-being of the City, we tend to think that he was speaking of no more than the absence of factions and civil war within it. But for the Greeks the essence of friendship consisted in discourse.[19]

Such discourse is more than a medium for expressing special interests, say, or for electioneering, or what have you. Discourse is to be taken in the broadest sense as responsible commentary or critique of the world, such that it comes fully to be only in being thus commented on or criticized: "For the world . . . does not become humane just because the human voice sounds in it, but only when it has become the object of discourse."[20]

The process offers no guarantees. There is nothing, for example, to prevent reductive, imbalanced, or otherwise irresponsible views of friendship. As noted above, the discourse of intimacy, brought to a peak of personal expression by Rousseau, too warmly embraces the alienated condition of the modern sensibility. Similarly, fraternity is redolent of the, as it were, prepolitical realm of domesticity and privacy. Not surprisingly, Arendt prefers the "classical" worldliness of a Lessing, whose *Nathan the Wise*, "modern as it is, might with some justice be called the classical drama of friendship."[21]

> What strikes us as so strange in the play is the 'We must, must be friends,' with which Nathan turns to the Templar, and in fact everyone he meets; for this friendship is obviously so much more important to Lessing than the passion of love; that he can brusquely cut the love story off short . . . and transform it into a relationship in which friendship is required and love ruled out. The dramatic tension of the play lies solely in the conflict that arises between friendship and humanity with truth.[22]

To approach that conflict, Arendt poses a hypothetical situation involving a "logical" argument for genocide. "Suppose that a race could indeed be shown, by indubitable scientific evidence, to be inferior; would that fact justify its extermination?"[23] Arendt answers, in part, that the divine commandment against killing one's fellow man provides too easy an answer, and the same may be said of other cultural perspectives, be they legal, moral, or religious. To face the question squarely, Arendt suggests, the question would have to be phrased as follows: "*Would any such doctrine, however convincingly proved, be worth the sacrifice of so much as a single friendship between two men?*"[24] Any response in the affirmative must suffer from, for lack of a better phrase, an excess of generality, or rather of "objectivity." The question can be addressed adequately only from a perspective beyond the familiar institutional prescriptions, whether in law, morality, or religion. That beyond is, paradoxically, at hand in the lived world: it is the realm, not of institutions, but of the human as such, the realm of the particular that should never be reduced to the "subjective" any more than the positive aspects of culture should reduced to the "objective." Again, the latter smacks of the individualistic, face-to-face intimacy popularized by Rousseau; face to face, individuals in the modern world are brought, or bring themselves, too close to one another. "We have seen what a powerful need men have . . . to move closer to one another, to seek in the warmth of intimacy the substitute for that light and illumination which only the public realm can cast."[25] In a state of intimacy, distinctions peculiar to any sovereign person slip into "the excessive closeness of brotherliness that obliterated all distinctions."[26] In the process, human beings, losing the freedom of speech and movement that are prerequisite to deciding and judging, find themselves deprived of the elbowroom of public that is the fitting arena of public expression and political activity. In such an arena, mere fraternity becomes the lesser prize, friendship the greater. Thus "Lessing was never eager really to fall out with someone with whom he had entered into a dispute; he was concerned solely with humanizing the world by incessant and continual discourse about its affairs and the things in it. He wanted to be the friend of many men, but no man's brother."[27]

The Concept of Responsibility

A famous remark by E. M. Forster, in his essay "What I Believe," invites comparison with the present line of thinking, especially as it approaches explicit problems of responsibility that will become increasingly prominent in the pages that follow. At a crucial point in his credo, Forster examines hypothetically the significance of the difference between responsibilities to friends and responsibilities to country. Before getting to these, however, it should be said that Forster's preferred term *reliability* amounts to what Arendt and Jaspers call *responsibility*. Forster writes: "I hate the idea of causes, and if I had to choose between betraying my country and betraying my friend, I hope I should have the guts to betray my country."[28] In *The Divine Comedy*, Forster points out, betraying a friend becomes a kind of capital offense: Dante "places Brutus and Cassius in the lowest circle of Hell because they had chosen to betray their friend Julius Caesar rather than their country Rome."[29] It seems hard to imagine a testimonial more congenial to Lessing's concept of friendship. The same may be said of Arendt's and Forster's views on discourse (the Englishman's term is "talking"): "Democracy has another merit. It allows criticism, and if there is no public criticism there are bound to be hushed-up scandals. . . . Parliament is often sneered at because it is a Talking Shop. I believe in it *because* it is a talking shop . . . I value it because it criticizes and talks, and because its chatter gets widely reported."[30]

On the other hand, when Arendt seeks a solution to the separation in democracy between the role of the private person and the role of the citizen, she requires the context of the state as Forster never would. Here she is closer to Jefferson's "Love your neighbour as yourself, and your country more than yourself."[31] The question becomes how to bring about a felt sense of the latter's presence comparable to the felt sense of the presence of one's neighbors? Such a sense could be obtained, Jefferson believes, by creating numerous little republics, of the type that emerged in the revolutionary societies in late eighteenth-century France, in modern workers' councils, in the system of soviets set up in Russia, and in the political wards existing in, but not always articulated with, the sovereign United States.[32] In civil life, private persons could be responsible citizens only if they could exert direct political influence through civic discourse.

Now the concept of responsibility is not without its difficulties. Entailing as it does virtually the entire sphere of the "ought," obligation, duty, and trust, it is conspicuously overdetermined. To be responsible is, in Forster's terms, as we have seen, to be reliable; Bakhtin's alternative is *answerable;* and currently much public discourse in education and government has discovered *accountable* to be a useful term. Responsibility, for Arendt, does not inhere in any single unilateral act or attitude, which perhaps is why she speaks in crucial passages of *coresponsibility.* That she does not do so consistently may imply that she did not recognize how felicitous the term would prove to be. Such a possibility is fitting insofar as she often brings to the fore ideas and attitudes that other thinkers have employed with little or no examination. In any case, her teacher Heidegger has provided in *Being and Time* some early insights into responsibility; in "The Question Concerning Technology," he goes on to provide the most economical and eloquent account I know of the general concept of coresponsibility.

In *Being and Time* responsibility is seen in relation to, but not limited to, a set of terms concerned with indebtedness and guilt. Ultimately, he seeks to delimit the concept of primordial human guilt; thus "*indebtedness becomes possible only 'on the basis' of a primordial Being-guilty.*"[33] Dasein, human being, is the kind of being that is thrown into the world; as thrown, "it projects itself upon possibilities into which it has been thrown," and it is this basis on which human being must assume as its own. In so doing, however, it finds that its projections have the capacity of outrunning it, as it were. "In being a basis—that is, in existing as thrown—Dasein constantly lags behind its possibilities,"[34] and this can be seen as in part what he is "guilty" of. To go further in this line of inquiry, helpful as that might be for an understanding of Heidegger's first major work, would lead us away from the present discussion. Here our concern is with the way in which "The Question Concerning Technology," drawing on concepts and terms in the earlier text, moves toward a general paradigm of responsibility and coresponsibility [Mitschuld].

Heidegger takes his point of departure from the traditional philosophical analysis of causality, consisting in the material, the formal, the final, and the efficient. In the first-named concept we find the matter of stuff from which something is made. Heidegger's example is a silver chalice. The form or shape of the entity being caused is then understood to fall within the modality of the formal. The third or final cause is the purpose or end to be served by the thing created; and the fourth is the efficient cause, "which brings about the effect that is the finished, actual chalice, in this instance, the silversmith."[35]

The revision of all this that Heidegger offers his reader stems from the differences that emerge when one compares the Aristotelian, Roman, and Germanic approaches with those of Greek antiquity: "What we call the cause [Ursache] and the Romans call [causa] is called *aition* by the Greeks, that to which something else is indebted [das, was ein anderes verschuldet]. The four causes are the ways, all belonging at once to each other, of being responsible for something else."[36] The translator of the essay helpfully notes that "The verb *verschulden* actually has a wide range of meanings — to be in-debted, to owe, to be guilty, to be responsible for or to, to cause. Heidegger seems intent on awakening all these meanings and on having connotations of mutual interdependence sound throughout this passage."[37] He continues:

Silver is that out of which the silver chalice is made. As this matter (*hyle*) it is co-responsible for the chalice. The chalice is indebted to, i.e., owes thanks to, the silver for that out of which it consists. But the sacrificial vessel is indebted not only to the silver. As a chalice, that which is in-debted to the silver appears in the aspect of a chalice and not in that of a brooch or a ring. Thus the sacrificial vessel is at the same time indebted to the aspect (*eidos*) of chaliceness. Both the silver into which the aspect is admitted as chalice and the aspect in which the silver appears are in their respective ways co-responsible for the sacrificial vessel.[38]

Having touched upon the two modes of matter and aspect, Heidegger pre-sents a third that he deems to be, if you will, *more* responsible. This is "that which circumscribes the chalice as sacrificial vessel. Circumscribing gives bounds to the things. . . . That which gives bounds, that which completes, in this sense is called in Greek *telos*. . . . The *telos* is responsible for what as matter and for what as aspect are together co-responsible for the sacrificial vessel."[39]

There remains the fourth participant in the fourfold of coresponsibility, and that is the silversmith, who is not, however, the efficient cause as that has been received by the philosophical tradition. Gathering together matter, aspect, and purpose (*hyle, eidos,* and *telos*), the "silversmith is co-respon-sible as that from whence the sacrificial vessel's bringing forth and resting-in-itself take and retain their first departure."[40]

In sum, "the four ways of being responsible . . . differ from one another yet they belong together."[41] Our understanding of their interrelationship remains incomplete until we consider what in general terms it occasions, or as Dewey would say, consummates. "The four ways of being responsible bring something into appearance. They let it come forth into presencing [An-wesen] . . . It is in the sense of such a starting something on its way into arrival that being responsible is an occasioning or an inducing to go forward [Ver-an-lassen]."[42] This could almost be an account of the background of Arendt's concept of natality, the phenomenon of new beginnings. For, in contemplating coresponsibility, we see that it does not cause but rather provides the necessary condition of worldly doing and making. As a cautionary note, it should be remembered that natality is a human event in the human world, whereas Heidegger concentrates here on made things, technological artifacts in the broadest sense, and on the differences that obtain within the *physis* that is nature, which, in its highest form, emerges as "*poiesis* in the highest sense."[43]

Guilt and Responsibility

In her 1945 essay "Organized Guilt and Universal Responsibility," Arendt begins with the difficulty of distinguishing between Germans and Nazis. As the war went on, political strategists among the latter had been doing everything they could to create the impression of a seamless national fabric, arguing that "there is no distinction as to responsibility, that German anti-Fascists will suffer from defeat equally with German Fascists, and that the Allies had made such distinctions at the beginning of war only for propaganda purposes."[44] At first the prerogative of the Gestapo and the SS, the operation of concentration camps eventually provided an arena of activity for ordinary members of the *Wehrmacht*. To weaken further any distinctions between Germans and Nazis, the latter carried out a terror campaign aimed at anti-Fascists, at the same time providing fellow Nazis with documentation to make it harder for the Allies or anyone else to tell the criminal from the noncriminal. In the midst of this fraudulent reconstitution of identity, orientation, and values, the interpersonal relations discussed above were in large measure damaged if not erased. The other could be a brother or friend only within definite boundaries (racial, political, biological) established by intranational enemies. The role of the member could at first glance appear to remain intact, but the merging of ordinary soldiers into fascist organizations had less to do with providing a satisfying sense of membership than with eliminating any traditional sense of belonging or solidarity. "That everyone, whether or not he is directly active in a murder camp, is forced to take part in one way or another in the workings of this machine of mass murder—that is the horrible thing."[45]

> How to determine identity, and hence responsibility, for the crimes in question? In this situation we will not be aided either by a definition of those responsible, or by the punishment of "war criminals." Such definitions by their very nature can apply only to those who not only took responsibility upon themselves, but also produced this whole inferno. ... The number of those who are responsible and guilty will be relatively small. There are many who share responsibility without any visible proof of guilt. There are many more who have become guilty without being in the least responsible. Among the responsible in a broader sense must be included all those who continued to be sympathetic to Hitler as long as it was possible, who aided his rise to power, and who applauded him in Germany and in other European countries.[46]

Those who were responsible in these ways showed themselves to be guilty of a signal incapacity similar to the thoughtlessness Arendt discerns in Adolf Eichmann. In each and every case, the indispensable connection between the ability to think and the inability to recognize moral distinctions, which requires a capacity for, and an exercise of, judging (the theme of the third and final volume of her study of *The Life of the Mind*), has been damaged beyond repair. In "Organized Guilt and Universal Responsibility," Arendt can nonetheless relieve the variously responsible "ladies and gentlemen of high society" from being labeled war criminals because "unquestionably they have proved their inability to judge modern political organizations,"[47] and judged on this ground they were not guilty as Hitler and his circle were guilty. They were simply, again, responsible—or rather, coresponsible: "Yet these people, who were co-responsible for Hitler's crimes in a broader sense, did not incur any guilty in a stricter sense. They, who were the Nazis' first accomplices and their best aides, truly did not know what they were doing nor with whom they were dealing."[48] That formulation would seem to allow a space in which Heidegger could appear, based on his early support for the

Nazi regime—of which he was certainly an explicit accomplice for a time—and his inability to realize, early on, the kind of operatives with whom he was dealing. Only on the occasion of his eightieth birthday does Arendt direct her full attention to this subject.[49]

Neither the Nazis themselves nor "those irresponsible co-responsibilities" evoke the ultimate horror, Arendt suggests; it is rather the fact that those key traditional roles that give a society cohesion, such as friends, brothers, members, or comrades are here obliterated or replaced: "In that organization which Himmler has prepared against the defeat, everyone is either an executioner, a victim, or an automaton, marching onward over the corpses of his comrades—chosen from any army unit or other mass organization."[50]

The Family Man

The familiar figure of the benign paterfamilias provides another disturbing instance of culpable role transformation. The groundwork for the transformation is laid in part by the neglect and subsequent decay of civic virtue and commitment to legitimate public activities and institutions. Add to this the social chaos and economic disruptions of the early twentieth century, especially in Germany after the First World War, and you have a formula for the emergence of the paterfamilias in the role of "an involuntary adventurer, who for all his industry and care could never be certain what the next day would bring. . . . It became clear that for the sake of his pension, his life insurance, the security of his wife and children, such a man was ready to sacrifice his beliefs, his honor, and his human dignity."[51] To survive, the man of the family, in becoming an unthinking functionary of the state and the party, might reduce or eliminate his role as friend, brother, member, and comrade. At the same time, he might take on any role that would help him avoid the sacrifice of his family, which would be expected to survive only as long as he survived. "The only condition he put was that he should be fully exempted from responsibility for his acts." At the same time he and other heads of household recognized only "responsibility toward their own families. The transformation of the family man from a responsible member of society, interested in all public affairs, to a 'bourgeois' concerned only with his private existence and knowing no civic virtue, is an international modern phenomenon."[52]

Jaspers, taking up the same or similar issues, draws distinctions among moral, criminal, political, and metaphysical guilt. To the sphere of moral guilt belongs responsibility for recognizing the purport and appropriateness of human actions. Criminal guilt is a sphere governed by positive law and the exercise of police power. "Political guilt involves at least (passive) co-responsibility in the case of every citizen of a state. . . . Everybody is co-responsible for the way in which he is governed."[53] The same coresponsibility obtains in the metaphysical sphere as that solidarity among human beings by virtue of which everyone becomes at some level coresponsible for any and every worldly deed. At the conclusion of "Organized Guilt and Universal Responsibility," Arendt states: "Perhaps those Jews, to whose forefathers we owe the first conception of the idea of humanity, knew something about that burden when each year they used to say 'Our Father and King, we have sinned before you,' taking not only the sins of their own community but all human offenses upon themselves."[54] Community in this broad sense holds out hope that the concept of the human can still embrace the threatened but vital social roles, from friend to member.

Any acknowledgment of the significance of the latter should come with the caveat that, as functionaries in violent times, members may experience in comradeship and fraternity a state of being "beyond" what is typically found in friendship. In times of collective violence, "We find a kind of group coherence which is more intensely felt and proves to be a much stronger, though less lasting, bond than all the varieties of friendship, civil or private."[55] Groups or masses caught up in such movements may experience, Arendt points out, a sense that insofar as members are committed utterly to coexistence with comrades, they may discover in their own deeds and dedications an augury of what will eventually be their own, which is to say their group's, immortality. But brotherhood of this sort presents significant dangers, for "it is true that the strong fraternal sentiments collective violence engenders have misled many good people into the hope that a new community together with a 'new man' will arise out of it. The hope is an illusion for the simple reason that no human relationship is more transitory than this kind of brotherhood."[56]

In Praise of Friendship and Responsibility

On the subject of friendship, we find in Cicero as well as in Arendt a belief in a distinctive moral quality that illuminates a given person and moves him or her toward a like illumination in another. "What unites friends in the first place," Laelius says to his friends Fannius and Scaevola,

> is goodness of character. All harmony, and permanence, and fidelity, come from that. When this moral quality appears, and reveals its brilliant light, and perceives and recognizes the same illumination in another person, it is impelled in his direction and receives his radiant beams. And that is how love or friendship comes into existence. Both words, *amor* and *amicitia* come from *amare*, to love. And love is precisely the nature of the affection you feel for your friend.[57]

In the midst of the Enlightenment, the influential F. W. Klopstock argued for the identity of love and friendship, probably influencing Heinrich von Kleist's views of both. As a participant in the eighteenth-century cult of friendship, Kleist, in any case, would employ erotic language in his intimate letters to a close male friend, though the element of idealization seems as notable as the amatory. The legitimizing of such sentiment and affect in the Storm and Stress movement may be seen as part of the same pattern. "The new emphatic, emotional grounding of subjectivity finds in the cult of friendship both an expression of itself and a budding need for community—indeed, some scholars see in the emphatic friendship of the eighteenth century a 'utopia of bourgeois community.'"[58]

Arendt, to be sure, would not subscribe to the view that love and friendship are identical. For the author of *The Human Condition*, love is unworldly and can prosper only in privacy. But precisely the opposite is the case with friendship: "love, in distinction from friendship, is killed, or rather extinguished, the moment it is displayed in public. . . . Because of its inherent worldlessness, love can only become false and perverted when it is used for political purposes such as change or salvation of the world."[59] On the other hand, Arendt agrees with Cicero regarding the affinity that draws two persons together in friendship, mutual responsibility, and affection, and the obligation of each to pay as much honor to the other as is humanly possible. In Cicero, this takes the form, for example, of Laelius's extended panegyric on the virtues of his longtime friend, Scipio, now dwelling in death, and anticipates Arendt's panegyric "Karl Jaspers: A Laudatio," in which she blends the role of friend and the theme of responsibility, and points to the same quality of illumination, which she calls "clarity," that we found in Cicero. For her old, loyal, and exemplary friend, Arendt explains,

> responsibility is not a burden and it has nothing whatsoever to do with moral imperatives. Rather, it flows naturally out of an innate pleasure in making manifest, in clarifying the obscure, in illuminating the darkness. His affirmation of the public realm is in the final analysis only the result of his loving light and clarity. . . . In the works of a great writer we can almost always find a consistent metaphor peculiar to him alone in which the whole work seems to come to a focus. One such metaphor in Jaspers's work is the word "clarity."[60]

Central to that work is Jaspers's general sense of historical mission, and the particular desire to achieve something of the cosmopolitan purposes entertained in the political philosophy of Kant. In the wake of the Second World War and the atom bomb, Jaspers is able to discern "the emergence of mankind as a tangible political reality."[61] Here, if anywhere, one can feel the spirit of Lessing and his commitment to full achievement of friendship in relationships of embodied responsibility. As she translates the thinking behind Jaspers's *Psychology of World Views,* her comments seem to lose some of their idealistic luster while gaining in sensitivity to more or less present realities. The following comments, for example, presciently describe the postmodern condition as envisaged by Jean-François Lyotard and Jürgen Habermas:

> The shell of traditional authority is forced open, and the great contents of the past are freely and 'playfully' placed in communication with each other in the test of communicating with a present living philosophizing. In this universal communication, held together by the existential experience of the present philosopher, all dogmatic metaphysical contents are dissolved into processes, trains of thought, which, because of their relevance to my present existing and philosophizing, leave their fixed historical place in the chain of chronology and enter a realm of spirit where all are contemporaries.[62]

Arendt's memorial essay on the passing of W. H. Auden is a passionate testimonial to friendship and the burdens of responsibility. She met the poet, she explains, "late in his life and mine—at an age when the easy, knowledgeable intimacy of friendships formed in one's youth can no longer be attained, because not enough time is left, or expected to be left, to share with another. Thus we were very good friends but not intimate friends."[63] As a poet who is political and public in the best sense of both terms, Auden portrays the threat and promise of the human creature in a homicidal age.

> Faces along the bar
> Cling to their average day:
> The lights must never go out,
> The music must always play,
> All the conventions conspire
> To makes this fort assume
> The furniture of home;
> Lest we should see where we are,
> Lost in a haunted wood,
> Children afraid of the night
> Who have never been happy or good.[64]

To such as these the poet shows the failed promise of universal love. For the children do not wish to love their friends, brothers, comrades, fellow members—not to mention members of their own families; they wish love only for themselves:

> For the error bred in the bone
> Of each woman and each man
> Craves what it cannot have,
> Not universal love
> But to be loved alone.[65]

Then the famous closing line of the next-to-last stanza: "We must love one another or die." Here is no mere wish for something unattainable, but a challenge to reach for something already in view. You find the same trying, for example, in Auden's efforts to make his friends happy: "When friends asked him to produce a birthday poem for the next evening at six o'clock," Arendt recalls, "they could be sure of getting it."[66] You find trying as well in Hermann Broch's powerful sense of responsibility for friends, especially when they experienced dire need, a sense of responsibility that Arendt rewards with high praise: "it was Broch who took care of everything. . . . It seemed to be assumed that all help would come from Broch, who had neither money nor time. He was exempt from such responsibilities . . . only when he himself landed in the hospital . . . and there obtained some repose, which cannot very well be refused to a broken arm or leg."[67]

Arendt's praise of others complements and compensates for the fear that she did not always meet her responsibilities to those who were closest to her. After the sudden death of her husband, she writes a tortured letter to her close friend Mary McCarthy in which she declares: "Am not at all sure if I should not be ashamed of myself. . . . Perhaps this is a process of petrifaction, perhaps not. Don't know."[68] The reader may detect at least an element of the "survivor complex" so familiar in this our age of mass destruction. Fear of failing others can become a fear of pity, as in Arendt's dilemma over Auden:

> Said he had come back to New York only because of me, that I was of great importance for him, that he loved me very much, etc. I tried to quiet him down and succeeded quite well. In my opinion: Oxford where he hoped to go for good has turned him down (I suppose) and he is desperate to find some other bearable place. I see the necessity but I know also that I can't do it, in other words, I have to turn him down . . . I hate, am afraid of pity, always have been, and I think I never knew anybody who aroused my pity to this extent.[69]

Arendt might have consoled herself with a piece of Goethean wisdom that she introduces into an essay on Bertolt Brecht: "The poet's relation to reality is indeed what Goethe said it was: They cannot bear the same burden of responsibility as ordinary mortals; they need a measure of remoteness."[70] Why should the same not apply to Arendt? Though not a poet, she is a poetic thinker in the mold of Heidegger and Walter Benjamin, and poetic texts play a significant role throughout her own writings. Certainly Arendt could be remote in these writings, as she could be in person; and precisely that fact may help to explain her sense of inadequacy, especially in the face of Auden's appeals for a help she is unable to provide.

In his poetry, at least, her friend could make a more disciplined, less poignant, but finally more bearable kind of appeal:

Follow, poet, follow right
To the bottom of the night,
With your unconstraining voice
Still persuade us to rejoice;

With the farming of a verse
Make a vineyard of the curse,
Sing of human unsuccess
In a rapture of distress;

In the deserts of the heart
Let the healing fountain start,
In the prison of his days
Teach the free man how to praise.

In a murderous age, the poet could offer something a little like consolation and a little like compensation, but somehow more than either; the "more" is praise, or has praise in it, and if we are surprised at Arendt's recognition of this, it is at least in part because of a certain militancy in Auden's, and in her, conception of it. As she observes, "Praise is the key word of these lines . . . praise that pitches itself against all that is most unsatisfactory in man's condition on this earth and sucks its own strength from the wound."[71] Auden goes even further in the encomiastic, italicized moment that lifts the following lines to a thrilling height:

I could (which you cannot)
Find reasons fast enough
To face the sky and roar
In anger and despair
At what is going on,
Demanding that it name
Whoever is to blame:
The sky would only wait
Till all my breath was gone
And then reiterate
As if I wasn't there
That singular command
I do not understand,
Bless what there is for being,

Which has to be obeyed, for
What else am I made for,
Agreeing or disagreeing?[72]

It is this singular command that is one of the great abiding gifts to those
who never met the poet as well as to those who were his friends.

NOTES

1. Hannah Arendt, *Love and Saint Augustine,* ed. Joanna Vecchiarelli Scott and
Judith Chelias Stark (Chicago: University of Chicago Press, 1996), 105.

2. Ibid., 105.

3. Ibid., 108.

4. Ibid., 108–9.

5. Ibid., 109.

6. Ibid., 110.

7. Ibid., 110–11.

8. Hannah Arendt, *The Life of the Mind* (New York: Harcourt Brace Jovanovich,
1978), 98.

9. Ibid., 99.

10. Fred R. Dallmayr, *Polis and Praxis* (Cambridge, Mass.: Massachusetts Institute
of Technology Press, 1984), 108.

11. Carl Schmitt, *The Concept of the Political,* 1932, trans. and ed. George Schwab
(Chicago: University of Chicago Press, 1996), 26.

12. Ibid., 26–27.

13. Ibid., 27.

14. Ibid., 27.

15. Cicero, *On the Good Life,* trans. Michael Grant (Harmondsworth: Penguin,
1971), 215.

16. Aristotle, *The Ethics of Aristotle: The Nichomachean Ethics* (Harmondsworth:
Penguin, 1955), 244.

17. Ibid., 244.

18. Hannah Arendt, *Men in Dark Times* (New York: Harcourt Brace Jovanovich,
1977), 24.

19. Ibid., 24.

20. Ibid., 24–25.

21. Ibid.,, 25.

22. Ibid., 27–28.

23. Ibid., 29.

24. Ibid., 29.

25. Ibid., 30.

26. Ibid., 30.

27. Ibid., 30.

28. E. M. Forster, *Two Cheers for Democracy* (New York: Harcourt Brace & Co., 1951), 68.

29. Ibid., 69.

30. Ibid., 69–70.

31. Hannah Arendt, *On Revolution* 1963 (Harmondsworth: Penguin, 1977), 253.

32. See David Halliburton, *The Fateful Discourse of Worldly Things* (Stanford, Calif.: Stanford University Press, 1997), 199–212.

33. Martin Heidegger, *Being and Time,* trans. John Macquarrie and Edward Robinson (New York: Harper & Row, 1962), 329.

34. Ibid., 330.

35. Martin Heidegger, *"The Question concerning Technology" and Other Essays,* trans. William Lovitt (New York: Harper, 1977), 6.

36. Ibid., 7.

37. Ibid., 7, n.5.

38. Ibid., 7.

39. Ibid., 8.

40. Ibid., 8.

41. Ibid., 8.

42. Ibid., 9.

43. Ibid., 10.

44. Hannah Arendt, *Essays in Understanding, 1930–1954,* ed. Jerome Kohn (New York: Harcourt Brace & Co., 1994), 120.

45. Ibid., 126.

46. Ibid., 125.

47. Ibid., 125.

48. Ibid., 126.

49. In "Martin Heidegger at 80," *New York Review of Books,* 17/6 (21 October 1971): 50–54, while not uncritical, she is relatively generous in her evaluation of Heidegger's thinking. She could be surprisingly severe, on the other hand, as in her argument that the political scapegoat, however unjustly treated, has political responsibilities of its own: "The so-called scapegoat necessarily ceases to be the innocent victim whom the world blames for all its sins and through whom it wishes to escape punishment; it becomes one group of people among other groups, all of which are involved in the business of this world. And it does not simply cease to be coresponsible because it became the victim of the world's injustice and cruelty." See Hannah Arendt, *The Origins of Totalitarianism* (Cleveland, Ohio and New York: World, 1958), 5–6.

50. Arendt, *Essays in Understanding,* 127.

51. Ibid., 127–28.

52. Ibid., 129.

53. Dagmar Barnouw, *Visible Spaces: Hannah Arendt and the German-Jewish Experience* (Baltimore, Md.: Johns Hopkins University Press, 1990), 137.

54. Arendt, *Essays in Understanding,* 131–32.

55. Hannah Arendt, *On Violence* (New York: Harcourt Brace Jovanovich, 1970), 67.

56. Ibid., 69.

57. Cicero, *On the Good Life*, 225–26.

58. Joachim Pfeiffer, "Friendship and Gender: the Aesthetic Construction of Subjectivity in Kleist," in *Outing Goethe and his Age*, ed. Alice A. Kuzniar (Stanford, Calif.: Stanford University Press, 1996), 215.

59. Hannah Arendt, *The Human Condition* (Chicago: University of Chicago Press, 1958), 51.

60. Arendt, *Men in Dark Times*, 75.

61. Ibid., 90.

62. Ibid., 85.

63. Arendt, "Reflections: Remembering Wystan H. Auden, Who Died in the Night of the Twenty-eighth of September, 1973," *New Yorker* (20 January 1975): 39.

64. W. H. Auden, *The English Auden Poems, Essays and Dramatic Writings, 1927–1939*, ed. Edward Mendelson (London, Faber and Faber, 1977), 246.

65. Ibid., 246.

66. Arendt, "Reflections," 40.

67. Arendt, *Men in Dark Times*, 113.

68. *Between Friends: The Correspondence of Hannah Arendt and Mary McCarthy, 1949–1975*, ed. Carol Brightman (Harcourt Brace & Co., 1995), 269.

69. *Between Friends*, 270.

70. Arendt, *Men in Dark Times*, 247.

71. Arendt, "Reflections," 45.

72. Ibid., 46.

15 On Friendship in Dark Times: Hannah Arendt Reads Walter Benjamin[1]

LILIANE WEISSBERG

> In the dark times, will there also be singing?
> Yes, there will be singing. About the dark times.
> —Bertolt Brecht

I. Critical Songs

Let us consider dark times first. Dark times, such as those of Europe's recent history, times that we have come to identify with the rise of fascism and the onset of World War II, its battles, its cruelties. Were these the times for philosophy? Or were these times that cast into doubt its task, its purpose, its continuity?

What would the place of a critic be in such times? We may wonder. But philosophy itself, Hannah Arendt seems to imply, experienced dark times often, perhaps as a caesura, or as a lack of orientation, and even early in the twentieth century. Indeed, this crisis of philosophy may have prepared the ground for a totalitarian state devoid of critical reflection. Thus on the eve of Martin Heidegger's eightieth birthday, in October 1971, Arendt writes an account of the 1920s when "the rumor of Heidegger's teaching reached those who knew more or less explicitly about the breakdown of tradition and the 'dark times' (Brecht) which had set in, who therefore held erudition in matters of philosophy to be idle play and who, therefore, were prepared to comply with the academic discipline only because they were concerned with the 'matter of thought' or, as Heidegger would say today, 'thinking's matter.'" Arendt compares Heidegger's early and strange fame to that of Franz Kafka, who, at about the same time (the 1920s) was un-

known to many but famous, and a "rumor," to a few. In the case of Heidegger, students would follow him to Freiburg or Marburg because of such
a "rumor that there was someone who was actually attaining 'the things'
[and not just theories or books] that Husserl had proclaimed, someone
who knew that these things were not academic matters but the concerns
of thinking men — concerns not just of yesterday and today, but from time
immemorial — and who, precisely because he knew that the thread of tradition was broken, was discovering the past anew."[2] On a different occasion,
Arendt would cite these "dark times" again, this time not as a reference to
the matter of thought, but perhaps to the matter of biography, to a matter
of a specific life, that of Walter Benjamin, a man who died quite literally
in darkness, on a night in 1940, after an ill-fated attempt to cross the border between France and Spain. Heidegger countered a broken tradition by
pursuing those philosophical questions that existed since "time immemorial"; he was trying to reconnect German philosophy to the Greeks, when
there was no other continuity at hand. Benjamin did not offer such a philosophical undertaking to find a place within eternal philosophical concerns.
Heidegger's contemporary arrived at the Spanish border a day too early perhaps or a day too late; he became simply a victim of bad timing. But he was
also a man who had blundered into these dark times belatedly, as Hannah
Arendt eagerly points out. Benjamin was unacquainted with the fast pace
of the twentieth century; for Arendt, he remained, despite all odds and all
chronology, a nineteenth-century flaneur.

Arendt, who first wrote about Benjamin for the *New Yorker* in 1968, reprinted her article as a preface to the first English anthology of his essays,
Illuminations,[3] and included it once more in a collection of her own work,
entitled *Men in Dark Times,* which was published in 1968 as well. There,
she qualifies the notion of "dark times" that she had taken from Bertolt
Brecht's poem "To Postery." Brecht, she writes, "mentions the disorder and
the hunger, the massacres and the slaughterers, the outrage over injustice
and the despair 'when there was only wrong and outrage,' the legitimate
hatred that makes the voice grow hoarse" (viii). This may be "real" enough,
but Arendt is eager to look at the less visible aspects of dark times:

"Dark times," in the broader sense I propose here, are as such not identical with the monstrosities of this century which indeed are of a horrible
novelty. Dark times, in contrast, are not only not new, they are no rarity

in history, although they were perhaps unknown in American history, which otherwise has its fair share, past and present, of crime and disaster. That even in the darkest of times we have the right to expect some illumination, and that such illumination may well come less from theories and concepts than from the uncertain, flickering, and often weak light that some men and women, in their lives and their works, will kindle under almost all circumstances and shed over the time span that was given them on earth—this conviction is the inarticulate background against which these profiles were drawn.[4]

Dark times, used in the plural here, are not unique. Even if history may never quite repeat itself, dark times can be found often distinguishing themselves paradoxically by unique shadows that are not cast by any light. But darkness is not the only quality that is both singular and a multiple occurrence. Arendt's emphasis shifts in this passage from darkness to a flickering—a hopeful glow, which carries a note of optimism. No specific historical situation is at stake here. The flickering candle, moreover, is neither one of mourning nor of memory; it shines ahead. And indeed, history is transformed by Arendt's pen into a scene reminiscent of that of the origin of painting, as described by Pliny in his *Historia naturalis,* or by Quintilian in his *De institutione oratoriae,* in which a woman held up a light to trace the shadow of her parting lover.[5] Are the dark times needed for illuminations to appear, do they themselves cast the portraits that she desires? In Arendt, history focuses on individual lives and works that counteract events that are both darker and more visible.

And in her collection of profiles, Benjamin is prominently featured while Heidegger is excluded—at least explicitly so. Brecht joins Benjamin's ranks, as does Rosa Luxemburg, Karl Jaspers, and the author who shared Heidegger's pattern of fame, Kafka. Perhaps it is not accidental that Arendt's collection would begin with that of an Enlightenment thinker, Gotthold Ephraim Lessing, although it is not necessarily the light of reason that is here at stake. For her, Lessing articulates a particularly important concept of *Humanität.*[6] And he, too, had a peculiar relationship to his own time (and place): "For Lessing never felt at home in the world as it then existed and probably never wanted to, and still after his own fashion he always remained committed to it. Special and unique circumstances goverened this relationship. The German public was not prepared for him and as far as I know never honored him in his lifetime. He himself lacked, according to his own judgment, that happy, natural concord with the world, a combination of merit and good fortune, which both he and Goethe considered the sign of genius."[7] Whereas Heidegger could gather a crowd of students, Lessing was deprived of students as well as of public honors. Did he choose his particular isolation at the Wolfenbüttel library voluntarily? Was he ahead of his time, or like Benjamin, quite simply behind?

In her essay on Lessing, as well as elsewhere in her collection, Arendt focuses on the notion of "illumination" that would, cast into the plural, provide the title for her collection of Benjamin's work. In regard to these dark times, illuminations occupy a peculiar temporal space, as they seem to waver between history and hope. Perhaps they are also able to provide the shadow that makes it possible for her to trace her closest, and perhaps already departed, friends.

History and hope do not always refer to general, common, "official" events. Thus illuminations, too, offer a trajectory to the private realm, or at least one that has been excluded from a public sphere: hence, perhaps the stress on Lessing's isolation, or on Heidegger's lonely voice. But it may be another reason why Arendt's men know of traditions yet live in dark times that commence in the eighteenth century, when our modern notion of a public sphere came into being.[8] "If it is the function of the public realm to throw light on the affairs of men by providing a space of appearances in which they can show in deed and word, for better and worse, who they are and what they can do," Arendt writes, "then darkness has come when this light is extinguished by 'credibility gaps' and 'invisible government,' by speech that does not disclose what is but sweeps it under the carpet, by exhortations, moral and otherwise, that, under the pretext of upholding old truths, degrade all truth to meaningless triviality" (viii). There is a public language of "mere talk," and in citing "mere talk," Arendt refers here again to her former teacher Heidegger, who had described this "mere talk" in Being and Time, a book that he completed in the twenties during their years of close friendship.[9] In Being and Time, Heidegger writes as well: "The light of the public obscures everything."[10] Thus Heidegger provides Arendt with an enlightening concept, much as another one of her teachers, who had been Heidegger's friend as well, Jaspers, had provided illumination for her. In Men in Dark Times, Arendt included not one, but two essays on Jaspers.[11] "What do you think is the greatest influence that Professor Jaspers has had on you?" Günter Gaus had asked Arendt a few years earlier in an interview. "Well, where Jaspers comes forward and speaks, all becomes luminous [da wird es hell],"[12] Arendt responds, and her phrasing echoes a Freudian case study. But in her collection of luminaries, it is not Jaspers, but Benjamin who clearly stands out. He did not just offer illuminations, he collected them, much as a diver would delve into deep waters that house secret treasures.

II. Pearl Fishing

Arendt knew Benjamin personally, of course. Although they had met in Berlin, they became good friends only in Paris. Arendt had fled Berlin in 1933 to join her husband Günter Stern, who arrived in Paris several months before her.[13] Benjamin was Stern's cousin. But even after the separation of Stern and Arendt seemed inevitable and final, Arendt's contact with "Benji," as she used to call him,[14] remained close. He befriended Arendt's lover and later husband, Heinrich Blücher, and when Arendt traveled to Geneva on behalf of a zionist organization, Blücher and Benjamin continued to meet for conversation and chess.[15] Both were sent in 1939 to the detention camp in Colombes.[16] In his letters, Blücher reported Benjamin's words to Arendt proudly. A statement made in October 1938, for example, gave evidence of their common point of view: "Benji is here and behaves in an extraordinarily rational manner. I have talked to him at length today. He is very much interested in Jewish issues, thinks highly of our cause [that is, Blücher's contact with communist groups] and would like to participate and really *do* things. Yesterday, he answered to a direct question in an almost moving way: I am learning Jew [ich lerne Jude], because I have finally understood that I am one. I think this is clear enough and seems to be a decent capitulation."[17] What Blücher seems to describe here is Benjamin's own turn toward "things," and his own "thinking matter."

In her letters to Blücher, to Kurt Blumenfeld (the former head of the German Zionist Organization), and to others, Arendt communicated a real sense of loss following Benjamin's death; and although she had been unable to protect his life, she ventured to protect and publish Benjamin's works. After the war, Arendt sought out the publisher Salman Schocken for this project and made use of her former connections, as she had worked as an editor for the Schocken publishing house in her early years in New York.[18] In pursuing her project, Arendt argued against her former husband Günther Stern and against Theodor Adorno, who both seemed hesitant to promote Benjamin's writings.[19] Adorno in particular seemed troubled by Benjamin's unorthodox reception of Marxism and his criticism of other members of the so-called Frankfurt School. Arendt, in turn, seemed intrigued by what she considered to be Benjamin's uniqueness: "Benjamin probably was the most peculiar Marxist ever produced by this movement, which God knows has had its full share of oddities," she writes (163). But Benjamin also appeared to be a "type." He was unique, because his work was, and Arendt borrows Hugo von Hofmannsthal's evaluation: "downright incomparable [schlechthin unvergleichlich]" (155).[20] He was typical, because his lifestyle and old-fashioned demeanor represented the German-Jewish bourgeois upper middle class.

In her essay, Arendt tells tales of Benjamin's book collecting, which outpaced his declining fortune and rendered him out of pocket more often than not. These stories become anecdotes about an individual, but cast a nostalgic glance at a bygone era, the nineteenth century, as well. Benjamin, moving from Berlin to Moscow or to Paris, seemed quite simply always out of place and out of time. When Benjamin replaced material goods with words, his collections multiplied and adjusted to new modes of exchange. Arendt is eager to point out the connection between the collector of books and the flaneur of words, as she sketches a picture of Benjamin placed in a Parisian coffee house, citing from a notebook filled with jotted-down quotations. But unlike Benjamin's gentlemanly book collecting, his planned project to construct a text entirely out of quotations gave evidence for his early interest in surrealism and contemporary aesthetics. Such a project would not only break with tradition, but review history from the present, and would construct an image whose historical significance would lie within the new. Arendt quotes Benjamin to illuminate this process: "The genuine picture may be old, but the genuine thought is new. It is of the present. This present may be meager, granted. But no matter what it is like, one must firmly take it by the horns to be able to consult the past. It is the bull whose blood must fill the pit if the shades of the departed are to appear at its edge" (199). This is the project that Arendt defines as unique. But in her Paris years, Arendt herself was occupied with a similar undertaking. In 1929, shortly after the completion of her dissertation on St. Augustine, Arendt had begun to work on a biography of Rahel Varnhagen that would be constructed from quotations of Rahel's writings. Arendt had emigrated with the manuscript from Berlin to Paris, where she discussed her project with Benjamin. He encouraged her to add two final chapters and to complete the book.[21]

Benjamin's esteem for Arendt's study is reflected in his correspondence with Scholem. Already in early 1937, Benjamin shows some familiarity with Rahel's letters,[22] and in early 1939, Benjamin sent Scholem a copy of Arendt's manuscript.[23] "I would very much like to know what kind of impression *Rahel Varnhagen* made upon you,"[24] Benjamin urges his friend, who would read the text "with a different emphasis,"[25] concentrating rather on the "fraud" on which the German-Jewish relationship was based. Scholem was not interested in a "hidden" Jewish tradition here,[26] but in the future. "[T]he future of Judaism is totally cloaked in darkness,"[27] Scholem writes.

Much like Benjamin, Arendt rejected psychoanalysis, but her string of quotations produced an interior monologue of sorts, a series of excerpts from Rahel's letters that would lose their original addressees but would insist on the integrity of Rahel's authorship. While Arendt may thus have felt a personal affinity to Benjamin's work, Benjamin had certainly no individual biography in mind. He wanted to construct an image of a topographical and temporal space, to describe the world of objects and their circulation. In his project on the Paris arcades of the nineteenth century, the city did not emerge as a historical reconstruction, but as an image of modernity. His sources were less contained and seemed to resist containment. Thus Arendt did not view him as a critic—a term that was, indeed, critically reflected upon by Benjamin himself—but as a diver who would rescue words the way that she would try to rescue biographical tales. In citing the image of the pearl fisher, Arendt replaced the textual construction of Paris with an image of a natural realm that was hardly touched by man: the sea. Despite his uniqueness, Benjamin could be compared to the philosopher of dark times—although their similarities might be invisible to most, not in the least to himself. Thus Arendt writes: "Without realizing it, Benjamin actually had more in common with Heidegger's remarkable sense for living eyes and living bone that had sea-changed into pearls and coral, and as such could be saved and lifted into the present only by doing violence to their context in interpreting them with 'the deadly impact' of new thoughts, than he did with the dialectical subtleties of his Marxist friends"

(201). Three years later, Arendt will write the following on behalf of Heidegger: "The rumor about Heidegger put it quite simply: Thinking has come to life again; the cultural treasures of the past, believed to be dead, are being made to speak, in the course of which it turns out that they propose things altogether different from the familiar, worn-out trivialities they had been presumed to say."[28] Benjamin's collecting and Heidegger's thinking share the mode of reviving cultural treasures, of diving for words, of making dead objects speak. For the political theorist Arendt, Heidegger's and Benjamin's search for truth and their reliance on language and linguistic probings seem to unite both beyond the question of ideology. And Arendt, recognizing this bond, becomes more than just a person to summarize similarities of thought; her own work searches for a place within this old and new world of "things."

III. Hunchback

In Arendt's essay, Benjamin enters the twentieth century as an endangered species. Still of a time past and unable to adapt to the present in practical ways, he acquires the uniqueness of a living artifact as well as of an original thinker. Both are in need of protection, and Arendt's essay turns into a curatorial space. She, too, becomes a pearl diver of sorts. It is Arendt who carries Benjamin's "Theses on the Philosophy of History," written on slim newspaper wrappers of the *Cahiers du Sud* and the *Schweizer Zeitung* from Paris to New York, perhaps to show them to Adorno, but ultimately to include them among her own papers, and they are now stored, together with her notes and correspondence, in the archives of the Library of Congress.[29] If she later described Rahel as "my closest friend, though she has been dead for some hundred years,"[30] it was certainly Benjamin's work during the late years of the war that should provide her with further guidance. In Lisbon, en route to the United States, Arendt and Heinrich Blücher read from Benjamin's "Theses" to each other as well as to other refugees, to discuss the possible practical implications of his concept of "messianic hope."[31] Her attempts to place Benjamin's writings posthumously follows those earlier efforts by Adorno (from New York) or Gershom Scholem (from Jerusalem) to keep Benjamin alive and working during the years of war. In her essay, Arendt describes Benjamin's resistence to Adorno's or Scholem's help as an awkward gesture of self-preservation, and as an insistence on some form of independent life. No doubt, her description reflects much of her own tense relationship with Adorno, as well as her troubled friendship with Scholem, which came to an end after the publication of her *Eichmann* book in 1964.[32]

For Arendt, Benjamin proves to be resisting help, as much as his texts resist a simple reading, cast as they are in a seemingly straightforward, simple language that would hide some of their complexities. In her essay, Arendt moves outside his work to an account of his life and tries to make sense of Benjamin's essays by integrating them into a biographical tale. Life stories are nothing new for Arendt. Following her book on Rahel Varnhagen, Arendt often employed different kinds of biographical narrative, most strikingly perhaps in her *Origins of Totalitarianism,* the three-volume study published in 1951 that established her fame.[33] There, Arendt tells the life stories of Rahel Varnhagen again, of Benjamin Disraeli, as well as other writers and politicians. While Benjamin's life is perhaps able to elucidate his work, life stories for Arendt should offer themselves as examples for political theory and actions taken, even in dark times. In his essay "The Storyteller [Der Erzähler]," Benjamin predicts the end of narrative due to the absence of experience, and more specifically, the experience of death.[34] In Arendt's essay, Benjamin's death not only takes a central position, but it is integrated in a general narrative of lucky coincidences and mishappenings. Benjamin's life becomes a tale about the good and bad turns of fate. Like the hero of a fairy tale, he can win with naïveté and remain blind to difficulties. And it is perhaps this blindness with which he could confront the dark times victoriously.

Indeed, to understand Benjamin's life and the instigation for his work, Arendt forms his life into a story with a simple plot line and chooses a children's tale as its leitmotif. This tale could have been culled from any of the children's books that Benjamin collected. It is the story of the little hunchback, published in Georg Scherer's *Deutschem Kinderbuch.*[35] "Wherever one looks in Benjamin's life, one will find the little hunchback," Arendt writes (168).

This story of the little hunchback appears in Benjamin's work as well, first in his own autobiographical text, *Berlin Childhood Around 1900. Berlin Childhood* consists of a sequence of brief vignettes that, brought into constellation with each other, provide a theory and practice for the remembrance of things past. There, Benjamin reminiscences about his youth and his mother's references to a "little hunchback" who would play tricks on persons and objects in the house (302–4). Indeed, the memories of the tales about the little hunchback conclude the memoirs of his youth. Arendt, who describes Benjamin's intense study of the Romantic period,[36] does not place the hunchback in a children's book, but traces its presence to a poem and folk song in Achim von Arnim's and Clemens Brentano's collection *Des Knaben Wunderhorn*.[37] "Mere children's talk" is thus elevated to the realm of German canonical literature. And, to stress the importance of this poem as an emblem, or even an allegory of Benjamin's life, Arendt quotes several verses:

> When I go down to the cellar
> There to draw some wine
> A little hunchback who's in there
> Grabs that jug of mine.
>
> When I go into my kitchen
> There my soup to make
> A little hunchback who's in there
> My little pot did break.
>
> . . . .
>
> O dear child, I beg of you
> Pray for the little hunchback too.
> (158–159)

These are the verses that appear as citations in Benjamin's autobiographical text, but are gathered and united in Arendt's biographical tale. Diving for these words, Arendt reconstitutes a poem.

IV. Kafka

The little hunchback trips the child in the role of an adult, drawing wine and making soup. His signature is one of mischief. He may cause damage inadvertently and is a sorry figure — one that should be included in a prayer for protection. If there is any political action inscribed in his deeds, it is perhaps indeed that of resistance. But something else becomes obvious as well. As in the tale of the race between the hare and the canny porcupine, the little hunchback is always already there waiting.

Arendt's essay on Benjamin was first written in German and then translated into English by Harry Zohn, who was also responsible for the translation of Benjamin's essays in *Illuminations.* Arendt was pleased with this
English version, for which she did some revisions,[38] but naturally, the German text came first. Mary McCarthy, to whom Arendt had sent the essay on
Benjamin and indeed all the pieces of *Men in Dark Times,* reflected on the
matter of translation, and finally evoked a third, secret language of powerful, hidden names that had preoccupied Benjamin himself within a theological framework. In McCarthy, however, it appeared as part of a fairy-
tale tradition and produced a German subtext of a different sort. "You turn
their lives into runic tales, with formulas like rhymes carpentering them
together: Rumpelstiltskin," McCarthy wrote to Arendt, recognizing as well
her friend's protective role: "[o]f course you are coaxing them to tell you
(and us) their secret name. This book is very maternal, Hannah, *mütter-
lich,* if that is a word. You've made me think a lot about the Germans and
how you/they are different from us. It's the only work of yours I would call
'German,' and this may have something to do with the role friendship plays
in it, workmanly friendship, of apprentices starting out with their bundle
on a pole and doing a piece of the road together."[39] Arendt agreed with
McCarthy about the fairy-tale-like properties of her essays but did not seem
to understand her remarks about their "German" nature[40] — and her exchange with McCarthy here is oddly resonant of the discussion on German
(and Jewish) essence that she conducted with Jaspers in earlier years.[41] But
if a "gnomic quality" marks Arendt's essay on Benjamin as one of apprenticeship and motherly protection, as McCarthy writes,[42] that quality is not
one that appears here for the first time. The hunchback did not only haunt
Benjamin's autobiographical sketch and Arendt's account, but it also structures Benjamin's own well-known essay on Franz Kafka.[43] Here, he cites two
other verses that Arendt faithfully included with his essay in *Illuminations:*

> When I come into my room,
> My little bed to make,
> A little hunchback is in there,
> With laughter does he shake.
>
> When I kneel upon my stool
> And I want to pray,
> A hunchbacked man is in the room

And he starts to say:
My dear child, I beg of you,
Pray for the little hunchback too.

(134)

At the end of the third section of this essay, entitled "Das bucklicht Männ-
lein [The Hunchbacked Little Man]," Benjamin does not refer to Rumpelstiltskin, but to the prisoner of "The Penal Colony." In Kafka's tale, this
prisoner is submitted to a sentence without knowing the reason for his conviction. His back is ornamented with letters that spell the "name" of his
crime in a manner that was unreadable to him. Benjamin compares the
hunchback—here no longer a figure of a children's poem, but of a folk
song—with the characters of Kafka's imagination. The hunchback is con-
demned to lead a displaced and disfigured life [entstellte(s) Leben][44] and
would only be released by the arrival of the Messiah. In the verse that Benjamin quotes, the hunchback does not break things, but interrupts another
person's actions with laughter and conversation; thus, he questions daily
tasks and prevents proper prayer. With his reference to the messianic tradition, it is Benjamin, not Arendt, who responds to McCarthy's claim. "In his
depth," he writes, "Kafka touches the ground which is given to him neither
by 'mythical speculation' [mythischem Ahnungswissen] nor by existential
theology. It is the ground for the German folk tradition [Volkstum] as well
as the Jewish one."[45]

Arendt does not comment on the occurrence of the figure of the hunchback in Benjamin's essay on Kafka, but it is precisely the figure of Kafka
that looms large in her essay on Benjamin. She herself had written repeatedly about the author. In her early piece, "The Jew as Pariah: The Hidden
Tradition" published in 1944,[46] and later included in a German collection
called Die verborgene Tradition,[47] "Kafka" itself becomes a secret name; and
its bearer is described as a writer who aggressively rethinks the problematic
of the pariah. Arendt refers to his novel The Castle whose hero, the land
surveyor K., fails to measure and establish borders but is intrigued by the
mysterious castle and the villagers' peculiarities. For Arendt, K. becomes a
Jew who lacks the pariah's innocence and awkwardness. In a second essay,
entitled "Franz Kafka," Arendt discusses a second novel, The Trial, but returns to The Castle as well.[48] She praises the author's simple language, which
gains perfection by the lack of adornment. It is a language in search of truth

that establishes the author both as modern and as a stranger among his peers (106).

In her essay on Benjamin, however, Arendt stresses Kafka's importance even more emphatically. Kafka, too, was "unique." "Innumerable attempts to write à la Kafka, all of them dismal failures, have only served to emphasize Kafka's uniqueness," Arendt writes, "that absolute originality which can be traced to no predecessor and suffers no followers" (155). Benjamin shares this originality, and the "downright incomparable" Berlin critic is constantly being compared to the slightly older writer from Prague. Both are unique, both offer a touch of the Romantic hero — if not genius — as they reflect on the modern world. One has to study Benjamin's "Theses on History" to understand Kafka's sense of progress and a fiction that predicts reality in a most gruesome way.[49]

Benjamin's reputation may have been greater during his lifetime, Kafka's greater after his death, but these differences seem slight. If Kafka wrote his fiction in the purest German, Benjamin's achievement as a critic was to think poetically, to focus on an allegorical mode. Indeed, Arendt feels unable to describe Benjamin without constant references to that other Jewish writer. It is perhaps not surprising that her file on Benjamin combines his manuscripts and notes on his work with her own research on Kafka. In a single folder, now part of the Arendt Papers, Benjamin and Kafka are inseparably bound together by Arendt's guiding hand and pen.[50]

Arendt's own sketch of Benjamin's life and work in turn does considerably more than rely upon quotations from Benjamin's essay or cite its figure of the hunchback. Like Benjamin, Arendt divides her work in sections that bear different headings, moving that of "The Hunchback" in first place. A Chassidic tale or the description of a photograph gain importance in Benjamin's piece; here, they are replaced by anecdotes from Benjamin's life. Arendt seems to slip into Benjamin's skin, rewriting his essay by restoring his life's story, producing a palimpsest of obvious names and secret ones that are inscribed beneath the essay's title and the author's signature.

Thus Arendt did not only write an essay on Benjamin. As an author of "dark times," Heidegger becomes his companion and his shadow. And as a "unique" author of German prose, he becomes Kafka's double. In turn, Arendt, who could not rescue Benjamin in life, becomes the writer of his fate. She publishes the story of his life together with a selection of his essays and enters thus herself into this intriguing constellation of the philosopher, collector, and writer. This may be Arendt's own way of thinking poetically, perhaps, that she had praised so much in Walter Benjamin. Perhaps this may be another way of writing history from the present, of approaching it allegorically. Thus Arendt does not only refer to Benjamin's illuminations. In her description of his life and work in those dark times, she tries to enact their lessons as well.

NOTES

1. A shorter version of this paper was first presented at the MLA Conference in Washington, D.C., December 1996, at a session on "Hannah Arendt and German literature." I would like to thank Paul Michael Lützeler, the organizer of this session, for his invitation to participate.

2. Hannah Arendt, "Martin Heidegger at Eighty," in *Heidegger and Modern Philosophy*, ed. Michael Murray (New Haven, Conn.: Yale University Press, 1978), 295. The essay was first published in the October 1971 issue of the *New York Review of Books*.

3. Hannah Arendt, "Walter Benjamin: 1892–1940," in Walter Benjamin, *Illuminations*, ed. Hannah Arendt, trans. Harry Zohn (New York: Schocken Books, 1969), 1–51.

4. Hannah Arendt, "Walter Benjamin," in *Men in Dark Times* (New York: Harcourt Brace Jovanovich, 1969), 153–206, here ix.

5. For a discussion of this myth, see Robert Rosenblum, "The Origin of Painting: A Problem in the Iconography of Romantic Classicism," *The Art Bulletin* 39 (1957): 279–90.

6. Arendt, "On Humanity in Dark Times: Thoughts About Lessing," in *Men in Dark Times*, trans. Clara and Richard Winston, 3–31.

7. Ibid., 5.

8. Compare Jürgen Habermas, *Strukturwandel der Öffentlichkeit: Untersuchungen zu einer Kategorie der bürgerlichen Gesellschaft* (Neuwied: H. Luchterhand, 1962).

9. Martin Heidegger, *Sein und Zeit*, erste Hälfte (Halle: Max Niemeyer, 1927); in regard to Arendt's relationship with Heidegger, see Elzbieta Ettinger, *Hannah Arendt/ Martin Heidegger* (New Haven, Conn.: Yale University Press, 1995).

10. Arendt translates and quotes Heidegger in the preface to her own collection *Men in Dark Times*, ix.

11. Arendt, "Karl Jaspers: A Laudatio," trans. Clara and Richard Winston, *Men in Dark Times*, 71–80, and "Karl Jaspers: Citizen of the World," *Men in Dark Times*, 81–94.

12. Arendt, "Was bleibt? Es bleibt die Muttersprache (1964). Ein Gespräch mit Günter Gaus," in *Gespräche mit Hannah Arendt*, ed. Adelbert Reif (Munich: Piper, 1976), 9–34, here 33, and trans. in *Essays in Understanding, 1930–1954*, ed. Jerome Kohn (New York: Harcourt Brace, 1993), 22.

13. See Elisabeth Young-Bruehl, *Hannah Arendt: For Love of the World* (New Haven, Conn.: Yale University Press, 1982), 115.

14. Compare, for example, the correspondence between Arendt and Heinrich Blücher, *Briefe 1936–1968,* ed. Lotte Köhler (Munich: Piper, 1996).

15. See Blücher, letter to Arendt, 15 September 1937, in Arendt and Blücher, *Briefe,* 82.

16. See Blücher, letter to Arendt, early September 1939, in Arendt and Blücher, *Briefe,* 93.

17. Blücher, letter to Arendt, 22 October 1938, in Arendt and Blücher, *Briefe,* 88.

18. Arendt and Blücher, *Briefe,* 128.

19. Arendt and Blücher, Briefe, 127, also 127n.

20. Hugo von Hofmannsthal published Benjamin's *Goethes Wahlverwandtschaften* in *Neue Deutsche Beiträge* 1928; with this thesis, Benjamin hoped to achieve a *Habilitation,* but was unsuccessful. Hofmannsthal's evaluation refers to this book; he was also impressed by Benjamin's dissertation, *Ursprung des deutschen Trauerspiels.* While Benjamin completed his essay on the *Wahlverwandtschaften* in 1924, he did not publish it that year, as Arendt writes (154). Thus Arendt alignes the publication of Benjamin's "incomparable book" with the date of Kafka's death (also cited on page 154).

21. In regard to the history and significance of Arendt's project for her philosophy and as a literary experiment, see my introduction to *Hannah Arendt: The Life of a Jewess,* first complete edition, ed. Liliane Weissberg, trans. Clara and Richard Winston (Baltimore, Md.: Johns Hopkins University Press, 1997), 3–69.

22. See Benjamin, letter to Scholem, 4 April 1937; *The Correspondence of Walter Benjamin and Gershom Scholem 1932–1940,* ed. Gershom Scholem, trans. Gary Smith and Andre Lefevere (New York: Schocken Books, 1989), 193; he refers to a letter by Rahel addressed to Leopold Ranke, of 15 June 1833, which is published in *Rahel: Ein Buch des Andenkens für ihre Freunde* III (Berlin: Humblot, 1834), 576–78; Arendt used this edition for her study. Benjamin refers to Rahel earlier, but in the context of an essay by Fritz Ernst, see Benjamin, letter to Werner Kraft, 25 May 1935; *Briefe* II, ed. Gershom Scholem and Theodor W. Adorno (Frankfurt am Main: Suhrkamp, 1966), 660.

23. See Scholem, letter to Benjamin, 2 March 1939; *Correspondence,* 245.

24. Benjamin, letter to Scholem, 8 April 1939; *Correspondence,* 251.

25. This refers primarily to Arendt, but Scholem's reading takes a different turn from Benjamin's interest in the book; see Scholem, letter to Benjamin, 30 June 1939; *Correspondence,* 257.

26. See David Biale, "Gershom Scholem's 'Ten Unhistorical Aphorisms on the Kabbalah': Text and Commentary," *Modern Judaism* 5.1 (1985): 71.

27. Scholem, letter to Benjamin, 30 June 1939; *Correspondence,* 255.

28. Arendt, "Heidegger at Eighty," 295.

29. David Suchoff writes that Arendt delivered the "Theses" "eventually into Theodor Adorno's hands"; see "Gershom Scholem, Hannah Arendt, and the Scandal of Jewish Particularity," *The Germanic Review* 72,1 (1997): 63. The "Theses" are included in the file on Benjamin, Hannah Arendt papers, Library of Congress, Washington, D.C.

30. Young-Bruehl, 56.

31. See Young-Bruehl, 162.

32. Compare Young-Bruehl's account of Arendt's relationship with Adorno and Suchoff.

33. Arendt, *The Origins of Totalitarianism* (New York: Harcourt Brace, 1951).

34. Benjamin, "Der Erzähler," *Gesammelte Schriften* II.2, ed. Rolf Tiedemann and Hermann Schweppenhäuser (Frankfurt am Main: Suhrkamp, 1977), 438–65.

35. Benjamin, "Berliner Kindheit um Neunzehnhundert," *Gesammelte Schriften* IV.1, ed. Tillman Rexroth (Frankfurt am Main: Suhrkamp, 1972), 235–304, here 302–4.

36. Indeed, Benjamin wrote a dissertation on the notion of "criticism" in the Romantic era, *Der Begriff der Kunstkritik in der deutschen Romantik* (Berlin: A. Scholem, 1920).

37. Achim von Arnim's and Clemens Brentano's collection of folk songs and poetry, *Des Knaben Wunderhorn*, appeared first in Berlin in 1805 and was published in many subsequent editions.

38. See Arendt's letter to Mary McCarthy, 21 December 1968 in *Between Friends: The Correspondence of Hannah Arendt and Mary McCarthy 1949–1975*, ed. Carol Brightman (New York: Harcourt Brace & Co, 1995), 231.

39. McCarthy, letter to Arendt, 16 December 1968 in *Between Friends*, 225.

40. See Arendt, letter to McCarthy, 21 December 1968 in *Between Friends*, 232.

41. Compare my introduction to Arendt's *Rahel Varnhagen*, but also Anson Rabinbach, "Negative Identities: Germans and Jews in the Correspondence of Karl Jaspers and Hannah Arendt," in *The German-Jewish Dialogue Reconsidered. A Symposium in Honor of George L. Mosse*, ed. Klaus L. Berghahn (New York: Peter Lang, 1996), 189–206, 292–95.

42. McCarthy, letter to Arendt, 16 December 1968 in *Between Friends*, 225.

43. Benjamin, "Franz Kafka: Zur zehnten Wiederkehr seines Todestages," *Gesammelte Schriften* II.2, 409–38, esp. 425–32. For a further account of Arendt's reading of Rahel, Benjamin, and Kafka, see my forthcoming essay, "In Search of the Mother Tongue," in *Arendt in Jerusalem*, ed. Steven Aschheim (Berkeley: University of California Press).

44. II.2, 432.

45. Ibid., 432.

46. Arendt, "The Jew as Pariah: The Hidden Tradition" is included in *The Jew as Pariah: Jewish Identity and Politics in the Modern Age*, ed. Ron H. Feldman (New York: Grove Press, 1978), 67–95.

47. Arendt, *Die verborgene Tradition: Acht Essays* (Frankfurt am Main: Suhrkamp, 1976). The title resonates quite clearly with Scholem's term.

48. Arendt's essay, "Franz Kafka," is included in *Die verborgene Tradition*, 88–107.

49. See Arendt, "Franz Kafka," 98.

50. See case 67, Arendt papers, Library of Congress, Washington, D.C.

16 Odysseus's Tattoo: On Daniel Ganzfried's *The Sender* and Binjamin Wilkomirski's *Fragments*

RAFAËL NEWMAN & CAROLINE WIEDMER

Mary Wollstonecraft Shelley remade the traditional trope of the "book as offspring" by dubbing her *Frankenstein* "my hideous progeny," thus rendering uncanny and monstrous what had been an innocuous metaphor, and positing the literary birth as unnatural and deformed precisely by virtue of its incongruously natural progenitor.[1] In what follows, we consider two texts that implicitly reverse this formulation: by shaping their very different narratives around or against the Holocaust, they implicitly acknowledge that extraliterary event as a hideous progenitor and as the monstrous sponsor of human histories (those of the survivors) that demand to be retold. Furthermore, the Holocaust has become productive of histories of another sort: those of the postwar, "second" generation, which through the operation of what Marianne Hirsch has called "postmemory" uses the experiences of the survivor generation as a means of fashioning a coherent identity in a globalizing world of weakened national, confessional, and humanist codes.[2] In a grotesque sense, the ethical self-fashioning made available by a relationship to narratives and memories of the Holocaust might be said to represent the literary construction of a progenitor. The Holocaust seems, in other words, to be the cause for the affects and symptoms felt in the post-Holocaust self that is in the process of coming into being through this very operation.

This metaphorical moment of autocreation has been given a literal turn with the discovery of fraud in the work of Binjamin Wilkomirski, who was found in his *Fragments* to have literally fabricated for himself a past as a child survivor of the camps.* The person responsible for the discovery,

---

*As this essay went to press, it was conclusively proved that *Fragments* was a hoax. The remarks in the second half of the essay should be read in the context of the debate over the book's authenticity still ongoing in 1999.

Daniel Ganzfried, is himself the author of a book, *The Sender,* a fiction-alized second-generation memoir in which these very temptations of self-fashioning, of self-authorization through the Holocaust, are thematized and worked through with subtlety and rigor. In the essay below, we take up first Ganzfried's novel, with its resistance to the lure of the Holocaust as liter-ary progenitor and its construction of an alternative memory, the subject of which will remain somewhere on the border between father and son, self and other, history and fiction. The second half treats Wilkomirski's text and the ramifications of its full-frontal and yet entirely fraudulent eyewitness re-counting of the events of the Holocaust for a late-postwar generation accus-tomed to blurring phenomenological boundaries in its aesthetic life-world. And yet it is precisely this generation, which will outlive the eyewitnesses and the survivors, that is in need of accuracy and truth for its appraisal of the disastrous past out of which it has arisen. As members of such a co-hort, and having been vexed for some time now with this same problem, we count ourselves fortunate to have had our own engagements formed by Stanley Corngold: to whom in grateful tribute this work.

At a crucial point in the climactic reunion scene with his father in Homer's *Odyssey,* Telemachus, the son of Odysseus, manifests doubt about the iden-tity of the man who has just revealed himself as the long-awaited hero, re-turned from his ten years of wandering following the end of the Trojan War. "Well," replies this man, effectively, "I am the only Odysseus you're going to get."[3] At this, Telemachus is reconciled to the man who is in fact present before him and who had until that moment consisted for him of little more than a collection of stories. The son has been tested by his own wanderings through the farther reaches of his homeland, as well as by an impromptu apprenticeship with his father's comrades Nestor and Menelaus. He is now prepared to lend his efforts to the task of reestablishing this Odysseus as king of Ithaca, husband to his mother Penelope, and rightful administrator of the patrimony Telemachus himself had earlier been called upon, in view of his father's long absence and presumed death, to bestow anew.

And yet Telemachus would not, in theory, have to make do with only this bald declaration as proof of his putative father's identity. Once Odys-seus, disguised as a wandering mendicant, has been smuggled into the be-sieged palace, his true identity is "read" and recognized conclusively by a faithful retainer. The servant, Euryclea, who has been called upon to give the stranger a footbath, notices a scar on Odysseus's leg and, since she had been that man's nurse when he was young, is able to recall the origins of the wound in an episode from her charge's gallant youth. The final seal is set to the process of recognition when Penelope herself, the faithful wife, tests and then formally recognizes Odysseus as her husband on the basis of his possession of a piece of information (the nature of their marriage bed) to which only the two of them had been privy.

These three stages of recognition—let us call them testimony, physical proof, and cross-examination—are also the subject of Daniel Ganzfried's novel of second-generation Holocaust memory, *The Sender,* in which a son confronts a long-lost father who happens to be a survivor of the Nazi work and death camps.[4] But the uses of these stages of recognition are significantly different in the epic poem and the contemporary novel, as much as the latter recalls the former thematically. Telemachus in the *Odyssey* moves through his putative father's testimony to an encounter with physical proof (the scar) and cross-examination (the shibboleth of the bed), respectively notarized and carried out by others more qualified than he, all of which will establish Odysseus as the counterpart to the corpus of stories Telemachus has heretofore had as the sole and undisputed legacy of his father. The hero of Ganzfried's novel, meanwhile, follows a path that is the reverse of this one. Faced with the solid and uncontroversial presence of a man he has no reason to doubt is his father, Ganzfried's Georg must himself carry out the cross-examination of this man, as well as the inspection of the physical proof of his identity, that will cause the store of anonymous tales to which Georg has gained access to fit this particular, undisputed father. Where Telemachus gives primacy to the man, in other words, Georg gives primacy to the story. Telemachus does not believe that the man he sees before him can be the actual hero of the stories he has heard, and he must be led to a belief in the authenticity of this all-important figure through the series of proofs evinced above: he must make the man fit the stories. Georg, meanwhile, cannot believe that the stories he has been listening to in his capacity as transcriber of taped accounts of concentration camp survivors can possibly refer to this figure, whom he knows beyond any doubt to be his father. He must struggle with versions of the same sort of proofs as confront Telemachus in his attempt to make the stories fit the man.

But Georg's stories have primacy not only because of the relatively uncontroversial identity of the man in question. The particular stories Georg has been hearing belong to the foundational history of his time, to the corpus of eyewitness accounts of the Holocaust, of its precursors, its effects, and its survivors, to what might be termed the *Iliad* of the modern era. Now, Telemachus's stories, the accounts of his father's exploits both on and off the battlefield, comprise in fact the original, veritable *Iliad*, as well as that saga's continuation in the equally celebrated but no longer extant cycle of *Nostoi*, or tales of return from the Trojan War. And yet even that seminal store of Hellenic myths pales in comparison with the flesh-and-blood hero of the *Odyssey* himself, with that Odysseus who continues to be the central and irreplaceable motive force in his own very much ongoing narrative. Faced by such a presence, Telemachus moves seamlessly from being a consumer of those stories (to whose accumulation he has devoted much of the earlier part of the poem) to becoming an actor in their sequel, in the poem's present time, with all of that frame narrative's notoriously *Iliad*-recapitulating intrigue and violence as Odysseus and his allies slay Penelope's suitors and take back the hereditary hall. For much of *The Sender*, by contrast, Ganzfried's Georg clings tenaciously to the accounts of the Holocaust, to its causes and its aftermath as evoked in the account he has been hearing, even in the face of his flesh-and-blood father. He does this in part because this particular man happens to be leading a life of no special distinction or urgency in the novel's present time, and in part, in a related sense that is famously true of survivors' accounts of the Holocaust in general, because the Holocaust did not — indeed does not — allow distinctive characters to emerge out of it (as do the *Iliad*, the *Odyssey*, and the lost *Nostoi*), and thus to take on heroic characteristics that might enable them to transcend their story's narrative world.

Georg's recognition of the sameness of the accounts of concentration camp survival comes early on in the novel, as he is about to happen upon the tape cassette containing what sounds like his father's voice but which bears, intriguingly, no return address. In a striking image, Georg is lulled by the series of identical testimonies he must hear and transcribe:

The more cassettes Georg had listened to since starting the job, the more often he had heard repeated years, places, countries, and the names of the concentration camps entered on the forms; for some time, in fact, he had had the impression, nearly dozing between the headphones, that

he was listening over and over again to one and the same story of survival of one and the same camp. When details did nevertheless stand out,
which was seldom the case, they would stir about on the stew of voices
like leaves torn from a tree that float downstream while one watches for
a while, until the next branch comes and they are forgotten. The fifteen-
minute breaks he took between sessions at his listening post had recently
been getting more frequent, without his noticing it, in proportion to the
extra effort it took him to get the headphones on again in his windowless,
soundproof studio.[5]

This is indeed the tape cassette that will provide the motive for the quest
that comprises the rest of the novel. And here, in what might indeed be
called a Homeric simile (relying as it does on a pastoral miniature to convey something workaday or unbeautiful), is evidence of what Dan Diner
has called the "statistics, but not the narrative" of the Holocaust. For "the
million-fold molding of life histories into one single fatal destiny, which was
carried out in a factory-like way, deprives the event in the consciousness of
posterity of any story-telling structure."[6] What the Holocaust was meant
famously to achieve, after all, was the elimination not only of the Jews but
also of their retailable, inheritable memory; and insofar as memory is one
of the phenomena most closely associated with the Jewish tradition, it has
even been suggested that memory itself formed a substantive target for the
architects of the "Final Solution."[7]

This nonnarrativity of the Holocaust is more pointedly foregrounded in
The Sender when Georg considers one of those people who lived through
the camps, a wealthy New York real estate developer who is now contrib-
uting money and prestige to the burgeoning museum project:

He was one of the "Survivors," as those who had lived through the concentration camps were familiarly known here. They made up their own
species, one referred to them with pride and gave them special privileges.
This was especially crucial in New York, where all the other communities,
after all, could only by stressing their alleged uniqueness avoid dissolving unnoticed into their surroundings. Some of them shrilly, others with
an elegant aloofness, each according to the share of authenticity reserved
to that uniqueness. On the other hand, no one was exactly sure what was
to be done with these "Survivors;" their own silence about their history

set them too distinctly apart from the rest of the family, which was concerned with nothing so zealously as the attempt to bear witness to the
rest of the world. (22)

What Georg is confronted with, then, is the singularly vexing problem of
a history so ethically privileged that it submerges its very actors within its
need to tell itself—to tell itself, in fact, through others who are less ethically
entailed in their own narrative than the sufferers of the events they relate.
And the Holocaust's ethically privileged history is of course so aesthetically
impoverished that it would in any case hardly afford the material for any one
of its actors to emerge from its grinding sameness as a distinct character.
Between the Holocaust's narrative unsuitability and its perverse compulsion to be narrated, then, there remains very little ground for meaningful
speech.

Ganzfried's solution to this conundrum, in the face of the survivor father
who stands before him upon the observation deck of the Empire State
Building throughout the novel's entire framing narrative, will be in fact to
free his protagonist gradually from the grip of the Holocaust testimony to
which he has been attending, and to construct for him instead a lovingly
detailed and perhaps entirely fictional account of his father's life before and
after the period of his internment in various of the Nazis' concentration
camps. For the reader will in fact never be allowed even to "hear" the voice
on the cassette recordings, but will only hear about it at the double remove
of Ganzfried's third-person account of Georg's listening. At most, the elusive phonic messenger or "sender" is sensually described: he is a "hoarse
tenor" with an "eastern accent," and is "probably a smoker" (31). The voice's
effect on Georg is evident on every page of his strand of this polyphonous
novel, but the first-person narrative that takes over from Georg's third-
person sections during roughly half of the book's considerable length, and
which even the careful reader may be forgiven for believing is equivalent
to the taped testimony, spends very little of its time recounting life in the
camps.[8] Much more of Ganzfried's care and attention is lavished on evoking, through that anonymous narrator's voice, the quality of the small-town
Eastern Jewish experience before and during the Nazi occupation of Hungary in 1944, on recounting without pathos the trials of rehabilitation in
a British army field-hospital established on the site of Bergen-Belsen following the Nazi defeat, and on detailing the poverty and continuing injus-

tices to be encountered in Palestine and Israel from the immediate postwar period and on into the 1950s.

This other narrative strand of the book will eventually dovetail, if only ambiguously, with the novel's present, set in 1991 at the height of the Gulf War and the imminent return of soldiers from a distant campaign. The martial background serves further to underline the Telemachean echoes of the novel's third strand. In the weeks leading up to the Allied attack on the Iraqi forces in Kuwait, during which period Georg searches for evidence to link the anonymous tape-recorded concentration camp testimony with his father, he consults veterans of the Hungarian-Jewish world, just as Telemachus visits his father's aging comrade Nestor to learn of his whereabouts; and he has recourse to the amazing if limited technological advances in memory storage, as at the Mormon Family History Center, with its genealogical data banks (248), in a wry inversion of Telemachus's experience of memory-altering magic at the home of Menelaus and Helen. But in the course of his research, Georg, like Telemachus once again, will be frustrated, for final confirmation of his father's identity will lie always just beyond his grasp, as indeed all guarantees of the ultimate return of the hero Odysseus will elude his son until that man stands before him and reveals himself. And as he tries once more to reconstruct the period following 19 March 1944, the date of the Nazi take over in Hungary, the beginning of the transports of Hungarian Jews to the death camps, and the occasion for the taped reminiscences, and thus to reserve for his father some connection with the master nonnarrative epic of their time, Georg grows to suspect that his own task may be doomed, and that his father may have to remain "without history, merely a left-behind" (128). As he attempts to recall his own early memories of his father, a vision of his restless eyes, he begins accordingly to doubt the possibility of retrieving what that man had witnessed, and indeed, of shaping from any such retrieved testimony an adequate or true narrative: for "no reality would arise from facts alone, since his sender was now threatening, if the facts did not add up, to disintegrate into an insubstantial trick of the mind" (128).

It is against such a threat of his father's evanescence, of his deterioration into a mere ahistorical chimera, that Georg — or rather, Ganzfried's novel, for the ultimate responsibility for the first-person portion of the story is never made clear — will construct the elaborate and yet unpathetically narrated history of a life, from its origins in prewar provincial Hungary through a most delicate and elliptical treatment of its concentration camp experiences, and thence to its Diaspora settlement in postwar Switzerland (although that destination is never explicitly named, but only cryptically suggested). In a parallel movement, however, Georg will for the entire duration of the novel's present–time frame narrative attempt to read upon his father's forearm the ultimate and most tangible proof of that man's identity with the privileged anonymous speaker of the Holocaust testimony: the tattoo Georg knows from childhood experience to be there. But the son is forced into a game of oblique scrutiny of his father's person since he cannot himself recall the number from past viewings, his father's physical presence in his life having been too brief and too early. It would be a simple enough matter to check his father's tattoo against the number recited clearly in the tape recording: only his father does not oblige, oblivious as he is to Georg's design.

This ongoing furtive struggle to glimpse the tattooed number signals Georg's unwillingness to relinquish the hope that some redemptive reality, some palpable history, may indeed arise from "the facts," from a discovered correspondence between the material testimony of the tape cassette and the material object of the writing on his father's body. This hope persists despite the novel's empirically attested option for another sort of truth, for a (re)constructed history that will in fact elide the privileged moment of the camps only to seek its wisdom in the quotidian of pre- and post-Holocaust experience. Indeed, Georg's attempts to glimpse his father's tattoo recall in one notable juxtaposition the pre-Holocaust marking of Jewish bodies in fascist Hungary by means of yellow armbands, only thereby to render suspect and illegitimate this even more indelible means of determining identity.[9]

And the novel will indeed ultimately equivocate upon the issue of this factual identity. For there will come no Euryclean moment for Georg, no recognition by means of the tokens and shibboleths of which Homer's epic makes use. The revelation of his father's tattoo will not have a chance to bring forth out of itself in vivid plastic detail the original scene of its inscription. In any case, the first-person account of the camp survivor and putative bearer of that tattoo notably leaves out much of its subject's camp experiences and avoids touching down in Auschwitz altogether.[10] For, as Erich Auerbach notes in "Odysseus' Scar," his foundational reading of the representation of reality in Greek epic and the Old Testament, treating the famous Euryclea scene in the *Odyssey,* the full-blown realism of the retelling of Odysseus's wounding by the wild boar in his youth, the cause of the scar that at a critical moment in his adventures threatens to reveal him, has the power to hold up Homer's frame narrative and suspend the impetus of his story's suspense.[11] In a related yet opposed fashion, Ganzfried's novel avoids such a realistic retelling of Auschwitz and a confrontation with the origins of the wound on the body of its survivor precisely because it knows that such a retelling, such a confrontation, would threaten to suspend the frame narrative that is underway.

Here then Ganzfried's novel reverses Georg's initial priorities, his privileging of the story—the Auschwitz testimony—over the man; or at least it substitutes now a new story for the one that had first caught the protagonist's attention by means of its generally acknowledged powers of ethical compulsion. For in place of the inevitably foregrounded and overshadowing style of the narration of Auschwitz, of the branding of his father's body, and of that brandmark's discovery within the present time of the frame narrative—the style of those numbing tape recordings Georg has been listening to, what in the context of Homer's epic technique Auerbach refers to as the sort of style that "causes what is momentarily being narrated to give the impression that it is the only present, pure and without perspective"[12]—Ganzfried's novel substitutes a lower-profile, less insistent, substantively subtler narrative. *The Sender* is in fact a special hybrid of past and present, vivid and less vivid, a veritable pastiche or cinematic montage of at least two different voices or perspectives in whose mingling revelation occurs, if at all, only at the margins of the story, without significant or leading recognition by any of its characters: for the connection between the two or three different story-strands is never made explicit, nor, if it is implied (in for instance the appearance of similar minor characters in the first- and third-person sections), is its significance emphasized.[13]

The novel effects thus a very artful blending of styles. It may indeed relinquish its right to revelation and the absolute vividness of identification through explicit shibboleths and the recognition of a wound. It does not, however, in those sections of the book in which the anonymous Hungarian Jew speaks in the first person about his life, wholly abandon elements of the vivid, plastic style that renders Homer so pleasurable to read, even as it supplements those sections with the flatter, more monochromatic scenes set in present-day New York.[14] Thus Ganzfried's novel is able to skirt the overwhelming narrative abyss of Auschwitz, yet must surrender neither its project of a vindicating recreation of the father's world disrupted by the Holocaust (and now likely to be overshadowed by the contemporary insistence upon narrating precisely and uniquely that event) nor its ethical commitment to a meaningful confrontation with the recognized survivor of the Holocaust (in contradistinction to the cynical professionalism with which his colleagues treat such witnesses[15]).

But the scenes in which father and son do in fact draw closer to one another, the stage for the fulfillment of this stern ethical imperative, are not, for all that, entirely devoid of literary antecedent or allusion. Indeed, they draw their power from a celebrated episode of another venerable tradition, an episode equally concerned with the estrangement and reunion of father and son, and it is in the admixture of this alternative style that *The Sender* will in the end find its oblique reconciliation with the difficult claims of Holocaust testimony. For in reading the sections of *The Sender* in which Georg researches his father's past, and especially those sections in which father and son spend an afternoon and evening atop the Empire State Building, one recalls Auerbach's parallel description, in that same essay in which he discusses the *Odyssey,* of "an equally ancient and equally epic style from a different world of forms," that of the Elohist author of Genesis as he relates Abraham's attempted sacrifice of Isaac.[16] There Auerbach speaks of a barren verbal landscape, one unadorned with epithets and externalized description, yet with an implied profundity of psychology and an unrelieved suspense in inverse proportion to such narrative austerity: all of this serving to provide the most extreme possible contrast with the genial foregroundedness of Homer's epic technique.[17] And indeed, the scenes atop the Empire State Building are remarkable for their dryness, their inarticulateness at the level of dialogue, their mystery regarding motivations and history, without thereby surrendering anything in the way of hinted psychological depth or narrative tension.

But the biblical episode, of course, is not evoked here in the context of the New York passages only as a marker of stylistic contrast with Ganzfried's Homeric world of the anonymous Hungarian Jew. What Georg and his father enact on the Empire State Building resembles the events of Genesis 22 thematically as well as stylistically. In both stories, a journey has been undertaken following a mysterious command (God addresses Abraham abruptly and without apparent location[18]; Georg receives an anonymous tape recording, and his father is perplexed and startled when he is unexpectedly given his son's number to call [9]); the journey takes the characters to a high place (God commands Abraham to take Isaac to one of the mountains in the land of Moriah, which Abraham will then call Jehovah-jireh, or "In the mount of the Lord it shall be seen," Genesis 22.14, while Georg and his father ascend to the observation deck of the equally portentously-named Empire State Building[19]); in both stories, a father and son are united by the necessity of a difficult and painful task (the imposed sacrifice, featuring the use of a knife and fire; the need for certainty regarding a wound inflicted by means of heated steel); and in both stories, the original goal is foiled or supplanted (the sacrifice is in the end not required, Abraham's faith having been proven without it; the tattoo is not inspected and the camp is not discussed, Georg having decided to accept his father as unknowably connected with the experience of the camps, and nevertheless unique for having lived a certain life before and after).

In place of the original goal of the biblical episode, of course, which is the immediate physicality of access to blessedness in the present through human sacrifice, there will be born a new conception of religious (and indeed cultural) identity through God's promise to Abraham of future blessedness,[20] while in place of the original goal of the novel, a reckoning with the indelible truth of the tattoo and Auschwitz, there is born a new kind of truth, a recognition that wisdom arises not from the facts, but from introspection, from an imaginative and perhaps fictionalizing encounter with memory, from a literary construction of one's own origins, and indeed of one's own father.

In both narratives, in Genesis 22 and in *The Sender,* there is thus a strongly redemptive strain. The Genesis episode will reprivilege, and thus redeem, Abraham's relation to his son, for Abraham's holiness had led him to a willingness to negate that relationship in favor of fealty to a spiritual father or Lord of his own, while at the episode's conclusion he is rewarded by that same Lord with a vision of limitless, felicitous, unscathed progeny ("I will multiply thy seed as the stars of the heaven"). Ganzfried's Georg, meanwhile, sees his father redeemed as a significant and valuable store of idiosyncratic memories quite apart from his involvement in the heretofore overprivileged world of the Holocaust, a world of monolithic narrative that had threatened to subsume his father in the all-important project of its own telling. What is ultimately redeemed in Ganzfried's *The Sender*—without however undoing or banishing either the specter of Jehovah's initial grim demand for human sacrifice, which informs the novel structurally, or that sacrifice's modern avatar, the Holocaust, which drives it at the level of its plot—what is ultimately redeemed is a fantasy of reunion with the world of the father, one that in turn privileges over his physical presence an imaginative and literary encounter with his memory.[21]

When Binjamin Wilkomirski's memoir *Fragments* first appeared in the summer of 1995, only a few months before Daniel Ganzfried's *The Sender,* it was widely received as one of the most important new works of Holocaust testimony, comparable in some estimations to the writings of Primo Levi and Paul Celan. Published by the Jewish Press of Suhrkamp Verlag in Frankfurt, it has since been translated into thirteen languages, made into two films and one theatre piece, and has received among others the National Jewish Book Award, the Jewish Quarterly Literary Prize, and the Prix de la Mémoire de la Shoah. Wilkomirski himself has toured countless schools and universities in Switzerland as well as other parts of Europe, the United States, and Israel to speak of his experiences in the camps and in postwar Switzerland as a child survivor of the Holocaust. *Fragments* is by all accounts the best-known book to have come out of Switzerland in the 1990s, and Wilkomirski himself had become the most visible Jew living in Switzerland.

The slim volume[22] is a record of the visions and affects of a Polish-Jewish child from Riga who survives Majdanek and a further unidentified camp (assumed by most critics to be Auschwitz) and is subsequently sent to Switzerland where he is given the brand-new identity of a Swiss citizen and is adopted by a well-to-do couple in Zurich. His early childhood experiences, writes Wilkomirski in the opening pages of *Fragments*, "are based in the first instance on the exact images of my photographic memory and the images that have been stored up along with them—bodily ones, too. Then comes auditory memory and the memory of what has been heard, also of what has been thought and at the very end the memory of what I have myself said. . . . If I want to write about it, I must renounce the organizing logic, the perspective of the adult" (8). Like partly recovered reels of old documentary film, these memories are marshaled into loosely ordered tableaux that resist the adult's will to an ordered chronology: Wilkomirski's father's skull crushed against a wall by the Latvian militia; his own body hurled into concrete by a camp guard; two dead children, their frozen fingers gnawed to the bone. This suggests a memory wholly un-edited by the ordering principles of the adult self and untouched by the enormity of Holocaust knowledge crowding the imagination of the mil-lennial mind. It is a form of memory, then, that for all of its fragmented-ness is unadulterated and pure, a memory for which fragmentedness is, the book implies, the very symptom of purity and, by extension, the proof of authenticity.

As if to underscore further the authenticity of the book, Wilkomirski differentiates between the activity of a poet or an author and his own work in the opening pages of his *Fragments:* "I am not a poet, not a writer. I can only try to set down in words experience and event as exactly as possible — as precisely, indeed, as my childhood memory has stored it up: without any knowledge yet of perspective and vanishing point" (8). More than anything else this seemingly modest disclaimer for the literary quality of his auto-biography is a further claim for its value as truth, a status that is of course elemental to the act of witnessing the Holocaust. The reader is led to be-lieve that it is not Wilkomirski himself who is responsible for the particu-lar structure and the particular memories of the book, but rather that the memories manifest themselves through the author, who is then left to trace their contours as a child would trace those of a picture under glass.

Given this relinquishing of authorial responsibility, the artful, indeed lit-erary, structuring of the book comes as something of a surprise: interwoven with Wilkomirski's earliest childhood memories in Riga and in Majdanek are those of his arrival and painful integration first in the Swiss town of Adelboden, and then in Zurich. What makes this structure most remark-able is that each strand of the narrative underscores the varying shades of memory the protagonist's former selves were capable of having. In the first distinct strand, the earliest flashes of horror glint against the faded and con-fused background of time and place: a boy bids his dying mother farewell in a desolate camp barrack; he gasps for air under crushed bodies in a train with an unknown destination; he finds himself yanked along by disembod-ied hands on endless marches to nowhere. In the second strand, that boy's impressions in Switzerland during the first few years are related by Wilko-mirski as a sort of double memory — that is, the adult remembers the older child's memory for whom the noncamp environment could only be inter-preted according to the remembered "normalcy" of the camps. In this view the adoptive parents' gas furnace appears to be just the right size for cremating a child; the Wilhelm Tell myth, as studied in school, is rejected as implausible because ammunition, after all, even for the crossbow, is much too precious to be wasted on children; and a ski lift on a school outing becomes a conveyor belt feeding children into the crematorium at the top of the slope.

The readers, in the meantime, are taken in completely by both strands of the memoir. While they busy themselves in the first half with supplying the missing contexts and details of the camps that the child Binjamin cannot understand or articulate, the second half of the book compels them to translate the most mundane events of everyday life into the stuff of nightmares. That is, the book's readers are called upon to "remember" and to apply their own Holocaust "experiences" in order to understand the book: to be, in Susan Suleiman's terms, both a referential reader, who asks what camp, what train, what city, and a universalizing reader, who interprets common objects and activities as icons for universalized suffering.[23] *Fragments* can only be read the way it is because of writers like Primo Levi, or Jean Améry, or Paul Celan, all survivors who report with mature and astute intelligence what occurred around them. And not only because of these last, of course, but more recently because of the numerous research centers, narratives, films, documentaries, and extravagantly outfitted Holocaust museums that have turned the Holocaust into a cultural reference point, a store of shared knowledge that unites a broad readership. It is this inundation that accounts for our growing competence in the Holocaust and that makes us greet eagerly any new perspective on the stories we've heard so many times before. *Fragments* itself is, in other words, at once a product and confirmation of our collective imagination. No wonder it has found such an echo around the world.

No wonder, too, that the suggestion that this book might be written by an imposter who took advantage of our eagerness has come as a shock. In the fall of 1998, three years after *Fragments* was first published, Daniel Ganzfried's research, published in a series of articles in the Swiss weekly *Die Weltwoche,* suggested that Binjamin Wilkomirski was really Bruno Doessekker, a Swiss musician with a penchant for the history of the Holocaust who had made up his "memoir" from whole cloth.[24] Ganzfried had not set out to prove this on his own initiative. Having been asked by the Swiss cultural foundation Pro Helvetia to write an article on Binjamin Wilkomirski and the phenomenon of children without identities for their house organ, Ganz-fried stumbled across biographical inconsistencies that were hard to recon-cile with the story told in *Fragments*. Bruno Doessekker, who only assumed the name Binjamin Wilkomirski when he began to write, had, according to the official registry of the city of Biel, been born there in 1941 as Bruno Grosjean, the illegitimate offspring of one Yvonne Berthe Grosjean. Rather than spending time in an orphanage in Cracow after the war, as *Fragments'* protagonist is supposed to have done, Bruno was given up for adoption by his birth mother and assigned to an orphanage in Adelboden, whence he was placed in 1945 with the Doessekkers of Zurich, who would become his foster parents. His still living biological uncle, by this account, the brother of Berthe Grosjean, confirms this information. In 1947 Bruno Doessekker, previously known as Grosjean, entered the public school system at the age of six bearing the name of his foster parents. Bruno's biological father con-tinued to support his son until the Doessekkers officially adopted him in 1957. When his birth mother Yvonne Grosjean died in 1981, he accepted her modest inheritance.

Wilkomirski's first, and to date only, public response to Ganzfried's reve-lations came in the form of an interview in the Zurich daily *Der Tagesan-zeiger*.[25] In this interview he points out that the seamless identity Ganzfried has unearthed is nothing new, but rather the driving force for writing the memoir in the first place. His biography, he maintains, is marked precisely by this tension between officially constructed identity and memories that could not be made to conform to the official story, a tension he had already thematized in the postscript to his book. There, in *Fragments*, he wrote: "I too received a new identity while I was still a child, another name, another birthdate, another birthplace. . . . But this date corresponds neither with my life history nor with my memory . . . The legally notarized truth is one thing, that of a life is another" (143). This tidy explanation, however, still leaves room for skepticism: if Wilkomirski was born in 1939, as is claimed in *Frag-ments*, instead of in 1941, as his birth certificate claims, then why was the age difference of two years neither noted upon school entry nor at any later date? If Berthe Grosjean is not his mother, then why did Bruno Doessekker accept an inheritance from her estate in 1981? And perhaps most curious of all: why had not Wilkomirski himself investigated the cirumstances of his allegedly fabricated official dossier? Why had he not insisted upon re-vealing the fact that the Swiss officials had switched his identity, and with it his entire background by falsifying documents after the war in an effort to integrate Jewish children who had survived the camps?

One of the unique aspects of *Fragments,* after all, is the attention it trains on the fates of children who survived the war either in camps or in hiding, and who were then alledgedly given false histories and identities by a number of European governments in the largely well-meant effort to prepare for them a life in societies in which anti-Semitism was still rampant. For the various organizations that attempt to help people recover their true identities—Amcha, the Children without Identity section at Yad le Yeled in Israel, the Children of Holocaust Society, the Contact Center for Children of Survivors of Nazi Persecution in Switzerland—the authenticity of *Fragments,* along with its legitimizing effect, had been as important as its potential fictitiousness is now shattering. Not surprisingly, it has been these organizations that have been most adamant in defending Wilkomirski.[26] His is indeed one of the few works that has thematized the problems that children without identities must confront: their often scanty memory; the absence in most cases of documents pertaining to their real pasts, even their names; and the psychological problems and insecurities arising from traumatic memories incommensurate with their assumed identity. Naturally a life history whose essential characteristic is that it consists of memories that are often impossible to trace would offer equally compelling material for someone whose intent it was to forge a Holocaust memoir, and for someone whose aim it was simply to excavate his past.

The verdict on whether the memoir is fictitious or not is still out, and it is not clear when or indeed if we will ever learn the whole truth in this matter.[27] While Ganzfried has suggested that Wilkomirski alias Doessekker take a DNA test to establish, or rule out, kinship with his only supposed living relative, the brother of Berthe Grosjean, Wilkomirski himself has appealed unsuccessfully to the Bergier Commission, the federal body investigating Swiss involvement in the Holocaust, to investigate his dossier. Since neither of these suggestions has to date been taken up, we are left with four basic scenarios: Wilkomirski is an imposter who has consciously constructed a survivor's memoir; Wilkomirski is an imposter but genuinely believes that he survived the camps; Wilkomirski survived the camps and his memories are inauthentic (that is, he was too young to have direct memories of his experiences, and his memories have therefore been constructed); or Wilkomirski survived the camps and his memories are authentic (that is, he has, as he claims in the book, direct memories of the camps). While many of the participants in the lively discussions sparked by the Wilkomirski affair have subscribed to and defended one or the other of these possible versions, we would like to focus on two generalizable questions, which, while emphasized by the current scandal, do not depend on its definitive resolution. First, what precisely changes in the function of the text within the larger sphere of cultural memory if it is revealed to be fictitious? Second, what sort of investment in a text's authenticity warrants the kind of outrage the revelations have generally elicited in readers?[28]

If *Fragments* is in fact invented, if Wilkomirski is, as Ganzfried believes, a born Swiss who saw the camps only as a tourist, the book, as well as Wilkomirski's oral testimony, now stored at the oral history archives at Yale and in the Spielberg archives, lose their testimonial value. This sudden change in testimonial status can also be seen to threaten other testimonies: Holocaust deniers have already begun to use the apparent effectiveness with which the story of the Holocaust was made up by Wilkomirski as evidence that the camps, and other survivor narratives, have been similarly invented. Even if Wilkomirski is indeed a child survivor from Riga, but the memory fragments he claims to have recovered from the time he was two to three years of age were constructed to such a degree as to render indistinguishable the line between authentic and inauthentic memory, his testimony would still prove of little help. The author's own description, in *Fragments,* of how he managed to recover the past is instructive in this respect: "Years of research work, many trips back to the presumed sites of the events, and countless conversations with specialists and historians helped me to interpret many inexplicable shreds of memory, to identify and rediscover places and people, and to produce a possible historical context as well as a possible, halfway logical chronology" (143).[29] Memories reconstructed under such circumstances, and with the retroactive input from so many sources (including a highly controversial psychoanalytic technique often used with adult victims of early childhood abuse to recover "deep" memory), are a testimony not so much to the Holocaust itself as to its proliferation as a cultural icon and system of reference in the late twentieth century.

While there is no doubt that the book's status as Holocaust testimony would change if it turned out to be fictitious, one might argue — and many have — that the book's literary and didactic merit remain the same whatever the outcome of the accusations. It would still be a vivid and moving story of the Holocaust, one that grippingly renders the horrors of the camps. Indeed, as Jurek Becker's novel *Jacob the Liar* amply demonstrates, books needn't be historically true in order to render an essential truth about the Holocaust.[30] Had *Fragments* been introduced as a novel from the beginning, it could have been received as a valuable contribution to Holocaust literature, a thematization of the fate of child survivors. The uproar about the text's authenticity has however shifted attention away from the subject of child survivors and onto other contemporary issues, thereby changing the text's cultural function and deflecting from its original context. Why, for instance, was the fraud made public when it was? In what way does the author's pychopathology, if he turns out to believe he is a survivor when he is not, block out the psychopathology of the two societies that have allegedly persecuted the novel's protagonist? And why, finally, did its readership make the "mistake" of receiving it with so much admiration and praise?

The book's initial reception and the dismay at the recent revelations bear some investigation, with particular reference to readers' investments in Holocaust accounts and the seeming double standard by which such accounts are judged. In the case of narratives that claim to tell the truth, there comes into being a tacit pact between author and reader. For Wilkomirski, who wrote to reclaim an identity, to reconstruct a memory, and to hold up a mirror to a cruel and insensitive society, it is essential that someone confirm, legitimize, and record this real identity and the memory that proves it. This is a role thousands of people have willingly played, reading the book, awarding it prizes, recording it as testimony, listening and watching raptly as Wilkomirski has told his story in auditoria, on television, and on radio. The payback for readers in the meantime consists in the opportunity to line up on the right side of the many ideological divides engendered by the Holocaust. For the way one positions oneself with regard to the Holocaust, that is, whether one believes it to have been unique, or that it should be historicized within the broader sweep of history, whether it has been remembered enough, as Martin Walser would have it, or whether its memory should be eternal, is a powerful determinant, at least in German-speaking countries, of one's political and ideological positioning within the general culture. This tacit pact, then, for the reader as well as for the author, in the case of a narrative that purports to tell the truth about the Holocaust, is crucial for the fashioning of a particular kind of identity.

The pact, of course, can only work as long as both sides hold to their respective obligations: if Wilkomirski is writing in an attempt to reclaim his lost identity, there must be a historical identity to reclaim; if he wants to reconstruct a life from the shards of memory, those shards had better be real. The uniqueness of the novel, namely that it is the account of one of the rare child survivors, rests with the authenticity of its author's claim. The reader's obligation, in the meantime, consists in believing and following the basic premises the author sets up. Contained in the sentence "I am not a poet, not a writer" is a disclaimer with regard to the literariness of the book, one which disallows criticisms on that score. In his postscript, Wilkomirski makes clear his expectations to the reader. He writes, "I grew up in a time and within a society that wouldn't or couldn't listen. . . . It was only seldom that I tried with timidity to share even a fraction of my memory with anyone, but such attempts constantly went awry. A finger tapped on the forehead or aggressive questions proffered in return would make me shut up in a hurry, and take back again what I had revealed. I wanted my security back, and I didn't want to be silent any longer. That's how I began to write" (142). To question the author's memories is to be aligned squarely with the boy's monstrous teacher and his ignorant adoptive parents, who stand for an entire society that wanted to hear nothing of the Holocaust or of a small child who had been in its camps. It would also mean denying him a security that can supposedly only come from the readers' acceptance and belief. But Wilkomirski ignores this pact in his single public response to Ganzfried's accusation when he says: "The reader was entirely at liberty to take my book as literature or as personal document. . . . Nobody must grant me belief."[31] Of course, once the claim of authenticity has been made, once readers have committed themselves to reading and participating in a true story of the Holocaust, there can be no backing out on the part of the author without breaching a trust, without breaking that pact.

If *Fragments* were conclusively revealed to be fictitious, however, all of Wilkomirski's faithful followers, the many schoolchildren who listened with awe, the many critics who wrote with enthusiasm, and the many readers who were haunted by the gnawed-off fingers, would be unmasked as dupes. If the horrific images were invented, then the emotions they elicited from their readers would take on the awful aspect of prurience, even pornographic pleasure, and turn commendable sympathy into disgraceful lechery.

When Daniel Ganzfried decided to make public the results of his research in August of 1998, he did so for numerous reasons, the three most important having to do with reader reception, with preserving the capacity for judgment even in the face of the Holocaust, and with the constitution of the memory we hand over as a legacy to the next generation. It is not surprising that Ganzfried, who in his novel *The Sender* resisted the impulse to dwell on the Holocaust proper in an effort to privilege Georg's father's postwar history, would insist in this nonfictional case that the person who embodies the position his fictional—and factual—father does in history be held to the stringent standards of testimony. The second-generation memory Ganzfried employs through his protagonist Georg is beholden to various postmodern phenomenological positions with special bearing on narrative: the blurring of the boundaries between truth and fiction, the acknowledgment of the constructedness of memory and the corollary constructedness of identity, and the contingent nature of the subject. In the case of Ganzfried's handling of *Fragments,* however, in the clearly marked nonfictional space of Wilkomirski's memoirs, the testing of the body of the witness that is so delicately avoided in the clearly marked fictional space of *The Sender* can and must be carried out. For in the case of *Fragments,* what has been posited is not only the trope or figure of the Holocaust as the hideous progenitor of scarred biographies, a rhetorical gesture to which all members of the postwar generation might lay equal claim, what Wilkomirski did with his memoir, if Ganzfried is right, was actually to elect the Holocaust as the archetype for his own undistinguished suffering. By the terms of the inverted Odyssean process adhered to and then abandoned by Ganzfried's protagonist Georg, Wilkomirski must have expected to have to undergo the scrutiny he has endured, having proposed the adequation of his particular self to that centrally privileged and grotesquely paternal body of history.

NOTES

1. "My hideous progeny" derives from the author's preface to the 1831 revised edition of her novel. See for an excellent variorum collation Mary Wollstonecraft Shelley, *Frankenstein, or The Modern Prometheus,* the 1818 text edited with an introduction and notes by Marilyn Butler (London: W. Pickering, 1993).

2. On "postmemory" see Marianne Hirsch, "Past Lives: Postmemories in Exile," *Poetics Today,* 17:4 (Winter 1996): 659–86.

3. See the *Odyssey* XVI 202–6: "Telemachus, it doesn't befit you to be too amazed nor to wonder overly much at your dear father being present: for no other Odysseus

will be coming hither, but here I am, just as you see me, I've suffered evils, quite a few in fact, and I've come after twenty years to my fatherland" (our translation).

4. Daniel Ganzfried, *Der Absender* (Zurich: Rotpunktverlag, 1995), hereafter referred to as *The Sender.*

5. Ganzfried, *The Sender,* 23. All subsequent references to the novel will be provided parenthetically in the text. All passages cited in English are from Rafaël Newman's unpublished translation, excerpts of which are forthcoming in his edited volume, *Jewish Writing in the Contemporary World: Switzerland* (Lincoln: University of Nebraska Press).

6. Dan Diner, *Kreisläufe: Nationalsozialismus und Gedächtnis* (Berlin: Berlin Verlag, 1995), 126 and 127 respectively; our translation.

7. See Gunnar Heinsohn, *Warum Auschwitz?: Hitlers Plan und die Ratlosigkeit der Nachwelt* (Reinbek bei Hamburg: Rowohlt, 1995). In his short essay "Gedächtnis und Institutionen," in *Kreisläufe,* 113–21, an implicit dialogue with Ernest Renan, Diner effectively lays the groundwork for such an idea in his identification of Germany's nineteenth-century anti-Napoleonic patriotism as that nation-to-be's opting for an *ethnic* collective memory over the *political* collective memory represented by the French Revolution: that is, for a national identity founded upon a rejection of the history of universal values and institutions, the very history that would in a later period come to be associated with "the Jews."

8. The notion of strands of narrative, with its attractively Penelopean connotation of a woven text, is owed to an essay treating Ganzfried among other young German-language Jewish writers in Sander L. Gilman, *Love + Marriage = Death?* (Stanford: Stanford University Press, 1998), pp. 184–202; there, however, the suggestion seems in fact to be that Ganzfried's first-person account is tantamount to the taped testimony, an imputation that clearly obscures the epistemological import of the novel. Other readers who have made this erroneous connection include some of Ganzfried's earliest Swiss reviewers: see Sandra Leis, "Ueberlebensmaske des Schweigens," *Die Weltwoche* (5 October 1995); Konrad Tobler, "Das Erinnern als Wissen um die Leerstellen," *Berner Zeitung* (25 November 1995); and Beda Hanimann, "Kindheit und Vergangenheit," *Der Kleine Bund* (9 December 1995).

9. At *The Sender* 75, during a discussion of military drill in 1940s Hungary, the first-person narrator describes his teacher's instructions always to wear the yellow armband on the left arm and to keep it at all times visible: "He showed us the place on the left upper arm—'Never on the right!'—and explained that it had to be visible at all times." On page 81, despite his father's having rolled up his sleeves, Georg is foiled in his attempt to see the tattoo on his left forearm: "Now he would have been near enough to him to be able to see more, but he found himself on the wrong side."

10. Ganzfried has in fact remarked that he "closed the doors of the cattlecar in Hungary and opened them again in Bergen-Belsen," the site of the last of his subject's three internments, soon to become a British army field hospital (personal interview). Auschwitz is of course remarkable in *The Sender* for its absence. At least one reviewer with a clear taste for exactly the sort of pathetic witness-bearing the novel decries has

gone so far as to lament the absence of echoes of Auschwitz, while forgiving the omission of the camp itself: "The story drifts more and more into banality; one simply cannot accept the thoughtless lust for life of a young man who has survived Auschwitz. Mustn't he have nightmares?" Lilian Leuenberger, "Beklemmende Suche nach der Geschichte eines Vaters," *Zürcher Unterländer* (17 February 1996); our translation.

11. See "Odysseus' Scar" in Auerbach, *Mimesis: The Representation of Reality in Western Literature,* trans. Willard R. Trask (Princeton: Princeton University Press, 1974, fourth edition), pp. 3–23.

12. Auerbach, *Mimesis,* 12.

13. Note that Auerbach (7) speaks of the lack of "perspectivistic connection" between scenes of past and present in Homer's *Odyssey,* as well, in which all is famously said to be foreground with no possibility of characters' remaining in the narrative's consciousness when not actually present. The difference of this disconnection from that of *The Sender* is that, in Homer, there is no question that the scenes so juxtaposed in fact do indisputably feature the same characters, while the point of Ganzfried's text is to cast doubt on precisely this sameness.

14. Ganzfried has in fact spoken of his will to disrupt the reader's pleasure, or consumption of the "ice cream" of the Hungarian Jew's detailed quotidian memoirs, by intercutting them with the more challenging passages set in New York (personal conversation). Compare Auerbach's account of scenes of description in Homer, in which "we may see the heroes in their ordinary life, and seeing them so, may take pleasure in their manner of enjoying their savory present, a present which sends strong roots down into social usages, landscape, and daily life. And thus they bewitch us and ingratiate themselves to us until we live with them in the reality of their lives; so long as we are reading or hearing the poems, it does not matter whether we know that all this is only legend, 'make-believe'" (13). Ganzfried's novel will not determine which of its strands is make-believe and which is truth, but neither will it allow us to be lulled into the security of a pleasurable indifference to this question.

15. See the scene (23–24) in which Georg's superior, Ben, conducts a disingenuous, fawning telephone conversation with an elderly lady whose estate he hopes to acquire for the museum, and then announces to his colleagues in mock encouragement: "'Have fun! And think about this: he who survives the Survivors has also survived the Holocaust!'"

16. Auerbach, *Mimesis,* 7.

17. Auerbach, *Mimesis,* 11–12.

18. ". . . God, in order to speak to Abraham, must come from somewhere, must enter the earthly realm from some unknown heights or depths. Whence does he come, whence does he call to Abraham? We are not told." Auerbach, *Mimesis,* 8.

19. Ganzfried has said that he chose to set his novel on the top of the Empire State Building, rather than anywhere in the land to which his family had emigrated from Israel, because "there is no place high enough in Switzerland from which to look down on the Holocaust with the right distance" (personal conversation). The key to interpreting this remarkable claim about a country within whose borders rise some

of the world's tallest peaks is perhaps then to be sought in precisely this biblical para-text, which demands an artificial, urban counterpart to its natural setting so as to underscore the novel's parallel but different implications.

20. "By myself have I sworn, saith the Lord, for because thou hast done this thing, and hast not withheld thy son, thy only son: That in blessing I will bless thee, and in multiplying I will multiply thy seed as the stars of the heaven, and as the sand which is upon the sea shore; and thy seed shall possess the gate of his enemies; And in thy seed shall all the nations of the earth be blessed; because thou hast obeyed my voice." Genesis 22:16-18.

21. Lest this conclusion seem to ascribe to Ganzfried a Gnostic disdain for the physical, like that suggested by Stanley Corngold of Kafka in "Nietzsche, Kafka and Literary Paternity," in Jacob Golomb, ed., *Nietzsche and Jewish Culture* (Routledge: London, 1997), 137-57, observe that *The Sender* ends in fact on a decidedly physical (and surprisingly tender) note, as Georg and his father step into the elevator that will take them back down to the less than sublime streets of New York. The father unwit-tingly preempts his son's ultimate attempt to examine his tattoo by begging Georg "for my sake," or, more literally, "out of love for me," to close his jacket and protect himself against the cold: which service the son wordlessly performs, in the novel's final line (368), and with a gesture of implicit respect for the loving imperative of the man whose past Georg may or may not have called back into literary life.

22. *Bruchstücke: Aus einer Kindheit 1939-1948* (Frankfurt: Suhrkamp Verlag, 1995). (Published in English as *Fragments: Memories of a Wartime Childhood,* trans. Carol Brown Janeway (New York: Schocken Books, [1996]) All references subsequently marked in the text; Wilkomirski's book will hereafter be referred to as *Fragments*. We have chosen to produce our own English versions of the passages here cited rather than to follow Janeway, as her translation has become controversial: see Philip Goure-vitch, "The Memory Thief," *The New Yorker* (14 June 1999): 48-68.

23. Susan Rubin Suleiman, "Monuments in a Foreign Tongue: On Reading Holo-caust Memoirs by Emigrants," *Poetics Today,* 17:4 (Winter 1996) 638-57. Suleiman is in turn influenced by Barbie Zelizer.

24. See the series of articles by Ganzfried, "Die geliehene Holocaust-Biographie," *Die Weltwoche* (27 August 1998), "Fakten gegen Erinnerung," *Die Weltwoche* (3 Sep-tember 1998), and "Bruchstücke und Scherbenhaufen," *Die Weltwoche* (24 Septem-ber 1998), forthcoming in English translation in Newman (ed.), *Jewish Writing in the Contemporary World: Switzerland.*

25. Wilkomirski, "Niemand muss mir Glauben schenken," interview by Peer Teuw-sen, *Der Tagesanzeiger* (31 August 1998).

26. Siegfried Unseld, who heads the Jüdischer Verlag at Suhrkamp, had received hints even before the book went to press that it might be fictitious. He accordingly sent the manuscript to Lea Balint, who heads the Children without Identity section at the Ghetto Fighters' House of Yad le Yeled in Jerusalem, for examination and approval.

27. See, however, the report aired on 7 February 1999 on CBS's "60 Minutes," with its presentation of evidence showing that Doessekker was in Zurich in 1945 in contra-

diction of his claim that he was at that time in a Cracow orphanage following his liberation from the concentration camp, as well as the testimony of Raul Hilberg, who maintains that it would have been virtually impossible for a small child alone to survive the camps. See also the long essays by Gourevitch, "The Memory Thief," and Elena Lappin, "The Man with Two Heads," *Granta* Nr. 66 (Summer 1999): 7–65, for sustained (if not uncontroversial) reflections on Wilkomirski's history and motives. Lappin in particular, although ultimately skeptical of Wilkomirski, still cannot entirely suppress her former friendship with him, which perhaps leads her to one-sidedness in her assessment of actors such as Ganzfried.

28. In this context we have benefitted from Birgit S. Erdle's presentation as part of the round-table discussion at the Theater Neumarkt in Zurich on 7 December 1998.

29. While he doesn't here specify the nature of the specialists, we know that he underwent psychoanalytic treatment using a controversial technique developed in the early 1990s to help adult victims of child abuse recover repressed memories. Elaine Showalter has collected and analyzed some of these "recovered memory" phenomena in her *Hystories: Hysterical Epidemics and Modern Culture* (New York: Columbia University Press, 1997).

30. Jurek Becker, *Jacob the Liar,* trans. Leila Vennewitz (New York: Schocken, 1990), orig. *Jakob der Lügner* (Berlin & Weimar: Aufbau-Verlag, 1969).

31. Wilkomirski, "Niemand muss mir Glauben schenken"; our translation.

17 Of Friends and Mentors

DONALD BROWN

No matter how well-matched the participants, in friendship there is always some disparity that must be overridden by affection. In situations where one of the two friends enjoys a more favored position than the other, is more exalted in rank, prestige, wealth, or knowledge, the relationship might more properly be considered as one of mentor to protégé. Such situations allow us to see the value of friendship as a bridge across the gap that separates unequals; the friendly hand extended from a superior or elder can in many ways do much more for one's self-esteem, professional standing, creative imagination, than all the more casual time spent in the company of contemporaries. The mentor's friendship can shape a character in ways that might otherwise have been left unexplored, unknown. In his famous epistle to Can Grande, Dante articulates a strong version of "the sacred bond" of friendship between unequals.[1] In offering to dedicate the *Paradiso* to his friend, Dante casts himself as an inferior and yet is able to assert the value of friendship between princes and "men obscure in fortune":

> Nor do I fear to incur the charge of presumption, as some may object, in assuming the name of friend, since no less than peers are those un-equal in rank united by the sacred bond of friendship. For if one looks at pleasant and profitable friendships very often upon observation he will see that eminent persons have been linked with their inferiors. And if he turn his gaze to true friendship, that is, friendship for itself, will he not observe that men obscure in fortune but great in virtue have been the friends of many illustrious and eminent princes? And why not, since even the friendship of God and man is not hindered by their inequality. If what is asserted may seem unworthy to anyone, let him listen to the assertion of the Holy Ghost, that certain men have participated in his friendship. For one reads of Wisdom in the Book of Wisdom, "For she is a treasure unto men that never faileth, in which they that use are made

partakers of the friendship of God." But the ignorance of the masses forms judgments without discretion: just as it thinks the sun to be a foot wide, so in one thing and another it is deceived by its credulity. But it is not fitting that we, to whom it is given to know the best that is in us, should follow in the footsteps of the herd, rather we are bound to oppose their errors. For those who are vigorous in intellect and reason and endowed with a certain divine freedom are constrained by no custom. Nor is this surprising, since they are not directed by laws, but the laws by them. It is clear, therefore, as I said above, that it is not at all presumptious to call myself your most devoted servant and friend.[2]

We can gloss Dante's thought about friendship as the assertion that any disparity between friends is dissipated by the very fact of friendship. Friendship equalizes the friends to the extent that each necessarily takes part in sustaining the valued relation. Dante's example of the "friendship of God" is in a sense incredible, but it is offered authoritatively to silence those who would find friendship between unequals incredible. If the Bible says there is at least some metaphorical way in which we can claim God as a "friend," then it justifies the possibility of friendship between princes and paupers, between the powerful and the lowly, between those who know and those who don't. Pursuing imaginatively the Book of Wisdom's quote about God, we might wonder what kind of friendship we might enjoy with one who is omnipresent and who would thus know all about us before we had a chance to introduce ourselves. More philosophically, we might consider such a highly hypothetical relationship in light of Maurice Blanchot's description of friendship as including a "common strangeness that does not allow us to speak of our friends but only to speak to them, not to make of them a topic of conversations (or essays), but the movement of understanding in which, speaking to us, they reserve, even on the most familiar terms, an infinite distance, the fundamental separation on the basis of which what separates becomes relation."[3]

I want to hold on to that final phrase: "an infinite distance, the fundamental separation on the basis of which what separates becomes relation," for it not only describes the distance that lies between one friend and another (particularly where disparities of class intrude), it also underlines the sense in which Dante's claim to the princely Can Grande's friendship occurs within a deliberate separation: that of Dante and Can Grande, as friends, in distinction from the "herd," the common run of person who might not perceive the basis of the friendship. Dante claims *that we two above the herd determine what is best for us* because the two friends enjoy a "divine freedom" that expresses itself in their willingness to recognize each other as friends, no matter that social convention might make such a bond seem unlikely. In other words, wisdom, which might here be glossed as the willfulness that permits one to exert divine freedom, makes one not only God's friend but a godlike friend, a friend who, we might say, is "beyond good and evil" in the sense that the values of common humanity, which would condemn the relation, are no longer taken into account: the friends "are not directed by the laws, but the laws by them."

The assertion of the possibility of such friendship seems to me congruent with Blanchot's understanding of how "what separates becomes relation." The friends exist in a realm apart, a realm called "friendship" that is not liable to the laws of the state or to the rules of convention but only to the dictates of wisdom, that is, what best serves the friendship. Blanchot says that in such friendship we do not speak of our friends but only to them; in other words, we do not hold the terms of the friendship up to a third person for inspection; we do not invite the witness of an interlocutor who may find cause to judge the worth of the friendship. In this again there is room for comparison with the divine friendship imagined by Dante, for whatever one may say about God, surely it is the case that, for the devout, what one says *to* God is much more important and constitutes one's true relation to a divine being. Indeed, Dante's comments about divine friendship are not said *of* Can Grande but rather *to* him, but we needn't interpret Blanchot's idea quite so literally. We may consider that, when speaking of friendship, one does not tell the world *of* a particular friend, but rather speaks only *to* friends. In so doing, one attempts to define (for the sake of one's friends) the relation formed by the separation of oneself and one's friends from the rest of humanity.

My use of the phrase "beyond good and evil" a moment ago was intended to create a certain context of hyperbole with which to characterize the bond between persons who are utterly committed to one another — "for better, for worse" as the marriage vow has it. But the phrase should bring to mind aphorism 153 in Nietzsche's *Beyond Good and Evil:* "Whatever is done from love always occurs beyond good and evil."[4] That statement may be read in conjunction with Nietzsche's characterization of friendship in I.14

of *The Gay Science* as "a kind of continuation of love" in which the "possessive craving of two people for each other gives way to a new desire and lust for possession" so that friendship becomes "a shared higher thirst for an ideal above" the friends.[5] Friendship such as that characterized by Dante and by Blanchot, also occurs, like love, "beyond good and evil," because friendship contains a "*shared* higher thirst" that aspires beyond the dictates of convention. In other words, the separation that becomes a relation is just this desire to, as Dante says, "know the best that is in us." The qualities in ourselves that we would most like to emphasize are those that the friend as mentor brings out in us, to the extent that we use the relation wisely.

Nietzsche's Zarathustra is the literary figure who may best be described as existing beyond good and evil, and his fourteenth discourse, in Book One of *Also Sprach Zarathustra,* is entitled "Of the Friend." There we find that the interlocutor or "third person" is the friend: "I and Me are always too earnestly in conversation with one another" for the situation to be endurable without a friend. The friend, then, is "the cork that prevents the conversation of the other two from sinking to the depths."[6] We can say that the friend is the witness to the hermit's argument with himself, the midwife to the birth of the philosopher's thought, the occasion for outwardly directed discourse.[7] But this is not a purely beneficial relation; Zarathusta suggests that friendship, by its addition of a perspective extraneous to one's own, may also be the means to one's downfall. Rather than leading us to find a mentor, "[o]ur longing for a friend is our betrayer" (82).

Dwight David Allman highlights the "contentious basis" for friendship in Zarathustra's discourse, pointing out the heavy emphasis on enemies and upon the enemy in the friend.[8] But the sense of enmity that Zarathustra evokes does not derive solely from the "agonistic conception of friendship" that Allman and others attribute to Nietzsche's attempt to revive a pre-Socratic ideal of friendship (126).[9] As Allman points out, Zarathustra's discourse on friendship is not simply Nietzsche's attempt to revive an ancient ideal (129), but is also "a testament to the fact that noble friendship is not yet possible" (130). This is indeed true and has its basis in Nietzsche's own experience: Zarathustra's sense of the friend as betrayer, particularly where women are concerned, and of woman's "injustice and blindness towards all that she does not love" (83), derives in part from the fact that Book One of *Zarathustra* was written early in 1883 while Nietzsche was still nursing his personal wounds, having been "ditched" by his friends Paul Rée and Louise

Andréas-Salomé after hopeful plans for a free-thinking *ménage-à-trois* went awry.[10] The experience clearly left Nietzsche bitter about the possibility of mutually sustaining a beneficial friendship. In his subsequent book, *Beyond Good and Evil*, Nietzsche treats friendship even more negatively, often placing the term "friends" in quotation marks to indicate either his irony toward the concept or to highlight the lack of sincerity in such relationships, or both. My point is that Zarathustra's views on friendship are somewhat paradoxical: on the one hand, there is a positive value to be gained (self-overcoming); on the other hand, there is a palpable danger in the possibility of betrayal, misunderstanding, and the malicious undermining of one's best efforts.

Zarathustra has been called "the loneliest man in literature," and much of that perception is due to the way in which he trumpets his isolation and his lack of friends and followers, a tendency that becomes more marked in Nietzsche's own situation from the mid-1880s until his collapse. But, even so, Zarathustra's dictum that "You should honour even the enemy in your friend" (83) and his insistence that slaves and tyrants cannot be friends both point to an understanding of the give-and-take of friendship as a positive value: friendship is not simply mutual admiration or a complacent "us against them" relation to the world, nor is it a relation of master/slave or primarily an agon between equals trying to outdo one another. Friendship, for Zarathustra, is a difficult test, something to be aspired toward, a task, a goal: "O my friend, man is something that must be overcome" (83). As Allman points out, Book One of *Zarathustra* conceives friendship "strictly in terms of its utility to the telos represented by the *Übermensch*" (125). The insistence is upon friendship as yet another relation that will fail; in that failure one must find the germ for something better, more fully achieved, more consistently itself. Zarathustra refers to his listeners as friends, but if they are so it is only because they accept him as their mentor and define themselves as the few who understand his teaching and are ready to sacrifice weak versions of happiness, reason, virtue, justice, and pity to become "hard," which is to say demanding of their friends and of themselves.[11]

Indeed, Zarathustra deliberately revises the Christian doctrine of "love of one's neighbour," for he finds in such "selflessness" a fear of the self and of the solitude of the strong: "Do I exhort you to love of your neighbour? I exhort you rather to flight from your neighbour and to love of the most distant!" (87).[12] The "most distant" then becomes synonymous with a certain kind of friend: "the creative friend, who always has a complete world to bestow" (88). It seems clear that this friend is Zarathustra himself who hopes to inspire in his listeners the love for the impossibly distant and a readiness for the doctrine of self-overcoming. But with regard to friendship as an ideal, it is equally clear that Nietzsche intends friendship to be a process in which one learns from one's betters, subjecting oneself to an ongoing inquiry into the values held in common — not least of which is each friend's evaluation of the other. As in Dante's friendship with Can Grande, there is a "divine freedom" in this creative friendship, a freedom that includes each friend's freedom to deny the other and even friendship itself should that become necessary.[13]

Dante, for all his creative genius, had need of friends, particularly as patrons and political allies; Nietzsche, for all his love of solitude, found cause to proclaim the creative friend as that individual who becomes an example for us, an incentive toward a higher relation. But there is a counterargument to these views of friendship's salutary inspiring power, particularly with regard to the creative individual, that has been stated quite forcefully by the narrator of Marcel Proust's *A la recherche du temps perdu*.[14] Late in *A l'ombre des jeunes filles en fleur*, the narrator attempts to justify the fact that he snubbed his devoted friend Robert de Saint-Loup in favor of hours of self-indulgent pleasure in the company of a troop of young girls; one of whom, Albertine, eventually becomes a major obsession in his life. The narrator, whom we will call Marcel for the sake of convenience, is often quite adept at justifying his indulgences by stressing the importance they will eventually assume once he arrives at a properly retrospective perspective on his past. But rather than excuse his indifference to his friend by referring to the romantic importance that Albertine will one day assume, Marcel instead pauses to offer his reasons for not valuing Saint-Loup's friendship:[15] "friendship is a dispensation from [the] duty [to live for oneself], an abdication of self."[16] Friendship is not only "devoid of virtue" but "fatal" because it deprives us of our own company, that solitude in which the "work of artistic creation proceeds in depth" (I.968). With friends, we remain on the surface of our thought, altering our most personal perceptions and individual ideas, so as to appear in accord with a friend who cannot add anything substantive to our search for truth.

Later, in Chapter Two of *Le côté de Guermantes*, Marcel even expresses his amazement that "men with some claim to genius—Nietzsche, for instance—can have been so ingenuous as to ascribe to [friendship] a certain intellectual merit" (II.409). Friendship makes us "sacrifice the only part of ourselves that is real and incommunicable . . . to a superficial self" (II.409–10). Once again the occasion for Marcel's disparagement of the "pleasure" of friendship, "half-way between physical exhaustion and mental boredom" (II.410), is the prospect of Saint-Loup's company. We might say that much of the tedium that Marcel finds in friendship can be attributed to his relations with Saint-Loup and that the latter's professed affection and obvious devotion act as the incentive to a perverse repulsion. Late in *Le Temps retrouvé*, Marcel learns of Saint-Loup's death and remains for several days shut up in his room, thinking of his deceased friend. Once again he recalls "the very special being" for whose friendship he "had so greatly wished," a friendship Marcel attained to an extent beyond which he could have hoped but which failed to give him "more than a very slight pleasure" (III.877–78).

Saint-Loup's meaning in the novel is very much predicated upon his natural superiority to most of his "race" (the term by which the narrator refers to the aristocracy in general and to the Guermantes family in particular). So, though we might take Saint-Loup to be the epitome of the serviceable and self-effacing friend, it is as a "personality more generalised than his own, that of the 'nobleman'" (I.791) that Saint-Loup remains fixed for the narrator as a "type," a figure to be circumscribed in its particularity—a particularity that retains a "relation of distance," as with Dante and Can Grande. Saint-Loup's superiority to Marcel is a matter of birth and of personal merit; it is based upon his status as an exemplar of the Guermantes family to which Marcel remains for many years utterly enthralled. The Guermantes, as aristocrats with prestige and influence, have the potential to perform for Marcel the act of patronage that one of their number, the infamous Baron de Charlus, performs for the violinist Morel. However, it is not as patrons but as idiosyncratic objects of the novelist's art that we find so much attention given to the Guermantes. With regard to relations within the hierarchy of the Faubourg St. Germain, we can find an irony in the fact that Marcel's social climb becomes the occasion for an increased sense of alienation, not because our hero climbs above his class and out of his element, but due to the inanity and superficiality he observes in the once grand figures with whom he becomes friendly. The very relation of distance that lifts friends above "the common herd" places Marcel into a relation with his chosen circle of snobs that reveals to him his own isolation while in their midst—not because they don't accept him but because they do.

The irony of finding what one wants superficial once one has attained it is complemented by a further irony: the fact that the figure responsible for the most important act of mentoring in the novel should emerge as the one character, outside of Marcel's immediate family, who has been known to him longest: Charles Swann. As a Jew, Swann is always something of an outsider despite his membership in the Jockey Club, and the rancorous division of society that takes place during the Dreyfus affair serves to make his isolation more obvious. Similarly, Swann's choice of a former courtesan for his wife also works against his status in the Faubourg, for he is never able to introduce his wife to his glittering acquaintances. But Swann is never entirely dropped socially, and his persistence in the novel indicates the extent to which his vision of the world remains in play throughout. Swann is a souvenir of Marcel's childhood visits with his own family to his aunt's home in Combray where Swann was a neighbor, a friend of Marcel's grandfather. Swann occupies a middle ground between the eldest and the most youthful generations in Marcel's family and is in his prime during the period that the narrator recalls with such immediacy after his episode with the madeleine. It is during the period of Marcel's boyhood that, besides disrupting the young Marcel's ritualistic bedtime kiss from his mother, Swann provides Marcel with a great lesson by presenting him with some reproductions of Giotto's depiction of the Vices and Virtues in the Arena Chapel at Padua.[17]

Habitual association of people with works of art causes Swann to identify the kitchen maid of Marcel's aunt with the figure representing Charity in Giotto's allegorical frescoes. Reading one's personal perceptions in terms of art—as with the kitchen maid or his wife Odette—and reading art in terms of one's personal emotions—as in the "national anthem" of Swann's love for Odette found in "le petit phrase" of Vinteuil's sonata—are characteristic tendencies of Swann's passed on in part to Marcel, while Swann's providing Marcel with reproductions of Giotto's frescoes is tantamount to a lesson in representation. Swann points out the resemblance between the "ample smock" of the pregnant kitchen maid and the "cloaks in which Giotto shrouds some of his allegorical figures" (1.87), but makes no further comparison to indicate a moral or symbolic meaning. It is up to Marcel to find a significance in Swann's somewhat whimsical identification: the power of the frescoes is found in their symbolism and in the fact that the intended virtue "was represented not as a symbol (for the thought symbolised was nowhere expressed) but as a reality, actually felt or materially handled" (I.88). The real meaning of the lesson is that abstract truths are best represented by mundane details and realistic figures — a lesson in the method of allegory that has significance for the narrative we are reading. The method is set forth outright, in the manner of Ruskin's moralizing readings of the carvings on medieval churches, when the narrator draws a comparison between the weight of the kitchen maid's belly and the "crushing burden" of death, not as an "abstract idea" but as something "painful, obscure, visceral" (I.88). The pregnant kitchen maid becomes then an allegorical figure for the confluence of birth and death as "burdens" that reveal the " 'seamy side' " of life. The "burden" is the pathos of real life, present as the underlying ground of allegorical abstraction.

Late in the novel, after the serial episodes of "mémoire involuntaire" en route to a reception at the home of the Prince de Guermantes, Marcel reflects upon the course of his life and, projecting the literary work he has been waiting his entire life to write, hits upon an idea that had not formerly occurred to him: "the raw material of my experience, which would also be the raw material of my book, came to me from Swann" (III.953). In the many thousands of pages of the *Recherche,* it may be possible for us to miss this necessary connection to the old friend of Marcel's grandfather, so the narrator spells it out for us: it was thanks to Swann that he became interested in Balbec and went there; there he met Albertine and also the Guermantes, Saint-Loup and M. de Charlus; he "thus got to know the Duchesse de Guermantes and through her [the Prince]" so that he owes to Swann "even my presence at this very moment in the house of the Prince de Guermantes, where out of the blue the idea for my work had just come to me (and this meant that I owed to Swann not only the material but also the decision)" to compose a grand narrative (III.954). The narrator remarks, "whoever it is who has thus determined the course of our life has, in so doing, excluded all the lives which we might have led instead of our actual life" (III.955). This may seem a fatalistic message to derive from Swann's friendly advice, but that is the point: people's comments can have repercussions quite beyond what was intended. The narrator himself remarks that this is a "rather slender stalk" (III.954) to support the causality of his life's devotions, but unless we see that this thread exists (at least within the retrospective realm in which the narrator exists), we miss what is inevitable in the seemingly fortuitous.

Returning to the question of friendship, then, we can see that it is the friendship of Swann, rather than that of Saint-Loup or any other Guermantes, such as the bizarre and overbearing Baron de Charlus, that means the most in the long run, not through what Hamlet, speaking to Horatio, calls "the consonancy of youth," but rather because of the elder man's grasp of what might interest a youth such as Marcel. Swann stands in the role of the friend as mentor, one with "a world to bestow," in Nietzsche's phrase. The irony (and there is always irony in Proust) is that Swann, who bestows upon his friend the incentive to pursue those chimerical and evasive dreams that will become the material for his book, is not able to turn his knowledge and taste to his own advantage. Like Moses, he may lead others to the promised land but not enter it himself.

Reflecting on the relation of Swann and Marcel as one of mentor to protégé in the light of Dante's and Nietzsche's ideals of friendship, we come upon what could be called the allegorical nature of friendship. In other words, we find that friendship always refers to an ideal that neither friend alone could possibly see, much less reach. We can call this relation allegorical because each friend must be read or perceived in relation not only to his other—his friend—but also in relation to the other that the friendship makes of him. Both members of the friendship are translated into more significant versions of themselves. This, of course, is the very method that Proust's Marcel seemingly spends his life trying to learn: how to translate his banal and ordinary existence into a work of literary art. He eventually realizes that the most important lesson in that peculiar *Bildung* came to him through the first adult, outside his family, to take any particular interest in him. Even if the narrator is willing to play imaginatively with the other possibilities that have been ousted, that might have been—were it not for Swann's intervention—his life's passion, we (his readers) know that there is no such alternative life. Marcel must become the narrator of the *Recherche* or there is no Marcel at all. Thus the entirety of Proust's great novel becomes something of an allegory of transformation, or rather an allegory by which, to use a profoundly significant phrase of Nietzsche, "one becomes what one is."[18]

The implications of the phrase are complex because of Nietzsche's view that no self or subject exists apart from acting, doing, becoming. And yet the phrase does seem to offer some version of a circumscribable and knowable self coming into being through activity. Proust's narrator is a fitting illustration of such a process because, in fiction, a narrator is no more than the sum of his effects; there never simply is a narrator, or rather, no character or person emerges as a single, stable subject within the narrative's long trajectory from the opening passages about trying to fall asleep to the closing passages about wanting to write a novel. The analogy between sleep, or dream, and literature holds because one cannot speak of sleep while one is asleep; one cannot "be" a narrator but only an agent of narrative. Without wishing to complicate the relation unduly, I want to make explicit that, in Proust's novel, transforming or becoming is always imagined as a process much like writing, much like friendship, and that both "activities" are allegories in that both stand for the process of becoming. Friendship may find its be-all and end-all in nothing more, ultimately, than an occasion or incentive for transformation, for becoming what one is: the person whom the creative friend bestows upon one. Encounters with mentors (even if, as with Marcel, not recognized at the time) are charged with possibility, with fleeting vision and vague apotheosis, for a self may emerge from such a process like a photograph from its pool of solution: each print, each self, different — but all bearing a relation to an image created through the friend's influence.

In a section of *The Gay Science* entitled *One thing is needful,* Nietzsche writes: "To 'give style' to one's character — a great and rare art!" (290) and insists that such art requires that a "single taste" have governed the development of the style. In the moment when Marcel accepts the opinion of Swann, he inaugurates a search for style that takes place within the bounds of a taste that his mentor bestows upon him. In the course of the long narrative, Marcel will learn much from his observations of others and of his recollection of their opinions, but his reflection that so much hangs upon the slender stalk of Swann's advice contains a recognition of how much his "great and rare art" owes to a single taste — a taste for Balbec, for seagirt Gothic churces, for frivolous women, for the pathos of living that lies beneath the formal beauty of the allegorical image — and this taste comes to him through a man whose friendship toward himself was disinterested, casual, provisional.

The friendship of the creative friend is by its nature provisional because it awaits the sequel to the seed or hint dropped at a propitious moment. Zarathustra cautions us to beware the betrayer or enemy in the friend, and the first place we may look for such betrayal is in ourselves when we fail to see the significance of what the friend bestows. We wrap ourselves up and guard our hearts in service to a "single taste": our taste for our own view, our own company, our own heaven and hell above all. We are wary of what the friend offers, for it may not be "the thing" sought for, the one thing needful of which Nietzsche speaks. And yet, to the extent that we find in friendship an opening for transformation, a Zarathustrian call to a higher self, a self embarked on becoming a work of art by giving style to character, we find in friendship the Dantean "divine freedom" that makes laws for itself rather than yield to those predetermined by lesser relations. Our friend then becomes an allegory through which we read another version of ourselves, as "through a glass darkly"—to use Paul's well-known phrase. If the friend is, as Zarathustra says, the cork that keeps the conversation between "I" and "Me" from sinking to the depths, the friend may also be the glass through which "I" see "Me" transformed into something other, a character, a style, a *fatality* "I" may still *become*.

In *Ecce Homo*, Nietzsche describes "what poets of strong ages have called inspiration" as the creative experience that allowed him to produce his Zarathustra: "one accepts, one does not ask who gives. . . . Everything happens involuntarily in the highest degree but as in a gale of a feeling of freedom, of absoluteness, of power, of divinity."[19] Nietzsche's evocation of the freedom and divinity of inspiration—which he considers an ancient ideal that one must "go back thousands of years" to find expressed elsewhere—reminds us of the "divine freedom" that Dante asserts in claiming, above and beyond the logic of the herd, the right to call his social superior his friend. The creative mind, whether Nietzsche's, Proust's, or Dante's, clearly seems to take upon itself the recognition of what matters, of what will give style to character. More to the point, each may claim an experience in which, as Nietzsche says, it appears "as if the things themselves approached and offered themselves as metaphors" (301), for such is the allegorical perspective par excellence: a sense of the things and persons of one's life and experience as mere signifiers in a text that one's own imagination must find the authority to write. The key to such authority, as Proust's narrator shows us, may be given to us offhand by a friend, a mentor who provides an added color or angle or contrast to our habitual mode of perception. Dante himself is such a friend when we consider that his letter to Can Grande is not famous simply because of its eloquent assertion of friendship between unequals, it is also known for the lengthy disquisition on the allegorical method of the *Commedia* by which Dante enlightens his friend as to the nature of the gift (that is, *Paradiso*) he would bestow. Dante implies that in bestowing his poem on his friend, he offers a vision that is significant for his friend's spiritual good. All three writers offer their readers a world of inspiration, of allegory, of the subtle transformation of experience into enduring form.

Of course friendship is not a work of art. The world that friendship bestows is not a static world in which each thing is identified and understood once and for all; neither is it the yawning abyss of boredom and social niceties that Proust's narrator describes upon occasion. Friendship, like the self one is always in process of becoming, is intermittent, as is all feeling, desire, and knowledge in Proust; but for friendship to exist at all one must be willing to assert the divine freedom of those who choose to make something out of nothing, shedding skins — shedding friends if necessary, like the lonely Zarathustra — in order to go further into "the infinite distance" that, in turn, creates a relation between the selves we once were and the "most distant" selves we may yet become, a relation that allows us to participate — even at a distance — in the growth of our friends as in the growth of ourselves.

NOTES

1. The question of the letter's authenticity has been in dispute at various times, most importantly in the early part of the century and again more recently, but most agree that the opening four paragraphs, at least, are authentically Dante's. See Robert Hollander, *Dante's Epistle to Cangrande* (Ann Arbor: University of Michigan Press, 1993) for a judicious weighing of the arguments for and against recognition of the entire letter as Dante's. In Hollander's view, the letter can be considered as a "companion piece" to *Paradiso* VI (91) in that "the procedures of [Dante's] poem exactly manifest [the letter's] insistence on theological allegory" (89).

2. "Dante's Letter to Can Grande," trans. Nancy Howe, ed. Mark Musa, in *Essays on Dante* (Bloomington: Indiana University Press, 1964), 34–47.

3. Maurice Blanchot, "Friendship," trans. Elizabeth Rottenberg, *Friendship*, (Stanford, Calif.: Stanford University Press, 1997), 289–92; the essay is a reflection on the death of Blanchot's friend Georges Bataille.

4. Friedrich Nietzsche, *Beyond Good and Evil: Prelude to a Philosophy of the Future,* trans. Walter Kaufmann (New York: Vintage Books, 1966).

5. Friedrich Nietzsche, *The Gay Science,* trans. Walter Kaufmann (New York: Vintage Books, 1974). Further references to Nietzsche's works in my text cite section number rather than page number.

6. "Of the Friend," in Friedrich Nietzsche, *Thus Spake Zarathustra. A Book for Everyone and No One,* translated with an introduction by R. J. Hollingdale (London: Penguin Books, 1971).

7. In *Beyond Good and Evil,* Nietzsche characterizes the "origin of a good conversation" thus: "One seeks a midwife for his thoughts, another someone whom he can help" (136).

8. Dwight David Allman, "Ancient Friends, Modern Enemies," *South Atlantic Quarterly* 97:I (Winter 1998): 113–35; from a special issue on friendship.

9. Allman cites John Coker, "On Becoming Friends," *International Studies in Philosophy* 25 (1993): 113–27; and Laurence Lampert, *Nietzsche's Teaching: An Interpretation of Thus Spake Zarathustra* (New Haven: Yale University Press, 1986), 57–58.

10. See R. J. Hollingdale, *Nietzsche: The Man and His Philosophy* (London and Boston: Ark Paperbacks, 1983), 130–42. Both Nietzsche and Rée had fallen in love with Lou Salomé, but she seemed to consider only Rée a romantic involvement. However, the three friends were planning to set up house together, despite the vehement protestations of Nietzsche's mother and sister (the latter had a violent antipathy toward Lou). "The *ménage-à-trois* was now [October, 1882] to be set up in Paris; Nietzsche had been making inquiries of his Paris friends for suitable accomodation, and he was mildly puzzled when, at the end of the month, Lou and Rée left for Stibbe without any definite date for another meeting having been fixed. At the beginning of November [Nietzsche's devoted friend Peter] Gast arrived in Leipzig, and during the following fortnight spent in his company Nietzsche gradually realized he had been ditched" (134). As Hollingdale points out, Nietzsche broke with his family due to Rée and Lou and then was abandoned by his friends. He was writing hurtful and confused letters to Rée and others in late 1882; the first part of Zarathustra was published in 1883.

11. Zarathustra's "transvaluation of all values" begins in the prologue where he proclaims that the "greatest thing you can experience" is the "hour of the great contempt" (42), where, in typically hyperbolic fashion, we find that happiness "should justify existence itself"; that reason should "long for knowledge as the lion for its food"; that virtue should drive one mad; that justice should make one a man of "fire and hot coals"; that pity is "the cross upon which he who loves man is nailed"; great contempt is directed at those who profess moderation in these things (43).

12. Hollingdale's translation alerts us of a play on words in Nietzsche's original German text: "Nächsten = neighbour and nearest, and throughout this chapter *Fernsten* (= the most distant), the opposite of nearest, is also made to mean the opposite of neighbour, i.e., the people of the most distant future. Hence the continual antithesis between 'neighbour' and 'most distant'" (339–40, n 11).

13. In section 279 of *The Gay Science,* "Star friendship," Nietzsche writes, "We were friends and have become estranged. But this was right, and we do not want to conceal and obscure it from ourselves as if we had reason to feel ashamed"; "That we have to become estranged is the law above us." Nietzsche goes on to express the poetic idea that this law above us "is probably a tremendous but invisible stellar orbit in which our very different ways and goals may be *included,*" and exhorts us to "*believe*

in our star friendship even if we should be compelled to be earth enemies." In other words, Nietzsche suggests that estrangement does not necessitate the renouncing of the friendship; it becomes more "venerable" as a moment along a path one should not be ashamed of having walked.

14. I do not mean to consider Proust's own personal view of friendship; he certainly had a wide circle of friends and acquaintances with whom he was on affectionate and at times intimate terms. In his letters, Proust sometimes makes statements that undermine the value of friendship, but this usually occurs as part of a protestation concerning his inability to engage in some social event; like Nietzsche, Proust was afflicted with ill health throughout his entire adult life and, in such circumstances, one is sometimes forced to depend on the forbearance of friends to an excessive extent — a fact that, on other occasions, can make one quite irritable about such dependence. Certainly the writer's need for solitude is so conventional as to be a cliché; what is more interesting is the question of how such solitude is possible in the midst of friends and family — a problem each writer must solve for him- or herself.

15. The repudiation of Saint-Loup's friendship, which is generally described in terms of complete devotion, is a recurring theme in the novel. Marcel's reticence figures, in part, as an important element in the narrator's refusal of homosexuality: eventually it is revealed that Saint-Loup has male as well as female lovers; the narrator is appalled and claims that he had always kept a certain distance in his relations with Saint-Loup. The eventual revelation, which comes as something of a surprise for the reader as well, could be said to be the reason behind the narrator's insistence on the pernicious effects of friendship. For a somewhat overstated but still interesting reading of Saint-Loup as the primary romantic interest in the *Recherche* and of the narrator's attempts to camouflage that fact, see Mark D. Guenette, "Le Loup et le narrateur: The Masking and Unmasking of Homosexuality in Proust's *A la recherche du temps perdu*," *Romanic Review*, vol. LXXX, No. 2 (March 1989): 229–46.

16. Marcel Proust, *Remembrances of Things Past*, 3 vols., trans. C. K. Scott Moncrieff and Terence Kilmartin (New York: Vintage Books, 1981), 968. All further references are to this edition and contain the volume number as well as the page number.

17. The original publication of *Du Côté de chez Swann* included the announcement that the *Recherche* would consist of three volumes. The announcement indicated the section titles of each volume and included "The 'Vices and Virtues' of Padua and Combray" as a section of the final volume, *Le Temps retrouvé*, projected for 1914. For a discussion of the importance of the configuration of vice and virtue in the *Recherche*, the analogies between Combray, Venice, and Padua, and speculation on why the restatement of the theme was removed from the Venice sojourn, see Beryl Schlossman, *The Orient of Style: Modernist Allegories of Conversion*, (Durham, N.C.: Duke University Press, 1991), 180–222.

18. "Wie man wird was man ist": the phrase is the subtitle to Nietzsche's *Ecce Homo*, an attempt to explain himself as a writer and thinker. The phrase is discussed at length in chapter six of Alexander Nehamas, *Nietzsche: Life as Literature* (Cambridge, Mass.: Harvard University Press, 1985). I am indebted to Nehamas's comparison of

Nietzsche's idea of becoming with the position of Proust's narrator: what Proust's narrator calls "the discovery of our true life" can, in Nehamas's words, "be made only in the very process of creating the work of art which describes and constitutes it. And the ambiguous relation between discovery and creation, which matches exactly Nietzsche's own view, also captures perfectly the tension in the very idea of being able to become who one actually is" (188).

19. Friedrich Nietzsche, *On the Genealogy of Morals*, trans. Walter Kaufmann and R. J. Hollingdale, and *Ecce Homo*, trans. Walter Kaufmann (New York: Vintage Books, 1969), 300–301.

18 Shprintze, or Metathesis: On the Rhetoric of the Fathers in Sholem Aleichem's *Tevye the Dairyman*[1]

HOWARD STERN

It would be hard to think of a novel more intensely concerned with the joys and sorrows of fatherhood than Sholem Aleichem's *Tevye the Dairyman*. In four of the novel's five central chapters, Tevye loses a daughter in marriage—whether hopefully, resignedly, reluctantly, or kicking and screaming—and in the fifth he loses a daughter to suicide when the engagement is broken. Needless to say, pathos abounds—more than enough for a relatively short novel; indeed, more than enough for a novel, stage play, musical, and movie. But the father-daughter relation is of tropological as well as thematic interest. Sholem Aleichem assigns to each daughter (more precisely: to each daughter's ambit) a characteristic figure of thought that derives from the limited repertory of Tevye's paternal discourse and that turns out to control, with astonishing rigor, the political and social thematics of that daughter's chapter. Thus *Tevye the Dairyman* combines features of the tearjerker and the handbook of rhetoric; it organizes a welter of highly charged material according to a grid of systematic tropes. To describe the novel in this way is to suggest affinities with other classics of the early twentieth century: Joyce's *Ulysses*, for example, or Berg's *Wozzeck*. One goal of the present paper is to confirm Benjamin Harshav's thesis that the virtuoso display of premodern modes of discourse in Sholem Aleichem paradoxically establishes a unique Yiddish variant of European modernism.[2]

It will have to suffice here to demonstrate the tropological system at its most explicit moment, the chapter "Shprintze [Hope]," and then to adumbrate connections with the rest of the novel. We begin with a rather puzzling conversation between Tevye and the happy-go-lucky Ahronchik, who has quietly been courting the eldest available daughter, Shprintze:

"A good evening!" I said to him.

"And to you, too," he replied. He stood there a little awkwardly with a blade of grass in his mouth, stroking his horse's mane; then he said, "Reb Tevye, I have an offer to make you. Let's you and I swap horses."

"Don't you have anyone better to make fun of?" I asked him.

"But I mean it," he says.

"Do you now?" I say. "Do you have any idea what this horse of yours is worth?"

"What would you price him at?" he asks.

"He's worth three hundred rubles if a cent," I say, "and maybe even a little bit more."

Well, Ahronchik laughed, told me his horse had cost over three times that amount, and said, "How about it, then? Is it a deal?"

I tell you, I didn't like it one bit: what kind of business was it to trade such a horse for my gluepot? And so I told him to keep his offer for another day and joked that I hoped he hadn't come just for that, since I hated to see him waste his time. . . .

"As a matter of fact," he says to me, as serious as can be, "I came to see you about something else. If it's not too much to ask of you, perhaps the two of us could take a little walk."[3]

What is the rationale of this proposed exchange, which is never mentioned again? One could certainly answer that there needn't be any rationale, since Ahronchik has already been richly characterized as the initiator of many acts of capricious or whimsical generosity—bestowing a fistful of money upon a beggar, taking a brand-new jacket off his back to thrust it upon a perfect stranger, and so on. Still the horse trade seems to be featured as especially pointless, and it leads directly (the "little walk") to Ahronchik's asking for the hand of Shprintze in marriage. The key to this scene is not Ahronchik's casual generosity—the disproportion of what he bestows on others—but the very principle of exchange: I take what you have and you take what I have. Only in a world governed by the principle of exchange can social relations be understood as reversible enough to permit the marriage of a millionaire's son and a milkman's daughter. As Tevye himself puts it, Ahronchik's mother would have no "reason to be ashamed of me . . . because if I wasn't a millionaire myself, I would at least have an in-law who was, while the only in-law she'd have would be a poor beggar of a dairyman; I ask you, then, whose connections [*yikhes*] would be better, mine or hers?" (92). Such a reading of the horse trade may seem extravagant at first, but it is supported by the text on every level from the narrative down to the phonological. It will be remembered that "Shprintze" begins with a discussion of Russia's liberal constitution of 1905, which triggered a series of pogroms and persecutions in the Pale of Settlement. The rich Jews of Yehupetz (Kiev) have abandoned their dachas in Boiberik and fled to other parts; Tevye's dairy business, however, has continued to blossom because rich Jews from other parts have been flocking to Boiberik: "But why, you ask, are they all running here? For the same reason, I tell you, that we're all running there! It's an old Jewish custom to pick up and go elsewhere at the first mention of a pogrom. How does the Bible put it? *Vayisu vayakhanu, vayakhanu vayisu*—or in plain language, if you come hide in my house, I'd better go hide in yours" (83). The Hebrew words quoted here ("and they journeyed and they camped, and they camped and they journeyed") are not to be found in the Bible in this configuration; the chiasmus that expresses reversibility here is directly attributable to the liberal constitution, which Tevye cannot pronounce and persists in fracturing as *kosnitutsye*— that is to say, chiasmus as a figure of words derives from metathesis as a figure of sound (ns/sn). The tragedy of "Shprintze" can thus be summarized as follows: a brief hope-dream of social mobility inspired rhetorically by a metathetic liberal constitution reveals itself as deceptive, and the world returns to its customary state of irreversible relations—which state is then explored in the following chapter, "Tevye Leaves for the Land of Israel."[4]

Since Tevye seems unable to discuss any issue for more than two sentences without quoting Biblical, rabbinic, or liturgical support—*vayisu vayakhanu* being only a slender pseudoquotation—it seems reasonable to expect the rhetorical system uncovered here to be anchored in some genuine holy-tongue material; and so it is. Late one evening Tevye is summoned to the dacha of Ahronchik's mother in Boiberik, and he speculates on the reason: "What can be so urgent, I wondered as I drove there. If they want to shake hands on it and have a proper betrothal, it's they who should come to me, because I'm the bride's father . . . only that was such a preposterous thought that it made me laugh out loud: who ever heard of a rich man going to a poor one for a betrothal? Did I think that the world had already come to an end . . . and that the tycoon and the beggar were now equals, *sheli shelkho* and *shelkho sheli*—you take what's mine, I take what's yours, and the Devil take the hindmost?" (92-93). The Hebrew here is taken from the (for our purposes marvelously titled) Mishnaic tract *Pirkey Avot* ("Ethics, or better: Sayings of the Fathers"). Chapter V, verse 10 reads as follows: "There are four qualities in a human being: he who says, what's mine is mine and what's yours is yours, that is the intermediate quality. And some say, that is the quality of Sodom. What's mine is yours and what's yours is mine — an ignoramus. What's mine is yours and what's yours is yours — a righteous man. What's yours is mine and what's mine is mine — a wicked man." How appropriate that Tevye associates Ahronchik, subconsciously perhaps, with the quality of an ignoramus! But the important reason for quoting this compass-rose of the Mishnaic fathers in its entirety is that each of the four quadrants plays a role in the novel: each designates in traditional Jewish terms the governing trope of a daughter (again, more precisely, of a daughter's ambit). There are four quadrants and five daughters because the youngest daughter, Beilke, repeats the story of the eldest, Tsaytl, with an alternative (tragic) outcome. It remains now to sketch these connections.

In the case of Hodl, who marries a communist and follows him into Siberian exile, "what's mine is yours and what's yours is yours" — the communist Peppercorn (Yiddish: Feferl) is memorably figured as a righteous man. Hodl maintains of him and his revolutionary comrades that "they were the best, the finest, the most honorable young people in the world, and that they lived their whole lives for others, never giving a fig for their own skins" (63). "Her husband, she swore, was as clean as the driven snow. 'Why,' she said, 'he's a person who never thinks of his own self! His whole life is for others, for the good of the world'" (68). (The key phrases in Yiddish here are *nor fun yenems vegn* and *yenems toyve*.) Many years later, in telling the story of Beilke ("Tevye Leaves for the Land of Israel"), Tevye actually brings himself to concur in this assessment: "At least that Peppercorn of hers is a human being — in fact, too much of one, because he never thinks of himself, only of others" (109). (*Er aleyn iz bay zikh hefker, un der gantser iker iz di velt.*) It must be admitted that the crucial formulation of righteousness from *Pirkey Avot* is not explicitly present in "Hodl" — whether because Sholem Aleichem preferred to submerge the tropological scheme in a wealth of figurative variations, or possibly because the explicit rabbinic theme of those variations did not occur to him until a later stage in the serial publication of the novel — but the structure is evident, given the explicit citation in "Shprintze" and the constant informing presence of "Sayings of the Fathers" throughout the novel.

To confirm our reading of "Shprintze" and "Hodl," we turn to Beilke's chapter, which invokes both of them, thematically as well as rhetorically. Beilke, the youngest daughter, has sacrificed her own happiness by marrying a very rich middle-aged vulgarian in order to make life easier for her father (this is the sacrifice that Tsaytl, the eldest daughter, was ultimately saved from making in "Today's Children"; hence the tropological congruence of these two chapters). Tevye attempts to forestall the sacrifice by pointing out that "'money is a lot of hooey, anyway, just like the Bible says. Why, look at your sister Hodl! She hasn't a penny to her name, she lives in a hole in the wall at the far end of nowhere—and yet she keeps writing us how happy she is with her schlimazel of a Peppercorn.' Shall I give you three guesses what my Beilke answered me? 'Don't go comparing me to Hodl,' she says. 'In Hodl's day the world was on the brink. There was going to be a revolution and everyone cared about everyone. Now the world is its own self again, and it's everyone for his own self again, too.' That's what she said, my Beilke—just go figure out what she meant" (103). The Yiddish here is more accurate in describing the condition of the world in Hodl's day: *hot men zikh gezorgt far der velt, un zikh hot men fargesn*—not "everyone cared for everyone" (reciprocity or reversibility = ignorance), but "one cared about the world and forgot oneself" (righteousness). Beilke often speaks as though her world were the exact opposite of Hodl's, and this move is understandable since Hodl was her father's choice of counter-example. Actually, though, Beilke's insistence on self-identity and social rigidity proves that "what's mine is mine and what's yours is yours"—her world is the exact opposite of Shprintze's (which of course had no stability).[5]

It must be admitted that this moment in the text achieves a maximum of tropological density and even ambiguity—partly because the story of Beilke not only revises the story of Tsaytl and rejects the story of Hodl, but also serves as a bravura recapitulation of all the previous episodes.[6] Nevertheless, we can adduce another powerful piece of evidence for the deep analysis according to four quadrants. Podhotzur, the rich vulgarian, who is naturally impervious to Tevye's theory of in-law reversibility (or *yikhes* relativity) as developed in "Shprintze," demands that his father-in-law either give up the dairy business or, better still, remove himself to either America or Palestine. Since Tevye has always wanted to see the Holy Land anyway (more precisely, to inhabit the five books of Moses), Palestine is decided upon. Later, mortified by her complicity in this attempted erasure of the father, Beilke bursts into tears and Tevye begins to comfort her: "'Have you forgotten that God is still in His heaven and your father is still a young man? Why, it's child's play for me to travel to Palestine and back again, just like it says in the Bible: *vayisu vayakhanu* — and the Children of Israel knew not if they were coming or going. . . .' Yet the words were no sooner out of my mouth than I thought, Tevye, that's a big fat lie! You're off to the Land of Israel for good — it's bye-bye Tevye forever" (112). Here the spatial and social reversibility of "Shprintze" is reinterpreted temporally, and the point is: it's no longer available (if it ever was). At the end of a series of tropological inventions on the theme of confusing mine and thine, everything is what it is. Such was already the condition of the world in Tsaytl's day; but at least it followed then as a consequence that people could be who *they* were: Tsaytl did not have to sacrifice herself by marrying the rich middle-aged vulgarian (the butcher Layzer Wolf), but could start a life of penurious felicity with her dreamboat of a tailor boy, Motl Komzoyl. Beilke is not so lucky: Podhotzur "has businesses everywhere. He spends more on telegrams in a single day than it would cost us to live on for a year. But what good does all that do me if I can't be myself?" (113). Now another saying from "Sayings of the Fathers" returns to govern the world as a spectral double of "what's mine is mine and what's yours is yours," namely, Hillel's famous "*im eyn ani li mi li?*" (113) — "If I am not for myself, who will be?"

It remains only to discuss the case of "what's mine is mine and what's yours is mine — a wicked man." The daughter in question here is obviously Chava, who marries the Christian scribe of the village, Chvedka Galagan, and is disowned by her father. It must be admitted that the evidence here is at its least explicit; what we find is a series of encroachments, subsumptions, misappropriations. Thus, for example, the village priest turns out to have knowledge of Hebrew — insisting, to Tevye's amusement and horror, that "he knew our Scriptures better than I did and even reciting a few lines of them in a Hebrew that sounded like a Frenchman talking Greek" (71). The Christian subsumes the Jew — both his religion and his authority. The priest claims to "think a great deal of you Jews. It just pains me to see how stubbornly you refuse to realize that we Christians have your good in mind" (74). Chava is in his "charge," his "custody" (*rshus, hazhgokhe*).

Naturally, Tevye is outraged: "I demanded to know . . . what he thought of a man who barged uninvited into another man's house and turned it upside down—the benches, the tables, the beds, everything" (77). As in the diametrically opposite case of Hodl, there is no distinction between mine and thine—Chava denies that "human beings have to be divided into Jews and Christians, masters and slaves, beggars and millionaires" (72). Tevye can only respond that such distinctions will not disappear until the Messiah comes; "but he already has come," says the priest (74). Everything is already "theirs."

This completes our sketch of the tropological system. It would be illuminating now to delve more deeply into the texture of the Yiddish. Our remarks on metathesis in "Shprintze" (*kosnitutsye* for "constitution") would have to be supplemented by aphaeresis in "Today's Children" (*stikratn* for "aristocrats"), prosthesis in "Tevye Leaves for the Land of Israel" (*natalye* for "Italy"), syncope in "Hodl" (*khlire* for "cholera"), and various types of ellipsis in "Chava." But space prohibits. A detailed rhetorical analysis of *Tevye the Dairyman* in Yiddish will be presented to Stanley Corngold— most generous of readers and writers!—on the occasion of his 120th birthday (*biz hundertuntsvantsik!*); or perhaps before.

NOTES

1. The author gratefully acknowledges the assistance of Anita Gallers and Susanne Fusso in developing the ideas and working out the details of the present paper. He thanks David Katz for allowing him to discuss a version of the material with his eager and perceptive students at Yale University. Quotations from Sholem Aleichem refer to *Tevye the Dairyman and the Railroad Stories,* trans. Hillel Halkin (New York: Schocken, 1987).

2. Benjamin Harshav, *The Meaning of Yiddish* (Berkeley: University of California Press, 1990) 98–107.

3. *Tevye,* 88–89. Subsequent references in parentheses.

4. Halkin's "Constantution" misses the point. In general, his translation is funny, ingenious, idiomatic, and a pleasure to read—highly recommendable. Nevertheless, it introduces a number of small errors that tend to obscure the tropological structure of the novel. For example, Halkin dubiously adds the name of Peppercorn to the passage about *vayse khevrenikes* (93). On the other hand, his hilarious metatheses on the name of Podhotzur (Hodputzer, Hodderputz), while not in the Yiddish, are attractive additions to "Tevye Leaves for the Land of Israel" and can be motivated by Tevye's nostalgic preference for the metathetic days of Shprintze.

5. In "Today's Children" the operative rabbinic expression is *"Odom koroyv le'ats-*

moy—charity begins at home" (39)—literally: "A man is closest to his own self." Money, of course, is normally understood as a medium of *exchange;* but not exchange in the sense of "Shprintze." According to the tropology of *Tevye the Dairyman,* the world of commerce is governed not by easy exchange but by obstinate hoarding.

6. Two examples of recapitulation: Efrayim the Matchmaker returns from "Hodl" (but recalls Motl Komzoyl—"the matchmaker, the father-in-law, and the groom all rolled into one" (48) from "Today's Children"); and the misunderstanding with Efrayim (101) recalls a similar scene of double entendre with Layzer Wolf (37–8), also in "Today's Children."

19 Middlebrowbeat

LAURENCE A. RICKELS

Here, too, I believe, is one focus of de Man's appeal to students: he was inviting into existence, among souls chained to the workbench of paper-writing, matter-of-fact rhetorical moods of violence, superiority, and dismissiveness.
—Stanley Corngold, "On Paul de Man's Collaborationist Writings."[1]

Because it "is generally considered to be the paradigmatic poem of modern consciousness," Paul de Man[2] argued in 1957, you would think contemporary criticism should have arrived at a consensus on Goethe's *Faust* by now and then. While it remains unclear from which general view de Man took down this tall order, at the end of his list of varying and contradictory receptions of the work, just for openers, he singles out the lack of determination of "the relative value of the two principal works based on the theme of Faust, namely, Marlowe's and Goethe's" (76) as strong indicators "that the critical placement of Goethe's *Faust* in world literature is not established once and for all" (77). It doesn't sound like Goethe's *Faust* was one of de Man's faves. But the thematic studies of *Faust* under review, on account of their nonsuperimposable variations or equivocations, are instructive for the inside view they afford of their own "different methodologies, and therefore permit, with Faust as touchstone, the bringing to light of their own respective virtues and insufficiencies" (77). De Man thus situates Goethe's *Faust* within or as the three-way intersection of thematic criticism linking and separating the outright historical, the intellectual-historical, and the mythological approaches to the "Faust theme." As text, Goethe's *Faust* is a transparent placeholder or "touchstone" for the limited reception of the Faust theme coextensive with it. Or it serves as transferential prop in session with de Man's resistance: "Faust" represents for de Man some "general" norm of "modern consciousness," a modern complex associated with Goethe's authority. De Man goes on to demean this complex as open-headed invitational to a host of "alien elements," "humanism, rationalism, literary nationalism, tradition, and so on." "Faust" thus doubles for de Man as the alienating middlebrowbeat where the complexity of these elements or ideologemes is not accorded "attentive study" (79).

Speaking for himself, de Man addresses the beginning of Goethe's *Faust* as an "end of the line" in its evocation of "an irrational, essentially dispersed character, whom only a chaotic will prevents from sinking into nonbeing," a finish line that is, however, "only a point of departure for Goethe, who situates his drama entirely on the opposite slope of this problematic."

> The depth and the novelty of *Faust* are not in the initial anguish of its central character but in the way he conquers that anguish, namely, in the recognition of the necessary copresence of Mephistopheles, in the conviction that Being is accessible only in the repeated negation of that through which Being reveals itself to him. When, through the experience of love, Faust finds that he has yielded to Being, he knows also that this path will be littered with parts of himself that his development has had to abandon along the way, will be marked by a series of cruel, degrading sacrifices that Mephistopheles will always be delighted to carry out on his account. (83)

This "dialectic" or couples theory does not impose "the separation from the real and the transcendent" as impediment to "formation of a path toward Being," and it is this "uniform direction" that harmonizes Faust's otherwise "diverse," even "catastrophic," "experiences." Goethe's *Faust I* and Hegel's *The Phenomenology of Mind,* which are "exactly contemporaneous," would appear to be parallel universals in the mainstream of received ideas. "In the development of the consciousness of self, as in the example of Faust's life, the passage from one stage to the next constitutes the central moment. Beyond their considerable differences, Hegel and Goethe do have this idea in common" (84). We either come full circle in booking this "passage," ending up with the splitting off of the middlebrow double, or we once again run up against the "trans-," the "across" we all must bear. When transference bears down on de Man's resistance as he's passing his review of Faust studies, he just splits. Because this is what we are left with: either all these journalistic points of review *are* Goethe's *Faust* or else they R us.

But first get to know the middlebrowbeat, get to know all about you. The "excessive continuity" of the thematic approach of one of the critics under review is exemplified by his characterization of "romanticism as an unconscious precursor of Nazism" (82). In the mythological third of the reception that is Goethe's *Faust,* the ultimate claim is staked, "the totalitarian position of absolute authority" (87). In both touchdowns we are within positions of resistance to psychoanalysis, which at the same time overlap with psychoanalysis. How can there be "an unconscious precursor" without Freud's science? And yet this psychohistorical connection, which at the same time elides the mediation of Romantic notions of the unconscious by psychoanalysis (and by resistance to or inversion of psychoanalysis), belongs to the supernatural realm of the unread. The myth criticism under review, which circumvents the mediation of repression that the intellectual-historical brand of thematic criticism invoked and then performed, comes to us via Jung's notion of archetypes, and thus from a whole history of negative transference onto Freud.

De Man reads these thematic positionings not for their resistance. He chooses instead to undermine the "totalitarian position" of the Jungian brand of thematic criticism, for example, by pointing out that poetic language, its origins notwithstanding, remains "mediate and temporal": "Art is not an imitation (or a repetition) but an endless longing for imitation, which by virtue of imitating itself, hopes finally to find a model. In other words, poetic language is not an originary language, but is derived from an originary language it does not know" (87). This "over-correction" of the mythic take on Faust serves to give it the dialectical benefit of releasing, now in its undermined form, the ultimate reading after all, that of critique of the mythic. The closing sentence of de Man's review article: "This critique of the mythic constitutes the first step in a true thematic criticism, which, contrary to what one generally assumes, should pass from myth to idea, and from idea to formal theme, before being able to become history" (87–88).

All this passing just passes by the task of translation (and of transference) that sets the stage of Goethe's *Faust.* Because imitation, however problematized, does not translate translation. Faust takes it from the top and opens his translation scene with retranslations of "word." It is through translation that Faust would seek "compensation" for having failed to meet match and maker in the earth spirit. It was in their botched exchange that first mention of the *Übermensch* was dropped in German letters, right before Faust passed on to the scene of *Übersetzen.*

Walter Benjamin's evocation of originary language as "pure language" in "The Task of the Translator" can't get around the Berlin street wisdom about "pure" or *rein,* which debunks it to mean "mere." *Reine Sprache* could also mean "just language." De Man can't get around getting around to translation. What goes beyond poetic language is translation: we have de Man's words for Benjamin's words for it on the taped record of his final 1983 Messenger Lecture, "Walter Benjamin's 'The Task of the Translator.'" "That is the naiveté of the poet, that he has to say something, that he has to convey a meaning which does not necessarily relate to language. The relationship of the translator to the original is the relationship between language and language, wherein the problem of meaning or the desire to say something, the need to make a statement, is entirely absent."[3] You can have your translation, but you can't translate it, too. Only the original can be translated: "The translation canonizes, freezes, an original and shows in the original a mobility, an instability, which at first one did not notice" (82). According to the media-technical analogies Freud uses in his earliest essays on transference, a transference is a reprintable cliché that it makes out of the original relationship it also freeze-frames and condemns as unstable.

One man's translation is another man's negative transference. Because even though de Man seems to be talking metaphor, he's suddenly in a spot of resistance in theory. Benjamin, de Man notes, says translation is not the metaphor of the original: "nevertheless, the German word for translation, *Übersetzen,* means metaphor . . . *Übersetzen,* I should say, translates metaphor—which, asserts Benjamin, is not at all the same. They are not metaphors, yet the word means metaphor. The metaphor is not a metaphor, Benjamin is saying. No wonder that translators have difficulty" (83). No wonder: it's some kind of wound or re-wounding (as the tape rewinds) that sends de Man to the corner of the class. The German and English words for "translation" also translate "tradition" and "transference."

Along the "intralinguistic" axis of Benjamin's understanding of translation—versus the extralinguistic coordinates of paraphrase and imitation—de Man lets go a striking reformulation of the "amazing" paradox that he is suddenly willing to accept, namely that a metaphor is not a metaphor: translations "kill the original, by discovering that the original was already dead" (84). But then he pulls himself together again and returns to Benjamin, and returns translation to the afterlife of the original.

The afterimage of translation shares in the techno logic Benjamin develops in "Some Motifs in Baudelaire." The gadget connection with technology, the flick of the switch, the push of a button, administers posthumous shocks, which, as shots of inoculation, safeguard systems of circulation and substitution against the massive psychotic breakdown and shutdown that would otherwise follow from direct contact with the pressures of our ongoing technologization and massification. As long as we keep it on a short control release, technologization ultimately provides a technology-free view of reality. Pure or mere language gives to translation what's due to the original. Aura is thus neither created nor incorporated; it is destroyed and then, by no default of its own, restored. In other words, let the taped record show: de Man's back, and his transference slips are showing. Either de Man split aura/or he's on both sides now.

In real time, de Man never takes the trans- to make the techno connections inside that hub of Benjamin's thought, which is wide open to Freud's influence. He underscores instead a posthumous sense of the pangs Benjamin's translators have unambiguously associated with birth and thus rebirth: "So if you translate *Wehen* by 'birth pangs,' you would have to translate it by 'death pangs' as much as by 'birth pangs,' and the stress is perhaps more on death than on life" (85). *Wehe* is an outcry of woe, of sorrow, also of warning that the outcome of your actions will come to grief. The pangs of one's own word in translation and the afterlife or fermenting decay of the original to which the translation also points find two examples in de Man's lecture, one intended, the other unattended. The intralinguistic *Wehen* are plunged into an abyss, for which de Man finds the French *mise en abyme* the best translation, because it is a structure and has a "non-pathetic technical sense": "The text about translation is itself a translation, and the untranslatability which it mentions about itself inhabits its own texture and will inhabit anybody who in his turn will try to translate it, as I am now trying, and failing, to do" (86). That is the open-and-shut example of where the woe goes. But when it comes to the French translation of *Brot und Wein*, de Man is disturbed by connotations of bastardization and cheap restaurants: "It is all right in English because 'bread' is close enough to *Brot*. . . . But the stability of my quotidian, of my daily bread, the reassuring quotidian aspects of the word 'bread,' daily bread, is upset by the French word *pain*. What I mean is upset by the way in which I mean — the way in which it is *pain*, the phoneme, the term *pain*, which has its set of connotations which take you in a completely different direction" (87). The woe comes back all right in English as the pain that de Man cannot accept in translation for his daily bread. And why not pick on "wine" for *Wein?* In the German there's no "whining," just the direct hit of *weinen,* of "weeping." Too close. In the taped question-and-answer period, Neil Hertz wonders how to account for the transition "from what's really a contingent impossibility—to reconstruct the connotations of *Brot*—to a major term, like the 'Inhuman'" (95). Let the recording show that de Man backs down: it was just an anecdote, and Benjamin gave the example—and "whenever you give an example you, as you know, lose what you want to say"—and what he gave, though it "comes from him," from Benjamin, he, de Man, gave "for the sake of a cheap laugh" (96). De Man has slipped, and covers what is now the butt of his joke, with a defense so brittle it keeps turning on the speaker. In other words, the anecdotal discussion of how *Brot* or interchangeably, de Man offers, *brood,* Flemish for bread (87), gets lost in the translation into *pain* "is still very human" (96). Stowaway in *Brot* is a certain melancholy brooding that can never cross over into the external or "human" expression of pain.

If we take Hertz, and take him at his word, then our question to de Man remains, Why not "transhuman" rather than "dehumanized" or "inhuman"? De Man: "If one speaks of the inhuman, the fundamental nonhuman character of language, one also speaks of the fundamental nondefinition of the human as such" (96). This all-or-nothing inhumanism informs de Man's reading of the end of Goethe's *Faust* in his 1957 review article. He takes issue with the born-again view of the crying-out warning shout of pain to come. The Jungian myth program sees poetry as "the language in which the divine is preserved and to which, therefore, one never returns to die; one returns to language to be reborn" (87). De Man issues the corrective: "The end of Faust is not a return to the divine (which, moreover, for Goethe, has never been absent), but is rather the evocation of the absolute interiorization that is death" (86–87). While it is true enough that the eternal is the internal (and likewise I'm sure), it is hard to imagine an absolute interiorization, perhaps as hard or impossible as imagining one's own death. Because the other always goes first, there can never be the closure of absolute interiorization. We are stuck between a loss—of the other—and the hard-to-imagine place of our own death. Or in a more political or genealogical setting: not even suicide realizes a self-relation but, in theory, takes along countless undisclosed others on the way out. The totalitarian attempt to project self-difference onto the despised other runs out of victims and up against the other within that must be offed—runs up against the suicide that was all along the starting point.

Goethe's Faust is doubled over by the suicidal ideation he extracts as inheritance down the corridors of the university from his father (the full-on transferential setting). The impulse is halted by a blast from the past, back to a future that uncontrollably comes toward us. Songs from childhood restore him to the doubly missing maternal connection. But the impulse isn't overcome; it is deferred (and prolonged) by the pact with the devil. Between the songs that flash Faust back to his childhood and the signing of the contract or wager, there remains the all-important transition of the translation scene. Faust's ultimate translation of Logos as performative deed prompts Mephistopheles to come out of his poodle disguise; he takes this to be the right time to make his proposition. Mephistopheles has a devil of a time serving as bureaucrat to Faust the thinker, genius, professor, and journalist. The devil or double translates into deeds by taking at their word certain thoughts that cross Faust's mind. Faust can thus not see that the deeds carried out by his double are in any way associated with him. In Benjamin's *The Origin of the German Mourning Pageant,* you can find, in vestigial form, an allegorical reading of Goethe's *Faust* that resonates with the endopsychic reading of *Faust* that Freud folds into his Schreber case study. In all three texts, a highest court of mourning or haunting places us before the law of our fathers—back in the transferential setting—and passes judgment on the striving bent on the splitting of the translation of words into deeds.

In the Messenger Lecture on "The Task of the Translator," de Man gives the floor to his student, Carol Jacobs, whose recently published article "The Monstrosity of Translation" is "precise and correct" on what thus, for de Man, can go largely without saying. Let her prove that they are both aware of the cabalistic meanings of Benjamin's texts. But then he can step in and take over once she arrives, back in Benjamin's "The Task of the Translator," at an error in translation, one that would make whole what remains, in the original, a broken part (90). She gets a break. We can recognize the transference gift—the famous teacher recommends his student by including her in his corpus—, but in the afterlife, translation, transmission of de Man's collected work, we are also reminded of another *Gift,* a "poison" indistinguishable from the medicine that Faust's doctor father hands down to him. We don't have to make the jump cut to a past we were left to not see. In

1978 de Man gave an introduction to Jacobs's *Dissimulating Harmony*,[4] a task or contract of translation that was one of the professor's more devil-ish performances. First he makes it all paraphrase, himself included, while managing, for want of burden of proof or understanding, to count himself and everyone else out, too: "Paraphrase is the best way to distract the mind from genuine obstacles and to gain approval, replacing the burden of understanding with the mimicry of its performance" (220). But then he has the last word of a survival that is not Benjaminian or Nietzschean, but in the terms of the transference, annihilating: "But whereas the apparent fluidity of Nietzsche's text turns out to be a stammer, the high quality of Carol Jacobs's readings threaten her with a worse danger. She cannot prevent her stammering text from being impeccably fluid. Parable turns into paraphrase after all, even and especially when one is as fully aware as she is of this inconsistency. The result is no longer the birth of something purely tragic, though it is certainly not benign. It may well be the birth of criticism as truly critical reading, a birth that is forever aborted and forever repeated but that, in the meantime, makes for indispensable reading" (223). With an endorsement like that, who needs newspaper reviews?

De Man's horror of the middlebrow, which in 1957 rushes him into conflation of Goethe with the appropriation of Goethe by Germanistik or by Thomas Mann, is what he was all along pushing away, projecting outward, and thus performing, too. We have only begun to read Goethe. The hands-off thematic criticism that the Goethe corpus has generated as the outer limit of defense dates way back, in fact to Friedrich Schlegel's essay on *Wilhelm Meisters Lehrjahre* in which art appreciation takes over where ambivalence had to be let off. That was Schlegel's devil deal with the journalistic, thematic, or middlebrow double. With the exception of the sketched reading stretched between Freud and Benjamin, by and large *Faust* has been given the appreciation treatment, which, just like idealization, conceals resentment, until that is what it turns around to become exclusively and up front. Friedrich Nietzsche teaches that Goethe's *Faust* gets it all wrong. But without Goethe's closing lines dedicated to the eternal feminine and to the *Gleichnis*, the mutable as "figure" of eternity, Nietzsche could not have pulled up the difference that the internal feminine can make, a mourning that must mourn even over the merely integrative and substitutive moments of successful mourning, a difference that goes with the flow of eternity as figure [*Gleichnis*] of transience into the formulation of *Die ewige Wiederkehr des Gleichen.* Karl Kraus dismissed *Faust* as an assembly of lines designed for decontextualized citing and recycling or paraphrase. But then Kraus's position as antijournalist was profoundly untenable, and when he took on *Faust* he was only going through another one of his phrases.

Developmentally speaking, journalism is adolescent, and often doubles as acting out. Journalism begins, over and again, with the journal entries jotted down by the teenager trying to contain the new-found interiority and energy of insight. Adolescence can be defined as the crisis brought on by insights and opinions, which are premature with regard to the teen's ability to give them a body and thus absorb and metabolize their shock value. Not to graduate from the mirror stage of journal writing commits you to the suicide drive. Every journal entry is here to serve you as the final line and dating of suicidal ideation. De Man lost his teenage brother and then his mother when he was a teen. We can't be sure about the brother, but let's assume *both* committed suicide. De Man's horror of adolescent journal-ism — the Teen Age — would give the momentum to his own splitting and acting out. It is tempting to consider the inevitable return of his bad press as the return also of the suicide pact. But the transference of the other stuck to de Man's corpus, taping it together, restoring it, and restoring it, for the first time, to a legibility we have learned to associate with what Benjamin called translation and what Freud identified as the transference. The resistance *in* theory was all along to the transferential setting, and thus to all the articulations of the trans-, to all the prefix launches that set us on our way, off into the externalizations of our pain, which attention to the transference, however, can, given time, translate and contain.

NOTES

1. In *Responses: On Paul de Man's Wartime Journalism,* ed. Werner Hamacher, Neil Hertz, and Thomas Keenan (Lincoln and London: University of Nebraska Press, 1989), 84.

2. "Thematic Criticism and the Theme of Faust," in *Critical Writings 1953–1978,* ed. Lindsay Waters, 1957 (Minneapolis: University of Minnesota Press, 1989), 76.

3. "'Conclusions:' Walter Benjamin's 'The Task of the Translator,'" in *The Resistance to Theory* (Minneapolis: University of Minnesota Press, 1986), 81–82.

4. "Foreword to Carol Jacobs, The Dissimulating Harmony" in *Critical Writings 1953–1978,* 1978, 218–23.

20 The Democratic Father (Credit and Crime in Metaphor)

A. KIARINA KORDELA

The moment in which the world grows increasingly literal is threatening and needs to be explained. Cervantes' *Don Quixote,* Flaubert's *Sentimental Education,* and Kafka's "The Judgment" describe different characters' responses to consternation. Don Quixote saves himself by enlarging his credulity, blaming magic, and summoning up religious patience: God will help His faithful knight. In *Sentimental Education,* Frédéric Moreau saves himself by constructing erogenous rhetorical fictions of selfhood; mastery of the Oedipus complex will save the consternated lover. In "The Judgment," Georg Bendemann consents to his own literalization and death; his hope lies in immersion in a sort of Dionysian capitalist flux, an urban rage of sex and commerce. In each case the anthropological moment shatters the reading relation: interpersonal distress in fiction is amplified into a reading trauma. Thereafter it is every hermeneut for her- or himself. Literature rewrites anthropology by suggesting that interpersonality is founded on the violent suppression of a more native unintelligibility. Interpersonality is the reward for the lost knowledge of the universal failure of reading.
— Stanley Corngold in *Franz Kafka: The Necessity of Form,* 175–76.

The Father

In all three cases, the early modern (Cervantes), the modernist (Flaubert), and the always already postmodernist (Kafka), at stake is the "Oedipus complex," which is to say, at stake is the Paternal Law—whether the father is Don Quixote's God, Frédéric's inaccessible, idealized woman, or Georg's capitalist and sexualized father. Specifically, Stanley Corngold raises here the question how this Law relates to the *literal* and the *figurative* or *metaphorical.* This question surprisingly involves the tension between what

Corngold calls the "anthropological moment" and the "reading relation." The one's death seems to be the other's life. A "failure of reading," a "violent suppression of a more native unintelligibility," a "reading trauma" is required for "interpersonality" to be attained. To focus on Kafka, who is one of the literary fathers of this piece as well as of postmodernity, the negotiation of this tension takes place "in a sort of Dionysian capitalist flux, an urban rage of sex and commerce"—in short, in what we know as Western, modern, capitalist democracies, up to and including our contemporary, transnational global capitalism, which, the totalitarian associations oozing in its global character notwithstanding, the Western liberalist discourse continues to equate with democracy. Concluding and paraphrasing, we may thus arrive at our introductory statement: At stake is the function of the father in the linguistic and discursive (and hence, ideological) disciplining of the subject as the subject of democratic (that is, noncoercively coercive or hegemonic) Law.

Corngold's linkage of the Oedipus complex to the literal and the metaphorical in language is analogous to Freud's bringing together, in *Totem and Taboo* (1913), of the murder of the primal father by the horde of his sons and the Oedipal incestuous desire for the mother—namely, "democracy." Mapping the modern male (Western) subject onto the historical birth of (French) modern democracy on the ground of the murder of the king, Freud generates both the son and the father as an Oedipus and a Laios without whom the mother would have remained irrevocably the exclusive privilege of the king. The moment that the king establishes the prohibition of the literal incestuous act with the mother coincides with the public recognition of the universal right, assumed to be shared by all sons, to the metaphorical incest with the mother—a mother disembodied as the body politic of democracy.

But at the roots of democracy lies not only Oedipus. There have always been two names—both of Methuselahian mythological force—that since antiquity haunt the Western discourse on Paternal Law and democracy: Oedipus and Antigone. If Oedipus epitomizes the ultimate subjection of the subject to the Paternal Law—a subjection necessary to save him from his eponymous complex—Antigone, her disobedience to the Law notwithstanding, remains paradoxically the woman of the prototypical democracy that has ever since haunted the imagination of any subsequent Western democracy. Sophocles' *Antigone* is traditionally read as the tragedy meant to justify democracy as the adequate social organization over against monarchy. Or, almost in Sophocles' words—in their translation—as the tragedy meant to use Creon's "misery" as a "witness to mankind what worst of woe / The lack of counsel brings a man to know!"[1] What "reading trauma" and what slippages between the literal and the metaphoric are required for an ideal democracy, programmed to serve as the *eidos* or idea (father) for any historically actual, future, Western democracy? What "anthropological relations" and "native unintelligibility" must Oedipus and Antigone, the son and the daughter, sacrifice in order for "interpersonality [to be] founded" for all democratic subjects?

Comparing the two seminal Sophoclean tragedies, one diegetic difference strikes us immediately: the occurrence of an actual crime (Oedipus's patricide), and its absence (Antigone's general innocence, including regarding the death of her brother). But Antigone, daughter and sister of Oedipus, differs from the latter in several other ways, one of which is the impossibility for Antigone to commit factually the incestuous act either with her father-brother, Oedipus, or with her other brother, Polynices, since both are dead. There is an additional brother, Eteocles, but he is not only dead, but dead and buried, and hence no good material for creating a narrative around: nobody cares, least of all Antigone. Furthermore, there is Ismene, a sister, who also remains fairly invisible, protected by her antiheroic, quasi-bourgeois readiness for noninvolvement. In any case, unlike her father Oedipus who did not know, Antigone knows that the father, as well as the brother, is dead. Finally, since their deaths lie beyond Antigone's responsibility, she, unlike Oedipus, should have no reason to feel guilt.

Antigone's part in the tragedy consists in the attempt to get Polynices' corpse buried, to render invisible this corpse (this embodiment of, among other things, the impossibility of incest), to force the king, Creon, to hide corpse and death, bury them, and thereby immortalize them. The king, Sophocles argues in his literary way, must come up to the times—the times of the Athenian democratic polis-state—by learning that corpses must be honored by burial ceremonies, that is, rendered at once invisible and immortal. In Corngold's terms, he must learn to transform literal death (the corpse) into metaphorical death (rituals, narratives, etc.). Rather than sheer *panem*, both Sophocles and Corngold argue, the democratic subjects need *panem et circenses*.

But Creon, who is an old-fashioned king, an authoritarian and decisionistic monarch, not yet adapted to the ideals of the Athenian democracy, does not know how to protect his authority, refuses to render this piece of flesh invisible, and is determined to derive all possible enjoyment from this literal death and its massacred body. He refuses, in other words, to learn that in democracy the laws of theater apply to reality, too, and that consequently, the prohibition to represent death literally on the stage means also the prohibition to represent death literally in reality. As if this were not enough, by prohibiting the burial, Creon transforms the literally impossible incest (between sister and brother) into a prohibition — something that paradoxically presupposes that the incest in question has somehow become possible, even if only metaphorically. In an interesting, democratic twist, the king's power to impose laws and effectively prohibit acts entails the subject's (Antigone's) power to commit other, impossible acts (for example, incest) — not, of course, factually (literally), since the concerned males are dead, but within the realm of imagination (metaphorically). Conversely, Antigone's imaginary power presupposes as its precondition Creon's factual authority and power.

This distinction between factual and legal authority and power on the one hand and imaginary power on the other is something that, however, was not systematically articulated by the fathers of ancient Greek democracy. Its theoretical representation originates, and not by mere fortuity, with Spinoza, one of the fathers (albeit one considered to be heretic and hence capable of only abortive, monstrous offspring rather than properly democratic kids) of an epigenetic democracy, that is, the modern, secular, Western democracy and its attempts to (re)establish itself out of the absolutist state, which had already struck root in sixteenth-century Europe. In lieu of any other kind of burial ceremony or funeral oration, Spinoza's literal death in 1677 is immediately followed by the posthumous publication of his *Ethics,* in which the distinction between these two forms of power was to outlive him. Even though, metaphysically and ontologically speaking, imaginary power (*potestas;* French *pouvoir;* German *Macht*) does not exist, Spinoza had argued, in historical, empirical reality, this nonexistent power has catalytically determinant effects on the real, existing power of authority (*potentia;* French *puissance;* German *Vermögen*).[2] Albeit not theoretically systematized, this distinction is already evident in Sophocles' *Antigone,* in which the eponymous heroine derives the force of her resistance precisely from her conviction, against all empirical evidence, that she indeed has power and can affect her historical reality. But imaginary power is not only the source of resistance, but simultaneously also the very ground of the authority that it presumes to resist. The fulfillment of Antigone's oppositional will would be tantamount to a breach of Creon's law and a subsequent infliction of his authority, but inversely, this authority and law derive their effective power and meaning in the first place only insofar as the possibility of their infliction and breach has already been opened up — something that presupposes that in spite of the unchallengeable empirical fact that Creon is the locus of historical authority, his subjects must be also loci of power. The establishment of his prohibition is what transforms this (literal) impossibility into a (metaphorical) possibility — just as it transforms the impossible incest into a possibility.

But the force of Creon's prohibition is not exhausted in this self-reflective power to ground thus tautologically and arbitrarily itself by means of supplementing its own law with the subject's power to break this law, whatever the latter may be. Creon's prohibition is also the cause and motor that in the first place set in motion the narration of Antigone's story, the action and plot of her tragedy, as well as all subsequent readings, rereadings, renarrations, and interpretations, including its translations and debates — not to mention the entailed production of material goods: books, articles, performances, pictures, films, and so on. In other words, a prohibition, set in the center of an impossibility, enables nothing less than exchange (discursive and economic) to proliferate and sustain the chain of circulation of both signification and commerce, thereby producing products and immortality, surplus value, and moral values alike. In this, the Sophoclean Antigone does not differ, as we know at least since Lévi-Strauss's analysis of myths, from, say, Goethe's Helen in *Faust*.[3] Both function not so much as real women but as signifiers that have the license to circulate freely across centuries and genres, fiction and theory, culture and economy.[4] But, whether in Sophocles, Cervantes, Flaubert, or Kafka, this "Dionysian capitalist flux" requires one more thing: corpses (literal, as are the knight's victims or Georg himself, or metaphorical, such as Frédéric's unattainable, spiritualized, immortal, ideal, and hence always already dead woman). To remain with the original father of democracy, however, the capitalist semantic and economic flux requires two dead bodies: first, the body that this prohibition presupposes as dead (Polynices), and second, the body that this prohibition eventually kills (Antigone). Only by rendering invisible these bodies can the events of their literal deaths be transformed into an unobstructed, infinite chain of free circulation of capital and signs. By contrast, to persist in focusing on theses corpses would prevent the development and production of the narrative—just as the obstinate focus on the commodity in exchange interrupts (brings death to) the ostensibly free circulation of capital. Briefly put, the democratic father must know well not only his Spinoza, but also his Marx.

The Daughter

Beyond the tension between corpse and narrative, *Antigone* points to another major, and currently perhaps more popular, tension, namely that between maleness and femaleness. If it can be said, as it often is, that *Antigone* is the drama about the abyssal gap or radical incommunicability between the two sexes, about the (Freudian) fact that males see females as blind to ethical and legal prohibition [*potentia*], while females see males as blind to impossibility—and hence to metaphorical possibility [*potestas*]—then it can also be said that *Antigone* is the drama about the gap between (Creonian) sadism, which kills, prohibits, and kills again, and (Antigonean) masochism, which disavows factual impossibility by means of imaginary possibility.[5] Seen in this context, the denouement of the tragedy states that the sadistic subject, Creon, with his prohibition, is the one who factually and literally destroys the masochistic subject, Antigone. For his part, Creon is destroyed only metaphorically, or by proxy, if you wish, since it is not he who kills himself, but his wife and son who kill themselves. And even in his metaphorical destruction, Creon is not only the master of Antigone, but as Luce Irigaray has pointed out, the "master of that destiny"[6]—his own and his family's, not to mention the destiny of democracy. In modern terms, invoking yet another unwanted and disavowed father of the generation of democracy out of the absolutist state, the Sophoclean king is a Machiavellian prince *avant la lettre*, who regards "that it is better to be rash than timid, for Fortune [destiny] is a woman, and the man who wants to hold her down must beat and bully her."[7]

Now Irigaray's comment is engendered as a reaction to Lacan's reading of *Antigone*, which itself is begotten by Heidegger's reading of *Antigone*, the procreator of which is Hegel's original and seminal reading of *Antigone*.

Allowing the mother (Irigaray) to function tacitly (as proper mothers are supposed to do) in the further development of this argument, and passing directly to the most recent father of this genealogical chain, Lacan turned in his seventh seminar, *The Ethics of Psychoanalysis (1959–60)*, to the immortalized, "beautiful," and dead Antigone, in order to elevate her heroism to the status of the ethical par excellence. Insofar as it involves a Creonian site of authority, an ethics of a state, such as the Athenian democratic state, Lacan argued, indeed demands a beautiful, heroic, and dead Antigone.[8]

Lacan's argument is structured around one basic thesis as the presupposition of any ethics pertinent to a post–World War II Europe, namely, that one should not separate the being from the signifier.[9] Antigone's persistence on burying Polynices' corpse testifies to her determination not to let this dead being be separated from the signifier, the rituals and narratives with which the state accompanies its subjects to death. By contrast, Creon's prohibition of this burial presupposes this separation, which allows the state to "finish off someone who is a man as if he were a dog,"[10] to treat being as if it were not attached to any signifier, as if it did not bear any name, and as if it were an animal, the cadaver of which can "legitimately" be eaten by dogs and birds. Yet again, antiquity, modernism, and postmodernism overlap insofar as the state, whether embodied in the king or in the vast bureaucratic, legislative mechanism, can arbitrarily let its subjects die "Like a dog!"[11] But, whereas Kafka's intention is to foreground that in this brutal, inhuman death of the subject, "the shame of it must outlive him" (229), Creon's intention in treating Polynices' corpse "like a dog" is that what outlives him is not the "shame" of Creon's own act but the "shame" of Polynices' historical past as a "traitor" of his country and as a "fratricide."[12] In other words, the difference between Creon and Antigone does not lie in their severing or not severing the being from the signifier, for Creon treats Polynices "as if he were a dog" not because the signifier has abandoned him, but, by contrast, because the signifier, manifest as historical and ethnic narrative (in which Polynices has become a figure of treason and fratricide), has stained him irrevocably. Creon's prohibition of the burial is not motivated by the assumption that the corpse in question does not bear a name, but by the historical fact that it bears *this* name as opposed to another, less infamous name.[13]

This forces Lacan to establish a further distinction, one which now pertains to the signifier itself. The signifier may be the one that circulates freely, transcending any historical determination, law, and authority, just as it can be the very designation of history, its laws, and its factual power dynamics. By analogy to the semantic ambiguity of "representation" (both representation in language as well as political and legal representation), the signifier is both: the ahistorical sign of imaginary power [*potestas*] and the historical sign of effective political power and authority. Creon severs Polynices' body from the signifier taken in its first aspect, which throughout history demands that human bodies be treated as bearers of names and as singular objects to which are assigned singular deaths and tombs. By contrast, Antigone, in her persistence to bury Polynices even if he had undoubtedly been a traitor and a fratricide, severs being from the signifier in its second aspect, which demands that death and posthumous treatment be determined by the specific historical past of each subject. Lacan's ethical imperative, by valorizing Antigone and discrediting Creon, in effect valorizes that specific function of the signifier, which affects that "purity, that separation of being from the characteristics of the historical drama he [who has lived] has lived through."[14] Returning to Corngold's terms, the metaphorical, imaginary, as opposed to the literal signifier, succeeds in suppressing not only "anthropology," but also history, while democratic "[i]nterpersonality is the reward for the suppression" of "a more native unintelligibility" or "of the universal failure of reading" of specifically the historical past and its actual power dynamics.

Thus, just as Cervantes, Flaubert, and Kafka allow redemption to emerge out of the separation of the metaphorical from the literal, Lacan allows out of the same separation, ethical purity to emerge and thus to ground ontological purity. After this separation and the redemptive purity that, in properly Hegelian fashion, emerges in all of these cases, Don Quixote, Frédéric, and Georg are like Antigone, who, yet again in Lacan's words "appears as *autonomos,* as a pure and simple relationship of the human being to that of which he miraculously happens to be the bearer, namely, the signifying cut that confers on him the indomitable power of being what he is in the face of everything that may oppose him."[15] Having thus attained the level of the pure, redemptive, metaphorical, and imaginary signifier and power, Don Quixote, Frédéric, Georg, and Antigone, unlike their enemies who always serve and please a certain historical authority, can serve and please ahistorical, divine authority, whether this is understood as the pagan Gods, the Christian God, or the secular "hermeneut."

But as we saw in our analysis of the relation between Antigone's (im)pos-sibility and Creon's prohibition, while metaphorically pleasing ahistorical being, our characters and their imaginary signifier and power [*potestas*] also please, feed, support, and ground historically factual power and its laws [*potentia*], and this is why one can object that neither divinity nor the her-meneutic act can be seen as ahistorical functions. Similarly, this is also why, as we shall presently see, Lacan's "ethical imperative" can be taken as such only insofar as it is assumed to address not only Creon but both Creon and Antigone—even if each of them from a different direction.

For Antigone, too, in her attempt not to let the "being," Polynices' body, be severed from the signifier, the burial honors that a culture ascribes to human dignity, ultimately separated being from signifier by turning both Polynices' and her own body into pure, ahistorical signifiers, that is, signi-fiers that signify nothing else except signification itself. Antigone invokes Polynices' name as the simple marker of bearing a name, as opposed to not bearing one, to not being inscribed in signification. By contrast, Creon invokes Polynices' name in its differentiation from all *other* names within universal signification. Thus Antigone is reduced to a "good," absolute mas-ochist, whose life or death is tantamount to pure signification (the highest signifier thereby being heroism). By contrast, Creon is reduced to a "bad," absolute monarch, for whom life or death is tantamount to pure history and effective relations of political power, within an always politically laden, and hence highly fragile, interpersonality.

All this means that in order for the normative statement, do not detach the being from the signifier, to function as an ethical imperative, it must be heard differently by Creon and Antigone, because it structurally has two meanings, contingent upon the ambiguity of the meaning of the terms "sig-nifier" and "representation." The one mode of hearing this imperative de-rives from the signifier in its absoluteness, the signifier as opposed to the nonsignifier. The other mode derives from the signifier in its differentiality and specificity (the signifier as opposed and in relation) to all other signi-fiers. Just as being [*être*] evokes both purity and separation [*inter-esse*], the imperative [*divide et impera*] itself bears both meanings, the historical and that which disavows history.

Consequently, ethics depends upon Creon's ability to hear the impera-tive as voiced from the imaginary disavowal of history and Antigone's abil-ity to hear it as voiced from within history. History, then, becomes tragedy (both literally and metaphorically) precisely insofar as neither man nor woman succeeds in doing what they should do. In other words, the precondition for the Lacanian normative statement to constitute an ethical imperative applicable to both genders—a universal ethical imperative—lies in our not mistaking Antigone for the realized embodiment of the ethical attitude par excellence. Her power as a corollary of Creonian power, far from signifying the advent of ethics in history, is limited to pointing to a possibility of ethics—a possibility to which neither she nor he alone can point. Antigone may arguably be heroic, but not yet ethical. Yet, she lies in the foundational tomb of the democratic (paternal) Law.

The Forefather

In the chain of *Antigone*'s readings, the maternal reading (Irigaray), more or less tacitly, points to the fact that Antigone's insistence to bury Polynices is a metaphorical version of not only a sororal incestuous (and necrophiliac) desire but also of the paternal incest—and hence directly analogous to Oedipus's desire for maternal incest. This reading presupposes two levels of metaphorical displacement and distance from the literal. The first level is introduced by the mere fact that the reproach of incestuous desire can in the first place apply to Antigone only metaphorically—unlike Oedipus who actually commits incest with his mother. By writing two separate tragedies, *Oedipus Rex* and *Antigone*, Sophocles distinguishes between literal and metaphorical incest and thus makes us notice that the latter requires our ability to metaphorize. Without this ability, Antigone's desire to bury Polynices is—just as a cigar may sometimes be simply a cigar—nothing more than what it says: the desire to bury Polynices. On the second level, Polynices can acquire the paternal position in relation to Antigone—so that Antigone's, already metaphorical, desire for incest is the desire of paternal incest—again only metaphorically. Polynices, who is, like Antigone, child of Oedipus and Jocasta, becomes metaphorically Antigone's father only via her other brother, Oedipus, who is also her father.

The crucial byproduct of this metaphorical sliding is a remarkable displacement of the bearer of incestuous desire, which has now shifted from Antigone to Creon. It is now he who desires, causes, and finally orders this double burial, in which finally both Polynices and Antigone, the literal siblings, literally lie in the tomb, thus metaphorically committing the incestuous act. This metaphorical incestuous act, finally, is not a substitute for any desire on the part of either Antigone or Polynices, but rather the metaphorical substitute for Creon's own desire to commit incest with his literal sister, Jocasta. What renders invisible both the literally tyrannical character and the metaphorically incestuous desire, which underlie Creon's prohibition and acts, is the attribution of a purportedly incestuous desire for Polynices to Antigone. By attributing this incestuous desire to her, by making his desire hers, Creon acquires (to invoke yet another great father of modern, specifically enlightened democracy) Antigone's "tacit consent" to her own burial.[16] Thus the attribution of the incestuous desire to Antigone at one stroke provides her with her *potestas,* and Creon not, of course, with his *potentia* (which from the outset is his and needs no provider) but with her "tacit consent" to his potentia. In short, the passage from *Oedipus Rex* to *Antigone* is the passage from coercive paternal authority and power to noncoercively coercive, hegemonic, paternal authority and power.

To pursue this metaphorical sliding to the end, by means of the metaphorical fulfillment of his incestuous desire at the *exodus,* the tragic denouement in which both Polynices and Antigone are buried, Creon fulfills by proxy not only his sororal incestuous desire—what he would get by actually committing the incestuous act with his sister, Jocasta—but also, finally, his parental incestuous desire, insofar as Antigone and Polynices are not only siblings but, metaphorically, also daughter and father. All of this boils down to the fact that, through this long series of incestuous metaphors, up to and including Antigone's "tacit consent," Creon's tyrannical act is transformed into an act of incestuous love. Consequently, tyrannical laws can henceforth be breached or canceled only metaphorically—something that reinforces their invisibility and literal force, protected safely behind the veil of metaphorical incestuous love.

A crucial detail must not be overlooked here. The node that both sustains the chain of metaphorical substitutions that move away from literal incestuous possibilities (incest between Oedipus and Jocasta, Antigone and Polynices, and Creon and Jocasta) and allows Creon to enter this chain of metaphorical substitutions is neither Oedipus nor Antigone (who are only nephew and niece, respectively, to Creon). Rather, it is Jocasta, who has first-degree (literal) relationships with all. Surprisingly, the forefather, whose voice Antigone is supposed to obey, in Lacan's reading, is after all the primordial mother, as both Lacan and Irigaray conclude. Crucially, however, it is not Antigone but Creon who follows her voice.

But if the forefather, the authentic father and king (Laios, king of Thebes and natural father of Oedipus, followed in the throne by his son, Oedipus, and then his brother, Creon) is already the foremother (Jocasta), can we really speak of a difference between the pre-Oedipal law of coercive tyranny and the incestuous, seductive, noncoercively coerced law of democracy, between *Oedipus Rex* and *Antigone*, and, finally, between the literal and metaphor? We can, of course, object that Laios's Law turns out to be Jocasta's Law only after *Antigone* and its metaphorical fulfillment of the incestuous desire of the already Oedipalized king, Creon. But in *Oedipus Rex* itself, Laios's Law, far from being determined exclusively by the effective relations of power [*potentia*], is already imbued by imaginary power and signifier. There, the cause and motor of the action is indeed Laios's inexorable order to kill his son, Oedipus, but—beyond the fact that from the outset this inexorable Law reveals itself as impotent, since the last slave can break it with impunity—this order is already programmed by a preceding order. This is the divine order, expressed in the Pythian infallible oracle, which prophecies that some day the son will kill the father and take his place, both the political and the conjugal. Thus Laios turns out to be an always already Oedipalized father who punishes his son as if he had already committed the incest and the murder for which he is supposed to be punished. But, as such, he proves to be also always already, like his successor Creon, a Machiavellian prince, who knows that crimes and evil deeds can be effectively rectified and prevented from threatening one's power only prior to their actual manifestation and exposure to the empirical, historical eye. In Machiavelli's own words: "That is how it goes in affairs of the state: when you recognize evils in advance, as they take shape (which requires some prudence to do), you can quickly cure them; but when you have not seen them, and so let them grow till anyone can recognize them, there is no longer a remedy."[17] As the specific early modern meaning of "prudence" indicates, and as any reader familiar with Machiavellian theory of state, overt or concealed, or with the linguistic concept of the performative function of language can discern, the crucial point Machiavelli makes here is not so much that the ideal prince is he who has Pythian prophetic abilities, but rather he who can use the latter as justification for attributing arbitrarily the intention of crimes to any subject, and to do so as effectively as if the subject had indeed already committed the crime.[18] This is Laios's feat and is what makes his attempt to kill his son appear as an entirely justifiable act. For, after all, it is clear that if Laios had not ordered his son's death, and if, consequently, the slave who had been ordered to execute the crime had not recoiled at the cruelty of this order and let Oedipus survive and be raised without ever having seen his father, then Oedipus could not ever run into his father and not recognize him, let alone kill him.

Concluding and bringing together *Oedipus Rex* and *Antigone*, we can infer that the overall, "cathartic" message is that metaphorical crimes (whether they are tyrannical orders that dissolve behind incestuous desires, or uncommitted crimes that function as if they had been committed) are the ground of democratic and tyrannical paternal authority alike, both of which are equally arbitrary. The ground of arbitrary authority, then, presupposes the desire for metaphorization. This guarantees not only the transformation of law into desire and the production of metaphorical crimes, but also the desire to fulfill desires (incestuous or otherwise) only metaphorically—that is, only insofar as they are not actually fulfilled, and this conversely means that the desire for metaphorization safeguards the literal unfulfillability of desire, that is, the obedience to and fulfillment of its (Creonian) prohibition. The prohibition of literal fulfillment of desire is sustained by the proliferation of its metaphorical fulfillments. The question then becomes: Are the father and his Law always alive and omnipotent behind the daughter's metaphorical and democratic fulfillment of desire and infringement of the Law?

The Gender of Democratic Epigones

"The contrast between the power, based on the personal relations of dominion and servitude, that is conferred by landed property, and the impersonal power that is given by money, is well expressed by the two French proverbs, 'Nulle terre sans seigneur [no land without a lord],' and 'L'argent n'a pas de maître [money does not have master].'"[19] Insofar as authority is arbitrary, paternal prohibition, set in the center of an impossibility, as we saw, enables nothing less than exchange (discursive and economic). In short, paternal prohibition is also the father of metaphor. To bury Polynices is to commit a metaphorical incestuous act, that is, to break metaphorically the prohibitive law—thereby sustaining and guaranteeing its literal prohibition. Furthermore, this metaphorical breach of the incestuous prohibition affects also the sexualization of the law and its inscription into the register of desire and *potestas*, rather than that of political power and legislation, *potentia*, in which it originates. This is no more and no less than a conclusion that could follow directly from Foucault's contribution in understanding psychoanalysis and, not least in it, Oedipalization. Psychoanalysis, as Foucault has argued, is part and parcel of the discursive and hegemonic, disciplining mechanism, by means of which coercive prohibitions and laws are internalized as one's own desire.[20] This process of disavowal of literal incest for the sake and by means of metaphorical incest merits closer attention. For what is ultimately disavowed here is less innocuous than sexual incest.

Even though there is arguably no essential difference between Laios and Creon, there seems to be one between Laios and Oedipus. This difference seems to lie between the actual attempt of the father Laios to kill the son Oedipus on the one hand, and on the other hand, the curse bestowed once and for all on any generation of the Labdakides family. In the face of this curse, the father Oedipus feels impotent and capable of only saying, as he is about to abandon forever his family, home, and city at the end of the tragedy: "Let our own fate wag onward as it may."[21] This impotence forces him to ask Creon for mercy, but, knowing that his position does not allow him to ask for anything and that anything he touches, by hand or tongue, is contaminated by him, he invokes gender difference and his socially determined physical distance from his daughters to justify his partial request:

And for my sons, Creon, take thou no care
Upon thee; they are men, so that they never
Can lack the means to live, where'er they be;
But my two girls, wretched and pitiable,
For whose repast was never board of mine
Ordered apart, without me, but in all
That I partook they always shared with me,
Take care of them; and let me, above all else,
Touch them with hand, and weep away my troubles!
Pardon, my lord; pardon, illustrious sir.[22]

The difference between Laios and Oedipus converges with the difference
between the constative and the performative power of language. Laios gives
his son Oedipus to the servant to kill him, thus becoming an agent of the
future (and letting the statement "the father has attempted his son's murder" become constative), whereas Oedipus, himself being subjugated to a
curse greater than he, can only reduce himself to the passive role of a virus,
through which his children are also contaminated. His only hope (but also
fear) is that his daughters be at least partly (or not at all) immune to this
virus, for, as he continues to say, even if the gods meant that "Such as must
be the bane, both of my sons," nothing prevents the people from wondering
whether it includes his daughters:

> And you as well? For what reproach is lacking?
> Your father slew his father, and became
> Father of you—by her who bare him. So
> Will they reproach you? who will wed you then?
> No one, my children; but needs must wither,
> Barren—unwed.[23]

Even though their gender may protect the two daughters against such a
violent and humiliating end as was his, it cannot protect them against its
female equivalent, an "unwed" and childless death—particularly when this
is also part of the father's bequeathed prophecy-curse. Indeed, in her tomb
Antigone does not lament anything else but having to die "Friendless, un-
wept, unwed," led "not as wives or brides are led, / Unblest with any marriage, any care / Of children;" in "Thou Grave, my bridal chamber!"[24] Interestingly, however, the lacking husband and children, potent as they would
be to mitigate the tragedy of her death, would never have had the power to
lead her to the same sacrifice:

> For never had I, even had I been
> Mother of children, or if spouse of mine
> Lay dead and mouldering, in the state's despite
> Taken this task upon me. Do you ask
> What argument I follow here of law?
> One husband dead, another might be mine;
> Sons by another, did I lose the first;
> But, sire and mother buried in the grave,

A brother is a branch that grows no more.
Yet I, preferring by this argument
To honour thee to the end, in Creon's sight.[25]

It is as if the antediluvian curse legated by Oedipus to his children affords no metaphorical substitutes or transitions within the range of its efficacy: no replaceable party, husband or child, can in any way be implicated in the law that concerns only his direct line of descent, on whom the curse befell. By suffering her unwed and rebellious death, Antigone remains up to the end faithful to both of her father's prophecies/curses.

This means that Oedipus has committed against his daughter only a verbal crime, as it were. Having never harmed her in any other way, he has only allowed the performative and suggestive function of his words to lead her to the fulfillment of their content. The difference between the two modes in which paternal authority transmits its Law is evident in the difference between the degrees of fatality and inevitability with which the tragic ends approach in each of the two Sophoclean tragedies. It is here that Ismene's invisibility proves operative in the dramaturgic economy of the play, by pointing to the fact that one can after all, like she did, evade the interpellation exercised by the performative power of the curse and its transmission by the father — unlike Oedipus who, haunted by factual crimes, cannot escape his fate.

But this ostensibly clear-cut difference is yet again undermined by the fact that the blurring of the two functions of language, the constative and the performative, already marks the initial moment of Laios's direct and factual attempt to kill Oedipus. For Laios, as mentioned above, wants to kill Oedipus only because he has been seduced by the performative power of the Delphic omen. Thus the primal, pre-Oedipal father Laios, he who should embody the literal, pre-Oedipal Law [*potentia*], has revealed himself to be a puppet of the metaphorical laws of the imaginary and performative power of language [*potestas*].

A puppet, but also an author. For what Oedipus says at his tragic end about himself ("O children, to have been / Author of you — unseeing — unknowing") applies doubly to Laios, since he nevertheless saw and knew. Oedipus's authorial father gives birth to his son by sending him to death as a criminal, penalized for a crime that he has not committed at the time of the punishment. This is literally a crime on credit that metaphorically functions as Oedipus's "tacit consent" to his being punished by the father. When a child is punished, the child is a woman, Rousseau would add. When the paternal punishment predates the crime, the son (who is always a daughter) owes a crime to the judge-father, I would add. The son owes revenge for the revenge taken on him. And this is exactly what Oedipus fatally does.

Yet if the son is always a daughter, Antigone then is a daughter of a different type. Unlike Oedipus who redeems his criminal debt to his father, Antigone owes nothing and will never avenge anything, for the father "punishes" her only verbally and performatively. No crime has factually been attempted against her; her credit relies only on words. But, and this was the point of speech-act theory, words are also acts. Yet, just as Antigone is a daughter of a different type than Oedipus, words are also acts of a different type than acts themselves are. To return to the terms of our local father, Corngold, they are metaphorical acts. For, unlike Laios's actual attempt of infanticide, the paternal attempt against her can be disavowed, incorporated, turned into all her own desire, but it cannot not be avenged, because there is no crime against her, unless she herself commits it, unless she herself decides not to make her own family and to remain faithful to her original, cursed family, as she does with absolute determination up to the end.

This then is the noninnocuously disavowed difference between the two fathers, Laios and Oedipus—a disavowal that converges with the currently popular disavowal of the difference between metaphor and the literal.[26] The former produces subjects who have at least the potential to redeem the crime, the credit of which has justified their arbitrary punishment, for it is a crime that has taken place literally. The latter, by contrast, by committing only metaphorical (verbal) crimes, does not fix the price required for the redemption of the credit. Oedipus's is an infinite credit, a credit about which the last judgment and the final price are indefinitely and infinitely deferred—so that Ismene, for instance, has eventually to pay nothing, whereas Antigone pays all. Oedipus's daughters encounter a crime that, like Marx's capital, is always suspended in eternal credit.

In other words, the daughter-daughter is subject to a metaphorical (and capitalist) law, whereas the son-daughter is subject to a literal (and feudal) law. As a result, whereas the son is committed to avenging the crime committed against him, the daughter is committed to incorporating the paternal law as her own (suicidal) desire, literal or metaphorical.

Which of the two is the properly democratic paternal law at the root of Western democracy?

Father and Crime on Credit

Shifting authorial register slightly, we may note that with Sophocles' *Antigone* we are conceptually already within the Athenian democracy of Socrates — and, performatively, within its legacy. We are, that is, in the state that requires for its self-sustenance an act of redoubled scapegoating. First, it requires scapegoating as an act of exchange, in which the citizens pay back Polynices, Antigone, Socrates, and the others to come, for "their" criminal debt. But given that "their" debt is precisely only a debt on credit — in fact, on an infinite and undefined credit, the price of which can be momentarily defined only retroactively, by the redemptive prices offered each time, to be reopened anew for the next subject in the metaphorical series of inheritance — scapegoating must also involve, secondly, the passive incorporation and active introjection of the guilt for "their" criminal debt in the first place. It involves the act of initial crediting, by means of which the father and the state ensure that the legacy continues to be transmitted, that the next generation be credited for their noncommitted crime. This becomes particularly evident in the case of Socrates because his crime and legacy are cast more explicitly as a future utopia (the Platonic polis-state) than are Polynices' and Antigone's.

This double scapegoating belongs to the everyday agenda of this state and its philosophy, as Derrida reminds us in the part of his *Dissemination* devoted to "Plato's Pharmacy." Of the "*pharmakon*," both poison and remedy, and the "*pharmakos*," the scapegoat, Derrida notes: "These exclusions took place at critical moments. . . . Decision was then repeated. . . . This ritual practice . . . was reproduced every year in Athens. . . . The date of the ceremony is noteworthy: the sixth day of the Thargelia. That was the day of the birth of him whose death — and not only because a *pharmakon* was its direct cause — resembles that of a *pharmakos* from the inside: Socrates."[27] The phrase "not only because a *pharmakon* was its direct cause" points to the inscription of the Socratic death in the frame of its notorious Hegelian reading. This, retroactively and from the inside of Socrates' death, bestows on it its own significance with paternal force the meaning of the death of Socrates—a man and a death who may or may not have existed, may be literal or metaphorical. In Hegel's words: "The sentence bears on the one hand the aspect of unimpeachable rectitude—inasmuch as the Athenian people condemns its deadliest foe—but on the other hand, that of a deeply tragic character, inasmuch as the Athenians had to make the discovery, that what they reprobated in Socrates had already struck firm root among themselves . . . and that they must be pronounced guilty or innocent with him."[28] Pointing to the double operation taking place in democratic scapegoating, Hegel tells us that the "legal" cause of Socrates' death is "rectitude," the Athenian people's revenge against its "deadliest foe," but its "psychoanalytic" reason, Hegel—an analyst *avant la lettre*—adds, lies in Athenians' own guilt. Thus is guilt introjected and incorporated. After that, the Athenians can arbitrarily make out of themselves "deadliest foes," upon whom they can confer "unimpeachable rectitude."

Passing now from Hegel to a later father in this legacy, we learn that what has thus "struck firm root among" the Athenian people, namely, their guilt, is also that which "is embodied or incorporated . . . [and] that which makes the body—the bodying—strong, sure and erect, and is simultaneously that by means of which we have become complete and that which conditions us in the future, the juice from which we draw our strengths."[29] This thinker is not Stanley Kubrick's Dr. Strangelove, but Martin Heidegger in his 1937 seminar on the importance of the Nietzschean notion of the "Eternal Recurrence of the Same" in Western thought. Hegel's "guilt" coincides with Nietzsche's "eternal recurrence of the same," and both are for Heidegger that which is "embodied or incorporated" as the curse, the real Law, the disavowed, but literal, eternal guilt for a metaphorical, noncommitted crime—which nonetheless being precisely metaphorical will always already have been committed. Eternal credit is the father of the eternal recurrence of the same.

Passing now to the father due to whom this discourse on paternity is in the first place possible, in Freud, too, trauma (the "crime" as the cause of an unspeakable guilt) transcends factuality and literality. The only psychoanalytic "fact" is "phantasies," and it is precisely their imaginary ontological status that bestows on them their paternal force—just as Polynices' and Antigone's phantasmic crimes do. In Freud's own words: "It remains a fact that the patient has created these phantasies for himself, and this fact is of scarcely less importance for his neurosis than if he had really experienced what the phantasies contain. The phantasies possess *psychical* as contrasted with *material* reality, and we gradually learn to understand that *in the world of the neuroses it is psychical reality which is the decisive kind.*"[30] Freud's statement reveals its rich significance particularly if we recall that, according to him, our "normal," modern and capitalist society is *"the world of the neuroses."* Now, the fate of "trauma" in psychoanalysis was to have always already been its "origin." In Lacan's words: "Is it not remarkable that, at the origin of the analytic experience, the real should have presented itself in the form of that which is *unassimilable* in it—in the form of the trauma, determining all that follows, and imposing on it an apparently accidental origin?"[31] Yet Lacan argues there is a radical difference between Nietzschean eternal recurrence of the same and psychoanalytic trauma, as well as the compulsion to repeat it—a difference that yet again converges with the difference between constative and performative, and above all, the latter's deceitful capacity to pass for constative. Nietzschean recurrence of the same (paternal law) is predicated, for Lacan, on Hegelian teleology. Freud opposes the Hegelian legacy at the moment when he "reopens the junction [joint] between truth and knowledge to the mobility out of which revolutions come."[32] For "revolutions" against any paternal authority, Lacan argues, are impossible as long as Hegel's "cunning of reason" presupposes epistemologically "that, from beginning to end, the subject knows what he wants" (301)—regardless of whether the subject is also assumed to know what the spirit of history (*the* Paternal Law) wants, as Polynices and Antigone are, or not to know, as the enlightened subject is. Freud's insistence on the ignorance of one's true desire "reopens" the "junction between truth and knowledge," thus also opening up the possibility that, against all accepted "knowledge" offered discursively to the subject, the subject always transcends the "truth" this knowledge entails performatively and presents to the subject as constative, as a *fait accompli.* Thus, recurrence proves to be not necessarily the father of his own eternal return, but also the possibility of his nonreturn.

To show the difference, Lacan turns to a Hegelian example, one that foregrounds guilt as the effect of specifically *literary* paternity. Prior to the disjunction between truth and knowledge, the statement "to be a philosopher means being interested in what everyone is interested in without knowing it"[33] appears to be an eternal truth, an unchallengeable constative statement. The reason for this, Lacan continues, is that this statement "has the interesting peculiarity that its pertinence [to philosophy] does not imply that it can be verified."[34] Into this gap of unverifiability Freud thrusts his sensitivity toward the performative function of language, thereby showing that it is a systematically concealed gap that, since the emergence of Logos, has always been open between knowledge and truth: so open that if one does not "reopen" it, it can be closed in such arbitrary ways that if, for instance, its "philosophical closure" happened to coincide with the end of the spirit of history, it could as well turn the entire world into philosophers (just as can the other notorious arbitrary closure, in which everyone, whether she knows it or not, is obsessed with the will to power). In fact, if the paternal law happened to be better sustained by the truth "that two and two make five," this is how the father would have closed the gap, and this is what he would have said, "since whatever he might have meant, would always be *the* truth."[35] For "eternal recurrence of the same" (Logos) guarantees nothing less than that the only absolute Law is Tauto-Logy—the father who arbitrarily performs reality, including all historical fathers. For the hypothesis that the philosopher does what everyone does without knowing it "can be put to the test only by everyone becoming a philosopher."[36] And this is to say, unverifiability and ignorance, far from being lack of knowledge, are effectively guaranteed truth. And, what is more, (performative) truth (unlike constative truth, which, according to our modern epistemology, is always doomed to miss reality in itself) *is* reality. For no sooner have we accepted the truth of the hypothesis than we ourselves have become philosophers. Just as no sooner have we accepted the truth of Hegel's other hypothesis, that "what [we] reprobated in Socrates had already struck firm root among [our]selves," than we ourselves have become Socrates.

In other words, as another father (who, like all fathers, is also a son) has put it, "Eternal Recurrence of the Same is not . . . some religious revelation or existential experience *outside* [the] semiotic" but "only a sign"[37]—as ambiguous as any other sign, as Ismene, Antigone, and Freud have shown us. The pertinent question becomes, then, Geoff Waite continues, what this sign "is a sign *for* in addition to being imbricated in this formal semiotic structure, what it is as *signifying practice*" (328). Moreover, we may add, what is the purpose, the thing that the sign produces performatively, by the "*signifying practice*" that cherishes eternal recurrence of the same as a constative truth, and what is the other thing produced by the "*signifying practice*" that foregrounds its arbitrarily performative, paternal power. For how else are we to have a minimally, however elusive, active function in adopting fathers unless we know the answer to these questions?

Or should we rather abandon the question of paternity altogether? The mere act of asking about literal, natural fathers suffices to perpetuate the authority of biological bonds and the entailed dichotomies between natural and adopted children, and so on. Is this the case also with metaphorical, literary fathers? Does it suffice to stop asking for the father to disappear? This is indeed a rhetorical question, not because it has and must have no answer, but because the answer is known: no—because when fathers are metaphorical, it is particularly the absent father who is omnipotent. Our silence about the father, far from "castrating" him, reinforces his potency.

I will conclude with a (post)modernist voice, this time not Kafka, but Lou Andreas-Salomé, who attempted to address the issue of the "absent" father. In Biddy Martin's succinct paraphrase, Andreas-Salomé "often used the differences between sons and daughters to show what had been subtracted from the conceptual world. For her, it was not only woman as materiality, phenomenality, or impossibility, but also as a figure of attachment and love. Whereas the son is forced to repress his love for the father in order to take his place, the daughter sublimates while remaining in love with an absent parent, which then allows for an ethics without murder."[38] Martin points out here that Andreas-Salomé's distinction "between sons and daughters" relies on the answer to the question whether or not the father indeed tried to kill the daughter or the son. Given that in our patriarchal society the answer is invariably "yes" for the son and "no" for the daughter, Andreas-Salomé infers that the daughter is therefore in a privileged position, and this allows her to remain "in love with an absent parent, which then allows for an ethics without murder."

Alas, as I have tried to show, unlike literal fathers, it is precisely the absence of the metaphorical father and his factual "murder" that opens up the infinite credit, which, as such, knows no limits in justifying any future murder as its own redemption.

Thus regarding the difference "between sons and daughters," we can proceed only nominatively and say that "daughter" is that subject who phantasmically constructs the trauma of the paternal murder as eternally credited, whereas "son" is that subject who constructs it as always already paid. The question after Antigone, however, is, as we saw, whether democratic subjects are always "daughters." Assuming that this is indeed the case, then woman's emancipation, whatever else it may involve, will not entail the omen's demand to the father to kill the daughter, too. For the point is that the democratic omen demands no child's murder. If in nothing else, it is in this that democracy keeps its promise for equality.

Therefore both "sons" and "daughters" are left with an "absent parent." What this effectively means is that nothing can be said about the father; nobody has thus far seen him. He eternally returns where he was from the beginning—his invisibility. Laios makes no appearance in either tragedy. He is metaphorical Law: pure and elusive.

NOTES

1. Sophocles 1993, 47.

2. Note that the English language, unlike Latin and other European languages, does not distinguish between these two forms of power. The Spinozian distinction between *potestas* and *potentia* is central in the work of major contemporary theoreticians of power and ideology, such as Michel Foucault, Gilles Deleuze, Félix Guattari, and Antonio Negri. For a philological approach to this distinction, see Giancotti E. Boscherini, *Lexicon Spinozanum* (The Hague, 1970) 2:850–57. For an ideological analysis of the relation between *potestas* and *potentia,* see Michael Hardt, "Translator's Foreword: The Anatomy of power" in *Negri 1991,* xi–xxiii. Moreover, note that this distinction corresponds to Lacan's distinction between the symbolic (*potentia*) and the imaginary (*potestas*) registers of the constitution of subjectivity—a correspondence that is not accidental since Spinoza was one of the major paternal figures for Lacan and his psychoanalytic theory. For more on the relation between Spinoza's distinction *potestas-potentian* on the one hand, and, on the other, Lacanian psychoanalysis, the philosophy of German idealism, and linguistic theory, as well as for a general reexamination of several of the Freudian concepts used in the present analysis, against the above theoretical background, see Kordela 1999.

3. See Lévi-Strauss 1963, particularly the chapter "The Structural Study of Myth," first published in the *Journal of American Folklore* 68:270 (October–December 1955): 428–44). There Lévi-Strauss reduces the other Sophoclean tragedy relevant to our issue of paternity, *Oedipus,* to the mythic negotiation of the irresolvable problem produced by the conflict between the tradition about the autochthonous origin of man (the conviction that we come from one) and the empirical evidence of sexual reproduction (according to which we come from two). By analogy to this mythic version of the logical incompatibility between one and two as origin, we can say that, on the level of political power, this incompatibility manifests itself as the conflict between one center of power (*potentia*) and two hegemonically conflicting and supplementary poles (*potentia* and *potestas*).

4. For more or less explicit accounts of the free circulation of meaning and truths (semantic value) between signification and economical exchange, as an inherent qual-

THE DEMOCRATIC FATHER : 377

ity of the discourse of secular and capitalist modernity, see in addition to Lévi-Strauss, Lacan 1991; Foucault 1970; and Barthes 1993.

5. This also means, as Deleuze has argued, that the counterpart of masochistic disavowal (the fetishistic act of believing in the existence or possibility of what one nonetheless knows to be nonexistent or impossible) is sadistic negation: the act of destroying (killing) and eliminating from reality that part of reality that does not fit in one's scheme of reality. For the linkage of sadism and masochism to negation and disavowal, respectively, see Deleuze 1989.

6. 1993, 119.

7. Machiavelli 1977, 69.

8. See Lacan 1992, particularly the chapter "The Essence of Tragedy: A Commentary on Sophocles' *Antigone*," 243–87. For the French original, see Lacan 1986, 285–333. Crucial in Lacan's argument is the analogy between Creon and Antigone, seen as functions within a democracy. This analogy emerges out of the fact that both the Creonian locus of legislative authority and the 'Antigonean' sites of resistance against this authority constitute exceptions to the democratic universality, according to which *all* subjects are subjected to the same laws and have equal rights. The inherently not-all structure of democracy is known as a logical problem in set theory, which exhibits the paradoxical undecidability about whether or not the set of all sets (for example, the state as representative of all subjects) includes itself as part of itself. Moreover, note that this paradox, as Zizek has shown, is expressed also in the Hegelian genus-species logic (in which one species appropriates the position of the whole genus) as well as in the logic of Freudian fetishism. The latter foregrounds that not only any positive set, but also nothing (the void set or zero) can appropriate the function of the whole—an insight that has been rearticulated in different ways by Lévi-Strauss and Roland Barthes. For a concise and conceptually precise presentation of the trajectory of the not-all logic from set theory (George Cantor, Bertrand Russel, Kurt Gödel) to the theory of signifiers and structural anthropology, as well as the relation between not-all logic and capitalism, see Karatani 1996, particularly the chapters "Structure and Zero," "Natural Numbers," "Natural Language," and "Money," 37–71. For a political and ideological function of the not-all logic in terms of Hegel's species-genus logic and Freud's fetishism, see Zizek 1996.

The issue of the exclusion as the ground of the universal, or the "not-all" structure of the "all," has been of central significance for some time now for certain trends within social theory. On the paradoxical, "not-all," structure of democracy as the societal organization of "citizens" with "equal rights," see Lefort 1988, particularly the chapter "The Question of Democracy," 9–20. On the same issue, with special emphasis on the paradoxical relation between the universal and the particular, see Laclau 1995. Again on the same issue, with emphasis on the semantically inherent paradox of "subjects" as "free and equal citizens," see Balibar 1991. Finally, on the function of the "not-all" structure in both social formations and sexual difference, see Zizek 1994, the chapter, "Otto Weininger, or, 'Woman doesn't exist," 137–64.

9. See Lacan 1992, particularly 277–80; 1986, 323–26. This presupposition even-

tually leads Lacan to his famous ethical, "categorical imperative," not to cede one's desire, which follows from the fact that, "From an analytic point of view, the only thing of which one can be guilty is of having given ground relative to one's desire" (1992, 319). The most central role in the general and institutionalized legitimation and encouragement of this compromise of one's desire (and hence of the induction of guilt) has been played historically by Christianity (see Lacan 1992, 319). Thus, if a kind "of ethical judgment is possible," this can be expressed by means of the question: "Have you acted in conformity with the desire that is in you?" (314).

    10. Lacan 1992, 279/1986, 325.

    11. Kafka 1968, 229.

    12. Recall that Polynices has also been the cause of the death of his buried brother, Eteocles.

    13. All cited phrases and words in this paragraph are repeated in Lacan 1992, 243–87.

    14. Lacan 1992, 279; 1986, 325.

    15. Lacan 1992, 282; 1986, 328.

    16. Jean-Jacques Rousseau, *Lettre à Mr D'Alembert sur les spectacles* (Ed. M. Fuchs, Geneva and Lille, 1984), 114, n. 1; cited in Fried 1980, 168. Rousseau uses this phrase referring to the woman as the willful victim of successful male erotic seduction.

    17. 1977, 8.

    18. "Prudence," being etymologically a contracted form of "providence," is used in early modern and Baroque literature, just as it is today, to indicate the king's "ability to govern and discipline oneself by the use of reason;" to exhibit "sagacity or shrewdness in the management of affairs," as well as "skill and good judgment in the use of recourses" and "caution or circumspection as to danger or risk" (*Webster's*)—all of which, however, were assumed, more explicitly than today, to derive from the king's primary ability to judge what is to be foreseen [*pro-videre*] and what not, depending on political expediency.

    Regarding the performative function of language, it is specifically speech-act theory (as defined by J. L. Austin in the William James Lectures at Harvard University in 1955; see J. L. Austin 1997, first published in 1962) that established within linguistics the distinction between this and the constative functions of language. Briefly put, the constative function of language refers to its passive function to describe or constate reality—a reality that is assumed to be already given. If the future were pregiven, a prophecy or oracle would be a constative statement. By contrast, the performative function of language, deriving "from 'perform,' the usual verb with the noun 'action,'" indicates, Austin continues, "that the issuing of the utterance is the performing of an action" (1997, 6). This is, for instance, the case in the statement "'I give and bequeath my watch to my brother'—as occurring in a will" (5). This distinction is crucial to psychoanalysis, insofar as the Freudian unconscious can be described as the discrepancy between the constative and the actual effects of the performative function of a statement. This discrepancy is possible precisely because the distinction between the performative and the constative functions of language is heuristic rather than empirically verifiable. With few exceptions, empirically it is in fact antinomically undecidable whether a statement fulfills only a performative or a constative function or both. As Austin remarks, when I say "'I apologize' . . . it is the happiness of the performative 'I apologize' which makes it the fact [constative] that I am apologizing: and my success in apologizing depends on the happiness of the performative utterance 'I apologize'" (47).

19. Marx 1967, 1:146.

20. See, for example, Foucault's *Madness and Civilization: A History of Insanity in the Age of Reason,* or *The History of Sexuality.* The same has been argued, albeit from a different perspective and with different consequences, by Deleuze and Guattari (see, for example, *Capitalism and Schizophrenia,* volume 1: *Anti-Oedipus* and volume 2: *A Thousand Plateaus*).

21. Sophocles 1991, 51.

22. Sophocles 1991, 51.

23. Sophocles 1991, 52.

24. Sophocles 1993, 33–34.

25. Sophocles 1993, 34.

26. Note that crucial in the establishment of this disavowal as an epistemologically legitimate, intellectual practice has been Paul de Man's systematic attempt to obliterate the difference between metaphor and metonymy, the literal and the figurative, the grammatical and the rhetorical (such as the distinction between a question meant literally to ask what it asks and one meant as a rhetorical question, the point of which is precisely to preclude an answer). Thus, de Man has argued—against the logic of his own argument, which points to the simple fact, deriving from the inherent ambiguity of language, that always both sides of the above oppositions are operative—that the question what is the difference between the literal and metaphor must be taken as only a rhetorical question. For, by concluding that whenever we try to discern a difference "[w]e end up . . . in the same state of ignorance," with "[t]he resulting pathos [of] an anxiety . . . of ignorance" (1973, 33), appearances to the contrary, in effect de Man opts for only one of the two sides, the rhetorical, which indeed guarantees the ignorance of differences. Having acknowledged that language produces always both functions, it is one thing to attempt to identify on what level, in what aspect, and to what end each is operative (as Corngold's above cited passage does), and another to ask conclusively (as well as ex- and pre-clusively) that therefore: "what is the use of asking, I ask, when we cannot even authoritatively decide whether a question asks or doesn't ask?" (de Man 1973, 29). Yet again, in terms of paternity, the difference converges with that between Laios and Oedipus as fathers.

27. Derrida 1981, 134.

28. Hegel 1899, 269–70.

29. Heidegger, 1986, 2/47: 79–80; as translated in Waite 1996, 11, without the emphasis. Brackets are mine.

30. Freud 1953–1974; 1917, 16: 369.

31. Lacan, 1981, 55.

32. Freud 1977, 301.

33. Lacan 1977, 292.

34. Lacan 1977, 292.

35. Lacan 1981, 36.

36. Lacan 1977, 292.

37. Waite 1996, 328.

38. Salomé 1996, 21. Implied here is mainly Lou Andreas-Salomé's "Was daraus folgt, dass es nicht die Frau gewesen ist, die den Vater totgeschlagen hat," *Almanach für das Jahr 1928* (Vienna: Internationaler Psychoanalytischer Verlag, 1928), 25.

WORKS CITED

Austin, J. L. *How to Do Things with Words.* Edited by F. O. Urmson and Marina Sbisà. 2. ed. Cambridge, Mass.: Harvard University Press, 1997.

Balibar, Étienne. "Citizen Subject." In *Who Comes After the Subject?* Edited by Eduardo Cadava, et al. New York: Routledge, 1991. 33–57.

Barthes, Roland. *S/Z.* Translated by Richard Miller. New York: Hill and Wang, 1993.

Corngold, Stanley. *Franz Kafka: The Necessity of Form.* Ithaca, N.Y.: Cornell University Press, 1988.

Deleuze, Gilles. *Masochism: Coldness and Cruelty.* New York: Zone Books, 1989.

de Man, Paul. "Semiology and Rhetoric." *Diacritics* 3:3 (1973): 27–33.

Derrida, Jacques. *Dissemination.* Translated by Barbara Johnson. Chicago: The University of Chicago Press, 1981.

Foucault, Michel. *The Order of Things: An Archaeology of the Human Sciences.* Translater anon. New York: Vintage Books, 1970.

Freud, Sigmund. *Standard Edition of the Complete Psychological Works of Sigmund Freud.* Translated by J. Strachey et al. London: Hogarth Press, 1953–1974.

Fried, Michael. *Absorption and Theatricality: Painting and Beholder in the Age of Diderot.* Chicago: The University of Chicago Press, 1980.

Hegel, Georg Wilhelm Friedrich. *Lectures on the Philosophy of History.* Translated by J. Sibree. New York: The Colonial Press, 1899.

Heidegger, Martin. *Nietzsches metaphysische Grundstellung im abendländischen Denken: Die Ewige Wiederkehr des Gleichen.* Edited by Marion Heinz. Frankfurt am Main: Vittorio Klostermann, 1986.

Irigaray, Luce. *An Ethics of Sexual Difference.* Translated by Carolyn Burke and Gillian C. Gill. Ithaca, N.Y.: Cornell University Press, 1993.

Kafka, Franz. *The Trial.* Translated by Willa and Edwin Muir. New York, N.Y.: Schocken Books, 1968.

Karatani, Kojin. *Architecture as Metaphor: Language, Number, Money.* Translated by Sabu Kohso. Cambridge, Mass.: The MIT Press, 1996.

Kordela, Kiarina A. "Political Metaphysics: God in Global Capitalism (the Slave, the Masters, Lacan, and the Surplus)." *Political Theory* 27:6 (December 1999): 789–839.

Lacan, Jacques. *Écrits: A Selection*. Translated by Alan Sheridan. New York, N.Y.:
W. W. Norton & Company, 1977.

———. *The Four Fundamental Concepts of Psychoanalysis*. Translated by Alan
Sheridan. Edited by Jacques-Alain Miller. New York: W. W. Norton & Company,
1981.

———. *Livre VII. L'Éthique de la Psychanalyse 1959–1960*. Edited by Jacques-Alain
Miller. Paris: Seuil, 1986.

———. *Livre XVII. L'envers de la psychanalyse 1969–1970*. Edited by Jacques-Alain
Miller. Paris: Seuil, 1991.

———. *Book VII: The Ethics of Psychoanalysis 1959–1960*. Translated by Dennis
Porter. New York: W. W. Norton & Company, 1992.

Laclau, Ernesto. "Universalism, Particularism, and the Question of Identity." In *The
Identity in Question*. Edited by John Rajchman. New York: Routledge, 1995.
93–108.

Lefort, Claude. *Democracy and Political Theory*. Translated by David Macey.
Minneapolis, Minn.: University of Minnesota Press, 1988.

Lévi-Strauss. *Structural Anthropology*. Translated by Claire Jacobson and Brooke
Grundfest Schoepf. New York: Basic Books, 1963.

Machiavelli, Niccolò. *The Prince*. 2. Edited by Translated by Robert M. Adams. New
York, N.Y.: W. W. Norton & Company, 1977.

Martin, Biddy. *Femininity Played Straight: The Significance of Being Lesbian*. New
York: Routledge, 1996.

Marx, Karl. *Capital: A Critique of Political Economy*. Translated by Samuel Moore
and Edward Aveling. Edited by Frederick Engels. 3 Vols. New York: International
Publishers, 1967.

Negri, Antonio. *The Savage Anomaly: The Power of Spinoza's Metaphysics and
Politics*. Translated by Michael Hardt. Minneapolis, Minn.: University of
Minnesota Press, 1991.

Sophocles. *Oedipus Rex*. Translated by Sir George Young. New York, N.Y.: Dover,
1991.

———. *Antigone*. Translated by Sir George Young. New York, N.Y.: Dover, 1993.

Waite, Geoff. *Nietzsche's Corps/e: Aesthetics, Politics, Prophecy, or, The Spectacular
Technoculture of Everyday Life*. Durham: Duke University Press, 1996.

Zizek, Slavoj. *The Metastases of Enjoyment: Six Essays on Woman and Causality*.
London: Verso, 1994.

———. "The Fetish of the Party." *Lacan, Politics, Aesthetics*. Edited by Willy
Apollon and Richard Feldstein. Albany, N.Y.: State University of New York Press,
1996. 3–29.

21 The Shadow of the Modern: Gothic Ghosts in Stoker's *Dracula* and Kafka's *Amerika*

MARK M. ANDERSON

I

One of the legacies of the Enlightenment in nineteenth- and twen-tieth-century European literature was the belief in the knowability of the human world and the related view that this knowledge could be codified in and through writing. The novels of Jane Austen, Honoré de Balzac, Charles Dickens, and Theodor Fontane, for all their obvious differences, share the fundamental assumption that human reason can decipher the initially con-fusing and perplexing world of personality, emotions, and social class. Lit-erature is a form of knowledge, with both author and reader exercising their common faculties of observation and reason. Social class, geography, gender and sexuality, historical generation, even the time of day: the en-tire world is presented as a closed system of forces that author and reader can understand and control. This last condition is crucial to the success of the realist enterprise, and for complex reasons often all too easily satisfied. For one of the tricks that reason plays on us is that knowledge, insofar as it orients us in the world and gives us a sense of mastery, *is also a form of pleasure,* not just cognition, and that, therefore, epistemological categories are not free from emotional, affective investments.

At the same time, the Enlightenment exploited another form of plea-sure in literature: that of *not* knowing something, of losing one's sense of orientation and mastery, of letting oneself fall prey to the emotions of fear and horror. Although Shakespeare and the Elizabethan dramatists had de-veloped this technique two centuries earlier, it was only in the eighteenth century that an aesthetics of obscurity, horror, and the sublime was explic-itly elaborated.[1] Edmund Burke's *Philosophical Enquiry* of 1757 is based on the premise that clarity is less suited to the excitement of strong aesthetic response ("emotion" or "affect") than is obscurity, or the "imperfect *idea* of objects"; lack of knowledge was for him a defining condition of the sublime.[2] Other contemporary philosophers investigated the "Pleasure derived from Objects of Terror" and "those kinds of Distress which excite agreeable sensations."[3] Starting in mid-century, an apparently anti-Enlightenment literature of darkness, ignorance, and terror flourished, elaborated first in the English Gothic novels of Horace Walpole, "Monk" Lewis, William Beckford, and Ann Radcliffe, as well as in the novels of the Marquis de Sade and all sorts of monster and ghost narratives (Mary Shelley's *Frankenstein,* Polidori's *Dracula,* the uncanny tales of E. T. A. Hoffmann and Edgar Allen Poe) that issued from this enormously popular genre a generation or two later. The pleasure here was not that of vision, mastery, and control, but of blindness, victimhood, and loss of self: the pleasure of being led into the dark, subterranean chambers of a medieval castle, of experiencing the torments of a helpless protagonist (especially the child-woman), of confronting an unknowable and all-powerful force of evil against which human reason, knowledge, and science are powerless.

Two modes of conceiving the world, two modes of exciting different forms of pleasure in the reader or spectator: this "sadomasochistic" model of aesthetic pleasure is one of the more paradoxical, and enduring, paternities of the Enlightenment. For long after the novels of Walpole and Radcliffe had become the objects of parody, the Gothic has constantly been updated and revised for new forms of modern experience, expanding its domain in the Victorian psychological and social novels, in detective and horror fictions of the *fin de siècle,* in German expressionist cinema of the 1920s, in the RKO horror movies of the 1930s, and in countless novels, films, television series, video games, and Internet Web sites in contemporary global culture. Indeed, recent commentators have even affirmed that American popular culture, from daytime talk shows and the eleven o'clock "slasher" newscasts, is peculiarly marked by its obsession with Gothic themes, vampires, and sadomasochistic narratives of victimhood and predator. The more virtual and high-tech we get, apparently, the more we retreat to the premodern fantasies of the Gothic.[4]

What is it about this genre, this set of stock settings and characters, this very mechanical means of exciting fear and terror that has made it such a dominant, even obsessive, force? Is there any logic to this uncanny paternity of the Gothic? In the following remarks I will focus on two turn-of-the-century narratives that make palpable this dual legacy of an Enlightenment-inspired modernity: Bram Stoker's *Dracula* (1897) and Franz Kafka's *Amerika (Der Verschollene,* 1912).[5] The first is no stranger to commentaries of the Gothic, for the text takes us from modern "rational" England — "up-to-date nineteenth century with a vengeance" — to a manifestly premodern and Gothic setting in Transylvania complete with haunted castle and vampire-ghosts. By contrast, *Amerika,* and indeed Kafka's work generally, has not been read in terms of the Gothic. Technology, bureaucracy, totalitarianism, decay of religion — these aspects rather have defined the ways in which Kafka has been read, interpreted, and handed down. What I will argue is that both Stoker and Kafka are Gothic writers precisely because technology and superstition, knowing and not knowing, mastery and victimhood, are presented not as mutually exclusive categories, but as parts of the same entity. The uncanny paternity of the Gothic lies in this recognition of a divided, self-warring inheritance, at work even when we may not initially recognize it: the Gothic as shadow of the modern.

II

Among its formal accomplishments, the eighteenth-century English Gothic novel famously reversed traditional narrative perspective, and with it concomitant gender and power relations. Rather than a questing male hero, the subject of Gothic narration and perspective is the pursued, vulnerable, fearful heroine. It is not simply the supernatural setting of feudal castle and midnight ghosts that makes a narrative Gothic, but this "female," victimized prism through which the dark, labyrinthine space of the Gothic site is perceived: a perspective that presupposes a link between external space and interior state of emotions, underground vault and the deep psychic levels of terror, architecture and memory. "Yet where conceal herself!" the heroine of the first Gothic novel asks when she finds herself the unwanted object of sexual aggression on the part of her fiancé's father. "How avoid the pursuit he would infallibly make throughout the castle! *As these thoughts passed rapidly through her mind, she recollected a subterraneous passage* which led from the vaults of the castle of the church of Saint Nicholas."[6]

With her flight into the depths of this suddenly remembered "secret passage," the first Gothic heroine initiates a kind of narrative exploration into the psyche as haunted castle (or haunted castle as psyche) that has become the staple of all Gothic fictions since: "The lower part of the castle was hollowed into several intricate cloisters; and it was not easy for one under so much anxiety to find the door that opened into the cavern. An awful silence reigned . . . through that long labyrinth of darkness. Every murmur struck her with new terror;—yet more she dreaded to hear the wrathful voice of Manfred urging his domestics to pursue her. She trod as softly as impatience would give her leave,—yet frequently stopped and listened to hear if she was followed."[7] Not the male, questing hero then, with his sight firmly fixed on the goal before him, but the anxious female heroine propelled forward by fear. Unlike the hero of epic, whose ego is predefined by his lineage and destiny, the child heroine of the Gothic romance is split between forward motion and anxious listening, between future and past. The boundaries between subject and world become fluid. Like the swooning subject of Füssli's celebrated Gothic painting "Nightmare," the Gothic heroine is literally haunted by apparitions, doubles, nightmares, and obsessive memories that take on a corporeality, a physicality of their own. The women (or the feminized Gothic men) are petrified by fear, they faint, fall into deep melancholy reveries and spells, become like wooden automata, speechless, insentient. At the same time, and in a parallel movement, inanimate buildings come to life, speak, and act with a will of their own: winds whistle through the corridors, rusty hinges squeak, even silence "reigns."

This blurring of self and world is particularly evident in the momentous passage from what is perhaps the most often imitated text of English Gothic, Ann Radcliffe's *Mysteries of Udolpho* (1794), in which the heroine, Emily St. Aubert, gets her first glimpse of her captor's property and her soon-to-be prison:

Emily gazed with melancholy awe upon the castle, which she understood to be Montoni's; for, though it was now lighted up by the setting sun, the gothic greatness of its features, and its mouldering walls of dark grey stone, rendered it a gloomy and sublime object. As she gazed, the light died away on its walls, leaving a melancholy purple tint, which spread deeper and deeper, as the thin vapour crept up the mountain, while the battlements above were still tipped with splendour. From those too, the rays soon faded, and the whole edifice was invested with the solemn duskiness of evening. Silent, lonely and sublime, it seemed to stand the sovereign of the scene, and to frown defiance on all who dared to invade its solitary reign. As the twilight deepened, its features became more awful in obscurity, and Emily continued to gaze, till its clustering towers were alone seen, rising over the tops of the woods, beneath whose thick shade the carriages soon after began to ascend.[8]

This description, which bears comparison with the celebrated opening to Kafka's *Castle,*[9] depends not only on a Burkeian evocation of a sublime Gothic edifice caught at that liminal moment of twilight, but on the subtle suggestion that the castle is a human, living presence, itself a phantom or specter on the margin of death and life. As the light "dies" away on its walls and the edifice is "invested" with darkness, it strangely comes to life, "standing" as a sovereign over the scene, its "features" "frowning" on potential invaders. Equally powerful is the uncertainty whether this animation of the castle is reflective of the actual sovereign Montoni, or, and perhaps at the same time, of the heroine's own melancholy consciousness. Time seems suspended as she gazes and gazes, as if paralyzed, at an increasingly "obscure" and "awful" image, her subjective consciousness merging with the "external" objects of her fears and obscure desires.[10]

This "supernaturalization of everyday life," and not the medieval claptrap of ghosts and goblins, is the true supernatural of Gothic fiction. As Terry Castle has remarked with regard to Radcliffe's novel: "Old-fashioned ghosts, it is true, have disappeared from the fictional world, but a new kind of apparition takes their place. To be a Radcliffean hero or heroine in one sense means just this: to be 'haunted,' to find oneself obsessed by spectral images of those one loves." Linking this narrative shift to a fundamental change in the Western attitude toward death (Castle speaks no less than of a "new phenomenology of self and other"), she notes that the "corporeality of the other—his or her actual life in the world—became strangely insubstantial and indistinct: what mattered was the mental picture, the ghost, the haunting image."[11] For the century that would take Freud's understanding of the human psyche to heart, the same century that would have to invent notions like the "simulacrum" and "virtual reality" to account for the increasingly abstract, insubstantial nature of human relations, this aspect of the Gothic novel perhaps best explains its longevity as the shadow of the modern: a Gothic paternity (or should we call it maternity?) whose end is nowhere in sight.

III

Historically, this regendering and spectralization of the Gothic narrative has been linked to the emergence of women writers, to an increasingly important audience of female readers, and to a progressive blurring of fixed gender identities. In this context, it is interesting to note that both Stoker and Kafka had strong homosexual leanings and that both were writing from a minority position vis-à-vis the dominant culture (Stoker was Irish, Kafka a Czech Jew). Is this one of the reasons why they both gravitated toward "victim" narratives, toward texts written from what Deleuze and Guattari have termed a "de-territorializing" and "masochistic" perspective: marginal, exposed, subaltern, toward the perspectives of the child, the outlaw, the foreigner, the animal?[12] Kafka's letters and fictions abound in such reversals of the questing Western conqueror into passive schlemiel, castrated son, or ritual sacrificial animal. Perhaps not surprisingly, desire is often figured in his writing as the vampiric, parisitic gesture of a simultaneous aggression and devotion. The enormous cockroach Gregor Samsa (an animal that, as Kafka noted to his father, not only stings its prey but sucks out its blood) lusts after the exposed neck of his sister Grete. The humiliated and violated Josef K. in turn attacks Fräulein Bürstner like a "thirsty animal," lapping at her face with his tongue before placing a long kiss "on the neck, right at her throat, and left his lips there for a long time."[13] Stoker's Dracula for his part shows a mesmerizing capacity for metamorphosis, a ghostly fluidity of being that can manifest itself as a dog, a bat, a wolf, and, in the first spectacular manifestation of his supernatural qualities, as a giant lizard that climbs down the castle wall "face-down," Samsa-like. His actual acts of aggression take place in England where he is a foreigner, an outsider-outlaw who will be hunted down by a veritable posse of Western scientists, technology experts, and symbolic representatives of the majority culture. Finally, the danger he presents to this culture involves the reversal of gender roles: chaste Victorian women become wildly erotic femmes fatales, while the male paragons of reason and authority become feminized, castrated acolytes of the master.

The opening chapters of *Dracula,* in which the young solicitor Jonathan Harker travels out to Transylvania in the classic "questing," exploratory manner of the Western hero, quickly reverses this identity and establishes a feminized position of vulnerability, dependance, and erotically charged terror. Depicted as a light-headed ingénue interested more in cooking recipes and sightseeing than the danger surrounding him, Harker quickly becomes a prisoner of the older, courtly, and virile Count Dracula in a castle marked by all the standard trappings of the Gothic: an impregnable, isolated position in a wild landscape; vast size and complex interior architecture; and spectral "hauntings." In chapters fraught with a sexual ambiguity not unlike the dynamics of captivity in Proust's *Albertine disparue* (Dracula cooks for Harker, makes his bed, and even wears his clothes), the novel describes an explicit gender reversal in the young Englishman. While wandering through the living quarters of a bygone age, Harker seats himself at an oak writing table "where in old times possibly some fair lady sat to pen, with much thought and many blushes, her ill-spelt love letter."[14] Reveling in the pleasure of disobeying the count, Harker decides to sleep where "ladies had sat and sung and lived sweet lives," giving in to a Gothic reverie of lascivious female vampires: "In the moonlight opposite me were three young women, ladies by their dress and manner. . . . All three had brilliant white teeth, that shone like pearls against the ruby of their voluptuous lips. . . . I felt in my heart a wicked, burning desire that they would kiss me with those red lips. . . . There was a deliberate voluptuousness which was both thrilling and repulsive, and as she arched her neck she actually licked her lips like an animal. . . . I closed my eyes in a languorous ecstasy and waited — waited with beating heart" (37–38). This scene, which concludes with the violent entry of the count declaring that Harker is "his" property, sets the Gothic terms of the narrative's subsequent exposition in England. For after this virtual gang rape of the central male protagonist by the three female vampires, *Dracula* shifts its setting back to England where there is not one but four main male protagonists (Seward, Arthur, Morris, and van Helsing) and two female protagonists (Lucy and Mina), all of whom are put into the same passive, subjected position of vulnerability that Harker occupies here and that the Gothic heroine generally occupies in the novels of Lewis and Radcliffe. Indeed, the terror represented by Dracula is that of an invasion of England, and especially London with its "teeming millions," by an alien enemy who is invisible and ubiquitous. In other words, after Harker's dream rape and possession by Dracula, the unified, single narrative perspective of his intimate voice (represented in diary entries and letters to his fiancée) gives way to a proliferation of disparate narrative voices, a veritable collage of letters, diaries, newspaper articles, and scientific reports written by many characters. This "castration" of the unified questing hero by the punishing father-imago and homosexual lover Dracula[15] results in a proliferation of feminized heroes and heroines whose competing narrative perspectives are partial, fragmented, and therefore impotent in the face of the ubiquitous, *totalizing* monster Dracula. Only when these various perspectives have been reunited by Mina into a single narrative collective (she collates their various diaries and letters into a single "master narrative") can they begin the chase that eventually drives Dracula from England back to his native soil.

On a narrative level, then, *Dracula* would seem to effect a self-transformation from Gothic novel to detective story, from a feminized "victim" perspective to that of the hyperlogical, punishing, "sadistic" pursuer à la Sherlock Holmes. The story seems to turn on a clear-cut opposition between the feudal, Gothic monster-devils from the East and, on the other hand, the Western doctors, lawyers, secretaries, and scientists familiar with the most up-to-date technological inventions. But this is not really how the novel is structured. Its ability to frighten the reader depends on a peculiarly Gothic complicity between predator and victim, a Gothic blurring of the boundaries of self and other. Dracula's castle is an enjoyable place to be: the food is good, the Count is interesting and courtly, the nighttime visions far more exciting than anything Harker has experienced (or will experience) in England. Just as Walpole's heroine in *Castle of Otranto* can "advance eagerly" into the underground labyrinth (63) and the classic Gothic heroine will inevitably "stray" into the hands of her aggressor, Harker *wants* to be in Dracula's old-world domain, wants to be cared for like a child, dominated, even terrorized. He (and the vicariously masochistic reader) seeks out that condition described by eighteenth-century aesthetics as a "distress which excite[s] agreeable sensations." Victimhood is a condition for extreme sensation: for a heightened, exalted sense of "reality."

Dracula, for his part, has no identity other than that conferred by the lifeblood of his victims; he is by definition a parasite, a ghost whose desire or will has no independent status but is a reflection of his victim's fears. A being without his own reflection, he not only sucks blood but appropriates Harker's voice and pronunciation, his knowledge of England, his *rational* functions. His goal (and England's fear) is to leave feudal Transylvania and to become indistinguishable from the average nineteenth-century, modern Englishman. Nor are the Western protagonists unambiguously on the side of modern technology and rationality. Seward is the head of a lunatic asylum, his rational faculties and technology dedicated to deciphering the signs of madness. The German-exclaiming Van Helsing, Seward's mentor in science, is also a kind of Faust figure versed in philosophy and black magic; it is his familiarity with vampire lore that is crucial in defeating the monster. Mina, after her near transformation into a vampire, enters into a telepathic "channeling" with the monster as he flees England that allows the men to track and destroy him. And, of course, Dracula is ultimately defeated not by Western technology but by the traditional symbols of superstition: garlic wreaths and crucifixes and stakes through the heart. Filled with references to telegraphs, phonographs, Kodak cameras, and telephones, this novel of modernity is haunted by nostalgia for Christian, premodern tradition.

To sum up: the force of Stoker's Dracula story lies in the prototypically Gothic reversability of self and other, of the continuity between feudal and modern conditions, "Gothic" site and modern, nervous, "female" interiority. In this regard Dracula's homoerotic relations with Harker, as well as the explicit identity reversals and exchanges that take place between them, establish a parallel for the relations between superstition and technology, "primitive" East and "progressive," scientific West — relations that the novel depicts as a kind of sadomasochistic relation between a passive, feminized subject and a punishing, repressed other. Like the Gothic novels of Mary Shelley and E. T. A Hoffmann, and even Goethe's *Faust, Dracula* portrays science itself as the origin of the ghostly and uncanny, the creator of the monstrous doubles that haunt our rational consciousness. The clicking of telegraph wires; the disembodied voices of the phonograph and telephone; the spectral reality of photographic and cinematic images; indeed, the increasingly "virtual," abstract quality of modern exchange so well described by Georg Simmel in his essays on modern urban life: these are the vampire-like "ghosts" or "hauntings" that make us fear for our own visceral, bodily reality and crave such an "agreeable source of distress."

IV

One of my working assumptions in the following remarks is that much of Kafka's prose also offers a radicalized version of classic Gothic fictions. His use of a "feminine" or "victim" subjectivity as his primary narrative perspective; of labyrinthine architectural structures and a "poetics of darkness" to foster the sense of claustrophobia, disorientation, and terror; of a "spectralization" of everyday life that makes his fictional worlds simultaneously real and unreal: all of these features are consistent with the paradigms of Gothic fiction first developed in the eighteenth century. To be sure, his writing exhibits peculiarities that cannot be reduced to or explained by this Gothic model, peculiarities that often have much to do with his analysis of modern bureaucratic and totalitarian power relations. But I think the special force of his writing stems from the deployment of these modern analyses into traditionally Gothic narrative conventions, resulting in what I would call the "bureaucratic Gothic" — a form of writing most easily recognized in *The Trial* and *The Castle,* but first developed *in nucleo* in *Amerika.*

Kafka was undoubtedly drawn to the American setting because of what he termed "das allermodernste" spectacle of modern technology and "traffic."[16] But after two chapters detailing this hypermodern world, the novel switches to the description of "A Country House near New York" that recalls the castles, haunted manors, and churches of the Gothic tradition. "Larger and taller than a country house designed for only one family has any need to be,"[17] the house is initially perceived by Karl at night in a state of confusion, so that he lacks any overview of its actual dimensions and shape. Once he actually enters the darker regions of the house, the Long Island setting (!) gives way to an explicitly premodern, Gothic interior: "[Karl] could scarcely credit his eyes at first, when at every twenty paces he saw a servant in rich livery holding a huge candelabrum with a shaft so thick that both the man's hands were required to grasp it" (66). Later in the chapter Karl must contend with a "long labyrinth of darkness" straight out of Walpole's *Castle of Otranto:* "[the corridor] seemed to have no end — no window appeared through which he could see where he was, nothing stirred either above him or below him." He passes "great stretches of blank wall completely devoid of doors; one could not imagine what lay behind them," and then comes to "one door after another," all of them locked, but the rooms behind them "obviously unoccupied" (74–75). Enveloped by a tomb-like silence, Karl suddenly comes up against an "ice-cold, marble balustrade" revealing a "great, deep chamber. One stood here as if in the gallery of a church" (75). In fact, the "country house" turns out to harbor a marble chapel with vaulted ceiling.

Other staples of the Gothic also mark this chapter: a letter from Karl's uncle has to be delivered "at the stroke of midnight" and is read by candle-light; an ancient servant with a long white beard arrives bearing a lantern; moonlight provides the only natural illumination; and an entire battery of menacing sounds and vaguely perceived shapes create an atmosphere of undefined terror. Perhaps most striking is the Gothic spectralization of figures, the effacement of their distinct contours, visible reality and "know-ability" into subjective perceptions and anxious intuitions. Karl's first im-pression of Klara is of a disembodied voice, a kind of ghost: "In the dark-ness of the chestnut avenue he heard a girl's voice saying beside him: 'So this is Mr. Jacob at last'" (55). Her misidentification of Karl Rossmann as "Mr. Jacob" underscores a misrecognition and fluidity of identity that con-tinues throughout the novel; a bit later Karl will note to himself "what red lips" Klara has, thinking of her father's lips and of "how beautifully they had been metamorphosed in his daughter" (57). And of course Klara's name is a slight orthographic variation of Karl's own — a semiotic version of their sadomasochistic, "jiu-jitsu" struggle that takes place on a narrative level.

The Gothic world is one of false appearances, mistaken identities, dou-bled selves. Karl initially thinks he must protect Klara from the unwanted sexual attentions of the sinister Mr. Green, attentions that her father crav-enly seems to allow (61). He imagines himself to be the questing hero of Western narrative, a knight who will break through the evil spell of this Gothic castle and rescue the virgin victim. Instead, Klara turns out to be a "wild cat" who uses jiu-jitsu to slam Karl onto the couch, a sadist who gets aroused while pummeling him and almost throws him out the window, and finally a sexually experienced woman who already belongs to Karl's (sup-posed) friend Mack, the shadowy figure who inexplicably seems to control everything in the Pollunder household from behind the scenes. Throughout the novel this reversal of gender identity and passivity will be replayed: Karl wants to initiate the typical American success story of the penniless young immigrant who makes good as a result of purposeful hard work, but instead is ambushed and ultimately dragged down by a complexly malevolent environment. The questing male hero is comically and tragically turned into the castrated, feminized, "Gothic" victim, trapped in the Castle: "This house was a fortress," Karl concludes at the end of his lengthy peregrination, "not a mansion" (75).

The point here is not simply to remark the incongruous presence of these Gothic tropes in the "allermodernste" American setting, but to understand their fundamental role in structuring the novel generally. The first is the passive stance of narration, which unfolds largely through the eyes of a boy who is a victim of events (starting with the seduction-rape that results in his initial expulsion from Europe). The slow groping walk through the labyrinth is a metonymic symbol for Karl's passive ignorance of the reality around him and of a narrative that only gradually reveals its secrets to him and the reader. Karl is literally "in the dark" about the actual "property rela- tions" governing this country house — who owns it, who is the lover of Miss Klara, what is "really" going on between Klara, her father, and his shady business associate Mr. Green. Semiotically, the labyrinth doubles the narra- tive maze of complex sentences and mixed plot signals that are designed to convey the disorienting effect of a vast, capitalistic, bureaucratic modernity. Karl gets lost, feels anxious, vulnerable, and helpless, as does the reader who has no choice but to experience the narrative through his passive, subjected perspective, to read through a text that obsessively reenacts essentially the same "deterritorializing" gesture of banishment and wandering in exile.

Critics have long noted the importance of Karl Rossmann's naive, child- like relation to his foreign, complex surroundings: his inability to learn from his experiences, to develop according to a *Bildungsroman* logic, to be caught in what Mark Spilka identified (with reference to Dickens's child protagonists) as a narrative perspective of "arrested childhood."[18] But Karl is not merely a child; he is a traumatized, "castrated" child who suffers precisely from the kinds of sexual abuse at the hands of adults that often underlie traditional Gothic novels. At the time he was writing *Amerika*, Kafka had already developed this notion of filial castration in two other texts: in "The Judgment," where Georg Bendemann is transformed back into a child by a father grotesquely mimicking a sexually aggressive woman, and in "The Metamorphosis," where a threatening fur-clad woman shakes a fist at Gregor Samsa lying on his back while his multiple little legs flutter helplessly. In *Amerika*, however, nothing less than the symbol of the new world, the Statue of Liberty, plays this role of giant castrating female: "As

Karl Rossmann, a boy of sixteen . . . stood on the liner slowly entering the harbour of New York, a sudden burst of sunshine seemed to illumine the Statue of Liberty. . . . The arm with the sword rose up as if newly stretched aloft. . . . 'So high!' he said to himself, and was gradually edged to the very rail by the swelling throng of porters pushing past him, since he was not thinking at all of getting off the ship" (3). Mesmerized by the sight of this giant female *cum* sword, the boy protagonist stands as if paralyzed, as mentally absent as Emily gazing up at the Castle of Udolpho, while a "swelling throng of porters" pushes him to the edge of the rail. The awe inspired by this gendered icon, and not the mere fact of the modern urban crowd, is what triggers Karl's passive stance.

To be sure, the transformed Statue of Liberty serves as a palimpsest for that other castrating woman in Karl's past, Johanna Brummer, the maid who "seduced" him and whose pregnancy resulted in his banishment from home, and, proleptically, for the formidable Brunelda, into whose dominating, domestic clutches he will later fall. The incident with Brummer, however, is key, for it explains, with an explicitness that Kafka would later shy away from, the traumatic sexual origin of Karl's reduced faculties for effectively remembering and learning from the past. The first mention of the maid in the text comes from Karl's uncle; but Karl, we are told, "had no feelings for that woman. *Hemmed in by a vanishing past,* she sat in her kitchen beside the dresser . . ." (27). It is not that Karl doesn't have a past, but that this past has vanished, has been repressed by the trauma of sexual aggression on the part of this much older, maternal woman (29) and, one supposes, by the violence with which his parents repeated and aggravated this aggression by packing him off to America. For a brief moment, prompted by Brummer's letter and his uncle's evocation of her, this traumatizing past resurfaces and we can see how the boy-child is undressed and forced to have sex with a woman whose groping proves so "disgusting" to him "that his head and neck started up from the pillows" and whose thrusting body provokes in him "a terrible feeling of helplessness. With the tears running down his cheeks he reached his bed at last . . ." (29–30).

This is the beginning, I would submit, of the Gothic in *Amerika,* the origin of the home as "unheimlich," familiar and uncanny at once, as the place of purported refuge that turns out instead to be a punishing, imprisoning source of fear.[19] Deprived of a secure sense of home and identity, Karl repeatedly makes his way in the American world by establishing inappropriately direct, personal relations with adult authority figures in the belief that they might exercise a benevolent and protective role in his development. But his actions are comically out of touch with reality. His relations are either with weak, marginal, vulnerable figures, like the stoker and Therese, or, more often, with capriciously malevolent figures, like his uncle, Klara, Brunelda, Delamarche, and the hotel manager. These are not incidentally evil figures. A student of Alfred Weber on bureaucracy, Kafka depicts the malevolence in America as a structural aspect of the entire social, economic, and political system. This, too, is in keeping with Gothic convention, where evil is not just located in the haunted castle but constantly threatens to pass into the "normal" world outside. For Karl, every attempt he makes to reestablish his lost family ties, to reorient himself within a particular configuration of personal and professional relations, results in the same initial gesture of public humiliation, banishment, and wandering with which his odyssey begins. If, as a recent commentator has suggested, "a fearful sense of inheritance in time" lies at the center of the Gothic view,[20] how not to see Karl Rossmann's story as the desperate attempt to escape from a past that refuses to let go? There is surely more than irony at stake when, at the end of the novel, he is turned away by every employment bureau of the Nature Theater of Oklahoma until he is engaged as a "European intermediate pupil" — precisely what he was in Prague before arriving in America. The undead spirits of the Gothic mean precisely this: the past is never over, there is no escape, the "American dream" will collapse back into the European nightmare.

V

The above remarks have attempted to trace a Gothic paternity in two very different literary productions of the *fin de siècle,* the one a potboiler that has spawned countless imitations and spin-offs, the other an unfinished, much less frequently read text that, insofar as it initiated what has come to be called the "Kafkaesque," has also permeated modern culture. More a structure of relations than a set of specific themes or images, the Gothic in this broad sense has a protean capacity for self-transformation and reinvention in areas where one might not expect it or even recognize it. Indeed, one of the more perplexing aspects of the Gothic — and perhaps a key to its uncanny ability to propagate itself—is the very spectral nature of the media in which it is played out. For if the defining trope of the Gothic is the ghost (or the shadow, or the double), this figure ultimately implicates the category of representation itself: the ghost as the uncanny space between presence and absence, reality and its simulacrum. Writing, no less than photographic or cinematic representations, is a mediation, and as such a kind of vampire sucking at the throat of the real—a specter that can be held at bay in cultures where only a small elite is allowed the power to read and write, but one that multiplies uncontrollably in technologically advanced democracies, with their large literate populations and modern means of communication. Perhaps this is what Kafka meant when he likened the writing of letters to an "intercourse with ghosts." Correspondence, he continues in a passage that applies equally to writing and representation per se,

> means exposing oneself to the ghosts, who are greedily waiting precisely for that. Written kisses never arrive at their destination; the ghosts drink them up along the way. It is this ample nourishment which enables them to multiply so enormously. People sense this and struggle against it; in order to eliminate the ghostliness between people and to attain a natural intercourse, a tranquility of soul, they have invented trains, cars, aeroplanes—but nothing helps anymore. . . . The opposing side is so much calmer and stronger; after the postal system, the ghosts invented the telegraph, the telephone, the wireless. They will not starve, but we will perish.[21]

Kafka's unfinished Gothic novels, as well as the unending proliferation of Stoker's vampire legend, continue to haunt the newly gendered modern even as it enters the next millennium.

NOTES

1. "[T]he Horrid, from being a category of the Beautiful, became eventually one of its essential elements, and the 'beautifully horrid' passed by insensible degrees into the 'horribly beautiful.'" Mario Praz, introduction to *Three Gothic Novels,* (London: Penguin, 1968), 10.

2. *A Philosophical Enquiry into the Origin of Our Ideas of the Sublime and Beautiful* (1757), ed. J. T. Boulton (Notre Dame: University of Notre Dame Press, 1958) (paperback ed. 1968), 60, Burke's emphasis.

3. A. L. Aikin, *Miscellaneous Pieces in Prose,* (London, 1778), as quoted by Praz, 10.

4. See Mark Edmundson, *Nightmare on Main Street: Angels, Sadomasochism and the Culture of Gothic,* (Cambridge, Mass: Harvard University Press, 1997).

5. First published in German by Max Brod under the title *Amerika,* the novel was originally intended by Kafka to be called *Der Verschollene.* See Stanley Corngold's discussion of the novel's title and his English versions of previously untranslated passages in "Rapture in Exile: Kafka's *The Boy Who Sank Out of Sight*" in his *Complex Pleasure: Forms of Feeling in German Literature* (Stanford, Stanford University Press, 1998), 121–38.

6. Quoted from *Three Gothic Novels,* ed. P. Fairclough (London: Penguin, 1968), 61, my emphasis.

7. *The Castle of Otranto,* in *Three Gothic Novels,* 61. All subsequent citations will be to this edition.

8. (Oxford: Oxford University Press, 1980), 226–27.

9. "There was no sign of the Castle hill, fog and darkness surrounded it, not even the faintest gleam of light suggested the large Castle. K. stood a long time on the wooden bridge that leads from the main road to the village, gazing upward into the seeming emptiness." Trans. Mark Harman (New York: Schocken, 1998), 1.

10. Kafka's Gothic opening to *The Castle* similarly sets the stage for an "as if" merging of the physical edifice with its human representative, Klamm, the obscurity or "nothingness" of the one functioning as metonymic index for the other. "When K. looked at the Castle, it was at times as if he were watching someone who sat there calmly, gazing into space, not lost in thought. . . . Today this impression was further reinforced by the early darkness, the longer he looked, the less he could make out, and the deeper everything sank into the twilight" (99).

11. "The Spectralization of the Other," in *The Female Thermometer: Eighteenth-Century Culture and the Invention of the Uncanny* (New York: Oxford University Press, 1995), 123 and 125.

12. See *Kafka: Pour une littérature mineure,* (Paris: Minuit, 1975).

13. *The Trial,* trans. Breon Mitchell (Schocken: New York, 1998), 33.

14. *Dracula,* ed. Maud Ellmann, (Oxford World's Classics, Oxford: Oxford University Press, 1998), 36.

15. Note that as a result of his adventure in Transylvania, Harker winds up half-insane in a convent in Budapest where his fiancée comes to rescue him; they are married with Harker literally prostate in a hospital bed, and any trace of an erotic relationship between them is strikingly absent throughout the novel.

16. For a fuller discussion of this key term in Kafka's writing, see my book *Kafka's Clothes: Ornament and Aestheticism in the Habsburg Fin de Siècle* (Oxford: The Clarendon Press, 1992), 19–49.

17. *Amerika,* trans. Willa and Edwin Muir (Schocken: New York, 1946), 55. Subsequent references are to this edition, which on occasion has been silently emended.

18. *Dickens and Kafka: A Mutual Interpretation* (Bloomington: Indiana University Press), 1963. Spilka looks primarily at the question of "a child's perspective" on corrupt adulthood, but one might also reformulate this relation in terms of Dickens's

own appropriation of the Gothic as a mode of characterizing the Law and the carceral aspects of modern English society. On this aspect of Dickens (and an unstated parallel to Kafka) see D. A. Miller's more recent *The Novel and the Police* (Berkeley: University of California Press, 1988).

19. Freud's reading of E. T. A. Hoffmann's "Der Sandmann" in his essay on " 'Das Unheimliche" is a key intertext in this regard. But see also Franco Moretti's attempt to combine Freudian and Marxist readings of *Dracula* in "Dialectic of Fear," In *Signs Taken for Wonders: Essays in the Sociology of Literary Forms,* (London: Verso, 1988), 83–108. Kafka's text also requires both psychoanalytic and social readings.

20. Chris Baldick, *Oxford Book of Gothic Tales* (Oxford: Oxford University Press, 1993), xix.

21. *Letters to Milena,* trans. Philip Boehm (New York: Schocken, 1990), 223, translation slightly modified.

SELECTED BIBLIOGRAPHY OF WORKS
OF STANLEY CORNGOLD

BOOKS

1. *The Commentators' Despair: The Interpretation of Kafka's "Metamorphosis."*
   National University Publications. New York and London: Kennikat Press,
   1973.

   1a. *The Commentators' Despair: The Interpretation of Kafka's
   "Metamorphosis."* National University Publications. New York and
   London: Associated Faculty Press, 1975.

2. *The Fate of the Self: German Writers and French Theory.* New York:
   Columbia University Press, 1986.

   2a. *The Fate of the Self: German Writers and French Theory.* Durham: Duke
   University Press, 1994.

3. *Franz Kafka: The Necessity of Form.* Ithaca: Cornell University Press, 1988.

   3a. *Franz Kafka: The Necessity of Form,* paperback. Ithaca: Cornell
   University Press, 1988.

4. With Irene Giersing. *Borrowed Lives.* Albany: State University of New York
   Press, 1991.

   4a. With Irene Giersing. *Borrowed Lives,* paperback. Albany: State
   University of New York Press, 1991.

5. *Complex Pleasure: Forms of Feeling in German Literature.* Stanford: Stanford
   University Press, 1998.

   5a. *Complex Pleasure: Forms of Feeling in German Literature,* paperback.
   Stanford: Stanford University Press, 1998.

6. *Lambent Traces: Franz Kafka* (in preparation).

7. *The Will to Art: Studies in German Literature and Thought* (in preparation).

EDITED BOOKS

1. *Ausgewählte Prosa by Max Frisch.* New York: Harcourt, Brace and World,
   1968.

2. *The Metamorphosis by Franz Kafka.* New York: Bantam Books, 1972.

3. *Thomas Mann: 1875–1975.* Edited with Richard Ludwig. Princeton: Princeton
   University Library, 1975.

4. *Aspekte der Goethezeit.* Edited with Michael Curschmann and Theodore
   Ziolkowski. Göttingen and Zurich: Vandenhoeck and Ruprecht, 1977.

5. *Franz Kafka, "The Metamorphosis."* Norton Critical Edition. New York: Norton, 1996.

TRANSLATIONS OF GERMAN LITERATURE AND CRITICISM

1. Rainer Maria Rilke. "Portrait" ("Bildnis"). In *Modern European Poetry,* edited by Willis Barnstone, 113–14. New York: Bantam Books, 1966.
2. Peter Beicken. "The Judgment" ("Das Urteil"). In *The Problem of "The Judgment," Eleven Approaches to Kafka's Story,* edited by Angel Flores, 238–51. New York: The Gordian Press, 1977.
3. Richard Thieberger. "The Botched Ending of 'In the Penal Colony'" ("La fin gachée de la 'Strafkolonie'"). In *The Kafka Debate: New Perspectives for Our Time,* edited by Angel Flores, 304–10. New York: The Gordian Press, 1977.
4. Gunnar Kaldewey. *German Romantics* (*German Romantics* [*sic*]). Hamburg: Gunnar Kaldewey, 1979.
5. Franz Kafka. *The Metamorphosis* (*Die Verwandlung*). In *The Metamorphosis by Franz Kafka,* edited by Stanley Corngold, 3–58. New York: Bantam Books, 1972.
   5a. Franz Kafka. *The Metamorphosis* (*Die Verwandlung*). In *The Norton Anthology of World Masterpieces,* vol. 2. New York: Norton, 1979, 1985, 1992.
   5b. Franz Kafka. *The Metamorphosis* (*Die Verwandlung*). In *World Masterpieces, Student's Edition and Annotated Teacher's Edition.* Englewood Cliffs: Prentice Hall, 1991.
   5c. Franz Kafka. *The Metamorphosis* (*Die Verwandlung*). In *Introduction to World Literature, Pupil's Edition.* Austin: Holt, Rinehart and Winston, 1993.
   5d. Franz Kafka. *The Metamorphosis* (*Die Verwandlung*). In *The Harper Collins World Reader.* New York: Longman, 1994.
   5e. Franz Kafka. *The Metamorphosis* (*Die Verwandlung*). In *Franz Kafka, "The Metamorphosis,"* edited by Stanley Corngold, 2–42. New York: Norton, 1996.
6. With Anthony Northey. Hartmut Binder. "Parable as Problem: Formal Aspects of Kafka's 'Before the Law'" ("Parabel als Problem: Eine Formbetrachtung zu Kafkas 'Vor dem Gesetz'"). *Journal of the Kafka Society of America* 10 (June/December 1986): 26–45.
7. Gerhard Neumann. "'The Judgment,' 'Letter to his Father,' and 'The Bourgeois Family'" ("Das 'Urteil' und der 'Brief an den Vater'"). In *Reading Kafka: Prague, Politics, and the Fin de Siècle,* edited by Mark M. Anderson, 215–28. New York: Pantheon, 1989.
8. With Michael Metteer. Friedrich Kittler. *Writing Networks, 1800–1900* (Chapter 1) (*Aufschreibesysteme 1800–1900* [Kapitel 1]), 3–24. Stanford: Stanford University Press, 1990.

SELECTED BIBLIOGRAPHY : 401

9. W. H. Auden, Bertolt Brecht, and Chester Kallmann. Essays and Letters. In *The Complete Works of W. H. Auden, Libretti and Other Dramatic Writings, 1939–1973,* edited by Edward Mendelson, 449, 675–78, 707–12. Princeton: Princeton University Press, 1993.

10. Franz Kafka. Letters and Diary Entries. In *Franz Kafka, "The Metamorphosis,"* edited by Stanley Corngold, 61–75. New York: Norton, 1996.

11. Hartmut Binder. *"The Metamorphosis:* The Long Journey into Print" ("Der lange Weg zum Druck"). In *Franz Kafka, "The Metamorphosis,"* edited by Stanley Corngold, 172–94. New York: Norton, 1996.

12. Walter Benjamin. "Two Poems of Friedrich Hölderlin: 'The Poet's Courage' and 'Timidity'" ("Zwei Gedichte von Friedrich Hölderlin. 'Dichtermut' — 'Blödigkeit'"). In *Walter Benjamin, Selected Writings,* edited by Marcus Bullock and Michael Jennings, 1:18–36. Cambridge: Harvard University Press, 1996.

13. Walter Benjamin. "Goethe's *Elective Affinities"* ("Goethes Wahlverwandtschaften"). In *Walter Benjamin, Selected Writings,* edited by Marcus Bullock and Michael Jennings, 1:297–360. Cambridge: Harvard University Press, 1996.

SELECTED ARTICLES AND ESSAYS

1. "Kafka's *Die Verwandlung:* Metamorphosis of the Metaphor." *Mosaic* 3 (1970): 91–106.

   1a. "Kafka's *Die Verwandlung:* Metamorphosis of the Metaphor." In *Franz Kafka's "The Metamorphosis," Modern Critical Interpretations,* edited by Harold Bloom, 37- 52. New York: Chelsea House, 1988.

   1b. "Kafka's *Die Verwandlung:* Metamorphosis of the Metaphor." In *Franz Kafka, The Metamorphosis,* Norton Critical Edition, edited by Stanley Corngold, 79–107. New York: Norton, 1996.

2. "The Rhythm of Memory: Mood and Imagination in the *Confessions* of Rousseau." *Mosaic* 6 (1972): 215–25.

   2a. "The Rhythm of Memory: Mood and Imagination in *The Confessions* of Rousseau." In *New Views of the European Novel,* edited by R. G. Collins and Kenneth McRobbie, 215–25. Winnipeg: University of Manitoba Press, 1972.

3. "Jerzy Kosinski's *The Painted Bird:* Language Lost and Regained." *Mosaic* 6 (1973): 153–67.

4. ""You," I Said . . .': Kafka Early and Late." *European Judaism* (Summer 1974): 16–21.

5. "Perspective, Interaction, Imagery, and Autobiography: Recent Approaches to Kafka's Fiction." *Mosaic* 8 (Winter 1975): 149–66.

6. "Mann and the German Philosophical Tradition." In *Thomas Mann: 1875–*

1975, edited by Stanley Corngold and Richard Ludwig, 9–16. Princeton: Princeton University Library, 1975.

7. "The Mann Family." In *Thomas Mann: 1875–1975,* edited by Stanley Corngold and Richard Ludwig, 46–53. Princeton: Princeton University Library, 1975.

8. "Where Babylon Ends: Nathaniel Tarn's Poetic Development." *boundary 2* 4 (Fall 1975): 57–75.

9. "*Sein und Zeit:* Implications for Poetics." *boundary 2* 4 (Winter 1976): 439–54.

   9a. "*Sein und Zeit:* Implications for Poetics." In *Martin Heidegger and the Question of Literature: Toward a Post-modern Literary Hermeneutics,* edited by William Spanos, 99–112. Bloomington: Indiana University Press, 1979.

10. "The Question of Law, the Question of Writing." In *Twentieth Century Interpretations of "The Trial,"* edited by James Rolleston. Englewood Cliffs: Prentice-Hall, 1976.

11. "The Hermeneutic of 'The Judgment.'" In *The Problem of "The Judgment": Eleven Approaches to Kafka's Story,* edited by Angel Flores, 39–62. New York: The Gordian Press, 1977.

12. "From Groundless Subjectivity to the *Homme-Rhizome:* Recent Kafka Criticism." In *The Kafka Debate: New Perspectives for Our Time,* edited by Angel Flores, 60–73. New York: The Gordian Press, 1977.

13. "Angst und Schreiben in einer frühen Erzählung Kafkas." In *Franz Kafka Symposium,* edited by Maria Luise Caputo- Mayr, 59–70. Berlin: Agora Verlag, 1978.

14. "Kafka's Narrative Perspective." *Newsletter of the Kafka Society of America* 21 (June 1978): 8–10.

   14a. "Kafka's Narrative Perspective." In Allen Thiher, *Franz Kafka: A Study of the Short Fiction,* 126–29. Boston: G. K. Hall, 1989.

15. "Freud as a Literary Text?" *Diacritics* 9 (Spring 1979): 84–94.

   15a. "Freud as Literature?" In *Critical Essays on Franz Kafka,* edited by Ruth V. Gross, 173–91. Boston: G. K. Hall, 1990.

16. With Howard Stern. "An American Rilke?" In *Yearbook of Comparative and General Literature,* 57–60. Bloomington, Indiana: Indiana University Press, 1980.

17. "Mann as a Reader of Nietzsche," *boundary 2* 9 (Fall 1980): 47–74.

18. "Dilthey's Essay *The Poetic Imagination:* A Poetics of Force." *Interpretation: A Journal of Political Philosophy* 9 (September 1981): 301–37.

19. "The Question of the Self in Nietzsche during the Axial Period (1882–1888)," *boundary 2* 3 and 10 (Spring/Fall 1981): 55–98.

   19a. "The Question of the Self in Nietzsche during the Axial Period (1882–1888)." In *Why Nietzsche Now?,* edited by Daniel O'Hara, 55–98. Bloomington: Indiana University Press, 1985.

20. "Metaphor and Chiasmus in Kafka." *Journal of the Kafka Society of America* 5 (December 1981): 23–31.
21. "Error in Paul de Man." *Critical Inquiry* 8 (Spring 1982): 489–507.
   21a. "Error in Paul de Man." In *The Yale Critics: Deconstruction in America,* edited by Jonathan Arac, Wlad Godzich, and Wallace Martin, 90–108. Minneapolis: University of Minnesota Press, 1983.
22. "Kafka's Double Helix." *The Literary Review* 26 (Summer 1983): 521–33.
   22a. "La doble espiral de Kafka." In *Franz Kafka: Homenaje en su centenario (1833–1924),* edited by Rodolfo E. Modern, 113–23. Buenos Aires, 1983.
23. "Hölderlin and the Interpretation of the Self," *Comparative Criticism* (Cambridge, England) 5 (1983): 187–200.
   23a. "Hölderlin's Poetry and the Persistence of the Self." In *Literature as Philosophy, Philosophy as Literature,* edited by Donald Marshall, 205–31. Iowa City: University of Iowa Press, 1987.
24. "Kafka's 'The Judgment' and Modern Rhetorical Theory." *Journal of the Kafka Society of America* 7 (June 1983): 15–21.
25. With Michael Jennings. "Walter Benjamin/Gershom Scholem, *Briefwechsel,* 1933–1940." *Interpretation: A Journal of Political Philosophy* 12 (May and September 1984): 357–66.
26. "Kafka's Challenge to Literary History." In *Rewriting Literary History,* edited by Tak-Wai Wong and M. A. Abbas, 198–218 and 26–27, 64, 158, 186–88, 227–28, 276, 307, 311, passim. Hong Kong: Hong Kong University Press, 1984.
27. "Restoring the Image of Death: On Death and the Figure of Chiasm in Kafka." *Journal of the Kafka Society of America* 9 (June/December 1985): 49–68.
28. With Michael Jennings. "Walter Benjamin in Recent Critical Perspective." *Modern Language Studies* 16 (Summer 1986): 367–73.
29. "Consternation: The Anthropological Moment in Literature." In *Literature and Anthropology,* edited by Jonathan Hall and M. A. Abbas, 156–88 and 111–12, 190, 193–95 passim. Hong Kong: Hong Kong University Press, 1986.
30. "Wit and Judgment in the Eighteenth Century: Lessing and Kant." *Modern Language Notes* 102 (April 1987): 461–82.
31. "Kafka's Other Metamorphosis." In *Kafka and the Contemporary Critical Performance: Centenary Readings,* edited by Alan Udoff, 41–57. Bloomington: Indiana University Press, 1987.
32. "Kafka's Challenge to Literary History." In *Change in Language and Literature: Proceedings of the 16th Congress of FILLM,* edited by Miklos Szabolcsi and Jozsef Kovacs, 350–51. Budapest: Akademiai Kiado, 1987.
33. "The Life of the Author in the Margin of His Breaks: On Kafka's Perspective." In *The Dove and the Mole: Kafka's Journey into Darkness and Creativity,* edited by Moshe Lazar and Ronald Gottesman, 179–97. Malibu: Udena, 1987.

34. "Nietzsche, Kafka, and the Question of Literary History." In *Nietzsche: Literature and Values* (*Monatshefte* Occasional Volume 6), edited by Volker Duerr, Reinhold Grimm, and Kathy Harms, 153–66. Madison: University of Wisconsin Press, 1988.

35. "The Curtain Half Drawn: Prereading in Flaubert and Kafka." In *The Comparative Perspective on Literature: Approaches to Theory and Practice,* edited by Clayton Koelb, 263–83. Ithaca: Cornell University Press, 1988.

36. "On Paul de Man's Collaborationist Writing." In *Responses: On Paul de Man's Wartime Journalism,* 80–84. Lincoln: University of Nebraska Press, 1989.

37. "Paul de Man on the Contingency of Intention," in *(Dis) Continuities: Essays on Paul de Man,* edited by Luc Herman, Kris Humbeeck, and Geert Lernout, 27–42. Amsterdam: Rodopi, 1989.

38. "Potential Violence in Paul de Man": a review-article of *Paul de Man: Deconstruction and the Critique of Aesthetic Ideology* by Christopher Norris. *Critical Review* 3 (1989): 117–37.

39. "Nietzsche's Moods." *Studies in Romanticism* 29 (Spring 1990): 67–90.

40. "Patterns of Justification in *Young Törless.*" In *Neverending Stories: Toward a Critical Narratology,* edited by Ann Fehn, Ingeborg Hoesterey, and Maria Tatar, 138–59. Princeton: Princeton University Press, 1991.

41. "Hölderlins 'Schneller Begriff.'" In *Bad Homburger Hölderlin-Vorträge 1990,* edited by Gerhard Kurz, 65–82. Bad Homburg v.d. Höhe: Stadt Bad Homburg v.d. Höhe in Zusammenarbeit mit der Hölderlin-Gesellschaft, 1991.

42. "Paul de Man's Confessional Anarchy." In *Textuality and Subjectivity, Vol. 2: The Poetics of Reading,* edited by Eitel Timm and Kenneth Mendoza, 36–50. Columbia: Camden House, 1992.

43. "Remembering Paul de Man: An Epoch in the History of Comparative Literature." In *Building a Profession: Autobiographical Perspectives on the Beginnings of Comparative Literature in the United States,* edited by Lionel Gossman and Mihai Spariosu, 177–92. Albany: State University Press of New York, 1994.

44. "Kafka and the Dialect of Minor Literature." *College Literature, Special Issue: Critical Theory in Post-Communist Cultures* 21 (February 1994): 89–101.
    44a. "Kafka and the Dialect of Minor Literature." In *World Literature,* edited by Christopher Prendergast. New York: Verso, forthcoming.

45. "On Death and the Contingency of Criticism: Schopenhauer and de Man." In *Intersections: Nineteenth-Century Philosophy and Contemporary Theory,* edited by David Clark and Tilottama Rajan, 363–77. Albany: State University of New York Press, 1995.

46. "The Subject of Nietzsche: Danto, Nehamas, and Staten." In *Nietzsche in American Literature and Thought,* edited by Manfred Pütz, 263–77. Columbia: Camden House, 1995.

47. "The Melancholy Object of Consumption." In *Violence and Mediation in Contemporary Culture*, edited by Ronald Bogue and Marcel Cornis-Pope, 19–38. Albany: State University of New York Press, 1995.
48. "Kafka's Zarathustra." *Journal of the Kafka Society of America* 19 (1995): 9–15.
49. "On Translation Mistakes, with Special Attention to Kafka in Amerika." In *Zwiesprache: Theorie und Geschichte des Übersetzens*, edited by Ulrich Stadler, 143–57. Stuttgart: Metzler, 1996.
50. "*Forum:* Defining Interdisciplinarity." *PMLA* 111 (1996): 286–88.
51. "Nietzsche, Kafka, and Literary Paternity." In *Nietzsche and Jewish Culture*, edited by Jacob Golomb, 137–57. London and New York: Routledge, 1996.
51a. "Nietzsche, Kafka und die literarische Vaterschaft." In *Nietzsche und die jüdische Kultur*, 145–64. Wien: WUV Universitätsverlag, 1998.
52. "Notes toward a Romantic Phenomenology of Poetic Mind: Rousseau, Wordsworth, Hölderlin, and Hegel." *Colloquium Helveticum* 25 (1997): 25–40.
53. "Fürsorge beim Vorlesen: Bernhard Schlink's Novel *Der Vorleser*." In *Signaturen der Gegenwart: Festschrift für Walter Hinderer*, edited by Dietrich Borchmeyer, 247–55. Würzburg: Königshausen und Neumann, 1999.
54. "Thoughts on Having Sold a Million Copies of 'The Metamorphosis.'" *Princeton Alumni Weekly* (Jan. 27, 1999): 24–25.
55. "Notes Toward a Phenomenology of e-mail." *Reading in the Media, Computer, and Internet Age* (June 2000): http://www.LiterNet.revolta.com/iser/corn1/htm.
55a. "Notes Toward a Phenomenology of e-mail" (in Bulgarian). In *Reading in the Media, Computer, and Internet Age*, edited by Ognyan Kovachev and Alexander Kiossev. Sofia, forthcoming.
56. "The Delay in Translation," *Forum:* "The 'Natural' Enemies of Comparative Literature." *Literary Research/Recherche littéraire* 17 (Spring/Summer 2000): 22–28.
57. "In the Circle of Kafka's 'Das Urteil.'" *Skrift* (Oslo) 12 (2000): 39–62.
58. "Disowning Contingencies in Hölderlin's *Empedokles*." In *The Solid Letter: Readings of Friedrich Hölderlin*, edited by Aris Fioretos, 215–36. Stanford: Stanford University Press, 2000.
59. "Anmerkungen zu Hölderlin und Hegel in Frankfurt." In *Hölderlin-Jahrbuch* 31 (1998/99), edited by Ulrich Gaier, 73–74. Eggingen: Isele, 2000.
60. "'Nu Bleu aux Bas Vers:' Reiner Aufrechter Südlicher Sezuan." In *Henri Matisse/Raoul Dufy/Correspondances*, edited by Michael Blaszczyk, 67–69. Bad Homburg: Michael Blaszczyk, 2001.
61. "Allotria and Excreta in 'In the Penal Colony.'" *Modernism/Modernity* 8 (April 2001): 281–93.
62. "Hegel's Aesthetics and the Difficulties of History." In *After*

Poststructuralism: Writing the History of Theory, edited by Michael O'Driscoll and Tilottama Rajan, 25–42. Toronto: University of Toronto Press, 2001.

63. "Adorno's 'Notes on Kafka': A Critical Reconstruction," *Monatshefte,* Special Issue: *Rereading Adorno,* edited by Gerhard Richter, 94:1 (Spring 2002): 24–42.

64. "Histories and Theories of French-German Relations: the Case of Hölderlin's Reception of Rousseau." In *Romantic Poetry,* edited by Angela Esterhammer, 457–73. Amsterdam: John Benjamins, 2002.

65. "Genuine Obscurity Shadows the Semblance Whose Obliteration Promises Redemption: Reflections on Benjamin's 'Goethe's Elective Affinities.'" In *Benjamin's Ghosts: Interventions in Contemporary Literary and Cultural Theory,* edited by Gerhard Richter, 154–68. Stanford: Stanford University Press, 2002.

66. "Aesthetic Will: Rethinking the Drive to Art from the Perspective of Hölderlin's *Hyperion." Eighteenth Century Studies,* 35:3 (Spring 2002): 497–509.

67. "Medial Allusions at the Outset of *Der Proceß;* or, *res* in media." In *A Companion to the Works of Franz Kafka,* edited by James Rolleston, 161–84. Rochester, N.Y.: Camden House, 2002.

68. "Bruno Freddi's *Vissuto";* also "*Vissuto:* eine Skulptur von Bruno Freddi" (Bad Homburg: Michael Blaszczyk, 2002).

   68a. "*Vissuto* di Bruno Freddi" (Sesto San Giovanni: Arti Grafiche Leva A.i.G., 2002).

69. "Von wegen der Wahrheit: Kafkas späte Aphorismen und Erzählungen." In *Franz Kafka. Zur ethischen und ästhetischen Rechtfertigung,* edited by Beatrice Sandberg and Jakob Lothe, 17–31. Freiburg i. Br.: Rombach, 2002.

70. "The Radical Modernist: Franz Kafka." In *Cambridge Companion to the Modern German Novel,* edited by Graham Bartram and Philip Payne. Cambridge: Cambridge University Press, forthcoming.

71. "1900: Sigmund Freud, *Die Traumdeutung." In The New History of German Literature,* edited by David Wellbery. Cambridge: Harvard University Press, forthcoming.

72. "1914: Franz Kafka, *Der Prozess." In The New History of German Literature,* edited by David Wellbery. Cambridge: Harvard University Press, forthcoming.

73. "Kafka's Later Stories and Aphorisms." In *The Cambridge Companion to Kafka,* edited by Julian Preece, 95–110. Cambridge: Cambridge University Press, 2002.

74. "The Thought of *Don Juan." In From Wordsworth to Stevens: Festschrift for Robert Rehder,* edited by Anthony Mortimer, forthcoming.

75. "Nietzsche's *Dionysus-Dithyrambs," A Philosophy of the Future: Nietzsche's*

Cultural Legacy and Critical Inheritance, edited by Sean Burke and Mark Sandy. Basingstoke, U.K.: Palgrave MacMillan, forthcoming.

76. "Tropes in Stendhal and Kafka." *Literary Imagination: The Review of the Association of Literary Scholars and Critics*, forthcoming.

77. "'Wie ein Fallbeil . . .': Kafka über Kunst und Ethik." In *Skepsis und Literatur*, edited by Bernd Hüppauf and Klaus Vieweg. Munich: Fink, forthcoming.

78. "Bookkeeping on the Modernist Model." In *Modernism*, edited by Astradur Eysteinsson and Vivian Liska. Amsterdam: John Benjamins, forthcoming.

79. "German Literature of the Great War." In *Cambridge Companion to the Literature of the Great War*, edited by Vincent Sherry. Cambridge: Cambridge University Press, forthcoming.

80. With Geoffrey Waite. "A Question of Responsibility: Nietzsche with Hölderlin at War, 1914–1946." In *Nietzsche: Godfather of Fascism?: On the Uses and Abuses of Philosophy*, edited by Jacob Golomb and Robert S. Wistrich. Princeton: Princeton University Press, forthcoming.

PRINCETON DISSERTATIONS IN GERMAN AND COMPARATIVE LITERATURE DIRECTED BY STANLEY CORNGOLD

Neil Chandler, "Artist-Philosopher: Nietzsche's Poetics and Thought," 1977.

Geoffrey Waite, "Nietzsche/Hölderlin: A Critical Revaluation," 1978.

Avital Ronell, "The Figure of Poetry: Self-Reflection in Goethe, Hölderlin, and Kafka," 1979.

Laurence Rickels, "The Iconic Imagination: Pictorial Signs in Lessing, Keller, and Kafka," 1980.

Vickie Grove, "The Burden of Exemplariness: Three 18th-Century Heroines," codirector J. Lionel Gossman, 1982.

Alice Kuzniar, "The Delay of an Ending: Narrating the Apocalypse at the Turn of the Nineteenth Century," 1983.

John H. Smith, "The Spirit and its Letter: The Rhetoric of Hegel's Early Writing," 1983.

Michael Metteer, "Desire in Fictional Communities," codirectors Ralph Freedman and Sandra Bermann, 1985.

Joel Golb, "Celan and Hölderlin: An Essay in the Problem of Tradition," codirectors Ralph Freedman and Eric Santner, 1986.

Curtis Bentzel, "With One Voice—The Effects of Silent Reading as a Mode of Reception in Eighteenth-Century German Poetics," 1988.

Angela Esterhammer, "Vision and the Limits of Language: The Poetics of Blake and Hölderlin," codirector David Quint, 1989.

Robert Tobin, "The Healing of Wilhelm Meister's Soul: Medical Discourse in the *Bildungsroman*," 1990.

Peter Musolf, "A Bare Bodkin for the Novel: Gottfried Benn's Critique of Realism and the Genesis of a New Aesthetic," 1990.

Jonathan Lang, "The Ends of Travel: Sexuality and Transgression in the Narratives of E. M. Forster and Andre Gide," codirectors Lee Mitchell and Sandra Bermann, 1992.

Eric Miller, "Fictional Representation: A Philosophical Study," codirector Thomas Pavel, 1992.

Neil Blackadder, "Offending the Audience: Modern Theater as Confrontation," codirector Thomas Pavel, 1994.

Steven Wlodek, "Adventure in the Works of Thomas Mann," codirector Ellen Chances, 1994.

Caroline Wiedmer, "Reconstructing Sites: Representations of the Holocaust in Postwar Literary Cinematic and Memorial Texts," codirectors Clarence Brown and April Alliston, 1994.

Karin Schutjer, "Community and the Individual Body: Kant, Schiller, Goethe, and Hölderlin," 1995.

Gerhard Richter, "Vital Inscriptions: Walter Benjamin and the Scene of Autobiography," codirector Michael Jennings, 1996.

John Lyon, "'Sie haben mich nach und nach verstümmelt': The Wounded Body and the Literary Self in Works of Goethe, Hölderlin, and Büchner," 1997.

Susan Bernofsky, "Writing the Foreign: Studies in German Romantic Translation," codirector David Bellos, 1998.

James Goldwasser, "Answering to the Name: German-Jewish Identity and Individual Identity in Franz Kafka, Gustav Landauer, and Franz Rosenzweig," codirector Eric Santner, 1999.

Sara Ogger, "Secret Hölderlin: The Twentieth-Century Myth of the Poet as Authored by the George Circle, Walter Benjamin, and Martin Heidegger," 2000.

Laura Deiulio, "The Promise and the Body: Marriage in German Literature around 1800," 2000.

Anne Jamison, "Form as Transgression: Structuring a Modern Poetics," codirector Claudia Brodsky Lacour, 2001.

Bernhard Kuhn, "Natural History and the History of the Self: Autobiography and Science in Rousseau and Goethe," codirector Claudia Brodsky Lacour, 2001.

Martin Dornbach, "Insight From Outside: The Authorization and Augmentation of Self-Understanding in Friedrich Schlegel, Kleist, and Hegel," in progress.

Joshua Gold, "Experience and Technique: History and Poetic Vocation in Hölderlin," in progress.

Mark Ilsemann, "Poetry of Excess: On Melancholy and the Elements in Hölderlin, Schelling, Goethe and Kierkegaard," in progress.

Michael Taylor, "Kant and the Discourse of Tragedy," in progress.

Brian Tucker, "Riddle and Enigma in Nineteenth-Century German Culture," in progress.

CONTRIBUTORS

Mark M. Anderson is Professor of German at Columbia University.

Donald Brown teaches English at Yale University.

Gail Finney is Professor of German and Comparative Literature at the University of California, Davis.

David Halliburton is Professor Emeritus of English at Stanford University.

Walter Hinderer is Professor of German at Princeton University.

Peter Uwe Hohendahl is the Jacob Gould Schurman Professor of German and Comparative Literature at Cornell University.

Jochen Hörisch is Professor of German at the University of Mannheim, Germany.

A. Kiarina Kordela is Assistant Professor of German at Macalester College.

Gerhard Kurz is Professor of German at the University of Gießen, Germany.

John Lyon is Assistant Professor of German at the University of Pittsburgh.

John Neubauer is Professor of Comparative Literature at the University of Amsterdam.

Rafaël Newman is a writer and critic in Zurich, Switzerland.

Herman Rapaport is Professor of English at the University of Southampton, United Kingdom.

Gerhard Richter is Associate Professor of German and Affiliate Professor in Comparative Literature at the University of Wisconsin, Madison.

Laurence A. Rickels is Professor of German at the University of California, Santa Barbara.

Mark W. Roche is the Rev. Edmund P. Joyce, C.S.C., Professor of German Language and Literature at the University of Notre Dame.

Karin Schutjer is Assistant Professor of German at the University of Oklahoma.

John H. Smith is Professor of German at the University of California, Irvine.

Liliane Weissberg is the Joseph B. Glossberg Term Professor in the Humanities at the University of Pennsylvania.

Caroline Wiedmer is Assistant Professor of English at the University of Zurich, Switzerland.

UNIVERSITY OF NORTH CAROLINA STUDIES IN THE GERMANIC LANGUAGES AND LITERATURES

For other volumes in the "Studies" see p. ii.

Several out-of-print titles are available in limited quantities through the UNCSGLL office. Orders for these titles only should be sent to Editor, UNCSGLL, CB#3160, Dey Hall, Chapel Hill, NC 27599-3160. They include:

33 WAYNE WONDERLEY. *Christian Reuter's "Schelmuffsky": Introduction and English Translation.* 1962. Pp. xii, 104.

58 WALTER W. ARNDT, PAUL W. BROSMAN JR., FREDERIC E. COENEN, AND WERNER P. FRIEDRICH, EDS. *Studies in Historical Linguistics in Honor of George Sherman Lane.* 1967. Pp. xx, 241.

68 JOHN NEUBAUER. *Bifocal Vision: Novalis' Philosophy of Nature and Disease.* 1971. Pp. x, 196.

70 DONALD F. NELSON. *Portrait of the Artist as Hermes: A Study of Myth and Psychology in Thomas Mann's "Felix Krull."* 1971. Pp. xvi, 146.

72 CHRISTINE OERTEL SJÖGREN. *The Marble Statue as Idea: Collected Essays on Adalbert Stifter's "Der Nachsommer."* 1972. Pp. xiv, 121.

73 DONALD G. DAVIAU AND JORUN B. JOHNS, EDS. *The Correspondence of Schnitzler and Auernheimer, with Raoul Auernheimer's Aphorisms.* 1972. Pp. xii, 161.

74 A. MARGARET ARENT MADELUNG. *"The Laxdoela Saga": Its Structural Patterns.* 1972. Pp. xiv, 261.

75 JEFFREY L. SAMMONS. *Six Essays on the Young German Novel.* 2nd ed. 1975. Pp. xiv, 187.

76 DONALD H. CROSBY AND GEORGE C. SCHOOLFIELD, EDS. *Studies in the German Drama: A Festschrift in Honor of Walter Silz.* 1974. Pp. xxvi, 255.

77 J. W. THOMAS. *Tannhäuser: Poet and Legend.* With Texts and Translation of His Works. 1974. Pp. x, 202.

80 DONALD G. DAVIAU AND GEORGE J. BUELOW. *The "Ariadne auf Naxos" of Hugo von Hofmannsthal and Richard Strauss.* 1975. Pp. x, 274.

81 ELAINE E. BONEY. *Rainer Maria Rilke: "Duinesian Elegies."* German Text with English Translation and Commentary. 2nd ed. 1977. Pp. xii, 153.

82 JANE K. BROWN. *Goethe's Cyclical Narratives: "Die Unterhaltungen*

deutscher Ausgewanderten" and "Wilhelm Meisters Wanderjahre." 1975. Pp. x, 144.

83 FLORA KIMMICH. Sonnets of Catharina von Greiffenberg: Methods of Composition. 1975. Pp. x, 132.

84 HERBERT W. REICHERT. Friedrich Nietzsche's Impact on Modern German Literature. 1975. Pp. xxii, 129.

85 JAMES C. O'FLAHERTY, TIMOTHY F. SELLNER, AND ROBERT M. HELMS, EDS. Studies in Nietzsche and the Classical Tradition. 2nd ed. 1979. Pp. xviii, 278.

87 HUGO BEKKER. Friedrich von Hausen: Inquiries into His Poetry. 1977. Pp. x, 159.

88 H. G. HUETTICH. Theater in the Planned Society: Contemporary Drama in the German Democratic Republic in Its Historical, Political, and Cultural Context. 1978. Pp. xvi, 174.

89 DONALD G. DAVIAU, ED. The Letters of Arthur Schnitzler to Hermann Bahr. 1978. Pp. xii, 183.

91 LELAND R. PHELPS AND A. TILO ALT, EDS. Creative Encounter: Festschrift for Herman Salinger. 1978. Pp. xxii, 181.

92 PETER BAULAND. Gerhart Hauptmann's "Before Daybreak." Translation and Introduction. 1978. Pp. xxiv, 87.

93 MEREDITH LEE. Studies in Goethe's Lyric Cycles. 1978. Pp. xii, 191.

94 JOHN M. ELLIS. Heinrich von Kleist: Studies in the Character and Meaning of His Writings. 1979. Pp. xx, 194.

95 GORDON BIRRELL. The Boundless Present: Space and Time in the Literary Fairy Tales of Novalis and Tieck. 1979. Pp. x, 163.

97 ERHARD FRIEDRICHSMEYER. Die satirische Kurzprosa Heinrich Bölls. 1981. Pp. xiv, 223.

98 MARILYN JOHNS BLACKWELL, ED. Structures of Influence: A Comparative Approach to August Strindberg. 1981. Pp. xiv, 309.

99 JOHN M. SPALEK AND ROBERT F. BELL, EDS. Exile: The Writer's Experience. 1982. Pp. xxiv, 370.

100 ROBERT P. NEWTON. Your Diamond Dreams Cut Open My Arteries: Poems by Else Lasker-Schüler. Translated and with an Introduction. 1982. Pp. x, 317.

101 WILLIAM SMALL. Rilke-Kommentar zu den "Aufzeichnungen des Malte Laurids Brigge." 1983. Pp. x, 175.

102 CHRISTA WOLF CROSS. Magister ludens: Der Erzähler in Heinrich Wittenweilers "Ring." 1984. Pp. xii, 112.

103 JAMES C. O'FLAHERTY, TIMOTHY F. SELLNER, AND ROBERT M. HELM, EDS. Studies in Nietzsche and the Judaeo-Christian Tradition. 1985. Pp. xii, 393.

105 JOHN W. VAN CLEVE. The Merchant in German Literature of the Enlightenment. 1986. Pp. xv, 173.

106 STEPHEN J. KAPLOWITT. *The Ennobling Power of Love in the Medieval German Lyric.* 1986. Pp. vii, 212.

107 PHILIP THOMSON. *The Poetry of Brecht: Seven Studies.* 1989. Pp. xii, 212.

The following titles are in print and can be ordered from the University of North Carolina Press, P.O. Box 2288, Chapel Hill, NC 27515-2288.

108 GISELA VITT-MAUCHER. *E. T. A. Hoffmanns Märchenschaffen. Kaleidoskop der Verfremdung in seinen sieben Märchen.* 1989. Pp. xii, 234.

109 GAIL K. HART. *Readers and Their Fictions in the Novels and Novellas of Gottfried Keller.* 1989. Pp. xiv, 144.

110 MARIAN R. SPERBERG-MCQUEEN. *The German Poetry of Paul Fleming: Studies in Genre and History.* 1990. Pp. xvi, 240.

111 DAVID PRICE. *The Political Dramaturgy of Nicodemus Frischlin: Essays on Humanist Drama in Germany.* 1990. Pp. xii, 152.

112 MARK W. ROCHE. *Gottfried Benn's Static Poetry: Aesthetic and Intellectual-Historical Interpretations.* 1991. Pp. xiv, 123.

113 JAMES A. PARENTE, JR., RICHARD ERICH SCHADE, AND GEORGE C. SCHOOLFIELD, EDS. *Literary Culture in the Holy Roman Empire, 1555–1720.* 1991. Pp. xiv, 290.

114 JILL ANNE KOWALIK. *The Poetics of Historical Perspectivism: Breitinger's "Critische Dichtkunst" and the Neoclassic Tradition.* 1992. Pp. xvi, 150.

115 ALAN C. LEIDNER. *The Impatient Muse: Germany and the Sturm und Drang.* 1994. Pp. xiv, 156.

116 GERHILD SCHOLZ WILLIAMS AND STEPHAN K. SCHINDLER, EDS. *Knowledge, Science, and Literature in Early Modern Germany.* 1996. Pp. xii, 312.

117 PETER R. ERSPAMER. *The Elusiveness of Tolerance: The "Jewish Question" from Lessing to the Napoleonic Wars.* 1997. Pp. xiv, 192.

118 ELLIS SHOOKMAN. *Noble Lies, Slant Truths, Necessary Angels: Aspects of Fictionality in the Novels of Christoph Martin Wieland.* 1997. Pp. xiv, 240.

119 BARBARA A. FENNELL. *Language, Literature, and the Negotiation of Identity: Foreign Worker German in the Federal Republic of Germany.* 1997. Pp. xvi, 170.

120 JOHN PIZER. *Ego–Alter Ego: Double and/as Other in the Age of German Poetic Realism.* 1998. Pp. xiv, 160.

Information for authors and a complete list of titles can be obtained from the Editor or from the departmental site on the World Wide Web (http://www.unc.edu/depts/german/index.htm).